D1602754

Free Market Criminal Justice

Free Market Criminal Justice

How Democracy and Laissez Faire Undermine the Rule of Law

DARRYL K. BROWN

OXFORD
UNIVERSITY PRESS

OXFORD
UNIVERSITY PRESS

Oxford University Press is a department of the University of Oxford. It furthers the University's objective of excellence in research, scholarship, and education by publishing worldwide.

Oxford   New York

Auckland   Cape Town   Dar es Salaam   Hong Kong   Karachi   Kuala Lumpur   Madrid
Melbourne   Mexico City   Nairobi   New Delhi   Shanghai   Taipei   Toronto

With offices in

Argentina   Austria   Brazil   Chile   Czech Republic   France   Greece   Guatemala   Hungary
Italy   Japan   Poland   Portugal   Singapore   South Korea   Switzerland   Thailand
Turkey   Ukraine   Vietnam

Oxford is a registered trademark of Oxford University Press in the UK and certain other countries.

Published in the United States of America by
Oxford University Press
198 Madison Avenue, New York, NY 10016

© Oxford University Press 2016

Library of Congress Cataloging-in-Publication Data

Brown, Darryl K., author.
    Free market criminal justice: how democracy and laissez faire undermine the rule of law /
Darryl K. Brown.
        pages cm
    Includes bibliographical references and index.
    ISBN 978-0-19-045787-7 ((hardback) : alk. paper)
1. Criminal justice, Administration of—United States. 2. Plea bargaining—United States.
3. Law and economics. I. Title.
    KF9223.B76 2016
    364.973—dc23

                                                                    2015023124

9 8 7 6 5 4 3 2 1

Printed in the United States of America on acid-free paper

Note to Readers

This publication is designed to provide accurate and authoritative information in regard to the subject matter covered. It is based upon sources believed to be accurate and reliable and is intended to be current as of the time it was written. It is sold with the understanding that the publisher is not engaged in rendering legal, accounting, or other professional services. If legal advice or other expert assistance is required, the services of a competent professional person should be sought. Also, to confirm that the information has not been affected or changed by recent developments, traditional legal research techniques should be used, including checking primary sources where appropriate.

*(Based on the Declaration of Principles jointly adopted by a Committee of the
American Bar Association and a Committee of Publishers and Associations.)*

To Carolyn, Guthrie, and Georgia, of course

SUMMARY CONTENTS

DETAILED CONTENTS

ACKNOWLEDGMENTS

Support from University of Virginia School of Law, through the good offices of Dean Paul Mahoney, particularly in the form of the E. James Kelly, Jr.– Class of 1965 Research Professorship, which provided time and resources that made this book possible. The unrivaled staff of research librarians at the University of Virginia Law Library were absolutely essential. Several law student research assistants were terrifically helpful as well. I was greatly aided by careful copyediting by Lori Vermaas, Almas Khan, Guthrie Brown, and OUP editors.

My colleagues at University of Virginia Law School read drafts of some chapters and offered valuable feedback, as did workshop participants in many places: Duke University Law School, the Hoffinger Criminal Justice Colloquium at NYU Law School, Fordham University Law School, University of Minnesota's Robina Institute, a CrimProf Summer Conference, and the AALS Criminal Justice Meeting. Some of the earliest ideas about this book, which turned out to play a big part in its final form, came during fruitful but all-too-brief visits at the Oxford University Centre for Criminology, made possible in particular by its director at the time, Ian Loader. Outside of workshop settings, Jenny Carroll, Michelle Dempsey, Brandon Garrett, Maximo Langer, Erik Luna, Dan Markel, John Pfaff, Richard Myers, Scott Sundby, and Jenia Iontcheva Turner read portions of the manuscript at various (often dreadfully early) stages and provided immensely helpful comments. Mike Redmayne saved me from some missteps in English law. Bettina Weisser did her best to educate me in German and European criminal justice. She also generously provided ideal accommodations for a research sabbatical, during which most of the first draft was written, at Westphalian Wilhelms University in Muenster, Germany. Through years of conversations and long email exchanges, Jay Stone educated me about political economy and democratic politics. For years Mike Klarman generously offered invaluable support for my work and career. Most indefatigable of all is my wife, Carolyn, who made this work possible in myriad ways, shouldering the heaviest burdens for both my career and our family life. Guthrie and Georgia provided their own unique encouragements, not always knowingly, while at the same time providing the best reasons *not* to spend time working on a book.

Charlottesville, Virginia
June 2015

CHAPTER 1

Introduction

JUSTICE IN A MINIMAL STATE

The Distinctiveness of the American Criminal Justice System

For decades, the United States has led all nations in its use of prison as criminal punishment. It incarcerates by far more people than any other country, with more than two million in prisons and jails in 2013, because it continues to have the world's highest incarceration rate, 716 per 100,000 in 2013. (In more than half of all nations, including nearly all in Europe, the rate is below 150 per 100,000.)[1] In addition, the United States remains the only advanced democracy that continues to employ the death penalty; it carried out thirty-five executions in 2014.[2] Despite the gravity of these practices, the criminal process by which U.S. jurisdictions determine guilt continues to prove itself to be disturbingly unreliable. Wrongful convictions are not unique to the United States, but their frequency appears to be no better than elsewhere. And the stakes are much higher, both because of the risk of wrongful *death* sentences and because of the sheer number of convictions leading to long prison terms. Exonerations from death row, or after decades of imprisonment, now number in the hundreds and recur almost monthly throughout the country.[3] Yet American law contains no explicit legal guarantee that a judgment of guilt will be *accurate*, nor that the factually innocent are assured of a process by which wrongful convictions can be corrected.

This severity and uncertain level of reliability are related to the singular institutions and practices that distinguish U.S. criminal process from justice systems elsewhere that share the same foundations in the common law and adversarial trial procedure. Only in the United States are most prosecutors and judges popularly elected. American prosecutors have much more influence over sentencing than do prosecutors in other nations. Plea bargaining is wide-spread and routine now in many national justice systems, but American rules for negotiated pleas are unusual in many respects. Guilty pleas are permitted for even the gravest offenses and harshest sentences; evidence disclosure is not required before a valid guilty plea; prosecutors have more negotiating power. Lawful convictions can be based on a "guilty plea" in which a defendant *denies his guilt*, and without a judicial finding that the evidence supports his convic-tion beyond a reasonable doubt. Most convictions now occur through guilty pleas rather than trials in England, Canada, Australia, and other jurisdictions, as well as in the United States. But U.S. courts embraced negotiated pleas earlier and less hesitantly than in other places, and the available data suggest that guilty pleas vanquished trial process in America more thoroughly than elsewhere. Despite the constitutional guarantee of a jury trial, only about 2 or 3 percent of criminal convictions occur by jury verdicts. More than 95 percent are the result of guilty pleas.[4]

These defining and disturbing features of American criminal justice follow, sometimes plainly but often subtly, from how criminal justice systems incor-porate distinctive traditions of American democratic governance and polit-ical economy. The American dedication to democratic process and political accountability is by many measures unmatched in other nations. National elections occur every two years. Voters rather than party officials mostly determine the candidates for general elections. Democracy runs deep: even minor local functionaries hold office by direct election. Civil service bureau-cracies are smaller than elsewhere, and as a result more officials are politically accountable—or, depending on one's emphasis, subject to political pressure. Voters in some states can enact laws by popular referendum, entirely circum-venting the legislative process. For these reasons and others, public policy, broadly speaking, is more closely attuned to politics and popular preferences. The durability of the death penalty is one example of such populist policy.[5]

This democratic tradition is one manifestation of an enduring skepticism about government power and its idealization, if not practical commitment, to a minimal state. The U.S. national government's powers are limited in ways not found in other countries. Political scientists sometimes describe the United States as a comparatively minimal or "weak" state in the sense that its central government lacks many powers and capacities long possessed by governments of European nations and elsewhere.

Aside from democratic governance, the aspiration for a minimal state sec-tor is most apparent in American political economy. Along with its affinity for democracy, the United States has long been distinguished by its strong alle-giance to a free market economy and to the kinds of public policies associated with robust capitalism in the laissez-faire tradition. Famously (or notoriously),

U.S. state and federal governments have comparably thin policies of social insurance and market regulation to moderate the disruptive effects of markets on their citizens: less generous unemployment insurance, weaker regulations governing employee discharge, less-than-universal health insurance. Consistent with its long-standing traditions of laissez-faire market policies and broad-based democratic politics, American society has always placed high value on personal liberty and individualism. A libertarian streak is apparent in laws protecting activities that are often more regulated in other countries, such as gun ownership, hate speech, campaign advertising, and private spending on political campaigns. The disposition toward individualism and a minimal state likely contribute to behaviors that are harder to measure. Levels of social solidarity or cohesion—broad notions of shared obligations and affinities among citizens—are lower than elsewhere, although rates of volunteering and charitable giving are higher than nearly anywhere else.[6]

The argument of this book is that these broader features of American government and political economy are central to American criminal procedure. Devotion to political accountability, individualism, and free markets provides organizing premises for criminal justice administration; they fundamentally determine which rules apply and how our criminal justice institutions are designed. Simply put, the ideologies of democracy and free markets lie at the heart of how American courts, lawyers, and legislatures define fairness, due process, and the rule of law. Yet however well it works as a means of public governance and economic policy, these strategies for minimizing state power have significant and sometimes perverse downsides for criminal justice. Market mechanisms and political accountability, as they are now incorporated into American criminal process, undermine the justice system's commitment to the rule of law. Criminal justice is administered less by rules grounded in public values and principles and more by private interests, partisan motivations, and political preferences. They are the primary reason why the rules, practices, and—to some degree—the outcomes of American criminal process differ from those of other common law jurisdictions.

Of course, democratic decision making and political accountability are hardly absent in other justice systems. The same is true of market-mimicking institutions. The adversarial trial tradition at its core has much in common with markets; it relies on the initiative of competing parties rather than the state to generate evidence. Yet the integration of market and democratic processes in American criminal process is deeper and more thoroughgoing. Prosecutorial authority has grown and judicial authority contracted because, in various ways, U.S. criminal process trusts political decision making over legal regulation. Plea bargaining is more freewheeling, more coercive, because its rules and rationales explicitly adopt those of markets and the private law of contract. Traces of the market appear as well in rules regarding pretrial evidence disclosure, and generally in the degree to which the parties control criminal procedure. Quite literally, proclivities for democratic authority and market processes in criminal procedure make American criminal justice more *lawless*. Instead of legal rules against illegitimate practices, the justice system trusts democratic or market-like mechanisms to prevent them. Legal criteria play smaller roles in decisions about evidence disclosure or proportionate punishment because political discretion plays a larger one. The cumulative effect is to reduce the state's responsibility—*public* responsibility—for the integrity of the criminal judgments rendered by its own courts. This position reaches its blunt apotheosis in the view of some Supreme Court justices, and perhaps the Court itself, that criminal defendants have no specific legal right to an *accurate* conviction.[7]

Recognizing the influence of democratic and market norms helps to clarify some of the central contradictions of American criminal justice, which has more than its share of seeming paradoxes. Americans highly prize individual liberty and are suspicious of government power. As much as anything else, that's why they rely so much on democracy and markets. Democracy limits and checks state power. Free markets displace and marginalize state control. Yet American criminal law enforcement is, by every reasonable measure, an unusually expansive and intrusive exercise of state power in its most coercive form. U.S. punishment policies are unique in the sheer quantity of liberty they take from offenders. Within trial process itself, the adversary system—and the constitutional right to confront witnesses—puts tremendous trust in cross-examination as "the greatest legal engine ever invented for the discovery of truth."[8] American trial process is notably adversarial even compared to other common law nations, which should make cross-examination even more potent. Yet the trial system reliant on this great engine far too often demonstrably fails to uncover truth, resulting in the gravest errors even in the most serious cases. Why does an unwavering faith nonetheless endure in adversarial efforts by private parties to produce "public goods," including comprehensive development of the facts needed for accurate court judgments? Beyond the inertia of long tradition, one reason is that this way of doing things echoes unmistakably of the market: parties are motivated by self-interest; party competition, not state officials, is responsible for producing evidence of the truth. To be sure, a full picture of criminal adjudication is more subtle and complicated. Yet to understand that process one must understand how the ideas of markets and democracy shape the structure of criminal procedure and lie at the heart of its rationales. Democratic and market processes can be *substitutes* to law—to prohibitions, commands, and specified decision-making criteria. The ways that American criminal procedure adopts democratic and market-based mechanisms in place of rule-based alternatives sets American criminal justice apart, even from its closest common law cousins. This fidelity to democratic and market ideology have profound and counterintuitive implications for the exercise of criminal enforcement power. They also reduce the state's responsibility for the integrity of judgments issued by its own courts. Sometimes forthrightly and sometimes inadvertently, opting for democratic and market-inspired mechanisms over legal rules expands that power and diminishes that responsibility. In doing so, it transforms public law norms and, fundamentally, what we mean by the rule of law.

Criminal Enforcement, Power, and Security

The system of adversarial process built around trial by lay jurors, which the United States shares with other common law countries, is a system designed to supervise and limit government power to mete out criminal punishment. Long before the U.S. Constitution, the English jury was a device to limit the authority of state (or royal) judges. Other features of the adversarial trial were slower to develop, but the eventual power of the defense to present and challenge evidence with the aid of a skilled attorney prevented state officials from monopolizing the investigation process and factual record.[9] The federal and state constitutions explicitly guaranteed most of the core features of the adversarial common law trial: a public jury trial, notice of charges, defense rights to present evidence and challenge state witnesses, and the privilege against self-incrimination. The adversarial jury trial is an example of separation of powers writ small: the judicial power is divided between judge and jury, both of whom serve, along with the defense, as a check on executive power to prosecute.[10] That system reflects some suspicion of government criminal enforcement authority, and acts on that suspicion by dividing authority in various parts of criminal *process*, rather than primarily by substantive rules, such as a mandate that detention be founded on some evidence of violating a preexisting law, a duty to determine the truth, or a bar against excessively harsh punishments.[11]

From early on, however, this government-hampering regime has faced a countervailing priority: the growing expectation of citizens, beginning in the nineteenth century, for the state to ensure greater "security." Broadly understood, security includes protection against not only traditional forms of violent and property crimes but from threats to evolving standards of public safety, social order, and new kinds of risks—from terrorism, technology-enabled frauds or privacy intrusions, environmental contamination, and more. The advent of prisons, modern police forces, and full-time prosecutors in the nineteenth century are examples of the state—in Great Britain, the United States, and other advanced and democratizing nations—expanding its role in ensuring order and security in this expansive sense. Where private citizens once took primary responsibility for identifying wrongdoers and initiating criminal charges themselves as private prosecutors, state officials gradually took over and eventually monopolized those roles. At the same time, the range of crimes expanded as new kinds of risks arose with industrialization, mass commerce and transport, and other manifestations of modernity. The state's power to regulate and discipline through criminal law expanded through new offenses that called for state intervention in earlier stages of apparent criminal activity. The growth of inchoate offenses—crimes of possession, conspiracy, attempt, and otherwise planning or preparing for wrongdoing in the future—aimed to *prevent* harms rather than merely respond to them and sanction past wrongdoing. All of this requires much more executive capacity for criminal law enforcement than eighteenth-century governments possessed, a capacity reflected today in public agencies' immensely sophisticated surveillance and investigative infrastructures.[12] With these expanded capacities and expectations comes greater legitimacy for this kind of state power.

The growing ambitions for criminal law enforcement—and basic public approval for it—stand in some tension with a system of criminal process that hinders state enforcement power, makes it more costly and serves purposes other than punishment and prevention. In that ongoing conflict, criminal process has given far more than enforcement agendas have. Some parts of that transformation look broadly similar across many national justice systems. Criminal courts seemingly everywhere, for example, have evolved some version of an abbreviated process akin to plea bargaining. But U.S. criminal justice adapted in distinctive ways and embraced distinctive rationales for doing so. It used its affinity for the norms and mechanisms of markets and democracy to devise modes of criminal process that, paradoxically, have *aided* and *expanded* state enforcement power—especially *executive* power, despite common law, constitutional, and political traditions that are suspicious of that power.

Democracy, Markets, and Law

I should clarify at the outset how the terms *democracy, markets*, and *law* are used throughout this book. Each is a shorthand way of referring to both a range of mechanisms, processes, or institutions, and also to a collection of norms and values, or to premises about what rule or system works best. Each can be used to *describe* or characterize particular rules or processes in criminal

justice systems, or may distinguish how one rule is different from an alternative possibility. Each also connotes *justifications* for rules or processes—why
one way of doing things is normatively superior to another.

DEMOCRACY

Democracy refers to the many practices that prioritize the political responsiveness of officials, political accountability for policies, and public participation in
governance by various direct and indirect means. Jury verdicts and prosecutor
elections are both democratic mechanisms in criminal justice. So is the power
of elected politicians to appoint and remove prosecutors who lack civil service
employment status. Making criminal law policy through the ordinary legislative process (or by popular vote through ballot initiatives) is more democratic
than a lawmaking process that gives significant agenda-setting or mediating
roles to politically insulated agencies or expert commissions; state and federal
policymaking on U.S. criminal justice is much more in the former mode than
the latter. By the same token, rules that give juries sentencing discretion (as
some states do, notably capital murder) are more democratic than a regime of
sentences set by judges who are constrained by guidelines.[13]

Beyond describing differences in institutions or practices, democracy also
refers to a set of norms and values that justifies preferences for those institutions. Democratic values support the claim that certain decisions *should* be
made in accordance with political preferences, the popular will, or community sentiment rather than, for instance, expert knowledge or legal criteria.
The value of lay juries follows from the idea that judgments are better when
fact-finding and law application are integrated with "common sense" or community norms. That is less likely if judgments are left in the hands of specialized experts or legally trained professional judges. By the same token, criminal
enforcement decisions are *better* when based on the discretion of politically
accountable officials, rather than on a system in which those decisions are
made by nonpolitical civil servants applying relevant legal guidelines.

MARKETS

I use *markets* to reference perhaps a broader range of ideas, norms, and practices. The word's usage is less familiar in discussions of criminal justice,
although it is widely used in studies of (or simply political debates about) public
policy generally. Most straightforwardly, the term refers to the core premises
and arrangements of markets in the general economy: private actors pursuing
their individual self-interests, competition among rivals, and cooperation with
others through contracts. Market arrangements describe an important mode

of "private ordering," decisions and outcomes achieved by the interaction of private actors, in contrast to "public ordering," meaning some kind of state regulation or management. Not all private ordering, however, is accomplished by market mechanisms. In the literature on corporate governance, for example, scholars distinguish between *markets* and *hierarchies*. A firm that contracts with other firms to provide it with goods necessary for its corporate mission relies on the market; a firm that produces those goods itself, as part of a larger, integrated operation under the control of a single management team, has chosen *hierarchical control* over markets. Drawing out the parallel to a public policy opting for state intervention in place of markets, corporate hierarchies opt for (private) managerial planning and administration over markets.

In discussions of public policy, market-oriented policies—especially those commonly labeled as neoliberal—suggest arrangements in which the state plays a smaller role in providing services or regulating the terms of private activities and contractual interactions, as well as situations in which the state contracts with private firms to provide public services. Relying on private firms to provide health insurance is market-based policy; state provision, as seen in the United Kingdom's National Health Service or U.S. Medicare, is not. (Although there are myriad shades of gray in the distinction: private insurance may be state regulated or subsidized; a government may provide insurance by contracting with private insurers to do so on its behalf.) The criminal justice system provides examples of the state contracting with private firms to administer public institutions such as prisons and probation services. State and federal courts also contract with private lawyers to provide indigent defense representation. (In New Zealand, the government contracts with private firms to serve as public prosecutors.)

Much of this book focuses on practices at the heart of adversarial adjudication—the procedures by which criminal charges are filed, evidence is produced for courts, and guilt and punishment determined. In Mirjan Damaska's classic characterization, the adversarial model is employed by less "activist" states, those less inclined to use courts to implement policy rather than merely resolve conflicts. For those reasons among others, state officials—especially judges—have less power and parties have more, especially regarding evidence production and the framing of legal issues.[14] Through a different lens, however, one can identify in these same core features of adversarial process the inspiration of the market. By making evidence gathering the parties' task, adversarial systems "privatize" responsibility for the evidentiary record on which public courts depend in order to render judgments and, ultimately, justify imposing criminal punishment. But it is only a *functional* obligation; no law imposes a duty on either party to conduct thorough investigations and provide the court with all available relevant evidence.[15] The motivation for parties to produce evidence and raise legal claims is fundamentally the same one that motivates private actors in the market. It is the incentive of self-interest, as defined by their rival partisan roles in the litigation (*partisan* in the sense of *party* and of *not impartial*). Holding aside for now the degree to which prosecutors' partisan orientation is moderated by public-regarding commitments (taken up in chapter 2), the parties pursue and produce evidence—and invoke legal rules and argue for opposing judgments—as rivals with competitive agendas. But they are also free, like market actors, to cooperate and enter de facto contracts, such as plea bargains.

In these respects, adversarial process shares elemental market premises and mechanisms. Defendants are literally private parties pursuing private ends, but their legal power to do so frees adversarial prosecutors to act more like private litigants too, by taking a more partisan orientation to counter the defendant's partisan efforts as well as to meet their burden of proof. An alternative, non-market-based model, characterized by a public-ordering rather than private-ordering in compiling evidence, would give state officials a dominant role in compiling the record. This is roughly the idea in a classic inquisitorial justice system that relies primarily on officials—investigating magistrates, prosecutors, and judges—who call and question witnesses while acting under a duty to objectively investigate all the facts. A central aim of this book is to assess the many ways that American criminal process extends its adherence to market premises and mechanisms beyond these basic features of adversarial process, as well as how it tempers some market-based mechanisms and consequences of adversarialism comparatively less than the justice systems of other common law nations.

As with democracy, the term *markets* not only describes institutions but also refers to normative tenets on which those institutions rest. Even the most zealous market advocates, after all, endorse moral limits on markets. Certain goods and services are excluded from the legitimate market realm—children, human liberty, a judge's or juror's decision. Heated debate surrounds whether many other things should be subject to markets, such as select drugs, sexual services, exorbitant consumer loan interest rates, or unsafe working conditions. Put differently, the debate is whether these things should be left to the preferences of private individuals rather than be governed by publicly defined criteria embodied in state regulation. Behind any basic market arrangement is the view that certain kinds of losses and injuries are permissible and should be tolerated. One justification is that people or firms *deserve* to suffer their losses, because those losses follow from voluntary decisions to participate in markets. Poor results often can be traced to a party's weak effort, judgment, or skill, but participants know that markets by their nature present risks even for the most diligent and sharp-minded. Another justification is that these losses have positive effects that outweigh their harms—they provide the incentive to work diligently in order to win gains and avoid losses. That creates competitive markets full of self-interested actors, which lead to public and collective as well as private benefits. Values such as these underlie adversarial legal systems. A party's failure to produce a witness, to invoke the application of an evidence rule, or to raise a legal claim *justifies* the adverse court judgment caused by that failure. More bluntly, a defendant's neglect in producing evidence or raising a claim justifies the state imposing a factually or legally inaccurate conviction, because the error is attributable to the defendant's own decisions. The more thoroughly a criminal justice system embraces the norms and mechanisms of the market, the more it embraces that implication.

LAW

Finally, a word to clarify the usage of *law*, especially in relation to the terms *democracy* and *markets*. Foremost, law refers straightforwardly to legal rules in some form—whether judicial doctrines or statutes, precise rules, or broad standards. But it also refers to "law-like" methods of administering rules, such as their application and enforcement by formally neutral judges. One example of this is the rule that prosecutors can initiate charges only after a judicial official has determined the evidence for those charges meets the probable-cause standard. By contrast, prosecutors' unregulated power not to file charges despite evidence supporting them (or to choose among charges when several options exist) is an example of a decision ungoverned by law. Law in this sense has close analogues in other institutions that aspire to neutral, nonpartisan decision making on specified criteria other than personal or political preferences—for instance, administrative agencies that act upon expertise or scientific analysis. Officials charged with "achieving justice" are more law-like than, say, legislators who are free to act on political values and to pursue policy preferences.

Using these terms in these ways takes advantage of familiar distinctions between law and politics, as well as between law—or regulation—and markets. This means setting aside different usages of the terms that would lead to confusion. Most important, distinguishing between law and politics or democracy is not to say that politically motivated decisions, or policies that follow majoritarian preferences, are not *lawful*. Of course they are, if they are in accord with the appropriate legal authorities (statutes, constitutions) that govern them. Likewise, legal rules define democratic procedures (such as jury decision making, elections, or political appointments).

Similarly, even "free" markets are not altogether free of law, as Bernard Harcourt has recently argued to incisive effect in *The Illusion of Free Markets*. Law is what defines and constitutes *free* markets. The misleading adjective "free" denotes that the law's primary role is to facilitate private interactions, which should largely determine market outcomes. Free markets are those in which the law does little more than enforce private contracts, bar fraud, and otherwise facilitate private sector exchanges. Nonetheless, distinctions between markets and government regulation, or between private ordering versus public ordering, are familiar, useful and meaningful conventions.

DEMOCRACY AND MARKETS VERSUS LAW

Clarifying this terminology improves recognition of how law, democracy, and markets become substitutes for one another. Each represents a mode of organization or decision making, so democratic or market mechanisms can serve as alternatives to legal regulation. Prosecutors can make decisions about what crimes to charge "politically"—according to policy preferences and in light of what they take to be community values or popular sentiment. Alternately, they can do so primarily by applying legal criteria and an experienced assessment of evidence, or the efficacy of punishment for goals such as deterrence. Likewise, as already noted, a legal system can generate evidentiary records for judicial decisions either by relying on private parties in market-like competition, or by imposing legal duties on officials (or to some degree even private actors) to objectively investigate and compile a comprehensive factual record. Some version of the latter approach describes the American regime of fact-finding by some regulatory agencies, as well as criminal justice systems in some civil law countries.

American adjudication gives both democratic processes and market processes larger formal roles, and gives law a correspondingly smaller role, than do legal systems elsewhere. In that specific sense, American criminal process is less *legal* than its counterparts in many other nations. The rule of law in U.S. criminal justice is more privatized and more politicized than elsewhere, because it relies more on politically motivated officials or market-like (self-interested, competitive) decision making to set enforcement priorities, adjudicate charges, reach convictions, determine punishments, and justify errors in judgments. In making these choices, the American rule of law regime relies less on legal rules, legal duties, and judicial neutrality.

This is also true for the rule of law in a somewhat broader sense. "The rule of law" is commonly used to describe the means by which a polity authorizes state authority as well as restrains it to prevent abuses of official power. The rule of law accomplishes this, most basically, by preestablished, legitimate rules that define entitlements for the state and private citizens, and which are enforceable by courts through due process. But judicially enforceable laws are not the only instrument by which to restrain and authorize state action. Some are the familiar features of common law and adversarial traditions. Juries are a democratic institution designed to check state officials—prosecutors and judges—and to authorize state-imposed punishment. Adversarial process reduces judicial power over trial evidence by putting evidence-production power in the hands of private defendants and their litigation competitors, executive-branch prosecutors. Throughout this book, I explore examples of how American criminal justice, in ways apparent and subtle, extends its reliance on democratic and market-based practices, rather than on legal rules, to carry out these rule of law ambitions, and also how the understanding of *the rule of law* changes in consequence of those choices.

This does not necessarily mean that U.S. criminal justice guards less effectively against official abuses of power. Like law, both democracy and markets can to some degree restrain or reduce government power. Political accountability is straightforwardly a means for citizens to supervise government. They can replace elected officials for (among other reasons) abuse of power; the same is not true for officials with life tenure or civil service status. Market mechanisms likewise can check state actors, as when the defense challenges state witnesses and produces rival ones. Markets can also prevent abuse of state power by simply displacing state power. That is a primary rationale for the minimal-state ideal, and it is one reason (on top of supposedly greater efficiencies) for privatization, or relying on the private sector instead of the state to provide goods or services.

However, neither democratic nor market processes—nor legal rules—are *necessarily* or consistently effective at restraining, or appropriately authorizing, state authority. Making officials responsive to popular sentiment is not the same as reducing their power. This is one key to understanding how American criminal justice retained a singular devotion to democratic governance while also greatly expanding its punitive capacity. Majorities even in the United States sometimes favor vigorous government. This has been readily apparent in the context of criminal justice, where the severity of punishment practices in recent decades has drawn support from "penal populism" and led to four decades of "law and order politics." Less apparent is how market-style norms and mechanisms have facilitated rather than hindered state criminal enforcement powers. The market-inspired rules for guilty pleas are one example. As I will consider in detail in chapter 4, the rules of plea bargaining embody a highly "deregulated," free market model, including the private market's moral indifference to effects of unequal resources among contracting parties, its exceedingly thin concept of coercion, and its minimal regulation of outcomes according to criteria of fairness rather than party consent. In these respects and many others, democratic and market norms in criminal justice simultaneously supplant legal rules and facilitate expansive state enforcement authority.

This basic orientation of U.S. criminal justice—less reliance on law, more on democracy and markets—has certain specific effects as well. Affinity for democratic and market-like processes rather than legal rules and the judicial enforcement of these rules affects the balance of powers between governmental branches. In particular, it works to the advantage of executive-branch officials, while significantly restraining judicial authority. Democratic and market-inspired rationales lie behind many of the rules and doctrines that constrain the criminal judge's role and lessen their capacity (and the juries' as well) to ensure accurate, fair, and proportional outcomes from trials and negotiated settlements. All of that weakens the judicial-branch check on prosecutors.

An additional effect follows from the embrace of market norms in criminal process, which relates to allocation of responsibility between public and private actors. Adversarial process by its nature puts power over—and thus responsibility for—the factual record in the parties' hands. Adversarialism does not necessarily also give the parties control over the procedural stages or components; through most of the nineteenth century, for example, parties could not waive the jury and agree by mutual consent to a criminal bench trial. Nonetheless the modern trend has been to expand parties' control over the adjudication process, and American justice systems have in some important respects gone further down this road, giving one or both parties the ability to waive nearly all rights and procedures. (They also bear the burden of demanding many procedural opportunities in order not to lose them, and for invoking governing law that they want courts to apply.) This is true from the earliest stages (defendants may waive judicial review of charges) through trial (defendants may waive the jury, the prosecution's evidence disclosure, or rules of evidence admissibility) and all postconviction challenges. But this strong model of party control entails a consequently smaller role for the state writ large (and probably better represented in this sense by the judiciary than the prosecution). Market rationality lies behind this regime as well; nearly all components of criminal process are tradable among the parties, or subject to private ordering by the parties. As party powers increase, so does party responsibility, including responsibility ultimately for the quality and content of the judgment. And as party responsibility increases, state responsibility decreases accordingly. As a result, responsibility not only for the process but also for the integrity of criminal judgments—orders issued by public courts—is privatized.

Other Accounts of Criminal Process

Parts of this picture resonate with other descriptions of the American political and legal systems, and parts are in tension with previous studies. A familiar account stresses American society as notably *legalistic* and litigation oriented. Tocqueville's enduring observation to this effect was that in the United States, all political questions eventually become legal questions.[16] Much more recently, scholars have emphasized the "legalistic" nature of American governance. Seymour Lipset has concluded that America is a more "legalistic and rights-oriented nation" than other advanced democracies, and "its people excessively litigious," a tendency he blamed in part on "the weakness of the state."[17] In Robert Kagan's influential account, the United States practices a distinctive form of "adversarial legalism" through which much public policy is made that, elsewhere, mostly is crafted in legislatures or bureaucratic agencies.[18]

Notwithstanding the claim here that American criminal justice is less legalistic, in a particular sense, than its counterparts elsewhere, this book has a good bit of common ground with those earlier analyses. There is no dissent here from the generalization that American courts are also more political than courts elsewhere and that "adversarial legalism is deeply rooted in the political institutions and values of the United States."[19] Kagan also emphasizes that adversarial legalism is a "party-dominated" style of litigation that permits and rewards party initiative and creative advocacy—a legal system, in short, in which parties have most of the power to frame legal issues, to control the factual record, and to adapt the process to their ends. Moreover, this book, like Kagan's, finds useful insights on American adversarialism by drawing contrasts with models elsewhere that are more bureaucratic or less political.

Despite these similarities, many of the characterizations and criticisms of American criminal justice in this book differ from prior accounts, including two recent, prominent accounts focused on the U.S. criminal justice system: William Stuntz's *The Collapse of American Criminal Justice* and Stephanos Bibas's *The Machinery of Criminal Justice.*[20] Although with different approaches and agendas, Stuntz and Bibas both attribute many of failings of American criminal justice to excesses of law and bureaucracy and to deficits of democratic accountability, especially at the local level. While parting ways on that point, this book shares some of their criticisms. Bibas and Stuntz both lament some dysfunctional parts of American democratic practice, especially politicized policymaking in legislatures, which has produced overly broad criminal laws and extremely harsh sentencing policies. Moreover, both emphasize the deleterious effects of justice systems dominated by prosecutors and judges, whom Bibas styles "insiders." Those two groups of officials have transformed adjudication into a largely nonpublic process that prioritizes speedy resolution of criminal cases through guilty pleas.

Unlike this book, Bibas and Stuntz argue that reform requires making criminal justice administration less legalistic and more democratic. As Bibas puts it, "the problem may be over-legalization of the system" and a "bureau-cratic ideal of justice" that "depends on expertise and rules." The key reason "America's criminal justice system is badly broken," Stuntz avers, is that it is "more centralized, more legalized and more bureaucratized" than in the past. Their common solution is (in Bibas's words) a "more local and democratic" and "a more moral, populist, participatory criminal justice system." Both are con-fident (in Stuntz's words) that if the United States will "make criminal justice more locally democratic, [then] justice will be more moderate, more egalitar-ian, and more effective at controlling crime."[21] Consequently, both urge more use of lay juries and other decentralizing strategies. Stuntz advocates more community input on policing, while Bibas emphasizes direct participation in criminal process by victims, defendants, and other interested parties. Such shared criticisms and prescriptions are particularly American. At bottom, their roads to a better—and they would insist more *lawful*—criminal justice system require more democracy, not more law.

Finally, despite the enduring insights of *The Faces of Justice and State Authority* since its publication thirty years ago, Damaska's study had a much different agenda and did not attempt to a fine-grained explanation of U.S. crim-inal process in relation to the American state, much less consequences such as high imprisonment rates, which had only started their ascent in 1986, when Damaska wrote. The United States was clearly a system he had in mind as an exemplar of a reactive rather than activist state, with a party-dominated proc-ess aimed at resolving conflicts more than implementing state policy. But if reactive still describes the American state in many respects, it is hard to argue that the term remains the best way to characterize its criminal enforcement authority, which is more proactive and invasive—measured by convictions and imprisonment, holding aside surveillance and investigation tactics—than any other nation. How did America's adversarial system, designed to *limit* official power, transform itself to serve a singularly potent state enforcement capacity? A big part of the answer, as noted earlier, lies in how the use of mech-anisms of democracy and markets rather than law has enhanced rather than checked state power.

The Power of Democratic and Market Principles

While sharing much in common with the aforementioned studies, it should be clear that this book focuses on a different set of explanations for dysfunction—the influence of market-oriented ideologies, especially as they interact with strong commitments to democratic governance. Democratic and market ideologies are pervasive in the doctrines, norms, and institutions of

American criminal process. They provide the background normative frameworks, or preconditions, that make the choices for some rules and institutions more intuitive and appealing than others. In ways obvious and subtle, the American system puts less faith in law and legality, and more in democracy and markets. The depth and breadth of those underlying rationalities in U.S. criminal justice explain why many parts of the American system look and operate so differently even in comparison to counterparts in other common law nations.

Why, for example, did plea bargaining take hold so much earlier and more openly in U.S. legal history? Guilty pleas have a long historical track record in American and English common law traditions. Explicit *bargaining* for those pleas has a shorter and somewhat more obscure history, at least outside the United States. Historical studies have documented widespread plea bargaining in various U.S. localities during the early nineteenth century.[22] By the 1920s, when scholars first documented and lamented "the vanishing trial," negotiated guilty pleas probably produced most convictions in most jurisdictions. The U.S. Supreme Court did not acknowledge plea bargaining until 1970, but it immediately gave the practice constitutional approval—earlier and more unreservedly than occurred in England, Germany, or probably any other jurisdiction. Why were negotiated pleas in lieu of trials so intuitively *appropriate* to American judges, lawyers, and legislators? Plea bargains met more resistance elsewhere (and in some places still do), and they stood in deep tension with the valorized tradition of jury trials. Several leading accounts convincingly attribute plea bargaining's triumph to how well it serves the professional self-interests of prosecutors and judges in the context of rising caseloads.[23] But were conditions so different elsewhere, or did American officials understand their interests differently and find those interests easier to reconcile with their conceptions of professionalism, fairness, and justice? Furthermore, why did American plea bargaining adopt its particular rules and norms, with almost no legal restrictions on negotiation tactics and only the most minimal in terms of bargains? The trend toward some version of consent-based conviction process in place of trials is worldwide, even in civil law jurisdictions where procedural traditions fit much less comfortably with negotiated nontrial judgments. Nevertheless, no nation has embraced America's "deregulated" rules of plea bargaining,[24] despite the remarkable uniformity on this point among the fifty-one different U.S. jurisdictions, each with the power to do otherwise.[25] For full answers one must look to the market rationalities that lead American jurisdictions to view plea agreements as closely analogous to private contracts, negotiated by autonomous, self-interested parties in a free marketplace.

The market model for plea bargains requires specific understandings of what prosecutors, judges, and defendants should do—what they are responsible for in criminal process, and what actions are professional or appropriate.

U.S. criminal justice systems are distinctive on these parameters as well, much of which can be traced to the trust in democratic governance in place of law. For example, U.S. prosecutors have more limited legal obligations for pretrial evidence disclosure, in good part it seems because they are more politically accountable than their counterparts elsewhere. In light of their political responsiveness, criminal process gives prosecutors more discretion over what evidence to disclose, rather than imposing broader legal duties to disclosure duties or even subjecting prosecutors' judgments to judicial review. This structural choice reappears elsewhere as well—discretion coupled with political accountability, instead of discretion limited by legal standards. Among other effects, this structure contributes to a more partisan, less ministerial conception of the prosecutor's professional role.

The implications of this preference for democracy over law extend beyond merely the prosecutor's role. One obvious consequence is that American judges have less capacity to supervise and check prosecutor decisions. In small but significant ways, English and Canadian judges—like the U.S. jurisdictions, adversarial systems with common law roots—have more supervisory authority over prosecutors. Judges lack even modest authority to review any aspect of charging decisions save for a minimal factual basis, and (depending somewhat on the jurisdiction) little or no power to order pretrial evidence disclosure. Prosecutors' political responsiveness is also a factor in the power they have gained at the expense of judges—unparalleled in other common law systems elsewhere—over sentencing. Both forthrightly and subtly, legal standards and judicial review play smaller roles in criminal justice because political supervision and market-like procedures and norms play larger ones.

Democratic and market rationalities, in these respects and others, strengthen the executive branch's criminal law authority. When crime is a perennially salient political issue, a strong and politically responsive prosecution corps leads easily to harsh enforcement and sentencing policies.[26] As between government officials, democratic norms favor prosecutors over judges. As between judges and parties, market-based norms in adversarial process favor parties over judges. Imposing fewer legal rules on parties (as laissez-faire or neoliberal deregulation minimizes rules on market actors) means judges have fewer grounds to supervise parties' decisions or efforts, and, ultimately, the efficacy of the adjudication process. More party autonomy and less judicial authority leads to less judicial—and *state*—responsibility for the integrity of court judgments.

Within this framework, it is easier to see why U.S. courts have done little to address practices that compromise the integrity of adjudication, from prosecutors' failure to reveal evidence favoring the defense to the widespread use of unreliable forms of forensic analysis, jailhouse informants, and eyewitness identifications. Responsibility for reforms lies more in the political process, and in some cases with the zealous adversarial process, than with judges' inherent responsibility for the integrity of judicial process. The more closely one looks at the implications of democratic and market-based principles in criminal process, the more convincing the case becomes that American criminal justice needs more *law*—more rules, a more active judiciary, and more state responsibility for the integrity of criminal procedure and its consequences.

The Organization of the Book

The remainder of the book first takes up in detail how democratic and market ideologies are fundamental to the design and practice of criminal process. It then examines the transformative power of those creeds in specific adjudication practices—plea bargains, trials, and appeals. The final chapters connect these choices to the expansive reach and power of the criminal justice system. First, chapter 2 describes how expansive commitments to democratic governance and political accountability shape core institutions of American criminal justice. The focus is on prosecutors, judges, and juries, and on the rules that define and limit their powers, especially against each other. Faith in political regulation over legal regulation lies behind much of what makes American criminal justice different from justice systems in other nations, including those based in the same common law and adversarial-trial traditions. Indeed, as already suggested, confidence in the democratic process has helped U.S. prosecutors win greater power over judges across time. Whereas other nations seek to reduce political influences on prosecutors and judges, U.S. jurisdictions embrace those influences as a virtue. The rise of politically accountable prosecutors—mostly through election, occasionally through political appointments—also helps suggest why public prosecutors were able to vanquish private prosecutors and related formal roles for victims in litigation more completely than did prosecutors in justice systems elsewhere. Democratic values are an important reason why state judiciaries uniformly signed on to a conception of separation of powers that constrains their authority to oversee any aspect of criminal charging. That choice was hardly preordained, given that state courts often supervised prosecution in their early decades, and that legislatures gave them powers by statute that they lacked at common law to review prosecutors' *nolle prosequi* (nonprosecution) decisions and to dismiss prosecutions "in the interest of justice." In these ways and others, legal standards and judicial supervision gave way to political supervision. Prosecutors' democratic legitimacy also plays a somewhat more indirect role in the marginalization of juries—the original institution of democratic governance in criminal process—through the rise of plea bargaining and bench trials. No other common law countries authorized waivers of the criminal jury nearly as early as did U.S. jurisdictions.

Chapter 3 takes up the topic of market ideas in criminal process, a topic less familiar than the role of democratic ideas. Partly to address that, I borrow descriptive insights from comparative political economists, who often characterize advanced economies as fitting into two broad groups—liberal-market and coordinated-market economies. In the first group, which includes the United States, state regulation tends to facilitate more private ordering. The state nominally is less committed to specific market outcomes (such as employment security or certain income distributions) and generally does less to ameliorate market outcomes through social welfare policies. Labor, antitrust, and corporate governance laws often disfavor longer-term economic arrangements by unions or industry-wide associations of firms. By contrast, policies in coordinated-market economies such as Germany rely more on public ordering. They usually have greater regulation of employment terms and more generous social welfare policies; they also are more favorable to unions and coordination by firms across industries. In different terminology, the first group follows a more neoliberal policy path than the second.

These broad policy differences rest on constellations of beliefs about the proper role of the state, the efficacy of market institutions, and what kinds of economic and social outcomes are desirable or tolerable. Chapter 3 develops the book's core argument that U.S. liberal-market traditions—the premises and norms of the nation's market ideology—fundamentally inform the rules, rationales, institutions, and values of criminal adjudication. Liberal-market ideas lead to rules that sharpen litigating parties' rival interests and incentives. The prosecutor's role is less ministerial, less oriented toward public values and interests beyond enforcement. The state—especially in the form of the judiciary, but in other respects as well—does less to "coordinate" certain kinds of outcomes, including, ultimately, the accuracy and proportionality of court judgments. Criminal process puts a priority on giving parties procedural opportunities but, as in the economic realm, the state is less committed to ensuring certain kinds of results.

Chapter 4 focuses on the core practice by which U.S. courts reach nearly all criminal convictions—negotiated pleas of guilty. The law of plea bargaining is a singular example of the influence of liberal-market norms in criminal process. Given the extensive literature on the history of plea bargaining and reasons for its ascendancy, such as rising caseloads, the focus here will be analyzing the particular set of legal rules for negotiated pleas that dominate U.S. practice but are less common (and sometimes controversial) elsewhere. The American law of plea bargains—constitutional, statutory, and common law—provides ample evidence of acceptance of and reliance on the norms and processes of markets and, somewhat more subtly, democratic ideology. Uniquely among the judiciaries of common law nations, American courts unabashedly describe plea bargaining as a "market" with rules drawn directly from the law of private contracts. This market-based rationality is likewise apparent in prosecutors' own descriptions of their goals and justifications for bargaining. The rationales for this law of negotiated pleas are, in the vein of economic arguments, thoroughly instrumental, and that rhetorical framework has displaced other normative conceptions of the practice over the last forty years in constitutional and common law. The instrumental aim of maximizing negotiated guilty pleas in lieu of trials has defeated rival rationales grounded in due process and fairness standards, which had given courts a greater role in supervising the parties' bargaining tactics and the substantive terms of plea-based judgments. A liberal-market model of party-dominated private ordering triumphed over a model with greater public (judicial) coordination and oversight. Judges have been relegated to little more than policing exceedingly narrow definitions of voluntary consent to the terms of negotiated pleas.

Chapter 5 shifts from plea bargaining to focus on the market-inspired, privatizing rules in trial and post-trial procedures. Even in adversarial trial systems, which are characterized by party rather than judicial control over the process, legal rules can vary greatly in the degree to which they safeguard accuracy and protect other public values. How strongly, for example, should the law protect defendants' individual choices for one defense lawyer over another? And how, if at all, may the state interfere with the role of private wealth in securing legal assistance? Right-to-counsel doctrines modestly compensate for defendants' poverty through state-funded legal assistance. At the same time, the law rigorously guarantees—at some public cost—wealthy defendants' freedom to retain any lawyer they choose in the private market for legal services. What limits should be placed on efforts to identify and correct erroneous judgments? How much should the state safeguard the integrity of judgments when they are jeopardized by litigants' inaction or poor decision making? To what extent should defendants suffer for the missteps of their lawyers? Criminal procedure rules must choose between allowing party decisions to undermine judgment accuracy, encouraging parties to take responsibility for the integrity of adversarial adjudication, providing chances to correct errors, and strengthening the state's role in safeguarding against such errors. State disclosure of exculpatory evidence, for example, could be mandatory before trials or guilty pleas, or it could be left to the party negotiation. Under "plain error" rules of review, courts will, in egregious cases, allow chances to correct errors despite some lapse by the defense. Under many other rules, defendants can increase the risk of wrongful or disproportionate judgments by waiving or inadvertently forfeiting various rights, and those errors go uncorrected. Throughout pretrial,

trial and appellate process, the logic and norms of markets influence choices among rules. The result is a procedural regime that favors private ordering and party responsibility, and diminishes judicial responsibility as well as the substance of public law norms.

Chapter 6 steps back from the details of procedure to assess the consequences of the fundamental ambition of market-oriented criminal process—to make the process of achieving convictions ever more efficient. The U.S. Supreme Court for decades has invoked efficiency as a powerful justification for rules that help replace trials with guilty pleas, as well as for rules governing practices from discovery to appellate review. Chapter 6 explores how the very concept of "efficiency," in criminal procedure as in other contexts, is more complicated than courts and policymakers generally recognize. A particular way of doing things may be efficient for one goal—such as achieving convictions quickly with minimal public cost—but poorly serve other goals, such as accurate outcomes or democratic supervision of criminal justice by juries.

More important, improving efficiency can have unintended, counterintuitive, and even perverse effects for the criminal justice system. Courts universally overlook these risks, although they are widely recognized in other domains outside of criminal justice administration. Producing something more efficiently lowers its price, which can in turn raise demand for it. Compared to trials, plea bargaining lowers the cost of adjudicating criminal charges, which makes criminal charges cheaper and easier to see through to conviction. The system's newly gained capacity for processing cases doesn't merely meet an external demand for processing some fixed number of cases. It induces more demand—it encourages more prosecutions. Chapter 6 presents evidence suggesting plea bargaining contributes both to increased rates of prosecution over time and provides savings in adjudication budgets that can be transferred to subsidize other parts of criminal justice, such as prisons.

Chapter 7 takes up a couple of broader questions raised by earlier chapters. Why did a country with an unrivaled devotion to local democracy and minimal state authority acquiesce in the practical demise of the jury, embrace an unusually strong form of executive power for prosecutors, and develop the world's most expansive and punitive carceral state? Chapter 7 argues that this system was a unique American adaptation to the steadily growing popular expectations about security in the modern era. Throughout advanced nations, people came to believe that the state must ensure an adequate security from an ever-expanding range of risks. Especially in the twentieth century, courts as well as policymakers began to speak explicitly of the state's duty to ensure safety and security by preventing and punishing crime. Replacing the jury box with the ballot box as the primary democratic institution of American criminal justice served this agenda well. Moreover, many of the criminal justice policies that led to record incarceration rates developed during a fraught period of American racial politics, in the years immediately after landmark civil rights advances in the 1960s. At the same time, the shift from trials to prosecutor-dominated settlements was pushed along by changes in the nature of evidence in the modern era. Modern technology often provides convincing evidentiary records long before trial. That diminishes the need for trials as a mechanism to *produce* evidence—one of the common law trial's original functions—and makes settlement based on pretrial records more feasible and more tempting. Finally, chapter 7 briefly surveys the differences in how market ideas and privatization have succeeded across various parts of the criminal justice system. States contract with private firms to run prisons and probation services, but not police and prosecution agencies, even though private security firms and law firms are capable of providing those services. The consistent theme seems to be that market mechanisms succeed not simply when they reduce public costs, but when they preserve state power.

In conclusion, chapter 8 connects the ideologies and reform trends in criminal justice to broader political and economic developments since the 1970s. During the same era that American criminal justice adopted its unprecedented policies of harsh incarceration, its national party politics began to sharply polarize and, in the wake of a neoliberal policy turn, income inequalities grew tremendously. The same vibrant market orientation that reshaped the political economy worked its way into criminal justice administration. The same lack of faith in the basic possibility of nonpartisan governance and skilled bureaucratic administration that increased in politically polarized society undermined aspirations for criminal justice administration governed by the rule of law rather than partisanship and private interests. Despite the depth of these commitments, events from the past and present confirm that harsh criminal justice does not inevitably follow from politically attuned criminal justice.

The focus on democracy and markets in these pages inevitably shortchanges other forces that contribute to the present-day structure of criminal procedure. Because so much of U.S. criminal procedure arises from the federal Constitution, much is explained by the peculiar methods and concerns of constitutional interpretation, in which courts variously weigh text, original meaning, contemporary practices, federalism or separation-of-powers concerns, practicality, and more. Several chapters discuss constitutional rules and their rationales, but always to draw out issues of democratic and market ideologies rather than to offer a more comprehensive constitutional analysis. Gliding over these considerations is not meant to suggest they are unimportant. The aim instead is to take advantage of the vast body of existing writing on these themes and assume familiarity with some of it. The same goes for issues of race, which get only very brief treatment here. Race is indisputably a central factor, if a complicated and contentious one, in U.S. criminal justice. For that reason it rightly continues to generate critical literature of nearly every genre, to which this work merely alludes rather than adds. No single volume (of modest length, at least) can do justice to all these disparate strands. What follows is an attempt to bring attention to overlooked influences on the U.S. criminal process, reinterpret some of its defining practices, and begin a new basis for critical assessment of an immensely important, far-reaching, but deeply troubling institution.

CHAPTER 2

Criminal Justice and Democracy

Community participation in the administration of the criminal law, moreover, is not only consistent with our democratic heritage but is also critical to public confidence in the fairness of the criminal justice system.
—*Taylor v. Louisiana (1975)*

[O]ur cases have cautioned against using "the aegis of the Cruel and Unusual Punishment Clause" to cut off the normal democratic processes. . . . [Only the] work product of legislatures and sentencing jury determinations . . . can be reconciled with the undeniable precepts that the democratic branches of government and individual sentencing juries are, by design, better suited than courts to . . . inform the selection of publicly acceptable criminal punishments.
—*Atkins v. Virginia (2002) (Rehnquist, C.J., dissenting)**

State Power and Democracy

The United States shares its status as a liberal democracy with nations in Europe, the Commonwealth, and elsewhere. But the nature of its democracy and its path of democratic development are distinctive. American democratic governments developed earlier than those in Europe and elsewhere, and the United States has generally led the world over the last two centuries in the expansion of its franchise. In contrast to most European states, which had strong central governments before they moved to broad-based democratic governance, in the United States democracy came first. As a result, many European states achieved "bureaucratic rationalization" before firmly established democratic institutions. That is, they had professionalized agencies to carry out various state functions, staffed by civil servants relatively insulated from politics. The United States did not, and so its state institutions developed in the context of democratic control, which led overall to more politicized, rather than nonpartisan, public administration—a difference of fundamental importance for American criminal justice. This history, combined with a generalized suspicion of centralized and nondemocratic state power from the founding era, set America on a unique path of democratic state development.[1]

Skepticism of central state authority is evident in the constitutional structure of the American state. Federalism creates a vertical division of authority, with power dispersed among the states and the federal government with limited authority. Separation of powers adds a horizontal division of authority within the federal and state governments. The result of these constraints on government power is in one sense *anti*-democratic. Compared to most parliamentary systems, where governing parties control government and can enact policies with majority support, the American presidential system of separated powers frequently frustrates efforts to enact majoritarian policies.[2] From another perspective, however, American government is unusually democratic. Elections are more frequent than in most other nations, and more officials take office by direct election, including minor local administrators and (in many state governments) cabinet officials. Suspicion of government power motivates both the obstacles to majoritarian decision making and the expansive electoral process, which allows citizens to check or influence more officials, including those who would be civil servants elsewhere.

As a consequence of American federalism, most criminal justice administration is handled by the states rather than the federal government, and the states—in the tradition of America's "persistent localism"—in turn devolve much of their responsibility to localities.[3] In nearly all states, among those locally elected offices are the primary criminal justice officials—prosecutors, judges, and sheriffs, as well as city council members, who typically appoint police chiefs. Direct election—or, in the federal system, political appointment—of those officials, most notably prosecutors, is the most obvious example of the ways in which American criminal process uniquely favors democratic responsiveness over politically insulated, nonpartisan bureaucracies. The same democratic preference extends to criminal lawmaking. Some states also permit legislation (including criminal justice policy) by popular initiative and referendum, and criminal law and procedure are otherwise crafted by legislatures through the ordinary political process, with comparatively little influence or agenda-setting power for expert bodies, nonpartisan officials, or specialized agencies. The same is true in institutions outside of criminal justice. Most advanced democracies use some form of nonpartisan process to draw boundaries of electoral districts; the United States leaves that task in the hands of the elected legislators, who design their own districts.[4]

Across common law jurisdictions, the use of lay juries (and sometimes lay magistrates) in criminal trials, rather than law-trained judges, is a different means of expressing the preference for democratic rather than professional decision making. Even in this widely shared heritage, American law over time came to place great emphasis on the locally representative and democratic nature of juries. "Those eligible for jury service are to be found in every stratum of society. Jury competence is an individual rather than a group or class matter," the Supreme Court declared by the 1940s. "To disregard it is to open the door to class distinctions and discriminations which are abhorrent to the democratic ideals of trial by jury."[5] Exclusion on the basis of status or group identity does "injury to the jury system, to the law as an institution, to the community at large, and to the democratic ideal reflected in the processes of our courts."

The long-standing commitment to democracy apparent in these familiar aspects of American governance is also evident, on close inspection, in the rules, doctrines, norms, and institutions of U.S. criminal process. The rationales behind American criminal process reveal a preference for politically responsive governance rather than objective or nonpartisan modes of governance, such as legal rules enforced by judicial review or administered by professional agencies and officials. In this chapter, attention is on the key non-legislative players—prosecutors, judges, and juries—whose roles shape many of the rules, norms, and institutions of the criminal process. Initially the focus is on the implications of political accountability for prosecutors' authority and on parts of the criminal process crafted in response to the prosecutor's role. Following then is a briefer consideration of how norms of democratic governance have affected the roles of judges and juries. Subsequent chapters explore reverberations of democratic accountability in other aspects of adjudication.

Throughout common law jurisdictions and in many civil law systems as well, prosecutors exercise broad discretion regarding whether or not to initiate criminal charges, and how to litigate, settle, or terminate them. But their authority is not unlimited or unsupervised. Criminal justice systems use a variety of tools to constrain, monitor, or otherwise regulate prosecutors. Some of these tools stem from the authority accorded to other criminal justice actors—judges, juries, victims, or other private parties. Some take the form of legal standards. Some arise from how prosecution agencies are organized and staffed. Even within common law nations, criminal justice systems mix these options in quite different ways. Observing how other systems make use of this range of possibilities clarifies how thoroughly American criminal justice relies on democratic rather than legal accountability—politics rather than law—to legitimize broad prosecution authority. What is less apparent is how political accountability for prosecutors has led to less power for others—for judges, juries, and victims—and has enhanced the power of prosecutors. Moreover, political accountability affects the professional norms within prosecution agencies. It encourages a more adversarial and a weaker "minister of justice" identity, because political responsiveness partially displaces bureaucratic professionalism both as a constraint and a source of legitimacy. Legislatures also take political oversight as a reason to forgo statutes or regulations that would guide prosecutorial discretion and reduce possibilities for biased judgments or abuse of power.

The Parameters of Prosecutorial Authority

POLITICAL VERSUS APOLITICAL PROSECUTION AGENCIES

The most obvious democratic structures of American criminal justice are well known. State criminal justice systems handle more than 90 percent of U.S. criminal cases,[6] and forty-five of the fifty states select prosecutors through direct local elections. Most states opted for this model during a wave of state constitutional reforms in the 1840s through the 1860s; many formerly appointed state and local officials (including judgeships) were transformed into elected positions.[7] The motivation, according to Jed Shugerman's study of state courts, was to *reduce* political influence from legislators, governors, and political parties who controlled appointments.[8] In many places, that ambition failed and party organizations influenced or controlled local elected officials into the twentieth century,[9] but the direct election of justice officials has nevertheless proven remarkably durable and influential. Of the five states that do not elect local prosecutors, three—along with the federal system—appoint prosecutors through processes mostly controlled by political officials: the president or governor nominates a candidate, who must be confirmed by the legislature.[10] Two other (very small) states, Delaware and Rhode Island, elect the state attorney general, who appoints a staff to handle all prosecutions.[11] Staff prosecutors commonly lack civil service job security; most serve, formally at least, at the pleasure of their elected chiefs.

On top of this democratic structure, U.S. prosecution authority is highly decentralized. State systems operate independently of each other and of federal authority (save for federal constitutional requirements), and most state attorneys general have little formal authority—in some cases virtually none—over locally elected prosecutors who handle all ordinary criminal cases.[12]

The political accountability that is nearly uniform throughout U.S. jurisdictions contrasts with virtually all criminal justice systems in other common law (and civil law) countries, where prosecutor elections are unknown, appointment processes are intended to be nonpolitical, job security is greater, and hierarchical supervision is typically more uniform.[13] All those features, of course, aim to minimize the political influences on prosecutors that American systems embrace. In this obvious way, the United States favors democratically responsive prosecution agencies, while other countries try to insulate prosecutors so as to maximize their professional or public-interested judgment. Where American jurisdictions worry about policymaking too remote from popular preferences, nearly all other systems put much more faith in objectivity, professionalism, and—as noted later—rules that restrict discretion. To be sure, realities can be different. Political concerns may be negligible day to day in many local offices in the United States, while political influence can work its way into nominally apolitical systems elsewhere. But as a matter of fundamental premises and values reflected in the structure of prosecution agencies, the differences are stark.[14]

LEGAL CONSTRAINTS ON PROSECUTORIAL DISCRETION

At the most basic level, justice systems make two sorts of choices about the scope of prosecution authority. One is whether and how much to restrain prosecutors' discretion with legal rules, such as charging guidelines or a mandatory duty to file charges for certain offenses whenever the state has sufficient evidence of a violation. A different kind of choice about prosecution authority lies in whether to give public prosecutors a monopoly over charging crimes, or whether private citizens will share some of that power—perhaps through an ability to bar certain prosecutions, or to press charges without a public prosecutor's involvement. Regarding both of these parameters, the rules across American jurisdictions are fairly uniform but differ from those in most European and common law countries. They also differ in ways that strengthen public prosecutorial authority.

Starting with the first point, the basic pattern of one kind of legal regime is relatively clear. In all common law systems and some civil law ones (such as in Denmark, France, and the Netherlands), prosecutors have always had discretion about whether to charge without a legal duty to pursue all well-grounded charges.[15] In other civil law systems—such as Germany, Italy, and Poland—a rule of mandatory prosecution long prevailed. Tellingly, that rule is often called the legality principle, on the premise that legality requires not only advance specification of offenses (the core of its common law meaning) but also consistent enforcement across similar cases.[16] Some doubt that the rule in reality ever consistently eliminated discretion, especially if prosecutors in practice are the ones making the call about sufficiency of evidence. But the mandatory prosecution rule remains a significant norm that signals wariness of wide-ranging prosecutorial discretion even in some systems such as Germany's, where the rule has been amended with the "opportunity principle" that authorizes prosecutorial discretion for certain crimes.[17]

Beyond this basic distinction in prosecution authority, other details can be important. Discretion can be accompanied by different kinds of limits or guidelines, and American jurisdictions uniformly follow the weakest model for governing prosecutorial discretion. Formal boundaries on prosecutorial decisions in statutes or administrative regulations are almost nonexistent. Judicial review under common law and constitutional standards is almost as rare, and when it exists it is exceedingly deferential. The U.S. Department of Justice comes closest to operating in a manner resembling non-U.S. systems. The department has extensive written policies that govern all federal prosecutors, that specify substantive criteria for charging decisions and that sometimes require approval from a supervisory official (often a political appointee) at the main Justice Department headquarters in Washington, D.C., or in a regional office. That hierarchical review can be meaningful, but departmental guidelines on enforcement decisions are never enforceable by judicial review. (The same is true for civil enforcement discretion exercised by other federal departments and executive agencies.) Although the federal system's level of formal hierarchy is unusual compared with other U.S. jurisdictions, even there supervision is ultimately, in effect, backed by politics rather than law.

LEGAL REGULATION, JUDICIAL REVIEW, AND PROSECUTORIAL DISCRETION

Common law jurisdictions have a weak tradition of regulating prosecutorial discretion directly through statute, common law, and judicial review.[18] Prosecutors at common law also controlled the power to *nolle prosequi*—to dismiss charges they filed in court, and thus those over which the court has jurisdiction.[19] But that tradition did not originate from a trust in the office of the public prosecutor. It arose at a time when private individuals effectively or literally initiated and pursued most ordinary criminal charges (discussed further later). Statutory or common law rules did not check abusive prosecutions because the structure of adjudication process was understood to provide adequate protection: the primary safeguard was the lay jury as fact-finder. Lay juries never had a significant role in the German system nor (with a few exceptions) in most civil law countries. Many civil law systems that adopted the legality principle chose a route of limiting prosecutors' authority through statutory constraint on discretion. But the common law model has long relied on lay juries to check misguided prosecutions. (Formerly the grand jury was an additional check on the initiation of serious charges, but the grand jury has been abolished in England and in many U.S. states, and rules changes have largely converted it to prosecutors' handmaidens in jurisdictions where it remains.) Instead of legal rules, common law systems opted for a procedural and *democratic* mechanism—popular review, in effect—of criminal charges.

Needless to say, times have changed. The marginalization of grand juries and trial juries is a familiar story in the United States, England, and other common law systems, due mostly to the rise of plea bargaining.[20] Once full-time public prosecutors came to dominate charging and the jury lost its role as the decision maker in most cases, common law systems needed to develop other methods to regulate prosecutorial power, such as by adding rule-based oversight by judges or by creating a real bureaucratic structure of prosecution agencies. In this respect, the English and American systems sharply diverge. U.S. prosecutors operate with more professional independence, while the English system codified prosecutor guidelines and incorporates some judicial review of their discretion. Despite American wariness of government power, no comparable constraint has emerged in American jurisdictions. The trend, in fact, has been broadly in the opposite direction—toward granting prosecutors greater unilateral authority, especially with regard to sentencing.

JUDICIAL REVIEW OF PROSECUTION DECISIONS IN ENGLAND

In line with the common law tradition, English judicial review of prosecutorial discretion is deferential: "judicial review of a prosecutorial decision is available but is a highly exceptional remedy,"[21] far from what one might expect under statutes that include a mandatory prosecution requirement. English courts, like courts in the United States and elsewhere, recognize that prosecution decisions typically "turn not on an analysis of the relevant legal principles but on the exercise of an informed judgment of how a case against a particular defendant, if brought, would be likely to fare in the context of a criminal trial before . . . a jury."[22] Nonetheless, English courts review both decisions to prosecute and decisions not to prosecute on several grounds, and "review is less rare in the case of a decision not to prosecute than a decision to prosecute (because a decision not to prosecute is final, subject to judicial review, whereas a decision to prosecute leaves the defendant free to challenge the prosecution's case in the usual way through the criminal court)."[23]

Decisions Not to Charge

Victims or other aggrieved parties in England can challenge decisions not to prosecute, and courts may overturn a prosecutor's noncharging decision under one of several sources of law. A decision not to prosecute may violate standards in the Code for Crown Prosecutors or equivalent prosecution policies, which are judicially enforceable. Judges may also reject the decision if it was reached by application of an unlawful policy,[24] or because they found it to be "perverse" under a general reasonableness standard.[25] Victim-challengers bear the burden of proving the prosecutor's decision was unlawful, which they might carry by pointing to clear facts in the case that present a conflict with the Code's charging criteria. Pursuant to this review power, judges may require disclosure of internal prosecution documents, but they assess the lawfulness of non-prosecution without examining the underlying evidence.[26] Judicial focus is on prosecutors' stated reasons for nonprosecution, conveyed either to the court or to victims or their families. (Under the European Convention on Human Rights, prosecutors in limited circumstances may have a duty to give reasons for nonprosecution.)[27]

Despite their deferential posture in this context, English courts have a long record of periodically disapproving prosecutors' decisions not to charge suspects. An important rationale for doing so is that "a decision not to prosecute, especially in circumstances where it is believed or asserted that the decision is or may be erroneous, can affect public confidence in the integrity and competence of the criminal justice system."[28] (For the same reason, courts give closer scrutiny to cases arising from deaths in state custody, where concern is about prosecutors' favoritism toward suspects who are law enforcement officials.)[29] The same standards apply to decisions to discontinue a prosecution after charging, despite the English law's adherence to the common law rule that prosecutors retain the power of *nolle prosequi*.[30]

Decisions to Charge

As noted, defendants in English courts—and in those of many other Commonwealth nations—can challenge decisions to initiate prosecutions, including decisions to charge a greater rather than a lesser offense. Courts rely on similar sources of law to review charging and noncharging decisions, such as whether a charge violates the prosecuting agency's own charging policies or is otherwise clearly unreasonable.[31] Additionally, English courts may prohibit prosecutions on various grounds that constitute "abuse of process" by police or prosecutors. Under one strand of abuse-of-process doctrine, courts will bar prosecution in response to various kinds of prosecutorial abuse of power. One example is a decision to prosecute after confirming to the defendant and the court that a specific charge would not be pursued, at least where the defendant can show reliance on the initial nonprosecution pronouncement.[32] If a judge finds pursuit of charges to be abuse on any of these grounds, she can order a stay of prosecution (preventing trial) or—at a later stage—reverse a conviction on appeal.[33] A stay can be justified for police misconduct as well, including *police* assertions of nonprosecution, even though only prosecutors formally control the decision to proceed with charges.[34] Abuse-of-process stays are an assertion of the court's inherent power to regulate judicial process and prevent it from being abused by litigants. For that reason, courts sometimes stay prosecutions on those grounds even when a fair trial is still possible. A leading decision describes this power in rule of law terms:

> [T]he judiciary accept a responsibility for the maintenance of the rule of law that embraces a willingness to oversee executive action and to refuse to countenance behaviour that threatens either basic human rights or the rule of law. The courts, of course, have no power to apply direct discipline to the police or prosecuting authorities, but they can refuse to allow them to take advantage of abuse of power by regarding their behaviour as an abuse of process and thus preventing a prosecution.[35]

Despite this sentiment, judicial power to bar prosecutions is sparingly used, and the law is clear that English judges (like their American counterparts) have no power to stay or quash a valid indictment on grounds that public resources are limited or that other cases in a crowded docket should take priority.[36]

In sum, English courts' supervision of prosecutorial discretion concentrates on extremes of unfairness and inconsistency, judged against a legal standard defined in the Code for Crown Prosecutors, or a clear-unreasonableness standard, and in light of reasons offered by prosecutors particular to individual cases. Courts do not second-guess broad enforcement policies or resource allocations.

REVIEW OF PROSECUTION DECISIONS IN THE UNITED STATES

Nothing comparable exists in the U.S. criminal justice system.[37] Four states give their courts limited and rarely used authority to assign special prosecutors when a public prosecutor "neglects" to pursue well-grounded charges.[38] In contrast to the English model, under which courts will to some degree examine the specifics of a case, the standard position across American jurisdictions is that "so long as the prosecutor has probable cause to believe that the accused committed an offense defined by statute, the decision whether or not to prosecute, and what charge to file . . . , generally rests entirely in his discretion."[39] American judges adhere more strongly than their English counterparts to the premise that "the decision to prosecute is particularly ill-suited to judicial review."[40] Consequently, they deny the feasibility of review based either on prosecution agencies' internal policies, constitutional law, or common law or courts' inherent judicial power.[41]

THE LAW OF SEPARATION OF POWERS

As a constitutional matter, the Supreme Court has repeatedly confirmed that "the Executive Branch has exclusive authority and absolute discretion to decide whether to prosecute a case." Nonetheless, once a crime is charged, "the primary constitutional duty of the Judicial Branch to do justice in criminal prosecutions" justifies some judicial authority over executive discretion. The Court has used that authority to reject generalized claims of executive privilege that would withhold evidence from a criminal proceeding.[42] At least in some aspects of criminal litigation, constitutional separation-of-powers doctrine is not a bar to judicial authority that overrides prosecutorial preferences, because "separate powers were not intended to operate with absolute independence," but rather with "interdependence" and "reciprocity."[43]

Blackledge v. Perry provides one example of how that reciprocal conception of separation of powers might have developed with respect to prosecutorial discretion. Perry was initially charged with a misdemeanor offense, on which he demanded a trial. *Blackledge v. Perry* held that the Due Process Clause barred prosecutors from responding to that demand by adding more serious charges for trial.[44] In order to protect a defendant from fear of retaliation—even if that was not the prosecutor's actual motive—the Court recognized judicial capacity to supervise particularly suspect exercises of prosecutorial discretion. But the Supreme Court effectively overturned the *Blackledge* doctrine in later decisions[45] and has subsequently never developed—or recognized a need for—meaningful constitutional grounds for judicial supervision of prosecutors. Although it acknowledged that "[t]here is no doubt that the breadth of discretion that our country's legal system vests in prosecuting attorneys carries with it the potential for both individual and institutional abuse," the Court repeatedly invoked the foundational premise that "[i]n our system, so long as the prosecutor has probable cause to believe that the accused committed an offense defined by statute, the decision whether or not to prosecute, and what charge to file . . . , generally rests entirely in his discretion."[46] This deference to prosecutorial discretion pervades federal constitutional law, and it renders even nominal constitutional limits on prosecutorial action—such as the bar against racially biased decision making—completely ineffective.[47]

It is important to recognize, however, that most of the Court's decision in this vein involved disputes about whether the judiciary should recognize or devise *constitutional* standards by which courts would review certain decisions by prosecutors. Among other hurdles, those arguments find some resistance in separation-of-powers doctrine. Notwithstanding periodic statements that each governmental branch's distinct powers are "not intended to operate with absolute independence," courts have long taken the view that enforcement discretion (of criminal *and* civil law) is a "special province of the Executive Branch." They cite reasons both textual and practical. The federal Constitution (followed in this respect by state constitutions) makes it the executive's obligation to "take Care that the Laws be faithfully executed."[48] Furthermore, enforcement decisions are "ill-suited to judicial review."[49]

Both state and federal courts often leave it at that. From those explanations for rejecting constitutional bases for judicial review, courts often draw the misleading implication that the Constitution, against the background of the common law's prudential deference toward prosecutors, additionally bars *any* kind of judicial review over criminal charges.[50]

This is especially true if the claim rests on common law or inherent judicial authority. As a typical example, when a federal district court rejected a petition for a writ of mandamus to compel a prosecutor to charge police officers with illegal wiretapping, it stated simply: "The federal courts are powerless to interfere with [the prosecutor's] discretionary power. The Court cannot compel him to prosecute a complaint, or even an indictment, whatever his reasons for not acting."[51] (To the extent this idea rests on the idea of prosecution as a power exclusively in the executive's control, it is in tension with practices in the nation's early decades, when federal crimes were sometimes prosecuted by state rather than federal officials, and private parties could pursue close analogs to criminal prosecutions in private *qui tam* actions on behalf of the federal government.)[52]

Broadly speaking, state courts endorse a similarly strong principle insulating executive enforcement discretion from judicial interference.[53] The California Supreme Court, for example, ruled that trial judges may not—without prosecutors' consent—instruct juries on a lesser-included offense, as an alternative basis for conviction to the greater-charged offense, because such an instruction "usurps the prosecutor's exclusive charging discretion" and violates separation of powers.[54] In Texas, separation-of-power doctrine means that trial courts lack authority to bar prosecutors from refiling charges after dismissing them or to require prosecutors to subpoena their witnesses (which enables the judge—upon an opposing party's challenge—to rule pretrial whether a witness may testify).[55]

More troublingly, federal and state courts' statements on prosecutorial authority are often so broadly phrased as to suggest that separation-of-powers jurisprudence would bar even *legislation* that authorizes judicial review of charging decisions. Case law on that point is rare, because such legislation is rare. One example comes from Wyoming. The state supreme court invalidated a statute that granted courts authority to order a prosecutor to pursue a charge when the judge found probable cause for a crime such as, in that case, in-court perjury by a police officer. The Wyoming court concluded that even the legislature could not alter the state separation-of-powers implication that "the charging decision is properly within the scope of duty of the executive branch."[56] In the federal context at least, it should be clear that separation-of-powers doctrine does not prohibit *legislatively authorized* judicial review. Congress surely can enact statutory restrictions, guidelines, or mandates for executive-branch enforcement actions, and provide for judicial review under those rules. This kind of statutorily authorized judicial review already exists for certain civil enforcement decisions made by federal executive-branch departments.[57] Thus, charging decisions are "ill-suited to judicial review" only as a practical or prudential matter, when no statute or regulation provides a basis for judicial review. Courts are well suited to review government action under sufficiently specific legal criteria. The difference in English and American practice, then, lies partly in the choice of legislatures not to provide courts with legal standards they can use to evaluate prosecutorial decisions.

Wyoming notwithstanding, there seems little reason to think the same is not true in the states. Some evidence for that lies in the examples from several states that *have* authorized limited kinds of judicial authority over prosecutorial discretion. In contrast to federal practice, a small number of states have statutes that authorize judges to dismiss criminal charges on their own motion, without the prosecutor's consent. Some state courts have narrowly construed their judicial power under those statutes. California courts, however, repeatedly reaffirm that dismissal is a "judicial function" and go so far as to warn that granting prosecutors a veto over that decision could violate separation of powers.[58] Statutes in an equally small number of states (perhaps three) require prosecutors to give reasons for *not* filing charges after a judge finds probable cause in a preliminary examination. Those laws also give courts authority to review those reasons and order the prosecutor to file charges, although—as they have with the power to disapprove *nolle pros* motions—courts have interpreted this power narrowly.[59] (Note that because this regime applies only to preliminary-examination cases, this judicial power is more confined than that exercised by English courts.) And at least two states have statutes that formally circumscribe prosecutors' plea bargaining authority by restricting their ability to reduce or dismiss charges.[60] All three types are examples of statutes that grant courts power over aspects of prosecutors' discretionary decision making, and thus they affirm state constitutional authority for courts to exercise such power with legislative authorization. (Whether courts take advantage of this authority is a different matter. Appellate decisions provide little evidence that they do.)

Furthermore, some state constitutions impose weaker hurdles to judicial review of prosecutorial action, because they depart from the federal model of separation of powers in various ways. As some of these constitutions draw less rigid distinctions between executive, legislative, and judicial roles,[61] a number of state courts have approved arrangements that likely would be barred in the federal context, such as expansive delegations of rulemaking authority to agencies, or the appointment of legislative candidates to executive boards.[62] Several state courts exercise greater authority than their federal counterparts by providing advisory opinions to other branches, and many have constitutional rulemaking authority.[63] Historically, public prosecutors in some places were originally appointed to their posts by *judges*, and some state constitutions placed prosecutors in the *judicial* rather than in the executive branch.[64] A few did so into the twentieth century; Louisiana still does.[65] That history sits uneasily with the view of prosecutorial decision making as a singularly executive function. (The same is true, as discussed later, of states' early reliance on private citizens to act as prosecutors.)

Despite many state systems having relatively better prospects for judicial supervision of criminal charging, only a few state supreme courts have assertively defined parameters of judicial power in a manner that modestly restrain prosecutorial authority. The New Jersey Supreme Court has taken a strong view of inherent judicial authority over sentencing. It held that statutes giving prosecutors power to invoke mandatory sentence terms (or to control access to diversion programs in lieu of trial) are constitutional only if that power is exercised under enforceable, statewide charging and plea bargaining guidelines, which courts can use as a basis to review prosecutorial decisions.[66] And the California Supreme Court has deemed as unconstitutional statutes that require a prosecutor's consent before judges could reduce certain offenses to misdemeanors, sentence offenders to drug treatment in lieu of prison, or strike prior convictions that trigger enhanced punishment.[67] But these decisions are unusual. Generally speaking, state justice systems closely track federal law and reflect a strong consensus against regulation or judicial review of prosecutorial discretion.

ENGLISH VERSUS AMERICAN PROSECUTORIAL GUIDELINES

From all of the foregoing, it is clear that legislatures in most, if not all, American jurisdictions could enact judicially enforceable restrictions for prosecutorial decision making. The difference between the U.S. systems and the English system in this respect is that American legislatures, with rare exceptions, have not chosen to do so. An emblematic example lies in the difference between the legal status of both the federal U.S. Attorney's Manual and equivalent Justice Department guidelines and England's Code for Crown Prosecutors. The latter is a *code*. It exists by statutory mandate[68] and has a status equivalent to federal administrative regulations in the United States. Changes to its provisions require a formal administrative process including public consultation—a notice-and-comment period, in U.S. parlance—before adoption. (That is a mechanism, it is worth emphasizing, of democratic input on prosecution enforcement policy.)[69] Prosecution policies in the U.S. Department of Justice are similar in their formality and substantive content but very different in legal status. They exist at the discretion of the attorney general rather than by congressional mandate. They lack the status of enforceable agency regulations. They are intended only as internal office policies, and federal courts uniformly treat them as such. Save for the limited exception in New Jersey, the same is apparently true in every state criminal justice system. A few legislatures have enacted general charging standards on their own, and a few have required local prosecutor offices to draft their own written charging policies,[70] but none is employed as a basis for judicial review.

In the end, U.S. jurisdictions lack English-style judicial review of prosecutorial discretion not as a function of distinctively American constitutional design but primarily as a matter of long-standing legislative choice. That policy is evident in other areas of law as well. U.S. prosecutors enjoy absolute immunity from civil liability for their unconstitutional conduct, regardless of the egregiousness of the violation or the severity of the injuries it caused; other government officials (save for judges) enjoy only partial or qualified immunity.[71] Indeed, the prospects of prosecutors facing criminal sanctions even for flagrant misconduct are vanishingly small.[72] (That sharply contrasts with felony-level punishments defined in the German Penal Code for the offenses of filing baseless charges or failing to pursue strong ones.)[73]

The question then becomes *why* this policy is so deeply and widely embraced. One reason is simply a deep trust that judges and legislatures have in prosecutors to use their discretion appropriately. The Supreme Court has repeatedly emphasized its confidence in prosecutors' professional integrity and trustworthiness as the reason it grants a strong presumption of lawfulness to their actions.[74] This presumption of prosecutorial integrity is not unique to the American criminal justice system. It is shared to some degree by other common law systems as well as many in the civil law tradition, although elsewhere that trust is grounded in the prosecution's insulation from politics and, in light of judicial review for some prosecutorial judgments, it is less unqualified.[75] Nonetheless, the depth and implications of this faith in prosecutors are greater in the U.S. system. The reason for *that* distinction lies in the American faith in democratic governance over enforceable legal standards. Trust in American prosecutors translates into exceptionally minimal oversight of their actions precisely because American prosecutors are supervised instead by political accountability.

U.S. MODEL: POLITICAL IN PLACE OF LEGAL SUPERVISION

Evidence for this reliance on politics in place of law runs throughout judicial discussions of prosecutorial discretion. Especially when rejecting arguments that the judiciary should provide better remedies for prosecutorial laxity or overreach, state courts often respond by observing, as a Wyoming court did, that "district and county attorneys hold elective offices; if their constituents are unsatisfied, they are free to express their feelings at the voting polls." Or, in the words of a Pennsylvania court: "The prosecutor is elected to run her office using her broad discretion fairly and honestly. If she fails to do so, . . . the remedy lies in the power of the electorate to vote her out of office."[76] Federal courts have long offered equivalent rationales for why they "are without power to compel" appointed prosecutors "to enforce the penal laws, whatever the grounds of their failure may be. The remedy for inactivity of that kind is with the executive and ultimately with the people."[77]

This confidence in democratic supervision is especially remarkable in light of the kind of prosecutorial actions that triggered these decisions. In the Wyoming case, the trial judge heard a police officer's testimony first-hand and, after all trial evidence was presented, became convinced that the officer clearly had testified falsely, yet the prosecutor refused to charge his own witness with perjury. In the federal case, the prosecutor moved to dismiss tax embezzlement charges because the defendant "is of a promi-nent pioneer family, is young, [recently married], is studying law . . . , *must of necessity plead guilty* if arraigned, and thus his 'career as a lawyer will be spoiled.'" The court correctly observed that "these 'reasons' . . . savor alto-gether too much of some variety of prestige and influence. . . . [T]hey incite, if they do not justify, the too common reproach that criminal law is for none but the poor, friendless, and uninfluential." But both courts could not see how to distinguish these scenarios from general second-guessing of pros-ecutors' enforcement priorities, so both pointed to the prospect of political accountability—either by local voters keeping in mind such actions at the next election, or the accountability working by means of presidential author-ity over federal prosecutors.[78]

COMMONWEALTH MODEL: LEGAL SUPERVISION IN PLACE OF POLITICAL SUPERVISION

By contrast, courts in England and other common law countries justify pros-ecutors' broad discretion by emphasizing their *insulation* from popular and political influences. "The primary decision to prosecute or not to prosecute is entrusted by Parliament to the Director [of Public Prosecutions]," a recent, representative Queen's Bench decision noted, "as head of an independent, professional prosecuting service, answerable to the Attorney General in his role as guardian of the public interest, and to no-one else."[79] A Privy Council decision is explicit about judicial scrutiny of politically tainted prosecution decisions: "The power to stay for abuse of process can and should be understood widely enough to embrace an application challenging a decision to prosecute on the ground that it was arrived at under political pressure or influence or was motivated politically rather than by an objective review of proper prosecutorial considerations."[80] Other common law countries—Ireland, Australia, Canada, New Zealand, and Caribbean Commonwealth nations—likewise emphasize that their prosecution agencies are independent from the influence of political officials.[81]

Over the last two decades, reform trends in these jurisdictions have only sought to strengthen prosecutors' political independence. Cornell Clayton's study of the U.S. attorney general describes an office more politically attuned than its counterparts elsewhere.[82] In England and Canada, the attorney general does not join the government's cabinet, and relatively recent changes in both places give prosecution agencies more political independence by making them accountable only at the level of general policy to the attorney general, and not at the level of decision making in particular cases.[83] (In a shift to increase democratic supervision of *police*, England and Wales in 2012 created locally elected police commissioners. These officials set policy, control budgets, and appoint chiefs for local police agencies; no analogous reform followed for prosecution agencies.)[84] Most U.S. states restrict their attorney general's authority over local prosecutors out of a preference for local political accountability rather than general aversion to political influence. (In New York, the elected attorney general lacks power to intervene in a local prosecution or to remove a local prosecutor, but the elected *governor* can order her to do either.)[85]

Canadian law now also mandates that the chief prosecutor—the Director of Public Prosecutions (DPP), who serves for a seven-year term—be appointed through a complex process that limits parliamentary influence; moreover, the DPP can be dismissed only for good cause by legislative vote.[86] Much the same is true elsewhere: chief prosecutors (usually titled the DPP but called the solicitor general in New Zealand) are appointed for a fixed term of years through a depoliticized process strengthened by norms that value professional experience and standing over political affiliation. Staff prosecutors below the DPP typically enjoy civil service protections, although New Zealand continues to rely on partners in private law firms to provide public prosecution services.[87]

CONCLUSION

The distinction between the American model and those of other common law nations plays out in contrasting conceptions of "disinterestedness." Courts elsewhere regard sensitivity to political influence as a potentially compromising form of "interest." American courts stress the importance "that the state wield its formidable criminal enforcement powers in a rigorously disinterested fashion." And they regularly invoke the possibility of abuse by—in the Supreme Court's oft-quoted phrase—a "corrupt or overzealous prosecutor."[88] But they implicitly define interestedness and corruption more narrowly. *Interests* seems to refer primarily to the prosecutor's family members, or property or business relationships, which create conflicts in specific cases.[89] Since the meaning of *corruption* must be cabined by the background assumption that prosecutors' political responsiveness is advantageous, it seems to primarily reference improper self-dealing, like bribery, and perhaps also a moral lapse. In any case, the foundational American view that political responsiveness is presumptively benign—a systemic virtue rather than a vice—restrains American courts from holding a broader idea of *interestedness* that permits much concern about politics.

Public versus Private Prosecution

Apart from the choice between democratic and legal constraints, criminal justice systems also can limit prosecutors' authority by denying public officers a complete monopoly over criminal charging and permitting aggrieved parties to share some of those powers. In all modern criminal justice systems today, public officials initiate and control the overwhelming majority of criminal prosecutions. But in all U.S. jurisdictions the public prosecutor's monopoly power seems to be more absolute than in many other advanced democracies. That is a bit puzzling in light of (1) the American affinity for privatizing state functions when feasible, (2) the political salience of crime victims' rights in criminal process, and (3) the fact that private prosecutions were common in state criminal justice systems in the republic's early decades—and remained the predominant English practice for much longer.

TRADITIONS OF PRIVATE PROSECUTION

England had no comprehensive public prosecution agency until the creation of the Crown Prosecution Service in 1985. Before then it relied mostly on private prosecutors, save for a small portion of cases handled by the director of public prosecutions. With the advent of police departments in the 1800s, police officers gradually came to dominate the job of charging crimes, creating—in Glanville Williams's description—a de facto public prosecution system, although one not controlled by lawyers.[90] American states departed from English practice in the early decades of the nineteenth century by employing public prosecutors (commonly called district attorneys). The break was not as sharp as it may seem, however, for two reasons. First, public prosecutors often shared authority with private prosecutors. Second, their roles were significantly different from those of their counterparts today in ways that made public officers in that earlier era more akin to private actors.

In accord with English tradition, American jurisdictions in the first half of the nineteenth century widely authorized private individuals to prosecute crimes, and they often relied heavily on them. In some places during this era, private prosecutions made up the majority of criminal cases. In Philadelphia, private citizens routinely charged fellow residents with crimes if magistrates confirmed a sufficient evidentiary basis.[91] As in England, a public officer—the attorney general or the district attorney—had authority to take over or to veto a private prosecution. But use of that power seems to have been unusual, and in some localities such as New York City, private prosecutions made up much of the docket into the latter nineteenth century, well after establishment of the district attorney's office.[92] Lawyers for private prosecutors sometimes appeared alongside a public prosecutor or even in place of him, in which case they were compensated by the court.[93]

It is also worth remembering that public prosecutors for much of the nineteenth century were in many respects functionally closer to private actors than today's officials. In his history of "the salary revolution in American government," Nicolas Parrillo carefully documents that until at least 1850 U.S. prosecutors everywhere were paid either by the case or by the conviction; conviction-fee pay continued in some states well into the twentieth century.[94] Under the fee-per-case model, especially before American cities had full-time police forces, a prosecutor's job often amounted to presenting whatever criminal allegations that private citizens filed or that magistrates had approved—the rough equivalent of an appointed counsel for victims. Payment-per-conviction sharply changed their role. Prosecutors gained an incentive to screen out weak complaints with low odds of success, and their adversarial posture was sharpened by personal self-interest.

CONTEMPORARY ROLES FOR PRIVATE PROSECUTORS

The nineteenth century saw the professionalization, in various ways, of prosecution and police agencies in all European and common law democracies. In the United States, the changes evolved into the nearly complete elimination of the victim and other private parties as a formal litigator in criminal prosecutions. Consequently, private individuals today lack legal standing to challenge prosecutorial decisions in practically all American jurisdictions. Nor can they retain counsel to act as formal advocates alongside the prosecutor during a criminal proceeding.[95] Individuals generally can file criminal complaints or request that judges issue arrest warrants, but the power to lodge formal criminal charges lies solely with the public prosecutor. Only modest remnants of the older model remain in a very few states. Rhode Island authorizes private prosecutors for misdemeanor offenses only, and Pennsylvania courts may approve a victim's request to take over prosecution from a district attorney who "neglects or refuses" to pursue a well-grounded charge (although victims lack standing to seek judicial review of a prosecutor's decision not to charge).[96]

That is not the case, however, in many other nations where criminal process is also dominated by public prosecution agencies, and those examples are reminders of the possibilities for integrating private and public prosecution authority. England and other Commonwealth countries still permit private prosecutions, where they now constitute a small but meaningful portion of cases.[97] Procedural codes of many civil law countries also authorize private citizens to initiate criminal prosecutions independently of public prosecutors.[98] Germany's code specifies several relatively minor crimes that *only* private parties can initiate, including trespass, bodily injury, property damage, invasion of privacy and defamation, as well as a range of commercial offenses such as copyright infringement.[99] German prosecutors are barred from charging these offenses without a private citizen's complaint. Additionally, for some more serious offenses, Germany and other European countries permit aggrieved parties formally to join a public prosecution as an accessory or auxiliary prosecutor, and private parties have standing to seek judicial review of a public prosecutor's request to dismiss (or decision not to file) charges in the wake of a private complaint.[100] Aggrieved parties under Italian law also have rights to request that police, prosecutors, or judges preserve evidence; officials who refuse those requests must provide written reasons.[101] Elsewhere in Europe, organized *groups* that have a special interest in certain offenses have standing to play a formal role in criminal proceedings alongside public prosecutors. The Spanish Constitution's right to "popular prosecution"[102] is understood to protect this form of participation, versions of which are also authorized in other nations. (Under the French code, groups are limited to a civil claimant role that is part of the criminal proceeding.)[103]

PRIVATE PROSECUTORS AND POLITICAL ACCOUNTABILITY AS ALTERNATIVES

Roles for private actors reduce the public prosecutor's monopoly. Private parties can trump a public decision not to charge by their authority to file charges themselves; they can block public officials' intention to charge when their consent is required; and litigation roles for private counsel reduce public control over trial tactics and evidence. All these are privately controlled devices to restrain or counterbalance public enforcement authority, although in ways quite different from legal regulation and judicial review.[104] They can also be understood as *democratic* devices for checking state enforcement policy and increasing lay (especially victim) participation in criminal justice. In that sense they contrast with both electoral accountability for prosecutors and with lay juries as a means of democratic supervision of state officials and democratic legitimacy for criminal process.

On that view, the consistent choice of U.S. jurisdictions to reject effectively all variations of private prosecution is a bit puzzling, at least if one takes seriously the traditional suspicion of government power and receptiveness to various models of privatizing public services. One might expect at least to see some inclination to contract with private law firms for prosecution services as the New Zealand criminal justice system still does and England formerly did.[105] Many U.S. jurisdictions do just that for probation services and prisons, and to provide indigent defense.[106] The uniform pattern instead is an unusually strong public prosecution monopoly that has held up against a powerful wave of victims' rights legislation in recent decades. Those reforms have expanded victims' rights to receive notice of court proceedings, to be present in court, to speak as witnesses at key proceedings such as sentencing, and sometimes to be consulted by prosecutors.[107] But uniformly such measures do not infringe on public prosecutors' monopoly of charging decisions, trial control, or settlement authority. (Much the same is true in English rules regarding a victim's right to be heard by judges or to be consulted by prosecutors.)[108] One explanation for rejecting private prosecution roles, at least as a way to supervise prosecutor discretion, might be that the lay jury can fulfill much the same function. Yet that claim has to ring a bit hollow when the jury has been so thoroughly marginalized by the triumph of plea bargaining. The more plausible explanation is the same one that also accounts for the minimal legal regulation of prosecutors—trust in the electoral process to adequately monitor politically responsive prosecutors.

"Ministers of Justice," Democracy, and Law

The dominant role achieved by public prosecutors has been accompanied in every justice system by a normative expectation that they should act as "ministers of justice." Unlike other parties in civil or criminal litigation, the prosecutor's aim is not merely for the client or interest she represents to prevail in the court's judgment, but to ensure that the process is fair and that the outcome is substantively just.[109] The stronger this ministerial norm is taken to be, the more prosecutors are presumed to act with quasi-judicial impartiality.[110]

This professional conception is not problematic in a nonadversarial system when the prosecutor's role and professional identity is understood to share more with the judiciary than with other lawyers. That roughly describes the French *procureur*, who shares the professional training and status as a *magistrat* with judges. Other civil law–based justice systems in Europe rely on their own variations of that conception.[111] (Even in the United States there is a broadly analogous idea in the use of neutral experts and professionals to carry out nonadversarial fact-finding in settings outside the courts, such as with some federal agencies, special investigating commissions, and inspectors general.) But the ministerial norm poses a special challenge for prosecutors in *adversarial* criminal justice systems. By design, adversarial parties are not expected to act evenhandedly or disinterestedly in choosing evidence and legal arguments to present in court. The process depends on parties acting in accord with rival interests, *partisan* interests. The partisan role—in the sense of interested *party*—is different in kind from the neutrality and objectivity of the judicial role.

Yet in adversarial systems the minister-of-justice norm requires prosecutors to combine a partisan role with a quasi-judicial one. Practically, if not conceptually, that can be a hard balance to strike. An adversarial prosecutor must marshal evidence and legal arguments that make the case for guilt and conviction, yet throughout must retain an overriding commitment to fair procedures that may work against conviction; she must continually reassess the case for conviction, to identify reasons that conviction may not in fact be synonymous with substantive justice.[112] That's no easy task for one who has invested considerable personal effort, and perhaps emotion or professional reputation.

From the foregoing, one can see how other common law systems support this aspirational role for prosecutors with institutional arrangements that U.S. jurisdictions reject. The justice systems of the major Commonwealth nations (as in most civil law systems) all foster the ministerial disposition by separating prosecutors from political influences.[113] Holding aside New Zealand, prosecutors are civil servants employed in nonpolitical agencies, a structure that aspires to strengthen professional norms and expertise, encouraged by devices such as England's Code for Crown Prosecutors and, more generally, some degree (albeit deferential) of legal regulation to guard against bias, incompetence, or misconduct. Even if those arrangements don't succeed at eliminating all undesirable political influence or other bad motivations (all systems have examples of prosecutorial lapses), this is a very different approach to strengthening the ministerial characteristics of dispassionate professionalism and quasi-judicial neutrality than one finds in most U.S. prosecution agencies.[114]

The U.S. model of democratically accountable prosecutors puts unique pressure on the ministerial norm. To be sure, professional norms and office cultures vary greatly across the United States and even within states, making for exceptions to every generalization.[115] Accepting that caveat, a common effect of that pressure is a different and weaker conception of what it means for a prosecutor to be a minister of justice—weaker because it accommodates a more partisan executive role, in at least two senses of the word *partisan*.[116]

First, political responsiveness makes prosecutors more inclined to a stronger partisan role in the sense of being an *adversarial party*, with specific interests to advance in a conflict between rival parties. This is implicit, for example, in the judicial endorsement of prosecution as a distinctly *executive*-branch endeavor best left to the state's law enforcement officials, with oversight coming from the people rather than the courts. (It is apparent also in the discretion granted to prosecutors in the law of plea bargaining, the subject of chapter 4.) When local electorates—or the political superiors of appointees—endorse sharply adversarial prosecutors who stress little regard for ministerial obligations, the remaining institutions that can work against such partisanship—legal education, professional norms of the local bar—may be, in any given locale, too modest to be effective. An outdated example is the California attorney general's 1935 argument to the Supreme Court in *Mooney v. Holohan* against a duty to disclose perjury by a state witness:

> The function of the prosecuting attorney is to prosecute, to act as an accuser, to be a partisan, to present the evidence on one side of the case. He has no power to adjudge, to sentence or, by his order, to deprive anyone of life, liberty or property. He is not part of the tribunal but a mere pleader before the tribunal.[117]

That view was a minority one even at the time and was implicitly rejected by the Court's holding in *Mooney*, but it suggests that any tradition of a strong quasi-judicial ministerial norm does not have deep roots in American criminal justice. More recently, prosecution organizations have resisted the authority of courts and bar associations, which can discipline all other lawyers for violations of law or professional ethical standards.[118] That record does little to suggest a ministerial commitment to abiding by a professional standard higher than that for other advocates. Likewise, the scattered but innumerable examples of illegal and ethically dubious prosecution tactics—such as concealing exculpatory evidence, or relying on dubious witnesses or forensic analysis, actions which lie behind so many wrongful conviction cases[119]—suggest that a strong ministerial norm has not taken hold in some local prosecution agencies.[120] When agencies are decentralized as in nearly all state criminal justice systems, the odds increase that at least some of those local offices will accommodate local political pressures to adopt a more adversarial and less ministerial posture.

The structure of U.S. prosecution agencies also increases the odds that prosecutors will be more partisan in a second, somewhat more political sense. Not in the crudest sense of using official power to advance the agenda of a particular political party, although isolated examples of this occur (surely outside the United States as well).[121] A more intermediate notion of *political* bias describes use of official discretion to serve the clear policy preferences of local voters, or one's own sincerely held ideological commitments, and, additionally, use of an office as a platform to advocate for politically contested policies.

Empirical evidence suggests that local political preferences affect professional discretion. One study finds that local constituencies' strong electoral support for Republican prosecutorial and judicial candidates leads to higher incarceration sentences in those courts. Several studies indicate that prosecutors' charging and sentencing choices vary with election cycles. In state-level studies, elected prosecutors dismiss fewer cases and seek harsher sentences in the year preceding an election than in other years.[122] It is hard to reconcile *that* pattern with a ministerial orientation that excludes political concerns from professional discretion. Prosecutors who are governed more by democracy than law or bureaucratic expertise are designed to respond to rather than resist media and electoral pressure. Recent empirical work by John Pfaff supports a related story about political preferences shaping prosecutorial behavior. In a series of trenchant studies, Pfaff concludes that much of the U.S. prison population increase over the last three or four decades is largely *not* due to familiar explanations such as longer median sentences, higher rates of offending, or zealous enforcement of drug crimes. His analysis of data from state criminal justice systems suggests that the most important reason for the jump in prison populations is a broad change in prosecutor behavior. At least from the early 1990s, state prosecutors collectively began filing serious charges in a significantly higher proportion of arrests made by police than they had before the incarceration boom.[123]

Perhaps politically insulated prosecutors also would have charged more frequently in the same circumstances, although the upward trend in filing began just as rates of offending began their steady downward trend after about 1990. Despite declining crime rates, this remained an era of populist, punitive "law-and-order" politics—precisely what popularly elected prosecutors are likely to respond to. (Historical studies suggest that more punitive prosecution in response to popular sentiment and political pressure is nothing new. Carolyn Ramsey's study of New York City prosecutions in the late 1800s found that the press focused heavily on crime and consistently urged in editorials that prosecutors adopt harsh charging and sentencing policies, which prosecutors in turn seemed to do.)[124]

Another contemporary example of prosecutorial partisanship—in the sense of strong, political policy preferences—can be inferred from the 2014 public protest by the National Association of Assistant U.S. Attorneys. Staff prosecutors in that group objected to a revised charging and sentencing policy issued by their boss, the U.S. attorney general. The new policy limited the circumstances in which federal prosecutors could use their discretion to charge certain drug offenses under a statute that carries long mandatory prison sentences. (It replaced a decades-old department policy to seek mandatory sentences much more frequently.)[125] Against a background of record U.S. incarceration rates, and with federal law imposing typically harsher sentences than state laws, the association protested that the policy would lead to undue leniency for some offenders.[126] The incident is interesting because assistant federal prosecutors are probably the most politically insulated of any American prosecution staff. Their appointments are nonpartisan, and federal law prohibits their dismissal on political (among other) grounds.[127] Their vocal disagreement seems to confirm their confidence in job security. At the same time, it reflects a professional-bureaucratic culture that inculcates little hierarchical deference or a strong professional consensus about policy independent of individual political leanings. Only about half of all assistant U.S. attorneys join the association, which suggests the group's policy positions follow more from its members' own political views than from broader professional expertise or culture.

State prosecutors as well sometimes use their office to pursue controversial enforcement policies, or even to lobby against judicial nominees and law reform proposals. To be sure, some prosecutors also push for less punitive policy reforms, such as drug-treatment programs in lieu of criminal sanctions and the recent federal policy on mandatory-minimum sentences.[128] One virtue of the decentralized American system is that it permits this kind of "democratic experimentalism," in multiple policy directions, by local officials.[129] Nonetheless, the weight of the evidence for at least the last generation is that collectively U.S. prosecutors have contributed more to increasing the punitiveness of American criminal justice than to moderating its severity. By comparison, German prosecutors took the initiative and adjusted their charging and enforcement priorities in order to reduce imprisonment rates when inmate populations strained national prison capacity in the 1980s.[130]

The broader point is that a system that oversees prosecution agencies through the political process is more sanguine about some kinds of political or ideological influences on prosecutorial actions. Accordingly, American criminal justice, unlike other common law systems, adapts the ministerial norm—and thereby prosecutors' professional identity—to be compatible with the reality of politically attuned officials. Political governance takes at least some degree of populist influence on discretionary judgments as a virtue. In this sense the U.S. ministerial norm is weaker. It is less quasi-judicial in order to forthrightly accommodate policy partisanship.

PROSECUTORIAL ROLES IN SENTENCING

Finally, consider briefly more specific, rule-based indicators of the adversarially oriented minister-of-justice norm in the United States. The first arises from the prosecutors' role in sentencing. The virtually uniform approach across U.S. jurisdictions is that prosecutors can and typically do recommend—and vigorously argue for—the court to impose particular sentences, in a manner more partisan than ministerial. Instead of providing judges with balanced summaries of aggravating and mitigating factors to support a recommendation, prosecutors stress only aggravating factors that support severity, leaving the defense to underscore mitigating considerations.[131] One federal trial court openly voiced its criticism of this routine practice: "The prosecution's sentencing memorandum . . . , not atypically for an advocacy piece by the prosecution, unduly emphasizes aggravating factors, while mitigating factors, substantial in this case, are largely ignored or treated dismissively. . . . As . . . a justification for the [proposed] 15-year sentence, it falls short."[132] In contrast, the rule or strong custom in England, Scotland, Australia, and Commonwealth Caribbean nations *prohibits* prosecutors from urging a particular sentence, because of concerns that they would improperly infringe on judicial sentencing authority. In a striking contrast to professional norms among U.S. prosecutors, their Scottish counterparts actively *opposed* proposals that offered sentence recommendations.[133]

PARTISAN RESTRICTIONS ON APPEALS

A second example of a rule that pushes the prosecution into a more partisan role, rather than the role of a justice-oriented minister, is the federal statute that limits appeals for review of sentences. A defendant may not appeal an erroneous sentence "unless the sentence imposed is *greater* than" sentencing guidelines specify, or than the one specified in a plea agreement. Correspondingly, the prosecutors may not appeal "unless the sentence imposed is *less* than" the guidelines' range or one set forth in such an agreement.[134] This is the symmetry of equivalent partisans. The law *prohibits* prosecutors from taking a ministerial role on behalf of the state's interest in justice, including its interest in avoiding *all* forms of sentencing errors. Formally, they must stand by even when they recognize a sentence is improper—and unjust—because it is excessively severe. Only the *defendant's* self-interested partisanship—not the state's dedication to fair process and lawful outcomes—protects him from unlawful punishment.

EVIDENCE DISCLOSURE AND ERROR-CORRECTION DUTIES

A final example can be found in regimes of evidence disclosure. That body of law is too complex to allow strong conclusions from a brief comparison between systems. Nick Vamos, however, examined English and U.S. federal rules on prosecution disclosure in some detail as they affect plea bargaining, and he concluded that the "limited defence rights to disclosure" under U.S. law are much weaker; the English "disclosure regime operates to ensure that a defendant should have full access to material that enables him, in [the plea negotiation] context, to assess as accurately as possible the strength of the prosecution case and any potential defences and, ultimately, his chances of acquittal."[135] Chapter 4 will take up this topic in more detail.

Considering only the primary constitutional obligation defined by *Brady v. Maryland* for the prosecution to disclose evidence favorable to the accused, one can see some parameters of that doctrine restrain the state's commitment to ensuring a full evidentiary record for the court and reflect a more adversarial, less ministerial notion of prosecutors. *Brady* decisions in state and federal courts limit the prosecutor's disclosure duty with regard to evidence that the defense could have found through its own "reasonable and diligent investigation" of public records, state witnesses, or other sources. The defense's "obligation to investigate the case" in an adversarial system, courts stress, justifies prosecutors' nondisclosure of exculpatory or impeachment evidence that diligent defendants could have found otherwise. The underlying principle is that *Brady* disclosure extends only so far as to ensure a fair adversarial trial *process*, including a fair defense *opportunity to learn* of evidence. The state need not ensure the defense or the court has all relevant evidence in hand. The purpose of the prosecutorial disclosure duty, according to the Supreme Court, "is not to displace the adversary system."[136] Thus, while prosecutors are ministers of justice in a general sense, the ministerial ideal does not require providing disclosure as a safeguard against a lapse in adversarial process that could undermine substantive justice.

Disclosure, then, is another part of criminal procedure law that reinforces either a robust ministerial role or the prosecutor's adversarial role as a mere partisan in a two-party competition. A stronger ministerial norm would include a broader disclosure duty as part of a more substantial state commitment to ensure full evidence records that maximize the odds of accurate judgments. The *Brady* doctrine narrows the prosecutor's asymmetric disclosure duty so as to depart as little as possible from the adversarial baseline of equal autonomy for both parties. A one-sided, ministerial disclosure duty runs counter to the role of an adversarial party that is expected to act according to its partisan interests.

This conflict is greatly reduced in systems grounded in inquisitorial process traditions, at least at the conceptual level. (Of course, law-in-practice may differ from law-on-the-books.)[137] The French justice system, for example, has a very strong ministerial norm in the shared *magistrat* status of judges and prosecutors, and also has a strong rule that the full evidence dossier compiled by state officials be shared with the defense attorney and judge.[138] Likewise in Germany, prosecutors have broader legal duties to objectively investigate exculpatory and inculpatory facts and to disclose all evidence to the defense at all stages of process.[139]

Making prosecutors politically accountable provides a rationale against legal regulation of their discretion, so it is unsurprising to see that U.S. courts are inclined to construe narrowly a legal command such as the *Brady* disclosure duty. Democratic governance also justifies prosecutorial discretion and countenances a role for political judgments in discretionary actions. All of this makes for a thinner ministerial norm, which U.S. courts tacitly endorse. The incentives of the partisan-advocate role nudge prosecutors to internalize a thin conception of the norm. The degree to which local prosecution cultures yield to that tendency varies in a highly decentralized system, but egregious examples are easy enough to find that federal appellate Judge Alex Kozinski, joined by colleagues, in a 2013 opinion blamed the judiciary collectively for failing to stop "an epidemic of *Brady* violations abroad in the land."[140]

As if to prove the point, only months later a *pattern* of such violations came to light in a state prosecutor's district near Kozinski's chambers. The district attorney's office for Orange County, California, failed to disclose numerous leniency agreements with its jailhouse-informant witnesses, and in some cases dismissed homicide charges rather than face judicial scrutiny of their practices. The district attorney had no problem winning re-election in 2014 amidst media coverage of the breaches.[141]

Effects of Democracy on Judicial and Jury Power

THE PARAMETERS OF JUDICIAL AUTHORITY

The effects of democratic ideology on the two key judicial players, judges and juries, can be recounted more briefly, because much has been covered already in the foregoing examination of prosecution agencies. As prosecutors gained power, much of it came at the expense of judges and juries. With the rise of public prosecutor offices, state courts (as well as, depending on the state, legislatures or governors) lost the authority to appoint prosecutors. As public prosecutors replaced private ones, judges lost their supervisory and management role over cases initiated by private complainants. In some places such as Philadelphia, the prior system had given judges a dominant role in city enforcement policies. In Steinberg's definitive history, Philadelphia judges until the 1850s defined public safety priorities, with a focus, for example, on alcohol-law violations. They ordered constables to investigate and charge certain types of offenders, and compelled those officials to appear in court and prosecute or face criminal sanctions themselves.[142] Judicial power in most places waned, although New York City judges through the 1860s still partially supervised prosecutors by exercising their power to appoint private attorneys when public prosecutors failed to appear. (Courts in about four states still have some power, rarely or never used, to appoint special prosecutors if a public prosecutor "arbitrarily" or neglectfully fails to press charges.)[143] Vis-à-vis prosecutors, judicial power never recovered; American judges never developed the modest authority to review enforcement decisions that English judges asserted.

POLITICAL VERSUS APOLITICAL JUDICIARIES

The story of the American preference for democracy over a politically insulated professional agency is also much the same for the judiciary as it is for prosecution agencies. Most states shifted to the direct election of judges in the middle decades of the nineteenth century, as they did for prosecutors.[144] A large majority of state court judges continue to face electorates through varying processes, although it is a smaller proportion than is the case for prosecutors: only thirty-nine states elect at least some of their judges. (Some states appoint judges on certain courts and elect judges to others.) And the rules vary: sometimes judges are appointed for a fixed term and then face a popular vote on a second term; some elections are nominally nonpartisan.[145] Where judges are appointed, the systems vary in how nonpartisan the selection process strives to be. A few states have versions of appointment commissions; in the federal system, the appointment process is often unabashedly political.[146] As with prosecution agencies, outside the United States elections for judicial posts are unheard of, and overtly political appointment processes are rare. In England, for example, the government's selection of judges is limited to candidates approved by an independent Judicial Appointments Commission.[147]

Given the relatively political nature of the American judiciary, it is unsurprising to find evidence that judicial discretion, like prosecutorial discretion, responds to political incentives. Studies find that elected judges impose harsher sentences in years preceding elections.[148] Because many local courts are responsible for appointing counsel to represent indigent defendants, evidence in some localities suggests that judges sometimes reward attorneys for support during elections with paid defense appointments.[149] These kinds of behaviors reveal how judges' democratic or political status sometimes weakens the *judiciary's* ministerial commitment to justice. Putting judges through the electoral process or otherwise heightening their political responsiveness weakens the judiciary's capacity for disinterested neutrality—for a *fully* judicial (rather than *quasi*-judicial) objectivity. Interpreting procedural and substantive law regularly entails some discretion. (For that reason, appellate courts review certain trial judges' decisions under an *abuse of discretion* standard.) Administrative duties such as counsel appointments can be wholly discretionary. Political judges have less capacity to carry out those tasks in ways that cut against either popular political preferences on crime policy or their own political interests.

CHANGES IN THE SCOPE OF JUDICIAL AUTHORITY

Despite its political rather than bureaucratic status, which should translate to deeper democratic legitimacy for judicial power, the judiciary has not seen this model redound to its benefit in terms of expanded authority as it has for prosecutors. To be sure, courts have over time gained some kinds of authority. Many state constitutions authorized the judiciary to promulgate rules of practice and procedure.[150] Many states have long departed from the common law with statutes that give judges authority to refuse prosecutors' *nolle prosequi* requests. (These statutes often predated judicial elections and often were a tool initially for judges to control private prosecutors, or public ones judges themselves had appointed.) Today courts consistently interpret that power to require nearly absolute judicial deference to prosecutors.[151] More generally, the relative autonomy that judges enjoy in decentralized systems provides leeway—as it does for prosecutors—for experiments in policy innovation. State and federal judges in many places have taken the lead in creating diversion programs, drug treatment courts, and similar alternatives to ordinary adjudication for charged offenders. In doing so, judges often take on significant administrative roles in place of their traditional, relatively passive duties in party-driven litigation.[152]

The fact remains, however, that judges' democratic pedigree did not earn them the same deference from legislatures that prosecutors enjoy. In the latter decades of the nineteenth century, most states enacted laws that prohibited the traditional practice of trial judges commenting on or "summing up" evidence for juries as a means to assist—and influence—jurors.[153] Judges lost other tools as well that had given them some ability to affect outcomes, notably their authority to order juries to reconsider verdicts.[154] (Another tool for some judicial control over juries, the special verdict form that confined jurors to answering specific factual questions, had never been as widely used by American courts as it had been in England.) Much later, legislatures began to enact mandatory sentencing rules, which directly restricted judicial sentencing power and, it was quickly recognized, increased prosecutors' power.[155]

One likely reason the judiciary gained less from electoral accountability than did prosecutors is that the judge's role is simply less compatible than the prosecutor's with decision making that responds to popular sentiment. Even though elected judges are more likely to be attuned to majority sentiments than judges with secure job tenure, if legislatures and citizens prefer criminal justice officials who are politically responsive, the judge's obligation of impartial fidelity to law is a greater constraint on responsiveness than the prosecutor's ministerial norms.

JUDICIAL POWER VERSUS JURY POWER

American criminal justice has not only increased its bias for prosecutorial over judicial power; some changes suggest a shift in favor of juries over judges, such as ending judges' power to comment on evidence. The American constitutional tradition expands the common law's recognition of the jury as a political institution, a local-democratic check on the power of executive and judicial officials. Building on common law tradition, the U.S. Supreme Court continues to emphasize the criminal jury's function as a "guard against . . . oppression and tyranny" and a "bulwark of . . . political liberties" that stands "between the accused and his accuser."[156] Shifts of power between judges and juries have been more of a two-way street, however, than between judges and prosecutors. Most notably, over the nineteenth century judges removed from juries the power to define the *law*. Legislatures together with courts dramatically reduced the jury's meaningful role in criminal justice by giving parties the power to waive the jury and to resolve even serious criminal charges either through bench trials or guilty pleas. In those reforms, the lay jury—the most venerable institution of democracy in criminal process—ceded most of its practical power to government officials—to judges, and especially to prosecutors.

Power over Law versus Power over Facts
The early rule was that juries are "*judges of the law* and the facts,"[157] a formulation still found in some state constitutions but no longer taken literally. Jury power to judge, find, or "determine" the law—meaning both the power

to specify the law's meaning and the power *not* to apply it—faded with the growth of common law, statutes, and modern rule of law norms that gave higher priority to consistency in law's meaning and application.[158] By the end of the nineteenth century, judges usually defined the relevant law for juries. (In that reform, at least, is a small move from a lay-democratic manner of defining law to a more professional-legal means.) But juries still determined the facts and had some leeway in how to apply the law through the general verdict.[159]

The modern division of authority between juries and judges follows the broader common law tradition. In contrast to the civil law tradition, the common law distrusts judges with fact-finding; parties control evidence and juries find facts. Yet common law is quite comfortable with some forms of judicial lawmaking;[160] after all, the tradition consists of judge-made law. But jury authority even with regard simply to fact-finding took a big hit, in practical terms, with the rise of bench trials and guilty pleas for serious offenses.

The Rise of Party Control over the Jury Trial

U.S. courts once took the virtue—or the *necessity*—of jury fact-finding much more seriously. Through the 1880s, the majority view among state supreme courts was that a *criminal trial* had to be a *jury trial*. The same was true in federal courts; the Constitution's Article III command that "The Trial of all Crimes . . . shall be by Jury" was not denied its literal meaning until the twentieth century.[161] Defendants did not have power to waive the jury and consent to a bench trial, even if the prosecutor and trial judge agreed. Conviction upon a guilty plea had long been a legitimate alternative to the trial (although not always for the most serious offenses), but the bench trial had not been. Courts—including the U.S. Supreme Court—insisted that the jury was either an essential *jurisdictional* feature of criminal courts or that it served an essential *public* interest that put it beyond the parties' control. An 1884 Iowa Supreme Court decision is representative. Trial without a jury, the court said, was not a question about "the waiver of a mere statutory privilege." Rather, the jury trial right is:

> an imperative provision, based, as we view it, upon the soundest conception of public policy. Life and liberty are too sacred to be placed at the disposal of any one man, and always will be so long as man is fallible. The innocent person, unduly influenced by his consciousness of innocence, and placing undue confidence in his evidence, would, when charged with crime, be the one most easily induced to waive his safeguards. There is no resemblance between such a case and that of a person pleading guilty. In the latter case there is no trial, but mere judgment upon the plea.[162]

Some states had permitted defendants to waive the jury for minor offenses. A Texas statute went further than most and barred jury waivers for all felony trials: "The defendant to a criminal offense may waive any right secured to him by law, except the right of trial by jury in a felony case."[163] Defendants could *plead guilty* to felonies but not assent to a bench trial. Most state courts in this era held that the legislature had the constitutional power to authorize jury waiver by statute, a view shared by the leading treatise writers. (A few took the view that trials without a jury required constitutional amendment.)[164] But the Iowa court's view was soon no longer to be the prevailing one. Usually by statute but occasionally by judicial decree, nearly all states authorized jury waivers.[165] Some carved out exceptions, however, and continued for a time to prohibit bench trials for the gravest offenses, or at least to require jury *sentencing* in those prosecutions, especially murder.[166]

After these reforms, guilty pleas even to murder were generally permissible except in cases of capital punishment, a limit that remains in effect in some states.[167] New Jersey seems to have been alone in requiring that murder convictions occur only through trial. In an 1874 statute that remained in effect well into the next century, the New Jersey legislature expressly prohibited guilty pleas for murder charges and mandated trial by jury.[168] In a few states including Texas and Washington, statutes required that, after a general guilty plea to murder, a *jury* must determine the *degree* of murder liability and the sentence.[169] But most states allowed judges to determine both liability and the sentence (except for the death penalty) after a basic guilty plea, although they often required judges to hold an evidentiary hearing before doing so. Under the typical statute, "the court must proceed, by the examination of witnesses, to determine the degree of murder, and award sentence accordingly."[170] This modest rule of a mandatory procedure, which serves the public interest in the accuracy of criminal judgments, is a type that (as chapter 4 will discuss) has now gone by the wayside.

Nearly all U.S. jurisdictions made this transition in the same couple of decades. The consensus at which they eventually arrived—and the era in which they did so—is remarkable compared to other common law jurisdictions. No common law justice systems outside the United States took the path of electing prosecutors or judges, but the most prominent Commonwealth nations all retained a much longer commitment to jury trials in serious offenses. England to this day does not permit waiver of the jury for trials in Crown Court, although defining many offenses as "triable either way" provide a functional substitute, as this classification allows such charges to be tried without juries (and with lower maximum punishments) in magistrate's court.[171] Hybrid offenses exist in other common law jurisdictions as well, where jury waiver also appeared much later. In Canada, jury waiver for serious offenses was permitted before 1985 only in the province of Alberta. High Court bench trials in New Zealand were authorized only in 1979, and they remain barred for offenses punishable by terms of fourteen years or more. The first Australian state permitted defendants to elect nonjury trials for indictable offenses in 1927; other states followed, but as late as 1986 the High Court of Australia held that the Commonwealth Constitution barred jury waivers in federal criminal trials.[172] It is no coincidence that U.S. jurisdictions were years ahead in allowing waiver of the jury and in their open encouragement of guilty plea bargaining.

The Demise of the Grand Jury

Before drawing conclusions from this history, it is worth recognizing the broadly similar evolution of the grand jury, the core function of which has been to screen the sufficiency of criminal charges. Few other common law nations still use the grand jury. It was never widely employed in Australia; England abolished the grand jury in 1933, New Zealand in 1961.[173] Even in the United States only nineteen states, plus the federal Constitution, retain a right to indictment by grand jury, and some limit the right to only the most serious offenses. Everywhere, the grand jury right (like the right to a trial jury) is frequently waived.[174] More revealing is the grand jury's transformation.

In the nation's early decades, state grand juries were frequently a central body of local government, especially in sparsely populated localities. That presents a parallel with state judges' broader powers in this era; in some places grand juries played wide-ranging administrative and policymaking roles far beyond screening criminal complaints. They oversaw tax assessments or building inspections and proposed legislation.[175] Gradually other state institutions evolved to take over these governance tasks. In the latter nineteenth century—again after the rise of elected prosecutors and judges, and at the same time that trial juries became waivable—grand juries fell from favor in many states, even for issuing criminal charges.

Where it survived, rule changes weakened the grand jury's independence and gave prosecutors much more control. Jurisdictions now overwhelmingly allow prosecutors to resubmit charges if a grand jury declines to indict. Most do not apply hearsay rules, which allows prosecutors to present one or two witnesses to summarize evidence and thus deprives jurors of a chance to assess witness credibility. Very few grand jury jurisdictions give defendants a right to testify or require prosecutors to disclose exculpatory evidence. These restrictions give prosecutors more control over the record and grand juries less information that might favor a decision not to charge.[176] The aphorism that a grand jury would indict a "ham sandwich" captures the prevailing view that grand jurors have become the prosecutor's rubber-stamp (and in federal practice, a powerful tool of prosecutorial investigations). Where it survives, then, the grand jury's fate shares much with that of the trial jury. The rules of criminal process have reduced the power and role of lay jurors in both contexts, while officials' power has increased. In light of all this, the grand jury is not plausibly a vehicle for significant lay-democratic supervision of prosecutors' investigation tactics and charging discretion. Nor is there consequential legal regulation or judicial review. Rather, the grand jury represents a transition from democratic supervision to control by democratically accountable enforcement officials.

TRANSFORMATION OF DEMOCRATIC GOVERNANCE

That same transition describes the broader changes in the criminal justice system beginning perhaps in the mid nineteenth century. Looking at prevalence of direct elections as the means to select prosecutors and judges, at who exercises more practical power, and at the jury's role in adjudication, one sees not simply a shift toward greater democracy but a strong transformation in democratic mechanisms. In short, the shift is from democracy by juries—direct citizen decision making at the level of individual cases—to democracy by elections. Now citizens mostly vote periodically for officials and implicitly judge the candidates' track records in office.[177] Formerly, much more voting occurred in the jury room, based on evidence from specific prosecutions and after some group deliberation.

What role the rise of politically accountable officials played in the near-demise of the jury is impossible to say. Perhaps little, given the modest role juries retain in other common law nations that do not elect prosecutors. Still, the two developments seem likely to be linked in the United States. Elsewhere, criminal justice systems rely more on (relatively modest) legal regulation of prosecutors, in addition to more substantial institutional frameworks to strengthen ministerial norms. Those are substitutes, of a sort, for the jury's institutional function as a check on overreaching prosecutors. U.S. jurisdictions chose a different model: guarding against prosecutorial excess by electoral supervision rather than legal rules, stronger ministerial norms, or supervision by juries.[178]

Among other implications of this change, one is particularly noteworthy. When criminal justice scholars argue that the answer to the excessive punitiveness and other dysfunctions in American criminal justice is more local-level democracy, they mostly have in mind restoring a meaningful role for juries. The predominant kind of local democracy, however, is practiced through the ballot box, the kind that is blamed—especially in discussions of penal populism and tough-on-crime politics—for increasing punitiveness.[179]

Conclusion

There are other ways to tell the story of the evolving balance between law and democracy in criminal procedure. Over the course of the twentieth century, U.S. criminal procedure added a lot of significant *law*—legal entitlements, duties, and prohibitions—that strengthened its basic legality, its character as a system of laws rather than men. Rules mandate more evidence disclosure and improve opportunities for appellate review; coerced confessions are inadmissible; defense counsel is constitutionally guaranteed; better rules limit unfairness from pretrial publicity, community intimidation, and advocates' appeals to racial biases. None of that was the case a century ago. Nineteenth-century conflict-of-interest norms for prosecutors and other attorneys look scandalous to contemporary eyes,[180] and the requirements of constitutional due process in criminal justice were exceedingly thin then. A century prior it was not yet clear that due process barred prosecutors from knowingly using false testimony. Leading jurists argued that defendants were entitled merely to a fair opportunity to uncover and to discredit perjury by a state witness.[181] In those ways and others, criminal procedure has moved decidedly toward a stronger rule of law ideal.

Those features are now firmly established, but taking them as indicators of a proper balance between law and politics in American criminal justice sets the bar too low, in much the same way that stressing the improved legal and social status of African Americans in 1950 compared to a hundred years earlier would say too little about mid-century racial justice. Criminal adjudication in the United States remains by many measures more democratic—or more political—than its counterparts elsewhere. Yet its structures of accountability are closely tied to some of its most problematic characteristics, most notably its uniquely expansive use of carceral punishment. In legal scholarship and judicial reasoning, democracy's virtues get more attention than its costs. Particularly in debates among scholars, the best arguments focus on improving underutilized democratic mechanisms, such as juries, which have been almost wholly supplanted by ballot-box accountability for criminal justice officials or those who appoint them.[182] Even so, discussions of democracy in U.S. criminal justice put more emphasis on the benefits of political judgment than its costs, while overlooking the advantages of more law and procedure—even more bureaucracy.[183] American justice systems have ignored or rejected even modest forms of legal regulation, with a modestly more substantial judicial role in criminal adjudication, which would be wholly consonant with a democratic criminal justice, would improve the rule of law in criminal justice administration, and would ameliorate some of the system's worst dysfunctions.

CHAPTER 3

Criminal Justice by the Invisible Hand

[I]f the prosecutor is interested in "buying" the reliability assurance that accompanies a waiver agreement, then precluding waiver can only stifle the market for plea bargains. A defendant can "maximize" what he has to "sell" only if he is permitted to offer what the prosecutor is most interested in buying.
—*United States v. Mezzanatto* (1995)*

Law versus Markets

Only commitment to free markets rivals democracy as a defining, foundational principle of American society and government. The United States has long been acknowledged by Americans and foreign observers alike to be just as strongly committed to a market economy as it is to democratic governance. Especially as understood in American politics and culture, democracy and markets share much common ground as ways of organizing public and private life. Both respond to skepticism of government power; both operate in service of individual freedom. Through democratic institutions, citizens can check (some) undue government infringements of liberty. Market economies likewise give people autonomy to pursue their chosen interests by their own strategies free from unnecessary state restrictions or commands. Both markets and democracy are mechanisms, or opportunities, for achieving ends, such as allocation of goods. Both give legitimacy to the outcomes they produce, and keep the state from otherwise having what those outcomes would be.

These are equally familiar features of American society generally. Within the structure of U.S. criminal procedure, however, the priority given to democratic principles is much better known, even though the influence of market norms and market-inspired mechanisms plays an equally significant role. One readily identifies the lay jury as a democratic institution at the heart of the common law trial, and America's singular preference for politically accountable prosecutors is nearly as well known, even to observers outside the United States. But what does criminal adjudication, a quintessentially public-law institution, incorporate from market institutions, which lie at the heart of the private realm?

To be sure, policies that aim to leverage private market efficiencies for the benefit of the public sector are central to the agenda of neoliberalism, which has had considerable success in a number of countries since the 1970s. Privatization of government services and functions is probably the most familiar market-oriented model for policy in this vein. In both the United States and the United Kingdom, governments have contracted with private firms to operate key institutions of the criminal justice system—prisons and probation services—as well as an innumerable range of other public-sector endeavors.[1] Variations on this theme are long-standing; nineteenth-century policies of leasing state prison inmates to private work-farms or to private firms with manufacturing operations inside prisons were precursors to private prisons. A large share of publicly financed indigent defense services in the United States are privatized in this sense; governments contract with private lawyers to provide legal services.[2] Behind these sorts of arrangements is an expectation that private actors driven by self-interest and disciplined by market competition will do the job more efficiently than public actors are likely to do.

In a different dimension, astute commentators such as Nicola Lacey, Katherine Beckett, and Bruce Western have recognized other connections between market policies and criminal justice practices. There are striking correlations between the political economy of a nation or U.S. state—its mix of social welfare policies and market regulations—and patterns of criminal punishment. Governments with policies that incline more toward unregulated markets and less generous social welfare provision have higher incarceration rates; conversely, those with more regulated economies and more generous public welfare programs tend to have lower imprisonment levels.[3] Finally, from another perspective, Bernard Harcourt's *The Illusion of Free Markets* traces harsh incarceration policies to widely influential ideas about private markets and the limited scope of the public sphere.[4]

When scholars' attention turns more specifically to the "political economy" of criminal procedure, however, the focus is strongly on the *political* rather than the *economic*; the operation and effects of market-based rules and rationales gets little attention. That is true of work as different (and insightful) as Stuntz's *Collapse of American Criminal Justice* and Jonathan Simon's *Governing Through Crime*. Even Damaska's classic *Faces of Justice and State Authority*, which distinguishes between *activist* and *reactive* states and links those differences in adjudication regimes, has little to say about the influence of market rationality or policy on legal systems.

One reason for this relative paucity of attention is that market rationality in American criminal procedure law is almost too obvious to warrant notice. The U.S. Supreme Court describes guilty plea agreements as "essentially contracts." It has explicitly designed the constitutional law governing those agreements so as not to "stifle the market for plea bargains" or put "arbitrary limits on [the parties'] bargaining chips."[5] Comparably explicit market metaphors are rare or nonexistent in the judicial opinions of other common law nations.

Market rationality is nearly as explicit in other branches of criminal procedure doctrine, but its influence extends beyond these kinds of overt references. The language of market economics is predominantly instrumental; the focus is on the likely or demonstrable effects of rules and practices rather than how they accord with moral norms or public law values. One modest indicator of a shift toward instrumental judicial analysis is evidence of the Supreme Court's use of the word "incentive" and its variants in reference to prosecutors and defendants over the last century. In the first thirty-three years after 1913, the Court never wrote of prosecutor or defendant "incentives." In the next thirty-three-year period, it did so twenty-six times. In the final thirty-three years before 2014, the Court's opinions used the word seventy-seven times in that context. That trend is consistent with dramatically greater usage of "incentive" or its variants in books and American public discourse in recent decades.[6]

Widening the scope, market metaphors, as well as rules intended to protect market-like institutions, appear in other constitutional doctrines, where they have attracted much more critical consideration. A ready example is the "marketplace of ideas" metaphor, which has retained a central conceptual role in free speech law for nearly a century. A more infamous one is the *Lochner* era of substantive due process doctrine, which recognized a fundamental right to "liberty of contract." For decades the Supreme Court leveraged that principle, in service of a strongly laissez-faire conception of capitalism, to strike down a range of economic and social welfare legislation—nascent steps in the direction of a coordinated-market economy.[7]

Within the law of criminal procedure but outside the context of plea agreements, the success of market mechanisms and market-inspired norms is usually more subtle, but only a bit. Some examples are developed in detail later, but one need only observe the symmetry between markets and adversarial legal process, which borrows its core structure and premises from the market. To render sound judgments that authorize the state to impose punishment, courts need sufficient evidentiary records. To produce them, adversarial process relies on competition between rival parties. Rather than state officials (even judicial officials) taking full responsibility for creating the factual record, that task is partially privatized by delegating it to the parties. The parties' motivation for taking on this task (most straightforwardly on the defense side) is the same as that for private market participants—self-interest, not legal obligation. This is most straightforwardly true for the defense, but it is true in a meaningful sense for the prosecution as well; the latter's partisan motivation is defined by prosecutors' adversarial role representing the executive's enforcement interests. Prosecutors have a "duty" to present evidence of a defendant's guilt, but it is a political or professional duty defined by their adversarial role. There is no enforceable legal duty for prosecutors to gather and present evidence of guilt; they do it because they want to win a conviction. Moreover, because adversarial process adopts market mechanisms (such as party competition) and market premises (such as faith in partisan- or self-interest as a reliable motivator), it implicitly borrows norms, or values, that accompany markets as well. One example is the moral view that parties have *responsibilities* to act in their respective, role-defined interests. If they don't, in large measure they *deserve* the consequences of failing to do so. It is no surprise then that, broadly speaking, more market-oriented societies tend also to rely on adversarial legal process; rationales for markets and adversarial trials have much in common.

The influence of market ideas extends much beyond the core structure of the adversarial trial to innumerable criminal process rules and the rationales that justify them. Emphasis on party self-interest, freedom of action, competition, and voluntary cooperation pervade criminal procedure. Parties' ability to challenge hostile witnesses through cross-examination is a species of Adam Smith's classic "invisible hand" idea by which private initiative also serves the public good—here, the judicial interest in determining the accuracy of testimony.[8] In the constitutional law on this right of confrontation accorded defendants, the Supreme Court has made clear that a judicial determination of a witness's reliability cannot substitute for party examination of the witness.[9] Truthful judgments do not depend on a state official's obligation to find that a witness is reliable; they depend on parties taking self-interested advantage of opportunities to investigate and demonstrate whether a witness is reliable. Even in a public law process in which the defendant's role is hardly voluntary, the state—as it does in the market—provides procedural opportunities, not a guarantee about outcomes. Rules of procedural default heighten party incentives to use those opportunities and make clear that favorable (even accurate) outcomes depend on them doing so. Other criminal procedure doctrines likewise embody the logic and practice of markets. Parties are free to waive—or, in the Supreme Court's forthright terminology, to "buy" and "sell"[10]—nearly all procedural entitlements; they largely control the specifics of process case-by-case through personal decisions or mutual agreement. In that sense the form of criminal process is "privatized." The same market-inspired form or structure is apparent in the law of evidentiary disclosure, appellate standards of review, and doctrines defining the right to defense counsel.

Norms from the market domain play a critical role as well throughout the law of criminal procedure. Markets carry their own values, which define what goods or services are *appropriate* for trade, what outcomes from trade are morally tolerable, and which tactics are the ethical ones in competing or negotiating with others. Market values justify legal rules that mimic market mechanisms, and they justify the consequences that follow from those rules. For example, final judgments are justified even if based on an incomplete or inaccurate factual record, as long as the parties had fair opportunities to contribute to that record. The norm that opportunity entails responsibility makes the legitimacy of judgments turn on party choices and conduct, rather than a rival norm, such as the state's obligation to ensure judgments by its criminal courts are substantively accurate regardless of a party's litigation skill or diligence.

This chapter develops the basic argument about market ideas in criminal process. Like the previous chapter, it focuses on some of the primary institutions of criminal process. The law and norms surrounding prosecutors, as well as the core structure of the adversary process, can be seen in a new light as a product of market-based as well as democratic commitments. Market premises are especially evident, for example, in the law guaranteeing defendants private counsel of their choice and in the means by which states provide publicly funded counsel to indigent defendants. Next, in large part because the power of market ideology is less familiar than democratic ideology in criminal procedure, the subsequent two chapters carry forward this examination of the role of market ideas—first in a critical look at the law of plea bargaining, then in a survey of other adversary-process rules that allocate responsibility for errors and outcomes between the state and private actors.

All this provides an insight into a seeming irony about the power of U.S. criminal justice. Much about American government arises from the original and enduring distrust of state power, famously including a federal government of limited powers, labeled as a "weak" state by political scientists when compared to European governments. As noted earlier, the strong tradition for democratic governance arises from that same concern. The basic choice for adversarial legal process does as well, by giving parties more power and state magistrates less. Yet despite these choices, the American state's criminal enforcement capacity is hardly weak in any meaningful respect, including by comparison to other advanced democracies. Incarceration rates alone make that clear, as does the broad reach of state and federal criminal law, correctly characterized as "over-criminalization" for, among other reasons, the wide use of strict liability and the punishment of very early-stage preparatory conduct.[11] Part of the answer is simply that U.S. jurisdictions embraced state power in one respect—by giving politically accountable public prosecutors a monopoly over criminal charging. But that is hardly the whole story. Public authority has gained advantages from the adoption of adversarial-process rules inspired by a model intended to limit the state—the model of markets. That turn has led to greater adversarialism, increased party autonomy, and reduced state responsibility for its own legal process. In that kind of system, it turns out, state enforcement capacity thrives.

Varieties of Market Economies

DISTINCTIONS AMONG CAPITALIST POLITICAL ECONOMIES

Criminal justice systems have long been examined through the lens of nations' "legal origins," referring typically to the common law and civil law traditions. Scrutiny through a framework of competing political economies, on the other hand, is relatively rare. Like legal traditions, political economies—state policies that shape, facilitate, limit, and displace markets, and that allocate roles of market and nonmarket institutions—also divide into relatively identifiable camps, although in both cases overly general categories obscure significant details. Moreover, whether or not we are all Keynesians now, we are all capitalists. Distinctions in how nations structure and regulate market economies provide considerable insight into how they organize criminal justice administration as well. Both domains present fundamental choices about the role of the state and private parties, and about the efficacy of hierarchies versus markets or public versus private ordering. Scholars of comparative political economy have done a great deal of work describing the "varieties of capitalism" among advanced nations, research that has mapped important differences in the scope and form of state regulation of markets. The most common categories of that literature—liberal-market and coordinated-market economies—are useful also in assessing criminal justice systems, because defining features of those variations, including premises about the efficacy of markets or state intervention, often tend to carry over into criminal procedure.

Liberal-Market Economies
National approaches to market organization and economic policy are commonly divided into two broad categories—liberal-market economies and coordinated-market economies. The countries widely seen as having a stronger free market orientation—especially among comparative political economists—are often described as *liberal-market economies* (LMEs). That description evokes the alternate label *neoliberalism*, which is often used to refer to the same set of economic premises and policies. The foremost example is the

United States, but the United Kingdom and most common law countries fit in this category as well.

Liberal-market economies generally give greater roles to private actors and market competition throughout their economies, and they often utilize competitive processes and private entities for providing state services (such as prisons and probation agencies) and social welfare (such as, in the United States, health care). "Free" markets, of course, are never free of state regulation. At bottom, markets, in Ronald Coase's words, "are institutions that exist to facilitate exchange, that is . . . to reduce the cost of carrying out exchange transactions." For "anything approaching perfect competition to exist, an intricate system of rules and regulations would normally be needed."[12] All states do much more to facilitate markets—and certain kinds of market outcomes—than simply enforce property rights and contracts. Antitrust laws, disclosure rules for securities markets or food products, limits on consumer loan interest rates, and regulation of private associational forms such as corporations or labor unions are all examples.[13] Nonetheless, LMEs put more emphasis on facilitating private exchange and competition. They start with a presumption for the private sector over the public sector as the most efficient way to produce and allocate goods and services. Very broadly, LME regulation is directed more at ensuring well-functioning, competitive markets, and it is less inclined to regulate overtly in favor of ensuring specific outcomes from markets, such as supporting particular industries or specific wage levels and distributions.

Not only does the state in liberal-market economies play a smaller coordinating role in the private sector; the same is true for large nonstate institutions such as unions and industry-wide employer associations. Labor laws in LMEs tend to disfavor unions, which are accordingly weaker, especially in the United States.[14] As a result, labor markets are more flexible, but labor-management relations are historically more adversarial, characterized more often by conflict than cooperation.[15] One consequence is that wealth inequalities are greater in LMEs, as is cultural tolerance of those inequalities. There is also greater acceptance of individuals' (and to a lesser degree firms') economic insecurity as a cost of more dynamic markets, so LMEs do less to mitigate harms from periods of unemployment.

Overall, in the labor sector as in other sectors, markets play larger roles; mediating institutions and state intervention, especially when it comes to defining market outcomes, play smaller ones. (Nonetheless, in practice state policies may favor some private interests over others. Established firms in a market, for example, may have significant influence over legislation or regulatory policymaking to the detriment of emerging rivals.)[16] In sum, LMEs rely more on mechanisms of private ordering than those of public ordering.

Along with these kinds of choices in market roles and organization, LME policies generally reflect specific market-related norms. Because liberal-market nations in general are more skeptical of the state's ability to improve social or economic outcomes by displacing or managing markets, it is a smaller step to the normative view that state intervention is *legitimate* only in limited spheres of social and economic life. Self-interest and personal responsibility are given wider scope; consideration for others' interests is more voluntary and less obligatory. Liberal-market nations tend to give less weight to nonmarket values, such as moral or social obligations, in private sector arrangements or exchanges, and these values play a smaller role in public policy.[17] For example, corporate governance rules tend to prioritize shareholder wealth more highly relative to interests of other stakeholders, such as employees or communities.[18] For the same reason, LMEs generally have fewer constraints—legal, cultural, or ethical—on high executive pay, and their social welfare policies are generally less redistributive. Both firms and the state carry fewer obligations for the welfare of employees or citizens; individuals consequently bear greater responsibility for their own interests and well-being. Market norms undermine social solidarity, notions of mutual obligation, and bourgeois habits of thrift, which has led even ardent advocates of free market capitalism to worry about the corrosive effects of markets on a society's moral order.[19]

Coordinated-Market Economies

By contrast, countries described as *coordinated-market economies* (CMEs) take a considerably different approach. Germany is commonly identified as a representative CME, although most other nations of west-central Europe as well as economically advanced Asian countries such as Japan fit under the label. In coordinated economies, states generally take a more active role in structuring private-sector interactions, notably by facilitating nonstate coordinating institutions. Looser antitrust laws may encourage industry-wide associations among firms, and labor laws (as well as, in some cases, labor traditions extending back to pre-capitalist trade guilds) result in stronger, industry-based (rather than employer-based) unions. Together these institutions play coordinating roles in market economies, for instance by working toward industry-based wage agreements. German corporate governance law (described as "codetermination") gives employees representation on corporate boards, which increases protection of workers' interests, including "nonmarket" ones such as security, relative most notably to shareholder interests. Employment law gives workers greater job security as well, rather than—as in a strongly liberal-market system—leaving security to individual employment contracts. Greater job security leads workers and firms to invest more in workers' firm-specific skills. Social welfare and other public services are relatively more generous.[20]

(Scholars sometimes distinguish a third national model, *social democratic economies* [SDEs], a label that describes Scandinavian countries especially well. SDEs share many of the cooperative institutions of CMEs but differ, for example, by linking social welfare, such as pensions or unemployment insurance, to citizenship rather than employment status.)

These features of coordinated economies reflect different public norms and different assessments of how well markets work to produce desirable outcomes with little state intervention. Broadly, CMEs accord greater legitimacy to a more expansive state role, both in social welfare programs and in other public interventions aimed at improving market outcomes.[21] Individuals' interest in employment security is more strongly valued, and firms have greater obligations to employees and other stakeholders who counterbalance the interests of shareholders.[22] An ethic of individual responsibility for one's own fate in the economic marketplace is implicitly somewhat weaker, while social norms of solidarity and mutual obligation are stronger. Self-interest is thus tempered by higher regard for competing interests, both for counterparties in a market relationship (such as firms and workers) and for third parties.

Competing Rationalities

To be sure, these two broad categories are generalizations that mask substantial differences among individual countries in regulatory priorities, institutional arrangements, and social values. The United States, for example, is more sharply market-oriented even compared to other liberal-market economies in policies regarding labor, health care, and unemployment insurance. At the same time, some U.S. policies reject this market orientation. The American agricultural sector is heavily regulated and benefits from considerable state price supports; and substantial federal funding (especially through the defense sector) goes to research in technology, medicine, and other fields that ultimately benefit private commercial development.[23] No nation consistently abides by a pure liberal-market model, and coordinated economies vary in their approach to managing markets. Yet nations that fall into both categories nonetheless remain predominantly *market*—or capitalist—economies. Despite generalizations that overlook significant differences, the basic distinction between liberal- and coordinated-market economies is a useful one—much like the dichotomy between adversarial and inquisitorial procedures—especially for what it highlights about ways to integrate state and market mechanisms. Those differences in state and market roles, and the competing value choices behind them, provide an important ideological background—an underlying rationality or worldview—that carries over to criminal justice systems.

The insights from comparative political economy are useful in a second respect as well. The fact that countries have the ability to adopt different market models with broadly similar economic success belies a claim of some economists and policy advocates, namely that globalization compels nations to follow neoliberal policies such as flexible labor policies, less generous social welfare policies and minimal regulation in other domains. The "varieties of capitalism" suggests that is not consistently true. Countries taking up variants of both liberal-market and coordinated-market economic policies have thrived to roughly equivalent degrees, measured by criteria such as per capita gross domestic product and average life expectancy.

In technical terms, this is possible when the world economy has multiple "points of equilibria"—that is, when various combinations of state and market policies provide equivalent paths to a successful economy. Moreover, something analogous is likely true with regard to criminal justice systems. Very different designs may all succeed sufficiently well at what adjudication is supposed to do—consistently render accurate judgments without undue delay or cost, in ways accepted as legitimate, while giving due regard to competing goals such as participation. So far we have fewer ways to measure criteria for success in criminal justice systems (accuracy and proportionality) than we do for national economies. If different arrangements succeed equally well, however, it would mean that criminal justice systems, like political economies, have multiple points of equilibria. That policy flexibility—in justice administration as in economic policy—means that a jurisdiction's choices can accommodate significant differences in tradition and culture, or simply "common knowledge" or shared beliefs about what possibilities are feasible and what outcomes are fair.[24] For both economic policy and criminal process, those differences include views about the efficacy of markets, the role of the state, and the scope of mutual obligation or solidarity versus the scope of individual autonomy and responsibility. Shared ideas and experiences condition, without determining, the institutional possibilities that appear both available and acceptable. Criminal procedure rules depend on answers to many of the same questions faced in economic and social policymaking. Both domains compel choices between public and private ordering, the relative responsibilities of the state and individual, and judgments about the kinds of outcomes taken as fair and legitimate.

AMERICAN POLITICAL DEVELOPMENT

In light of the differences highlighted in the previous chapter between the American and English criminal justice systems, one might wonder how meaningful the relationship is between a nation's political economy and its mode of criminal adjudication. The United States and the United Kingdom are both leading examples of liberal-market economies. Clearly, a nation's commitment to liberal-market policies and norms is not the sole determinant of all key details of its procedural rules and institutions. For one, important differences follow from choosing whether to regulate public officials through democratic accountability or through some mix of legal rules, bureaucratic or judicial supervision, and professional norms. Moreover, a related difference between nation states matters as well, one earlier acknowledged in passing: whether government is relatively centralized or decentralized. While the United States and the United Kingdom have a lot in common as liberal-market economies, they differ considerably in their degrees of centralized governance. The United States is comparatively more decentralized, with a federal structure that preserves significant power for state governments, in addition to a strong separation-of-powers structure that limits the effectiveness of the national government. The United Kingdom—even after some devolution of state functions to Scotland, Wales, and Northern Ireland—remains a nonfederal centralized state.[25]

As noted earlier, scholars (particularly in studies of American political development) have described the U.S. national government as a comparatively "weak" state, at least compared to the classic Weberian model of European states with strong central authority, wide-ranging administrative capacity, and large, professionalized bureaucracies.[26] More recently, scholarship tends to reject or avoid characterizing the American state as "weak" for various reasons, including its exceptionally large military capacity and strategies for achieving policy goals with less centralized management through public-private and federal-state partnerships. (Health care is a prominent example: federal—or state—government is not the direct provider of health insurance for most residents, but government regulates insurance contract terms and subsidizes private insurance through tax deductions or credits and direct subsidies.)[27] Nonetheless America retains a decentralized government structure, as the existence of fifty-one different criminal justice jurisdictions confirms. That fragmented and decentralized design reflects the much-noted distrust of centralized state power that started in the founding era. It is intended, among other things, to preserve individual liberty, by keeping much public power at a state or local level, and also by leaving more room for a larger nonstate sector, as Tocqueville among others has noted—for civil society, markets, and other forms of private ordering.[28]

Decentralized government has been one factor facilitating the liberal-market orientation of American political economy. For example, some view the U.S. Constitution as intentionally creating a common market among the states by limiting state governments' regulatory power over interstate commerce and immigration.[29] Without abilities to restrain interstate trade through tariffs or the like, states are inevitably in competition with other states for capital and people, which effectively constrains their leeway for public regulation within their own borders. Many types of firms can move to another state if they dislike one state's regulatory environment.[30]

From the nation's earliest years, market-oriented features of U.S. government mingled with a strong practical and ideological support for a market economy. "By the 1830s, most citizens believed that divinely inspired bounty and a powerful set of natural laws—illustrated by the market—ordered social actions," Brian Balogh has written, and "energetic governance came to be regarded as the exception in an otherwise self-regulating society."[31] The rapid expansion of commerce in the early nineteenth century was the era of the American "market revolution,"[32] and the law adapted as markets and industry expanded. Corporations were allowed to transform from special-purpose entities in service of specific public needs (such as building a bridge or toll road) into general-purpose vehicles for purely private commercial endeavors.[33] Throughout this early period, legal doctrines evolved from a regulatory focus on, say, the fairness of terms in private exchange, to putting priority on the rights of individuals to determine fairness for themselves. That shift helped to broaden and to normalize commercial competition, although courts retained some power to scrutinize private actions for their effects on broader public interests.[34] Overall, despite periodic challenges over time from populist or labor movements, the liberal-market orientation in American political economy gained support from decentralized government, broad popular sentiment, and evolving legal ideology.

This is not to say that a more centralized state such as the United Kingdom necessarily inclines toward a less liberal-market, more coordinated-market model. That debate doesn't matter here. Particularly in criminal justice, some English policies such as private probation services demonstrate a strong liberal-market or neoliberal orientation.[35] The point for now is a narrower one: American political development provides an additional window on why the United States is so firmly committed to liberal-market policies, and—more important—why market ideas so thoroughly pervade even domains like criminal process, where their salience is not as obvious. The much-noted American distrust of the state leads to both the bias for democratic/political administration over politically insulated bureaucracies and the bias for private markets in the provision of public or social goods. The multilayered, decentralized structure of U.S. criminal justice agencies—fifty state criminal codes and state-administered prisons, plus locally elected prosecutors and locally appointed police chiefs—is designed to increase democratic accountability. But the same fragmentation also impedes agency coordination and managerial hierarchy, both of which (as is commonly recognized in the context of corporate governance) are alternatives to markets as organizational strategies. American political development has been guided—arguably from the founding—by the ideas of, and experience with, a liberal-market economy. Its state structure is especially well adapted to that model in which the state facilitates a wide scope for markets, sometimes using policy to fine-tune private actors' incentives yet mostly minimizing its own coordinating role. The same ideas inspire and justify many procedures and norms of U.S. criminal adjudication.

Criminal Process and Market Ideology

With these broad grounds for comparison in mind, consider more closely how the criminal justice system incorporates the favored mechanisms, premises, and norms of specific political economy types. The influence is apparent at the broadest level of institutional design. Painting again with a broad brush, it is no surprise that nations with liberal-market economies are largely also those within the tradition of adversarial legal process. Nations with coordinated-market economies, by contrast, generally have legal systems with roots in traditions of inquisitorial legal process, even though in recent decades many reforms have incorporated various aspects of adversarial procedure. The basic differences between adversarial and inquisitorial approaches can be described in terms very much like those that distinguish liberal-market and coordinated-market economies. Adversarial process is fundamentally based on the principles of liberal-market economies; systems with strong inquisitorial components share the fundamentals of coordinated-market policies.

ADVERSARIAL PROCESS AS A LIBERAL-MARKET SYSTEM

The broad similarities of adversarialism to market institutions are plain to see. Adversarialism places most power and responsibility in the "private sector"—in the hands of the parties. The parties have opposing interests; they seek opposing judgments. In pursuit of those disparate interests they compete with each other to produce evidence for the court, and to convince the court about the applicable substantive and procedural (e.g., evidence) law. However, parties—like market actors—can elect to cooperate or to reach an agreement if both conclude that such options best serve their interests. Practically, this means in the criminal justice context that the prosecution's role is to marshal the evidence and legal arguments in favor of guilt, leaving to the defense the task of undermining that case and producing evidence and arguments favoring acquittal.

This commitment to legal process dominated by competitive parties comes at the expense of nonpartisan (non*party*) public authority, specifically judicial power. As one would expect in a liberal-market economy, the government regulates with a light hand. No judge or magistrate has a duty—and little if any authority—to develop the evidentiary record, or to closely supervise the adequacy of party evidence gathering (as opposed to managing the parties with the aim of reducing delay or abusive behavior). That would smack too much of public ordering, of state control over the evidence record. The same is true regarding application of law. Adversarial judges do not enforce on their own initiative, for example, evidentiary law when they notice a party offer inadmissible hearsay, nor are they likely to flag a defense (such as the absence of *mens rea* on an element of the offense) that is suggested by testimony but overlooked by a defendant and his counsel. In this weak judicial role is an echo of the liberal market: state regulators do little to coordinate competitive interactions with an eye toward favoring a certain kind of outcome. No official steps in to fill gaps in the factual record created by a party's lapse.

In adversarial process, as in other market settings, the law—the state—sets the fundamental terms of engagement, at a minimum by defining the parties' underlying property and other entitlements.[36] Law defines, for example, the prosecutor's charging entitlements—the range of offenses that apply to any given act of wrongdoing—and the breadth of her discretion in choosing among them, which are critical sources of prosecution leverage in U.S. plea bargaining. Law likewise defines a defendant's privilege against self-incrimination and many other ground rules that distribute advantages in criminal adjudication. More to the point, the rules of adversarial process itself define—or literally *create*—the parties' motivating interests. At bottom, what motivates parties is their aversion to an unfavorable judgment. As in any well-functioning adjudication regime, parties should suffer an adverse judgment if that is, as a matter of objective truth, the correct outcome. However, they can incur an adverse judgment if (subject to modest limitations discussed later) their own efforts at evidence gathering and legal advocacy fall short for any number of reasons. Particularly under federal law, as Justice Scalia takes pains to emphasize, the state does not guarantee that judgments of its courts will be *accurate*; it merely guarantees parties the opportunities to participate in a process designed—if they fulfill their roles—to maximize the odds of accurate judgments.

Here too legal process mimics free markets: the state does not assure individuals a specific quality of outcome regardless of individual effort. Adversarial systems, like markets, provide an opportunity to compete and pursue one's interests. But just as a firmly liberal market economy promises no guaranteed minimum income, adversarial procedure does not promise an accurate court judgment. Free markets and adversarial process both rely on the possibility (or threat) of bad outcomes to motivate private initiative. Adversarial frameworks incentivize parties to produce *public* goods—evidence and legal argument—by making the content of court judgments dependent on their own efforts. In this way, as if by an Invisible Hand, adversarialism harnesses competing pursuits of partisan interests for goods the state requires and otherwise would have to produce directly. Adversarialism seeks to replicate markets' vaunted capacity to collect information and allocate resources better (often but not always) than public or private hierarchies.[37] Party rivalries create factual records and focus legal issues on which courts need to render state-enforced judgments. It seems no surprise, then, that adversarial process arose in the crucible of modern capitalism and political liberalism—the Britain of John Locke, David Hume, and Adam Smith.

LIBERAL-MARKET REGULATION

Throughout many sectors of market economies, law does more than set basic entitlements and leave parties otherwise free for private interaction. Even in a strongly liberal-market economy like the United States, regulations are pervasive. Rules define permissible, required, or prohibited behavior with the general aim of improving how markets operate, whether by preventing "market failures," in the familiar phrase, or by favoring—usually modestly—certain kinds of outcomes. Long-standing rules against fraud and coercion are basic examples. Many market sectors have information disclosure requirements as well. Consumer products must warn about risks or disclose their materials or contents. Securities markets have significant disclosure obligations, in addition to rules barring trades based on nonpublic "inside" information; regulations further limit sale of some products to "accredited" investors only.[38] Occupational licensing requirements prohibit customers' voluntary, fully informed transactions with unlicensed practitioners. Various auction or competitive bidding formats adopt various rules with the aim of managing prices and outcomes; some conceal offers from other competitors, others restrict the revision or frequency of bids.[39] Some market interventions by the state are more substantial. Through tax policies, the United States heightens incentives for private actors—employees and employers—to accumulate retirement funds and secure health insurance. (Those markets operate alongside state-run retirement and insurance programs, like Social Security and Medicare.) The state also creates private markets for pollutants such as sulfur dioxide through "cap-and-trade" policies that set emissions limits on private firms and encourage them to trade emission credits.[40]

Thus it is no surprise—and no departure from the reality of free markets—that adversarial process relies on comparable rules that impose some duties on parties and restrain them from no-holds-barred tactics. Most common are requirements of notice and disclosure. Prosecutors must announce charges with sufficient specificity; defendants must give notice of some defenses, such as alibi or insanity. Both parties must give notice if they plan to use expert witnesses. Though they vary widely among jurisdictions, discovery rules generally obligate both sides to reveal anticipated witnesses and other sources of potential evidence. These are simply "information-forcing" rules, which are familiar in many market settings. Such rules prevent a party from concealing information that, if guided solely by partisan interest, the party would likely not disclose.[41] The deeper purpose of these rules is to improve the functioning of markets or contractual exchanges. When all sides have access to relevant information, markets are more likely to produce optimal outcomes. In criminal process, as in other domains of public policy, the liberal-market state favors market-inspired mechanisms of private ordering—even though, in the context of public adjudication, the state provides a degree of coordination that is familiar even in liberal market economies.[42]

INQUISITORIAL PROCESS AS A COORDINATED-MARKET SYSTEM

More briefly, the paucity of market-inspired features that exist in classic inquisitorial legal process provides more evidence of the influence of political economy on criminal procedure. Many contemporary legal systems based in this tradition have now integrated substantial features of adversarial models. Nonetheless, in its strong form inquisitorialism relies much less on parties and much more on judicial officials to oversee fact investigation and evidence production. Commonly much of this job rests with prosecutors as well as (or more than) judges. The prosecutor, however—as the previous chapter noted, citing French and German examples—is a more quasi-judicial official than is familiar to most lawyers from adversarial traditions; the prosecutor's professional identity is more closely aligned with judges than the advocacy role of defense attorneys. While defendants in European courts now usually have powers to produce (or request production of) evidence, prosecutors or investigating magistrates have a formal duty to investigate the case fully and objectively, in contrast to the adversarial prosecutor's focus on gathering incriminating evidence. Prosecutors should be less partisan; their professional-bureaucratic culture is less adversarial and more ministerial, more closely aligned with the judiciary and a duty of impartiality. In another sharp contrast to adversarial process, inquisitorial procedure gives judges an affirmative obligation to ensure judgments that reflect the objective truth, rather than merely the best decision in light of the evidence produced by the parties. Partly for that reason, judges usually have pretrial access to evidence dossiers and take a more active role in questioning or even calling witnesses.[43]

Even though European justice systems vary considerably from each other and now depart in important ways from classic inquisitorial forms, the tradition's influence nonetheless remains significant in providing nonmarket-inspired principles. The inquisitorial model emphasizes management and responsibility by public officials rather than competing parties. Motivations, especially with regard to information gathering, are in theory based in legal and professional duties rather than partisan or self-interests and competition between rivals. Defendants' (and victims') participation should be less critical to accuracy. All these features require trust in the state and bureaucratic expertise that is much weaker in common law adversarial systems, and particularly in the United States. Overall, the state's role in coordinating adjudication process to maximize the odds of accurate judgments is substantially greater in inquisitorial jurisdictions than in typical adversarial ones, especially in American jurisdictions.

THE UTILITY OF ERRORS IN MARKET-BASED PROCESS

In any justice system, it is the parties—particularly defendants—who suffer from erroneous judgments, regardless of whether the fault lies with the judge, prosecutor, or defense. Yet adversarial process, unlike inquisitorial process, *needs* parties—especially defendants—to face some risk of erroneous judgments because, like markets, it depends on parties to be motivated by self-interest. Errors have *utility* in adversarial process, because they provide an incentive for parties to avoid mistakes by diligently fulfilling their adversarial roles. The prospect (or threat) of wrong outcomes motivates parties to zealous and skilled pursuit of their interests, because their lapses or tactical missteps can lead to erroneously adverse judgments. That motivation would be undermined if parties could, postjudgment, easily correct their own failures or miscalculations, through appellate review, new trials, or otherwise. All justice systems must limit chances to correct errors or relitigate cases for the same reasons—to gain the benefits of finality and to limit public resources devoted to litigation. But adversarial process also needs to limit error-correction opportunities—perhaps more sharply—in order to increase parties' commitment and diligence to the first trial process.

Inquisitorial models have their own risks and trade-offs, but they do not share the need to let erroneous judgments stand. By contrast, that need is built into the conceptual foundation of adversarial process, at least to the degree adversarial process depends on defense participation for accurate judgments. It shares that conceptual foundation with markets, where the prospect of failure in trade or competition likewise looms, alongside the prospect of rewards for market success, as a motivating force. The difference is that, in markets, there is no necessarily *correct* outcome, although some are more appealing (and morally acceptable) that others. In criminal cases, however, there *are* right and wrong answers about past events that led to criminal charges, as well as errors about the legal significance of those past events. That is why we speak of *errors* in judgments but merely *losses* in markets. The possibility of letting errors stand uncorrected fits uncomfortably in a public law regime committed to just outcomes. It endures because this market mechanism is implicitly accompanied by a market *norm*: that parties deserve to lose—meaning that they deserve to bear erroneous judgments—if they fail to take full advantage of opportunities to protect their own interests.[44]

Prosecutors and Defense Counsel in U.S. Adversarial Process

THE PROSECUTOR'S ROLE REVISITED

Adversarial process nominally gives control to *parties*, but the *counsel* for each side actually makes most of the decisions. The lawyers' interests or motivations are critical; most rules seeking to affect incentives are directed at them. This is plainly true for prosecutors, who represent abstract public interests rather than individual clients. To restate an earlier point, prosecutors in an adversarial jurisdiction are *partisan* in at least two senses. Straightforwardly, they are advocates for one *party* in a bilateral competition between partisan rivals. That role is a *partial* one—partial to the executive's enforcement interests. It is sharply different from the impartiality of the judicial role, notwithstanding however much the ministerial norm distinguishes it from lawyers for ordinary private parties. The obligations and the cultural norms of adversarial process, and professional immersion in the executive's enforcement agenda, create a role-based partisan interest analogous (at least in many cases) to private self-interest.

As advocates within an adversarial structure, prosecutors, like other advocates, can take less responsibility for the substance (including accuracy and proportionality) of outcomes. Like other advocates, they can plausibly take the view that the *process* is responsible for the outcomes. "My job is to present the state's case; the defendant has to present his and the jury makes the decision." The ministerial norm should cut against this perspective. To the degree it does, notice its function in political economy terms. The norm is a modest mechanism of public coordination, superimposed on a process otherwise driven by rival private, or partisan, interests. The stronger the ministerial norm, the more the state intervenes in the process of party competition. The more impartial the prosecutor's role is made by the effect of this quasi-judicial norm, the less "private" or partisan it is, and therefore more conceptually distinct from ordinary adversarial parties. Seen in that light, it is unsurprising that the American tendency is for a weaker ministerial norm. More modest state intervention is what one expects in a strongly liberal-market political economy.

Local prosecution agencies' relative autonomy from judicial or hierarchical supervision is one reason for the weaker norm (and for variation across local professional cultures), and another reason is procedural rules that approve more partial conduct such as partisan sentencing advocacy (if not sentence *engineering*). But a more important reason is more obvious—the political nature of U.S. prosecution offices. The effect of democratic politics more often than not is to increase rather than moderate prosecutorial partisanship. In this way, making prosecutors politically accountable works against norms that would play a stronger coordinating or regulatory role in adversarial process.

Prosecutors' more "private" or partisan style contributes to the sharper adversarial culture of U.S. litigation, described by Robert Kagan and others. That adversarial culture borrows more from the model of free markets than other adversarial systems do. Marginally less ministerial and more partisan prosecutors are indicators of a regime that stresses party competition somewhat more and public ordering somewhat less. U.S. courts, with less sentencing authority than English judges and lacking even the modest authority to review charging decisions, mark the weaker scope of public coordination as well.[45]

THE LAW OF DEFENSE COUNSEL

Unlike the prosecutor, the defense lawyer has an actual, individual client. That relationship is not only governed in multiple ways by the law defining the right to counsel, it is also deeply affected by the market economy and by how right-to-counsel doctrine takes account of the market. Individuals differ widely in personal wealth, disparities that precede the moment they may become criminal defendants. The right to counsel responds to those disparities most obviously with a public subsidy for the poorest suspects—the guarantee of defense representation provided by the state for those who lack private resources to hire counsel. Beyond that "market intervention," however, the constitutional law regarding right to defense counsel gives considerable deference, even reinforcement, both to preexisting wealth distributions among defendants arising from the market and to the market-like structure of adversarial process.

The Relevance of Resource Disparities

Liberal markets are defined by the state's more modest role regulating market trades and engineering preferred market outcomes. That hands-off approach extends to wealth disparities between market actors. Market rules generally let stand the competitive advantage that large-scale purchasers have over smaller ones. Thus the benefits stemming from vastly larger capital resources that Wal-Mart, for example, enjoys over small independent retailers include more bargaining power with product suppliers. In lending markets, wealthier people and firms borrow on more favorable terms than those with lower incomes and fewer assets.[46] Across many contexts, those able to hire expert agents or advisers gain advantages over those who cannot.

We would expect a criminal justice system deeply aligned with liberal-market ideas to likewise do little to mitigate the effects of private wealth disparities on legal outcomes. Yet wealth differences clearly affect adjudication, and the impact grows as the importance of the parties' role in the process grows, and as safeguards against party lapses diminish. Parties with more resources can invest more in fact investigation, evidence production, and legal research. Parties with few resources do fewer of those things, perhaps not enough for the process to function reliably.

In theory, the structure of inquisitorial process means that party wealth matters less. State officials (whether prosecutors, judges, or magistrates) have an obligation to ensure a comprehensive, nonpartisan evidentiary record, and courts have formal responsibility for ensuring the accuracy of judgments. Although European states today guarantee defendants various means to offer evidence, challenge witnesses, and the like, inquisitorial process depends much less on the defense to play a role in producing fair and accurate judgments. Consequently, differences in defense resources (and legal skill) should matter less. Even the practice of judges, prosecutors, and the defense all having access to the evidentiary file (roughly what common-law lawyers would call open-file discovery) mitigates wealth effects. Pretrial information does not turn on defendants' ability to gather such evidence on their own.

By contrast, adversary process relies more on parties, in particular the defense, to gather facts themselves, produce evidence, frame legal issues, and identify relevant law for the court. Courts and lawyers have long acknowledged this. Adequate defense counsel "'is critical to the ability of the adversarial system to produce just results,'"[47] the Supreme Court recently stressed, reaffirming a long-standing premise. At least since the 1930s, the Court has expanded the constitutional right to counsel on the recognition that adversarial process requires a skilled defense to counterbalance the prosecutor's partisan role:

> Left without the aid of counsel, [an individual] may be put on trial without a proper charge, and convicted upon incompetent evidence, or evidence irrelevant to the issue or otherwise inadmissible. He lacks both the skill and knowledge adequately to prepare his defense, even though he has a perfect one. He requires the guiding hand of counsel at every step. . . . Without it, though he be not guilty, he faces the danger of conviction because he does not know how to establish his innocence.[48]

The dependence of adversarial process on the defense creates the risk that defendants' wealth will affect outcomes. As the Court implies, the roles of public officials in adversarial process are not expected, regardless of defense contributions, to ensure just outcomes. Judges are more passive and do less to develop the evidentiary record or otherwise compensate for any defense inadequacies. Prosecutors have a weaker obligation and disposition to actively seek out evidence favorable to the defense, rather than merely disclosing it whenever state agents possess it. In political economy terms, the state does less to "coordinate," regulate, or structure adjudication process and ensure desirable outcomes. The market-like, competitive-party structure of adversarial process counts on the defense counsel acting zealously in her client's interest, and in having the financial means to do so.

Public Defense as Market Intervention

Although American adversary process is vulnerable to effects following from defendants' wealth or poverty, criminal procedure rules in the United States (and elsewhere) mitigate those effects at one extreme through state funding of defense counsel for indigent defendants. Although the doctrine is widely criticized as inadequate, courts are required to invalidate convictions if the defense counsel's performance was deficient in ways that undermined confidence in the reliability of the judgment.[49]

While this entitlement reduces the adverse effects of economic markets on adjudication, it does not disturb the fundamental market-like premises and operation of adversarial process. The purpose of providing competent defense counsel is to ensure sufficient competition between the parties, which is the heart of adversarial process. The entitlement does not change that competitive structure, and it does not regulate how parties play their adversarial roles (beyond a deferential requirement that defense lawyers perform "reasonably"). The state does not, by guaranteeing the right to counsel, coordinate adversarial process and outcomes more directly. The defense lawyer, after all, remains the agent solely of the defendant, even though the state pays her fee. Her role and obligation is solely to serve the client's private interests. Defense counsel's public-regarding duties (as an "officer of the court") require little more than not destroying evidence, knowingly offering perjury or other false evidence, or lying to the court. In sum, state provision of defense counsel is meant simply to improve the party competition by which adversarial process produces judgments.

In that sense, the right to counsel looks a lot like state policies in many other domains of liberal-market economies. In many market contexts, people need skilled agents to pursue their interests effectively, especially when they engage with others who have expertise or have skilled agents of their own. An information or skill imbalance can cause market failure, which regulations in many settings seek to prevent. Outside of criminal prosecution, the state rarely compels people to participate in competitive markets or market-like processes, and therefore it rarely subsidizes assistance for the poor in doing so. (To the degree U.S. law requires participation in health insurance markets, notice that contract terms are heavily regulated and low-income purchasers get public subsidies.) But people are barred from some markets if they lack sufficient private resources and skill to compete effectively. Recall that certain securities markets are limited to certified (i.e., *sufficiently skilled*) investors as well as to licensed sellers—that is, the equivalent of litigants able to act as their own counsel.

Licensing requirements provide a partial analogy, along with common requirements for information disclosure or specific safety practices in all sorts of service-provider markets—from medical care, legal assistance, dentistry, architecture, and brokerage services to building construction, hair styling, auctioneering, and much else. In many contexts service providers have legal obligations akin to strong minister-of-justice duty: they must do things that protect the interests of others, things which they might not do out of self-interest. In all cases licensing requirements bar people from markets in which they lack the ability to sort out skilled from unskilled counterparties. Allowing anyone to contract freely with anyone else for certain services is a recipe for market failure.[50] Licensing rules, in short, are one public policy for improving market outcomes. Subsidizing skilled agents for market participants is one step further to the same end, which was in effect the Supreme Court's stated rationale for requiring state-provided defense counsel in adversarial criminal process.

Inadequate Public Funding for Defense
Seen in this light, the right to counsel is a conceptually conservative intervention in the criminal justice system, wholly consistent with both the

adversarial process tradition and contemporary liberal-market policies. In the context of criminal litigation, it is also the primary check on government power—something Americans claim to especially favor. Why then has the state failed so frequently in providing indigent defense services? There is hardly any debate that it has, given the widely, repeatedly documented inadequacy of funding for defense services in many jurisdictions. As with all generalizations about U.S. criminal justice, there are exceptions. Decentralized administration leads to wide variations. Funding in the federal courts, and in the state courts of select cities, is generally good. But study after study, year after year, reveals inadequate support for public defense in many localities and whole states.[51] Courts mostly do little to address the problem, in large part because the constitutional right to counsel has not been interpreted to give courts much ability to find the right violated before trial based on defense resources (rather than because no lawyer appears for the defendant at all). A very few exceptions notwithstanding, U.S. courts are reluctant to stay prosecutions based on inadequate state funding for defense services.[52]

Reasons for the perennial inadequacy of indigent defense funding are not a mystery. Those funding decisions, like everything else in American criminal justice policy, are rarely insulated from the political process. Majoritarian political sentiment never strongly favors spending public money on the defense of accused criminals. Law abiders always outnumber law offenders. The nation's troubled history of race relations, particularly acute in the criminal justice system, undoubtedly contributes to this sentiment. Durable cultural stereotypes that link criminality disproportionately with African Americans or other minority groups, and enforcement patterns that generate disproportionate arrests of minority suspects, do not make majoritarian political processes a promising venue for consistently adequate indigent defense funds.

An additional, less noted reason adds to the explanation for inadequate defense funding: the norms of the free market. Although state funding for defense looks much like other policies in liberal-market economies that improve markets' operations rather than replace them with the state, such a subsidy nonetheless is a marginal disruption of market outcomes, that is, of individual gains (or lack of them) in the market economy. Liberal-market economies generally accept not only wealth disparities produced by markets but also market outcomes in which one party's greater wealth gave it big advantages over others. Liberal-market policies that tolerate the market consequences of wealth disparities, or simply some participants' failures in a market economy, require norms that justify those policies and view those consequences as legitimate. One version of liberal-market norms builds on a view that whatever advantage one has from market success is a fair one; likewise one's prior lack of success—even one's poverty—is to some extent earned or deserved, especially to the degree it stems from lack of diligence or skill. In that normative framework, a defendant's lack of resources to protect his interests in adversarial process is less troubling. Here markets and democracy combine to produce this component of criminal justice policy. Market norms strengthen views that favor less defense funding. Through democratic policy-making, those views influence policy.

Regardless of whether that kind of moral logic plays much of a role in indigent defense funding, there is stronger evidence that wealth and its advantages gained in the economic marketplace carry real normative weight in other aspects of the law governing defense counsel. For that, one must look at another component of the constitutional law of defense counsel—the right to spend private funds on the attorney of one's choice.

CONSTITUTIONAL RIGHT TO THE LEGAL SERVICES MARKET

From the Sixth Amendment assurance that in "all criminal prosecutions, the accused shall enjoy the right . . . to have the Assistance of Counsel for his defence," the Supreme Court has defined several distinct entitlements. The best known guarantees are those just noted: the guarantee that indigent defendants receive state-funded defense counsel and the right for all defendants to constitutionally adequate legal representation.[53] Additionally, for the small portion of defendants who have done well in the market economy and accumulated enough personal wealth to retain attorneys with private funds, the Counsel Clause holds an additional guarantee: a right to hire the private counsel of one's choice. *This* right—the right to access the private market for legal services, free of state interference—enjoys greater constitutional protection than the right to *effective* counsel.

The common law has a long tradition of permitting privately retained counsel; state-funded counsel is the comparatively recent development. As early as 1932, the Court, in *Powell v. Alabama*, implied that the long-standing common law rule has constitutional status. It was "hardly necessary to say," *Powell* noted, "that, the right to counsel being conceded, a defendant should be afforded a fair opportunity to secure counsel of his own choice."[54] In its more recent and important decision on this point, *United States v. Gonzalez-Lopez*, the Court confirmed that the right to counsel expressly includes "the right of a defendant who does not require appointed counsel to choose who will represent him."[55] The "right to counsel of choice" is conceptually distinct from the right to be provided with counsel or the right to effective assistance. The Court describes it variously as simply "the right to a particular lawyer,"[56] or as a right that "commands . . . that the accused be defended by the counsel he believes to be best."[57]

Despite such statements, a defendant is not *really* entitled to whichever "counsel he believes to be best." The right to publicly funded counsel does not encompass the right to choose a particular lawyer. And well before *Gonzalez-Lopez* it was clear that judges could deny defendants an attorney who is not admitted to the bar (a licensing limit on market transactions) or who has a conflict of interest, even when the defendant expressly waives any claim to nonconflicted counsel.[58] The right to counsel of one's own choice is really a right to hire a lawyer using private funds, and it merits expansive deference. Considered alongside the *Strickland v. Washington* right to effective counsel, the *Gonzalez-Lopez* right "to secure counsel of [one's] own choice" is remarkable in at least two respects. The first is the unusual strength of the guarantee that the Court's doctrine provides to this entitlement to purchase legal services on the private market. The second is the exceptional degree to which the Court has endorsed the ability to participate in the legal-services market *as a specific criterion of fundamental fairness.*

In both the limits and rationale for the right to counsel of choice, the central place of the private market for legal services is just short of explicit. For one, the rules of the market provide the only limits on this entitlement. No attorney can be required to enter a contract with a defendant merely because a party has chosen him over all others, even if the defendant stands ready to pay the lawyer's fee. Additionally, a defendant's right to choose a particular lawyer is limited by his means to pay the market price for legal services. A "defendant may not insist on representation by an attorney he cannot afford,"[59] because "the Sixth Amendment guarantees a defendant the right to be represented by an otherwise qualified attorney *whom that defendant can afford to hire.*"[60] This right, in other words, extends only to those with private wealth sufficient to successfully contract for legal services in the private market (although the law presumably would also protect those defendants who can retain counsel through nonmarket private ordering, such as a lawyer who will agree to work *pro bono*, without pay). Chief Justice Roberts recently confirmed the obvious: "It is of course true that the . . . defendant has no right to choose counsel he cannot afford."[61]

The "right to select counsel of one's own choice," then, is more accurately characterized as the right to participate in the free market for legal services. Closely considered, its only purpose and effect is to assure that a defendant's market access is unimpeded by the state; the doctrine is indifferent to other limits on one's capacity to secure the legal services that one prefers. Put differently, the right to select one's own lawyer is a targeted right against state interference in the private sphere of market transactions. It is a negative right—freedom *from* state intervention in private exchange. By contrast, the market-correcting right to appointed counsel is a positive right, funded by the state. As such it is a right, in effect, only to a competent attorney of the *state's* choosing. The case law on the right to appointed counsel expressly rejects a guarantee that a defendant will have a satisfactory or "meaningful relationship" with his attorney.[62]

The right against state interference in private market transactions for legal services receives notably stronger support than that for the right to effective assistance of counsel. It is not an overstatement to say that the Supreme Court's decisions are fiercely protective of legal representation provided through the market.

Specifically, state interference in a defendant's choice of a privately retained attorney falls into the narrow and privileged category of *structural* error, which triggers reversal of a conviction regardless of whether the error had any effect on the proceedings. "A choice-of-counsel violation occurs whenever the defendant's choice is wrongfully denied,"[63] regardless of whether a court can identify any harm, and regardless of the lawyer's "comparative effectiveness."[64] That is not the same standard that applies for violations of the right to effective assistance of counsel. Under the flagship decision of *Strickland v. Washington*, a defendant bears the burden of proving he suffered some prejudice from his lawyer's poor performance, because the Constitution provides, in the Court's words, only a right to "effective (not mistake-free) representation."[65] A structural-error rule, then, is more costly to the state; it means more frequent reversals of judgments and retrials. There is arguably a small irony in this. The public treasury bears greater expense, in relitigation costs, to preserve this unfettered market-access right than it does to preserve the right to effective counsel.

The difference between those two standards follows from the view that the two rights serve different purposes and distinct ideas of fairness. The right to effective counsel was "derived . . . from the purpose of ensuring a fair trial" in an adversarial system; good defense representation, again, "'is critical to the ability of the adversarial system to produce just results.'"[66] This justification is entirely consequentialist, and the right is limited by this justification. An effective defense lawyer is assured only as long as seems likely to matter. The guarantee is not violated if the trial was fair despite the defense attorney's ineffectiveness. A fair trial is one in which the defendant cannot demonstrate, in retrospect, that he suffered enough prejudice to undermine judicial confidence in the conviction.

The right to choose any private counsel, by contrast, rests on a different kind of justification and serves a different interest. The right to choose private counsel "has never been derived from the Sixth Amendment's purpose of ensuring a fair trial."[67] Instead, it is essential to a separate "particular guarantee of fairness—to wit, that the accused be defended by the counsel he believes to be best."[68] Of course, the right is not to any attorney that a defendant "believes to be best," but only to any attorney a defendant has successfully contracted with in the private market. Much like classic *Lochner*-era substantive due process jurisprudence, the Constitution protects a conception of fairness grounded in the value of state noninterference in market exchange—independent of whatever actual effect (or noneffect) interference might have on the fairness of the *trial*.

This rationale is deontological rather than consequentialist. It is grounded in a moral priority for access to the free market for legal services rather than on the right's beneficial effects on criminal justice outcomes. Freedom to contract for legal services is an *intrinsic* component of fairness that the Court finds to be "the root meaning of the constitutional guarantee" to counsel.[69] The effective-counsel guarantee rests solely on its utility to improve adjudicative accuracy or the odds of "just results," but there is scant reference to the practical good that the right to privately hired counsel might contribute to better judgments or even to the fairness of *trial process*, independent of better outcomes. The right to the legal services market is not alone in this kind of justification. Other rights, such as the right to silence, rest on fairness rationales unrelated to trial accuracy or other utility. But the right to choose one's own counsel is really a guarantee that one is free to participate in markets—free to benefit from the private trade in legal services if one has the means to do so—without interference from rules or the state's discretionary authority in the public adjudication.

From one viewpoint, this is unexceptional. In the Anglo American traditions of both liberal markets and common law adjudication, it would be surprising for the state to restrict access to the market for legal services other than through traditional licensing or bar-admission requirements and conflict-of-interest rules. It is hard to imagine, for example, legal limits in the United States on private spending for defense services, much less state control over the selection of *all* defendants' choice of counsel (as opposed to state control merely for those defendants relying on publicly funded counsel).

The unacceptability of such as an extreme policy reveals the political morality and the rationality shared by the common law, adversarial, and liberal-market traditions. Plausible arguments exist in favor of such limits, after all, and certainly for subjecting privately retained defense representation to more substantial regulation. But the basis for those arguments lies elsewhere in the law. One source includes the precedents that define some private endeavors as "affected with the public interest." Another includes the balancing tests applied elsewhere in criminal procedure and due process doctrines. Following those models, the right to private counsel would be weighed against competing interests such as resource constraints on the criminal courts, adjudicative accuracy, or even effective criminal law enforcement.[70] In other contexts (notably forfeiture of defendants' crime-related assets), the Court has suggested that leaving a suspect with ample resources to spend on his defense is not an unambiguous public good; top-quality counsel with ample resources can unduly frustrate enforcement and in that way assist (albeit lawfully) criminal wrongdoing.[71] In fact, until recently four of nine Supreme Court justices favored a bit more limited definition of the right to counsel of one's choice,[72] one that would restrict remedies for violations of the right—like the right to effective assistance of counsel—to cases in which the trial judge's interference with counsel was likely to have affected the final judgment in some way detrimental to the defendant. The majority in *Gonzalez-Lopez* rejected that alternative because it put too much emphasis on the defense lawyer's *public* function. Instead, as the doctrine now stands, the right to retain counsel with personal funds gives the fullest protection to a *private* interest on which the law places great value within criminal procedure and beyond: the individual right to unfettered market access.

Conclusion

The law of privately funded defense is unusually forthright in its embrace of market values—the norms that inhere in and justify liberal market political economies. That body of law is all the more striking because of its indifference to the efficacy of privately chosen counsel as market *mechanism*. The state must fully respect individual autonomy to pursue private preferences at private expense, even without evidence that this form of private ordering leads, in some sense, to better adjudication outcomes. Elsewhere in U.S. criminal procedure, the values of the market are more subtle and implicit. Market norms reinforce a more sharply partisan, adversarial conception of the prosecutor's role. They also add conceptual support for decisions to inadequately fund indigent defense services. The right to state-funded legal assistance, after all, is the kind of public intervention that liberal market economies disfavor and minimize—state interference with the market's distribution of wealth.

Of course, faith in market mechanisms is pervasive in U.S. criminal adjudication as well, starting in the core structure of adversarial trial process, which gives the real power to competitive parties rather than to the judge, the official who ultimately renders the state's judgment but does so only upon whatever evidence and law parties provide, and largely through the procedures that they choose to invoke. Elsewhere across the law of criminal procedure, the liberal-market confidence in market mechanisms, and its acceptance of market values, is either apparent or implicit. Chapter 5 will survey a selection of trial-related rules in which the logic and rationality of the market lie barely below the surface in judicial reasoning that is preoccupied with party incentives and private responsibility for consequences that follow from one's own choices or inadvertence. First, however, the next chapter takes up the central practice of contemporary criminal adjudication—plea bargaining. In the distinctive body of rules and norms that define this practice in U.S. jurisdictions, the power of market rationality is again explicit and unambiguous. For the closest real-world instance of the Platonic ideal of liberal market criminal justice, one need look no further than the American law and practice of negotiated guilty pleas.

CHAPTER 4

The Free Market Law of Plea Bargaining

Plea bargains are essentially contracts.
—*Puckett v. United States (2009)*

The prosecutor's interest at the bargaining table is to persuade the defendant to forgo his right to plead not guilty.
—*Bordenkircher v. Hayes (1978)**

The Singular American System of Plea Bargaining

American criminal justice embraced plea bargaining much earlier with fewer reservations than criminal justice systems anywhere else. In the process, it developed a distinctive set of rules and rationales for plea agreements. Some follow from features of U.S. criminal process previously noted, such as prosecutors' wide charging discretion and freedom from binding regulations or judicial oversight. But those rules also follow the overt, enthusiastic embrace—remarkably uniform across U.S. jurisdictions—of the market as the metaphor and framework for the law of negotiated guilty pleas. The rules for party negotiations closely track the rules of most liberal-market transactions, which is to say the state regulates, or coordinates, very little. More important, market rationales guide rule development and administration, and market norms justify negotiation practices and outcomes. Following the model of the market, American law barely acknowledges risks of coercion and contains no meaningful notions of unfair party advantage. The Supreme Court worries much more about *not* bargaining. More specifically, it worries about criminal procedure rules that would excessively regulate party negotiations and terms of agreement in ways that would impede the efficiency that criminal process achieves by replacing trials with settlements.

Plea bargaining, or some comparable form of abbreviated process, is now common in many nations and on the rise in criminal justice systems worldwide.[1] But U.S.-style bargaining rules are not. Plea agreements flourish in quite different legal regimes. That fact confirms that a lesson from the study of "varieties of capitalism" extends as well to the criminal justice context. Plea bargains, like market economies, succeed under very different rules and institutional arrangements. Resolving the vast majority of prosecutions through negotiated convictions does not require a set of rules that closely mimic free markets. Nevertheless, American courts routinely assert the opposite, and market-oriented rules prevail with remarkable consistency throughout U.S. jurisdictions. But the rationality of free markets dictates those rules, not the practical necessities of criminal justice administration.

Criticisms of Plea Bargaining

For the better part of a century, plea bargaining has drawn the attention—largely critical—of legal scholars, historians, social scientists, and law reformers. Excellent archival studies have documented many details from plea bargaining's early origins, which date back nearly two centuries in some U.S. localities.[2] Observational studies do the same for contemporary practice.[3] Research on both the past and present tries to explain why plea bargaining is so widespread: whether it is a necessity to deal with rising caseloads, a tool of lawyers' and judges' self-interests and desire for control, or a way to enhance the role of law enforcement officials and reduce the power of juries or judges.[4]

Critics have also given a lot attention to the many problems and risks inherent in plea bargaining, especially under American rules.[5] The foremost concern may be coercion. Defendants who face a choice between a long sentence if convicted at trial and a much shorter one if they plead guilty sometimes choose the latter even if they are actually guilty only of some lesser offense—or even if they are wholly innocent. A disturbing number of confirmed wrongful convictions occurred through guilty pleas, in the United States and elsewhere.[6] There is little debate that pleading guilty in spite of one's innocence can be a *rational* decision under the right conditions, and the rules of plea bargaining aggravate those conditions. Some people are risk averse when the stakes are high enough. Indeed, hundreds of wrongful convictions confirm the reasonableness of defendants who plead guilty because they doubt a trial will reach the right outcome, perhaps because circumstantial (or even fraudulent) evidence misleadingly points toward guilt, or because the defense lacks the resources to gather conflicting evidence the state overlooked.[7]

Another concern about plea bargains is that they produce inaccurate convictions and punishment of the guilty, which is probably their more common consequence. Criminal charges to which a defendant pleads guilty sometimes misdescribe his wrongdoing. Sometimes, to be sure, this occurs in order to grant leniency to the guilty—in exchange for pleading guilty, for cooperating with law enforcement against other offenders, or to offset collateral civil penalties triggered by convictions. The more worrisome form of inaccuracy, of course, arises from charges that are unduly severe in light of an offender's wrongdoing, but to which defendants nonetheless plead guilty. Expansive criminal codes, which make a variety of charges possible for the same wrongdoing, undermine a consistent relation between punishment and culpability. Plea bargaining then makes it harder to identify the right level of liability and punishment, because by definition it punishes identical wrongdoers differently depending on whether their conviction occurs by trial or guilty plea. The ambiguity increases when defendants' liability varies depending on *how quickly* they plead guilty, whether some refuse to waive particular rights (such as evidence disclosure), and whether some provide valuable assistance to law enforcement. These differences leave it uncertain whether bargaining involves a *discount* for pleading guilty or a *penalty* for refusing to do so; in other words, they make ambiguous which is the *right* outcome and which is the departure from it. In short, plea bargaining further undermines the connection between punishment and actual wrongdoing and culpability.

Moreover, plea bargains cut out lay juries from criminal process. They redirect decisions about criminal convictions into the hands of professionals—prosecutors, defense lawyers, and judges. Discretionary judgments are inevitable in many cases, and bargaining changes the one who exercises that discretion. By definition, achieving convictions through guilty pleas rather than trials reduces public participation in criminal process; as a practical matter the same is true for the participation of victims and other interested parties.[8] As public trials are replaced by private negotiations—private in no small part because prosecutors are allowed to conceal their reasons and tactics—criminal process becomes much less transparent.

Routine plea bargaining has an additional effect, implicit in the problems discussed. As practiced under the free market rules that prevail in U.S. jurisdictions, plea bargaining corrupts. It compromises the professional roles and norms of prosecution agencies and (perhaps to a lesser degree) the judiciary, and it corrupts the purposes and principles of criminal justice. It does so in much the same way that markets corrupt nonmarket institutions and values, such as religious faith or customary bonds of social solidarity, as even the free market's strongest advocates concede. Thus gaining an advantage at another's expense can be rationalized as "just business" and "nothing personal." Guided by this norm, contracts between employers and employees are less informed by customs of mutual obligation, and creditors can charge whatever usurious interest rates markets will bear, free of once-powerful religiously grounded constraints. Professional norms such as judicial neutrality and the ministerial commitment to justice are grounded in values and institutions outside the market. But market-based rules undermine those norms by encouraging participants to view plea negotiations as instrumental practices driven by partisan interests, rather than as public law adjudication committed to public principles (such as punishment in proportion to guilt), public criteria for fair process, and public responsibility for the integrity of criminal court judgments.

American Law of Plea Bargaining

THE MARKET MODEL OF PLEA BARGAINING

The U.S. Supreme Court did not explicitly acknowledge plea bargaining until about 1970, when it affirmed the validity of guilty pleas induced by charge reductions or the prospect of sentencing leniency.[9] It used the phrase "plea bargain" for the first time a year later. That was late in bargaining's long American history, but still decades earlier than judicial recognition of the practice in England and continental European jurisdictions. (In the same year, 1970, *R. v. Turner* in effect prohibited plea bargaining in England by banning defendants from receiving advance notice of the sentence that would follow a guilty plea—a rule not formally reversed until 2006.)[10] The Court later regarded plea negotiations before the 1970s as a "clandestine practice," and said court practices surrounding plea bargaining "reflected [an] atmosphere of secrecy."[11] That is probably an exaggeration, but the Court's 1971 decision in *Santobello v. New York* legitimized the practice by holding that prosecutors who reach plea agreements with defendants are constitutionally required—once defendants plead guilty—to keep their side of the bargain.[12]

The established understanding of guilty pleas, reconfirmed by *Santobello*, is that their effect is greater than that of a mere confession of guilt. A guilty plea—once accepted by a court—"is itself a conviction. Like a verdict of a jury it is conclusive."[13] Its legitimacy rests on the defendant's consent to conviction. Together with the decision in *Alford v. North Carolina* a year earlier, *Santobello* made clear that the same is true of a plea *agreement*—a guilty plea on terms negotiated with the prosecution. The standard for validity "was and remains whether the plea represents a voluntary and intelligent choice among the alternative courses of action open to the defendant."[14] That familiar rule has an important implication. For convictions following a trial, either a judge or jury has made fact-findings that support conviction beyond a reasonable doubt. For judgments based on guilty pleas, the defendant's voluntary consent displaces the constitutional requirement for proof of guilt beyond a reasonable doubt.[15] That basic alteration in criminal process places the legitimacy and integrity of judgments in the hands of the parties, reducing the responsibility of courts for the integrity of their own judgments. For American courts, it provides the premise for a law of plea bargaining that gives the parties—especially prosecutors—wide freedom in an almost wholly unregulated negotiation process. Courts are required to do little to confirm the accuracy or fairness of plea-based convictions, and little judicial process is required beyond confirming the voluntariness of a defendant's decision to plead guilty.

There is a symmetry of sorts here with prosecutorial discretion. The defendant's freedom of choice—*his* discretion—lies at the heart of guilty plea legitimacy, much as the prosecutor's lies at the core of criminal charging decisions. Courts enforce formal requirements of voluntariness and right to counsel for defendants, and probable-cause requirements for prosecutors' charging decisions, but parties are otherwise free of legal regulation. Courts have little supervisory role because few rules set bounds on either party's autonomy in their respective realms, even though both implicate public—rather than merely partisan—interests. Parties have the power. Public regulation—the law and the judiciary—put few bounds on their autonomy. That sounds a lot like the model of a free market. And market ideas, including this commitment to party autonomy and the free pursuit of partisan interests, guide the development of U.S. plea bargaining law after *Santobello*. Most important, market ideology defines the rules for negotiations. Even after *Santobello* the Court—as Justice Douglas observed—had "not spelled out what sorts of promises by prosecutors tend to be coercive."[16]

Consistent with its organic origins in trial courts, the law of plea bargaining is the product much more of judicial than legislative policymaking. Even for the state justice systems, the federal constitutional law of plea bargaining has come to define the most important premises as well as ground rules. In only relatively minor ways do statutes, common law, or state constitutions reshape the practice of plea bargaining from that authorized by federal constitutional law. As it defined that law in recent decades, the Court has consistently concluded that the U.S. Constitution prohibits almost no tactic in party negotiations, beyond that "the agents of the State may not produce a plea by actual or threatened physical harm or by mental coercion overbearing the will of the defendant."[17] Conceptualizing party negotiations in free market terms leaves little basis for public rules coordinating those interactions and the outcomes they produce. In the context of wide prosecution discretion, expansive criminal codes, and mandatory sentencing laws, prosecutors have the capacity in many cases for coercive bargaining tactics despite courts' lack of a conceptual framework that enables them to recognize these tactics as such.

Prosecutor Control of Trial Penalties

The Court made this clear in *Bordenkircher v. Hayes*, which arose from Paul Hayes's indictment in a Kentucky state court for writing bad checks. Because

Hayes had two prior felony convictions, his prosecutor would agree to nothing less than a five-year prison term in exchange for a guilty plea. Hayes refused. The prosecutor then obtained an additional indictment charging Hayes as a habitual offender. That charge meant that Hayes now faced a mandatory sentence of life without parole if convicted. He nonetheless insisted on a trial, at which he was found guilty and sentenced to life in prison. The Supreme Court concluded that the prosecutor's tactic of charging Hayes more in the wake of Hayes's refusal to plead guilty—to pressure him into changing his plea—was constitutional.[18]

Bordenkircher means that in effect there is no constitutional limit on the "plea discount" or "trial penalty"—that is, on the disparity between the sentence a defendant faces after pleading guilty and the one he faces after conviction at trial. When statutes create wide ranges of charges and penalties for an act of wrongdoing, the choice among them—and the magnitude of the trial penalty—lies in the prosecutor's discretion. The Constitution does not restrict a prosecutor's choice between two statutes that criminalize the same conduct but carry different punishments. Nor does it limit the disparity between liability and punishment options that defendants can face, which can be extreme enough to lead innocent defendants to plead guilty.[19] The Court has accepted that prosecutors "offering substantial benefits in return for the plea" or "confronting a defendant with the risk of more severe punishment" for insisting on a trial "clearly may have a 'discouraging effect on the defendant's assertion of his trial rights,'"[20] though it has not acknowledged that this "discouraging effect" may be so strong as to prompt false guilty pleas. The wide difference in penalty options of the sort faced by Hayes—plea bargain offers accompanied by the prospect of post-trial sentences that are five or ten times greater—appear not to be the norm, but they are not uncommon. Data on their frequency are not available, but recent federal and state cases provide many examples of defendants who declined to plead guilty in exchange for sentences as low as four to eight years, and who subsequently received life-without-parole sentences after trial.[21]

Expansive criminal codes—typically enacted by legislatures without input from law commissions such as one finds in the United Kingdom and many other nations—increase prosecutors' opportunities for confronting defendants with hard choices. Those choices are made much starker when offenses carry mandatory sentences, or when judges otherwise have limited sentencing discretion. (The proliferation of such sentencing policies is one consequence of politicized policymaking.) Fixed penalties put punishment decisions largely in the prosecutor's control. In *Corbitt v. New Jersey*, the Supreme Court approved a state criminal statute that authorized a lower sentence only for convictions based on guilty pleas; the law also required a mandatory life sentence for guilt determined at trial. The Court was "unconvinced" that the statute "exerts such a powerful influence to coerce inaccurate pleas *non vult* that it should be deemed constitutionally suspect."[22]

Courts have approved additional pressure tactics as well. Prosecutors can lawfully threaten to indict *other* people, such as the defendant's family members, if he does not plead guilty. Or they can make a defendant's plea agreement contingent upon *another* defendant also pleading guilty, so that each defendant will urge the other to take the plea bargain.[23] Prosecutors' motives—their good or bad faith—do not matter, nor does consistency over time in the use of these tactics. This is true as a matter of constitutional law, but no other source of law provides a basis for U.S. courts to intervene in these plea bargaining tactics—not common law, statutes, or judicial authority to bar abuse of process. Sentencing law additionally restricts courts' discretion in many cases, and the legislative trend in recent decades has been in that direction—to give prosecutors more control over mandatory sentencing rules.[24] Constitutional rules against excessive or disproportionate punishment are too weak to give courts a meaningful role on that basis.

Guilty Pleas without Admissions of Guilt

If guilty pleas are confessions plus consent to conviction, the latter component—though it can be extracted under severe state-induced pressure—is nonetheless the only necessary one. The Supreme Court made this clear in the case of Henry Alford, who was charged in a North Carolina court with capital murder. Alford insisted he was not guilty, although prosecutors presented considerable evidence indicating otherwise. Prosecutors sought the death penalty—at least if Alford insisted on a trial. They offered a plea agreement for a life sentence if he would plead guilty. Alford wanted to consent to conviction in order to take that deal, but he steadfastly refused to admit his guilt. The trial court permitted Alford to plead guilty—perhaps more specifically, to consent to conviction—without admitting guilt, and the Supreme Court affirmed that a conviction and sentence on this basis are constitutional. Although the trial judge is required by statute to find a factual basis for the conviction, constitutional doctrine has never specified a procedure or standard of proof for doing so. Proof beyond a reasonable doubt is required for trial convictions but not for convictions based on a guilty plea—even when the defendant explicitly denies the factual basis for his guilt.[25]

Waiving Rights to Disclosure and Appeal

In this plea bargaining system, the law regulates as little as possible in order to maximize party power and responsibility. It is no surprise then that nearly every other component of criminal process, beyond the trial itself, is also on the table as a bargaining chip. Prosecutors have a constitutional duty to disclose *at the trial* any evidence favorable to the defendant regarding either guilt or punishment. But because that duty does not apply until trial, prosecutors can insist that defendants waive disclosure as part of a plea agreement.[26] Nearly all other procedural entitlements may be waived for forfeited as well, including rights against double jeopardy and to appellate review of the validity of a guilty plea or the legality of a sentence.[27]

THE RATIONALITIES OF AMERICAN PLEA BARGAINING

The pattern in all this is apparent: nearly unregulated party autonomy. Rules authorize party negotiations and do almost nothing to restrict tactics or terms. The state *qua* state (as opposed to the prosecution) plays no significant affirmative role in the guilty plea process analogous to the duties of courts to provide indigents with counsel and prosecutors to disclose certain evidence at trial. Judges must ensure simply that defendants knowingly waive their rights. Voluntariness requires little more than the absence of criminal coercion such as physical force, and that prosecutors keep any promises they have made in exchange for the guilty plea. Although even broken promises are excused if a defendant does not object in time to the breach.[28] As a result, the law does little to protect public interests or defendant interests that are not always well served by parties pursuing partisan interests, including more robust conceptions of substantive and procedural fairness, and strong commitments to the consistency, accuracy, and proportionality of criminal judgments.

All of this plea bargaining law is constitutional. Nevertheless, just because the federal Constitution puts no limits on prosecutors' hard bargaining and requires little from courts that order convictions based on guilty pleas, legislatures are not prevented from enacting laws to govern plea bargaining practices. Nor does the federal Constitution prevent state courts from developing such rules as a matter of state constitutional or common law. Yet across U.S. jurisdictions, few laws of this sort exist. Nearly everywhere, the constitutional "floor" for plea bargaining largely *is the law* of plea bargaining. In a federal system that licenses procedural diversity, that is a striking consensus.

An important reason for this uniformity is the nature of the Supreme Court's reasoning in its plea bargain decisions, which overwhelmingly stress political or moral norms and policy justifications rather than constitutional text. It could hardly be otherwise. The Constitution guarantees trials and several trial-related rights, but it says nothing about guilty pleas. No history of plea bargaining from the founding era exists to inform originalist accounts of constitutional meaning. Instead, the Supreme Court—followed by lower courts—builds the constitutional law of plea bargaining on its assumptions about the necessity for bargaining and about what rules are essential to facilitating the practice. It endorses the fairness as well as practical advantages of leaving party negotiation over criminal judgments unconstrained by public law or judicial supervision. And the Court speculates, a bit ominously, about the danger to public safety that could follow if judicial interference in the bargaining process hinders law enforcement effectiveness.

Constitutional scholars and political theorists have long suggested that, in democracies where courts have final authority on questions of constitutionality, judicial decisions have feedback effects on the manner of legislative and executive policymaking. James Thayer made part of this point in his classic argument that political officials proceed with less reflection about the constitutionality of policies where courts have the final word.[29] The influence surely runs in a second direction as well. Practices that courts deem constitutional can gain moral and political legitimacy from that judgment. Coupled with judicial assertions of practical necessity, policymakers are less inclined to forgo advantages from those practices.[30] One piece of suggestive evidence is this: until about the mid-1970s, a government commission, and some local court systems, urged the abolition of plea bargaining. One is hard pressed to find an example of that since the 1980s, once the constitutional law of plea bargaining was largely settled.[31]

Even if the Supreme Court deserves credit for defining the American vision of plea bargaining, that still does not answer the question of why the Court adopted that vision in the first place, or why that view proved so persuasive to other policymakers. The best answers to those questions are that the Justices and most other professionals in criminal justice systems were convinced (1) that plea bargaining became, at some point in history, an absolute necessity for criminal justice administration; (2) that plea bargaining could meet the justice system's demand for it only if practiced within the minimal constraints on party interactions that characterize free markets and private contracts; and (3) that this market-style bargaining also had a lot of normative appeal as the right and fair way to resolve most criminal charges.

Necessity

Legislators, prosecutors, and nearly everyone else eventually came to share the Court's assumption that "plea bargaining is an essential component of the administration of justice," because without it "the States and the Federal Government would need to multiply by many times the number of judges and court facilities."[32] This consensus has only grown with time. "The reality is that plea bargains have become . . . central to the administration of the criminal justice system. . . . [O]urs 'is for the most part a system of pleas, not a system of trials.'. . . '[P]lea bargaining is . . . not some adjunct to the criminal justice system; it *is* the criminal justice system.' "[33] "[W]e accept plea bargaining because many believe that without it . . . our system of criminal justice would grind to a halt."[34] In sum, for whatever reasons—rising crime rates, rising caseloads, changes in law enforcement agendas, demands on public coffers from programs outside criminal justice—governments will no longer fund justice systems at levels to permit trials for more than a very small percentage of criminal cases. If budgets or caseloads won't change, criminal process must.

With resource constraints in mind, the Court increasingly emphasized in its plea bargaining decisions "the interest of the State in efficient criminal procedure." That interest quickly transmuted into sanguine acceptance of "the simple reality . . . that the prosecutor's interest at the bargaining table is to persuade the defendant to forgo his right to plead not guilty."[35] The forthrightness of that assertion tells us something about the judicial views of the prosecutor's ministerial norm. The prosecutor's role in this account is bluntly adversarial rather than ministerial, and it implies a purely instrumental idea of prosecution aims in plea negotiations. Even so, the need to resolve most cases by plea agreements does not speak to *how high* that portion of cases must be, although the Court seems to think that number needs to be very high. In *United States v. Ruiz*, it feared that not letting the parties bargain over pre-plea evidence disclosure "could lead the Government to abandon its heavy reliance upon plea bargaining in a vast number—90% or more—of federal criminal cases."[36] Yet the state interest in efficiency through guilty pleas does not unambiguously dictate what the bargaining rules should be. The Canadian Supreme Court, for one, made precisely the opposite inference about what practices lead to more pleas. In *R. v. Stinchcombe*, the Canadian justices required prosecutors to disclose all relevant evidence before defendants chose between a guilty plea and trial, citing "compelling evidence" that disclosure would save time and reduce delays by causing an "increase in guilty pleas."[37]

In a criminal justice system that needs to produce most of its convictions without trials, the right to a jury trial is a problem. It is the wrong *default rule*—a rule that applies unless the parties agree otherwise. Default rules exist throughout many areas of law.[38] Ideally they define the option that works best (or that the parties prefer) in *most* cases, so that they save the effort of having to contract around them. The jury trial right, however, is not that kind of default rule. On the premise that trials need to be rare events, the state has to devise ways to convince defendants to routinely waive their trial rights.

The law of plea bargaining allows the state to use every possible tool for that end short of criminal fraud and coercion, from grossly disproportionate differences between plea and trial sentences to the threat that prosecutorial leniency (or absence of vindictiveness) for a defendant's family member hinges on his plea of guilty.[39] In affirming the constitutionality of these practices, the Supreme Court does more—it insists that they are both necessary and morally appropriate. Prosecutors' "imposition of these difficult choices [is] an *inevitable* attribute of any legitimate system which tolerates and encourages the negotiation of pleas," the Supreme Court has asserted, without recognizing that "difficult choices" of *any magnitude* are in fact not inevitable.[40] Virtually every procedural component and legal entitlement must be available as bargaining chips. Whatever the costs to competing public interests—fairness, accuracy, proportionality, or consistency—anything less "could seriously interfere with . . . the efficient administration of justice."[41]

Market values provide the normative justification: plea agreements reached in this process are "desired by defendants" because they voluntarily consented to them.[42] The prosecution merely "offers substantial benefits" to defendants in exchange for a guilty plea. Bargains are inherently characterized by "mutuality of advantage," so the judiciary need not assure the fairness of bargains that are by definition "mutually beneficial."[43] Within the transaction-maximizing logic of the market, any other view is literally irrational: "As a logical matter, it simply makes no sense . . . that mutual settlement will be encouraged by precluding negotiation over an issue that may be particularly important to one of the parties to the transaction. A sounder way to encourage settlement is to [remove] any arbitrary limits on their bargaining chips . . . [so as not to] stifle the market for plea bargains."[44] The law of bargaining aims not merely to authorize or facilitate but to *maximize* plea agreements. It condemns any rule that could hinder that aim—rules that would serve competing public interests, such as fairness, accuracy, proportionality or consistency.[45] This is a legal regime wholly conceived as a free market, within which parties, free from state regulation, zealously pursue their rival interests.

Despite the eventual triumph of this vision, however, for several years after the Court initially began to craft plea bargaining doctrine, none of the doctrine's core assumptions was self-evident, at least in the eyes of many judges and state criminal justice systems. Many contested that plea bargaining was a benign and desirable way to achieve convictions, that guilty plea rates had to exceed 90 percent and remain at whatever level prosecutors insisted upon, and that negotiated pleas could thrive only under the rules for private contracts and free markets, unhindered by judicial interference and meaningful standards of fairness or due process. It was the Supreme Court's preference for the market model of bargaining—often announced in closely divided decisions such as *Bordenkircher*[46]—that led this model to prevail. The Court's influence on the norms and policy assumptions surrounding plea bargaining, as well as the larger political-cultural context of the American liberal-market economic tradition, explains why most other policymakers went along.

Due Process Regulation of Plea Bargaining

While *Santobello* called plea bargaining "essential" to criminal justice, it also signaled that the Constitution puts limits on some tactics and terms. The principles that justify plea bargaining, the Court wrote, "presuppose fairness in securing agreement between an accused and a prosecutor." Plea agreements "must be attended by safeguards to insure the defendant what is reasonably due [in] the circumstances," and—citing a 1927 decision—federal courts "will vacate a plea of guilty shown to have been unfairly obtained."[47] That seemed to open the door to plea bargaining but also to judicial supervision of bargaining.

Many lower courts took that *Santobello* language seriously, and in the 1970s, they began to develop more specific fairness standards for plea negotiations, standards grounded in requirements of due process. For a time courts used those doctrines to exercise modest but meaningful judicial supervision over plea bargaining. In particular they devised means to modestly supervise prosecutors' actions so as to hold those actions to "the 'most meticulous standards of both promise and performance . . . in plea bargaining'" and thereby "both to protect the plea bargaining defendant from overreaching by the prosecutor and to insure the integrity of the plea bargaining process."[48]

To that end, courts scrutinized plea agreements for implicit prosecutorial promises that might have induced a defendant's guilty plea, and they required prosecutors to create records that enabled judicial review of some aspects of their discretionary decisions that led to agreements. In *United States v. Bowler*, the plea agreement included a government promise to exercise its discretion in reviewing certain mitigating factors—such as a defendant's cooperation and his health—before making a sentence recommendation. Although that discretionary judgment "is an evaluative function normally performed internally within the office of the prosecutor," the Seventh Circuit required that "the Government's evaluation of the specified mitigating factors must be set forth in the record at the time of sentencing."[49] To enable judicial review in a charging context, the Eighth Circuit Court of Appeals required that prosecutors provide reasons to justify additional charges against a defendant after he rejected a plea bargain offer.[50] Notice in both examples the resemblance here to English courts' review of prosecutor decisions for abuse of process. Making prosecutors' discretionary decisions transparent in this way permits a court to "ascertain whether or not the Government had in fact performed the promised evaluation, and it is not the privilege of the Government to make the determination as to whether or not it has honored its promise."[51]

Other federal appellate courts imposed similar requirements that enabled meaningful judicial review of plea bargains.[52] Some made explicit that constitutional fairness regulated the public law process of plea negotiations more stringently than the ordinary law of contract did for private parties in the marketplace. The Fourth Circuit held, for example, that while mere contract *offers* are ordinarily not enforceable in private settings, due process required enforcement of prosecutors' plea agreement *offers*.[53] That is, fairness barred prosecutors from withdrawing offers before a defendant is able to respond with his acceptance—a sharp distinction between the law of plea bargains and private contracts that was subsequently abandoned in judicial reasoning as well as much scholarly writing.[54] Here again is an example of U.S. courts exercising power over prosecutors akin to English rules that enforce certain prosecution promises to prosecute or to decline prosecution. The difference between the systems is not inherent in different rules for separation of powers or judicial capacity. The difference is what rules courts (with the acquiescence of legislatures) choose to develop when available sources of law permit more than one possibility.

Needless to say, this line of due process doctrine did not last. One hurdle is the unswerving commitment (in federal and state law) to prosecutorial discretion unchecked by judicial scrutiny, which the *Bordenkircher* decision in particular reaffirmed. Justice Powell dissented from that decision; he was willing, in that extreme scenario, to impose a modest constraint on executive discretion. Yet even his starting point for such a limit was this: "if the system is to work effectively, prosecutors must be accorded the widest discretion . . . in conducting bargaining. . . . Only in the most exceptional case should a court conclude that the scales of the bargaining are so unevenly balanced as to arouse suspicion."[55] Without judicial control of sentencing discretion or a well-crafted criminal code of the sort no American jurisdiction is able to produce, plea bargaining regulation can never get very far absent some limits on prosecutorial discretion. The other hurdle is the Siren-song appeal of free market bargaining. One of many examples is the Supreme Court's 1984 decision in *Mabry v. Johnson*, which shut down a public law obligation of "scrupulous fairness" for prosecutors during plea negotiations and instead relied on contract law treatises to justify constitutional parameters for plea bargaining that closely tracked the private law of agreements between ordinary parties.[56] As a consequence of *Mabry* and other decisions in the same vein, U.S. courts today have no meaningful role supervising the plea bargaining process, and prosecutors negotiate without any meaningful constitutional limits.[57] State courts have largely adopted the same approach.[58]

After *Mabry*, if not before, the Supreme Court, followed by other courts and policymakers, focused on the mutual benefits of bargains, discounted "difficult choices" prosecutors create for defendants, and worried much more about hindering plea agreements than whether the state "exerts such a powerful influence [as] to coerce inaccurate pleas." A court's concern is only to ensure that a defendant had a chance to receive competent counsel and that he had not "*misunderstood* the choices that were placed before him"—not whether those choices were fair or unduly coercive.[59] After *Mabry*, the *Santobello* requirement of fairness in forming plea agreements means little more.[60]

Challenges to "Necessity": Local Limits

The brief post-*Santobello* era of due process regulation showed possibilities for an alternative to the free market law of plea bargaining. In broadly the same era, however, criminal justice systems in a number of localities—and one state—resisted the practice of plea bargaining itself. Their successes suggested that plea bargaining is not—as the Court and many others insisted—an inevitable necessity, at least not in all places or at rates of 90 percent or more of a criminal docket.[61]

Numerous studies from the 1960s through the 1980s confirmed comparatively low rates of guilty pleas in various jurisdictions. Several urban court systems—generally more overburdened than rural ones—reduced guilty pleas to rates of less than 40 percent of all convictions.[62] A landmark study by Stephen Schulhofer in the 1980s found that the Philadelphia criminal courts devised a custom of efficient bench trials largely by keeping parties from perceiving a need to plea bargain.[63] Earlier studies of Philadelphia and Pittsburgh courts found unusually low guilty plea rates—under 35 percent—due to the same basic strategy: use of bench trials made possible by widespread waivers of only the jury. Albert Alschuler's nearly two decades of exhaustive research on local plea bargaining practices beginning in the late 1960s includes an account of a successful ban on plea *bargains*—but not guilty pleas—imposed by local judges in El Paso, Texas, with no evidence that the judges imposed harsher sentences following trials than they did for guilty pleas.[64] In the 1990s, Ronald Wright and Marc Miller found a similar practice in New Orleans—many guilty pleas but few plea *bargains*. There, the bargaining ban came from the city district attorney's office, which avoided bargaining by rigorously screening charges so that defendants knew that filed charges were strong ones prosecutors could prove at trial.[65] Some defendants still pled guilty, with no apparent increase in the number of trials.[66] Similarly, Alaska's attorney general, with the support of the state courts, imposed a statewide ban on bargaining for several years in the 1970s.[67] Alaska is one of the few states in which the state attorney general appoints local prosecutors and can dictate policy for them.

The studies of these very different contexts suggest nothing was unusual in the caseloads, resources, or other circumstances in these jurisdictions. The common characteristic seems to have been the motivation of key officials. Plea bargaining limits arose from the initiative of local trial judges or prosecutors, or by collaborations among local officials and attorneys who developed local practice norms to displace bargaining. The avoidance of bargaining by "front line" practitioners who confront most directly the exigencies of caseloads and resource constraints undermines claims of bargaining's necessity. Consistent with long-standing common law tradition, all these jurisdictions permitted guilty pleas without the inducement of an explicit bargain. Collectively, they suggest not only that some jurisdictions do not *need* to do as much plea bargaining as they do but also that officials in these jurisdictions once disapproved of the practice of plea *bargaining*, although not of guilty pleas per se.

To be sure, that discomfort was not widespread even in the 1970s and 1980s. Still, all evidence suggests there is much less of it now. Greater acceptance of bargaining, however, is not necessarily because bargaining was "essential" to the justice system—although it may be because many *believed* it was essential. Well-regarded studies found that plea bargaining thrived in some places even when caseload pressures and resource constraints did not force officials to use it. Separate studies of Connecticut courts by Milton Heumann and Malcolm Feeley provide perhaps the best-known examples. Guilty pleas accounted for roughly 90 percent of convictions in both studies. Other historical evidence indicates roughly the same percentage for nearly a century in the state's courts. But a natural experiment strongly suggests that this guilty plea rate was not compelled by caseload pressures. The small percentage of trials did not increase even when caseloads declined dramatically (due to a statutory change in Superior Court jurisdiction) during the period of Heumann's study. Feeley discovered the same thing by comparing two similar local court systems. Trials were no more common in one local court system that had low caseload-per-judge ratios than they were in a nearby one with much higher caseloads. But interviews revealed that local court officials in lower-volume courts still *believed* that bargaining was compelled by their caseloads.[68] Reliable evidence that judges, prosecutors, and defense lawyers *believe* plea bargaining is essential for criminal justice administration is much easier to come by than evidence that it actually is. The fact that a justice system gets 90 percent of its convictions from guilty pleas does not prove that it *must* resolve 90 percent of cases that way—a topic explored further in chapter 6.

Paths of Plea Bargain Regulation

Operating a justice system with guilty plea rates below 90 percent is possible when the right officials are committed to it, but examples of prosecutors who voluntarily abjure plea bargaining (or of judges who encourage them to) are increasingly rare. The Supreme Court's consistent cheerleading for plea bargaining reflects—and surely contributed to—a broader cultural and professional acceptance of negotiated guilty pleas. Yet plea bargaining still flourishes even under rules that better regulate its practice and reduce the worst risks it poses. Some reforms, in fact, do not directly regulate *bargaining* at all, but simply change the context in which it occurs. The best examples are sentencing laws that give judges discretion over punishment terms, rather than putting control over sanctions in prosecutors' hands through mandatory-incarceration statutes and restrictive sentencing guidelines. Other options to regulate bargaining exist as well. All affect in some way the parties' discretion and control over aspects of procedure and punishment, which are "chips" that parties trade in plea negotiations. What all these reform options have in common is that they move plea bargaining away from its prevailing market-based model, by reducing the parties' autonomy and power (unilaterally or in concert) to control the criminal process and its outcomes.

REGULATING DISCRETION

The most straightforward way to reduce most risks that arise from plea bargaining would be to limit incentives to plead guilty. Sentencing laws that give judges wide discretion to determine the sentence tend to operate as this kind of limit. At least, that is true as long as judicial sentencing practices—or explicit sentencing indications before the plea—do not make clear that the incentive is in fact great because the difference in the post-plea and post-trial sentence is great. This effect of discretionary sentencing is reinforced by the presumption, common in U.S. jurisdictions and elsewhere, that sentences on multiple offenses will run concurrently rather than consecutively. Judicial sentencing control and concurrent sentencing together hinder prosecutors' ability to define the consequences that will follow from defendants' choices between trials and guilty pleas. Concurrent sentencing reduces the impact of dropping or adding charges, and judicial sentencing makes it impossible for prosecutors to confront defendants with the choice that Paul Hayes faced—"five years or life"—in *Bordenkircher*. That kind of overt pressure to plead guilty requires punishments fixed by statute (although sentencing guidelines that tightly constrain judges' options can have nearly the same effect).

Judicial sentencing authority makes it easy to limit the differences defendants face between sentences after a plea versus after a trial conviction, because rules that constrain judicial sentencing discretion are now widespread and in principle uncontroversial. It is easy, in short, to regulate the incentives *judges* create to plead guilty. It is much harder in the common law tradition, and in American systems in particular, to regulate *prosecutorial* discretion. When sentences are fixed for specific offenses, rules would have to restrict prosecutors' power either to add new charges to the initial ones if a defendant declines to plead guilty (as *Bordenkircher v. Hayes*) or restrict their power to drop some of the initial charges. Either kind of rule is feasible and constitutional, but in practice such rules are rare.

California and New York have statutes that ostensibly impose these kinds of controls on prosecutor bargaining tactics. They either prohibit bargaining altogether on serious offenses or restrict the magnitude of the charge reduction prosecutors can offer. (Unsurprisingly, officials have found ways to avoid both rules, and neither state's legislature has attempted to close those loopholes.)[69] Recall that there are precedents for those statutes in the nineteenth-century laws that barred bench trials or guilty pleas for serious crimes.

The same kind of restriction also existed for a time as a due process doctrine that guarded against prosecutorial vindictiveness by barring the government from adding more charges against defendants after they decline to plead guilty or after they exercise other procedural rights, unless the government provides good reasons such as discovery of new evidence. The Supreme Court endorsed that doctrine for a time, notably in *Blackledge v. Perry*. It eventually changed course and shut down this constraint on bargaining tactics as a matter of constitutional law, in a line of decisions that included *Bordenkircher*.[70] No jurisdictions have chosen to adopt similar restraints by statute, which is why, with the rise of mandatory sentencing statutes, American prosecutors gained power over sentencing and thereby greater power in plea bargaining.

MANDATORY INFORMATION DISCLOSURE

An alternative, perhaps more modest approach to bargaining regulation would aim to improve the quality of plea agreements simply by ensuring that both parties are better informed. The key step would be to make the prosecutorial duty to disclose exculpatory evidence apply before plea agreements and make it nonwaivable; prosecutors now can bargain around that obligation. On the model of mandatory "information forcing" rules in innumerable commercial settings,[71] statutes could expand disclosure requirements for both prosecutors and defendants. Removing nondisclosure as a "bargaining chip" means the parties would negotiate only after both are better (and more equally) informed. All else equal, full, symmetrical information improves the quality of agreements. For that reason mandatory disclosure rules govern in many private market domains. Nonetheless, such rules have not gained as much traction in American criminal procedure; because they depart from the implicit free market model that dominates judges' and policymakers' reasoning in this context. That framework assumes that nothing prevents the competitive litigation process from working perfectly and so parties will bargain for as much information disclosure as has value to them, relative to what else they might be able to gain by trading away their right to information.

BARGAINING RULES OUTSIDE THE UNITED STATES

Because plea bargaining is now common worldwide but the American liberal-market approach to the regulation is not, jurisdictions outside the United States give some indication of how feasible these kinds of bargaining regulations can be.[72] When the English courts and Parliament eventually embraced bargaining,[73] they adopted rules for its practice that contrasted sharply—and intentionally[74]—with American rules and practices. The Criminal Justice Act of 2003 created the Sentencing Guidelines Council and authorized sentence discounts for guilty pleas. The council's regulations limited sentencing discounts that judges could give for guilty pleas to no more than a one-third reduction from the post-trial sentence, shrinking it to as little as 10 percent if the defendant delays his guilty plea until the trial date.[75] Chapter 2 noted that English prosecutors' charging decisions are subject to modest judicial review and that the Code for Crown Prosecutors has an enforceable legal status that American prosecutorial guidelines lack. How much more constrained English prosecutors are in charge bargaining compared to their American counterparts is hard to measure. But their charging discretion matters less because English plea bargaining occurs against a body of sentencing laws with many fewer mandatory punishment terms than in U.S. jurisdictions, and with sentencing guidelines that give English judges more leeway than U.S. judges enjoy under the federal guidelines. As a result, the constraint on judicial plea discounts does much more to define plea bargaining parameters generally than an equivalent rule would in U.S. jurisdictions.

Equivalent sentence-discount limits exist for guilty pleas in other systems further afield from the common law tradition. The Italian criminal procedure code—reformed substantially in the 1980s to incorporate more features of U.S. adversarial process—limits the guilty plea sentence discount to one-third, and it bars any discount for serious offenses, defined as crimes punishable by more than five years in prison. Spain also mandates a one-third sentence reduction.[76] German statutory law has no explicit cap, but Germany's Federal Court of Justice found that a negotiated conviction for a three-and-a-half-year sentence, against the prospect of a sentence twice that long after trial, was a prohibited threat.[77]

England's rules restrict only judicial sentencing practice. Limits on prosecutorial discretion are less rigorous, but still somewhat greater than in the United States. In *McKinnon v. United States*, the House of Lords suggested a plea bargain could constitute "unlawful pressure" and prosecutorial abuse of process, although only if the plea sentence discount was "substantially more generous" than 50 percent below the authorized post-trial sentence.[78] (*McKinnon* addressed whether English law permitted the defendant's extradition to the United States in light of a plea agreement offered by American prosecutors.) But the abuse-of-process standard in English courts also applies more broadly; its function resembles the federal due process doctrine developed in some lower courts between *Santobello* and *Mabry*. English courts enforce prosecutor offers or promises to defendants at a stage before a court approves of a plea agreement. English courts can demand reasons from prosecutors that justify criminal charges after, for example, prosecutors announce an intention to drop a domestic violence prosecution in the wake of a civil restraining order. Without sufficient reasons, courts will bar the renewed prosecution as an abuse of process.[79] The underlying commitment is more to a principle of fair play by public officials than to private contract law. Additionally, the Code for Crown Prosecutors forbids overcharging as a tactic to induce guilty pleas. To be sure, the U.S. Attorneys' Manual does much same for federal prosecutors, and the law in practice often varies from law on the books. But the English Code for Crown Prosecutors has the status of enforceable regulations that U.S. Justice Department policies do not,[80] and English evidentiary disclosure rules are somewhat stronger in the plea bargain setting than their U.S. counterparts.[81]

Whatever the explanation, negotiated convictions thrive in national criminal justice systems worldwide under a variety of mandates, restrictions, institutional forms, and professional norms.[82] English plea bargaining in particular is routine, which suggests that the chilling effect of regulating it is marginal. (Indeed, inducements to plead guilty under English rules have been sufficient to cause some documented wrongful convictions.)[83] Comparisons of guilty plea rates alone do not account for the possibility of other variables at play, but the contrast is still notable. In U.S. federal courts during 2009, 96.7 percent of convictions came from guilty pleas, and 88 percent of charged defendants pled guilty; others either went to trial or had charges dismissed. (Figures for state jurisdictions, for which data are less comprehensive, are approximately the same.)[84] In the Crown Courts of England and Wales in 2009–2010, guilty pleas accounted for 91 percent of convictions, and 73.5 percent of charged defendants pleaded guilty.[85]

In spite of all this, the widely shared American presumption persists that even modest regulation of bargaining would be fatal because "if the system is to work effectively, prosecutors must be accorded the widest discretion . . . in conducting bargaining." This is not a plausible claim. It is a product of a worldview constrained by the ideology of the free market and a singular faith in prosecution governed only by politics.

GREATER JUDICIAL SCRUTINY

A separate path to improving the integrity of negotiated pleas has a different focus. Criminal procedure rules could require that judges consistently play a more substantial, responsible role in confirming the factual and legal integrity of convictions that are achieved through party negotiations over the defendant's guilty plea. A more active judicial role in the plea hearing aims at different interests than do rules limiting charging discretion or the size of plea discounts. Judicial scrutiny of the factual foundation and legal accuracy of a guilty plea would do little or nothing about the coercion from gross disparities between plea and trial sentences. But an active judicial role in which the court, rather than merely the parties, takes meaningful responsibility for the integrity of convictions based on guilty pleas can prevent some improvident pleas and also add some qualitative integrity to the plea process.

The primary step in this reform is one that some trial courts already follow voluntarily but that is far from a requirement or from a widespread practice. The duty to "determine that there is a factual basis for the plea"[86] would require conducting an active, careful colloquy with the defendant to elicit his detailed account of all the relevant conduct and circumstances, including his *mens rea* (e.g., intention as to conduct or results, awareness of circumstances), that are required for liability. The same inquiry would extend to any facts relevant to plausible defenses. Requirements that plea agreements be in writing, as is common in federal courts and mandated by statutes in a few states[87] serve similar ends, at least if they include detailed factual accounts in addition to the rights waived by the defendant and any promises between the parties. Another, probably less common approach to investigating the factual basis of convictions without a trial is to require the government to provide on the record sufficiently specific summaries of its evidence and sources of that evidence. A further judicial inquiry to assure the factual integrity of convictions is more unusual still. Within the bounds of client confidentiality and attorney work-product privilege, judges could demand that prosecutors and defense attorneys provide a meaningful account of how they have adequately investigated the facts, assessed the evidentiary sources of the case, and otherwise prepared for the disposition. In the common law tradition, judges depend on the parties to investigate the facts and compile the evidence. Attorneys on both sides have professional obligations to do so, and defendants have at least a modest legal *entitlement* to the defense attorney's efforts under effective-assistance doctrine. Yet in the shift from trials to guilty pleas, adjudication loses the transparency that enables judges to see both the evidentiary record and some of the party efforts to develop its scope and quality. The nature of this judicial process entitles—or arguably, should obligate—judges to inquire that the court has been adequately well served by the parties' adversarial efforts before the court enters a judgment of conviction based upon those efforts.[88]

The predominant norm, especially in state courts, is to engage in a much less careful and thorough inquiry to ensure the plea's factual basis and legal accuracy. Because a guilty plea's constitutional validity rests primarily on the defendant's consent rather than on judicial fact-finding, judges are not required to be convinced beyond a reasonable doubt that a guilty plea is factually accurate.[89] The text of Federal Rule 11 makes apparent that the validity of guilty pleas depends much more on the defendant's knowing waiver of his trial-related rights, which the judge must specifically confirm, than on the rigor of the judicial finding about the plea's factual basis.[90]

This prevailing practice for accepting guilty pleas tracks the underlying priorities of the adversarial process, which put more responsibility on parties than judges for ensuring proper outcomes. Still, more rigorous alternatives to prevailing practice are consistent with adversarial tradition as well. Fact investigation and settlement negotiations remain with the parties. Nonetheless, it is always only the court that enters a judgment of conviction and an order of punishment. Choices about the guilty plea process address only how actively and responsibly judges will fulfill their role in issuing judgments based on party-defined evidentiary records. Consistent with common law tradition, and implicit in criminal procedure rules, American judges have the authority to demand that parties produce some evidence before accepting a guilty plea.[91] (In England, *R. v. Newton* explicitly confirms judges' power to order an evidentiary hearing for pleas even if the parties' factual accounts do not conflict.)[92] One U.S. jurisdiction goes further, however, and has adopted explicit rules that ensure primary judicial responsibility for the accuracy and fairness of guilty pleas: the U.S. military justice system.

U.S. MILITARY JUSTICE

Under the Uniform Code of Military Justice,[93] service personnel can be charged the full range of criminal offenses in military courts (or courts martial). Negotiated guilty pleas are permitted for all but capital offenses[94] (a rule reminiscent of nineteenth-century state laws), and they are routine.[95] But the procedural requirements for entering a judgment based on a guilty plea are orders of magnitude more rigorous than in state and federal courts. Military law largely does not limit bargaining terms and tactics, save in a few important respects. Parties cannot make an agreement contingent upon a specific sentence (although they can agree to a maximum sentence), because sentencing can occur only after an adversarial hearing. The Military Code also prohibits prosecutors from adding additional charges if defendants refuse to plead guilty (that is, it bars the practice *Bordenkircher* approved). Plea agreements also cannot waive appellate review, because appellate review is *mandatory* even if neither party alleges error.[96] The fact investigations that precede charges occur in a rigorous framework akin to an adversarial preliminary hearing: defendants are notified of the investigation, granted counsel to cross-examine or to call witnesses, and retain access to records of the investigation.[97]

As in civilian courts, military judges give primary attention to assuring a defendant's voluntary confession and his knowing waiver of trial rights. But there is a critical additional obligation, which appellate courts unfailingly scrutinize: before accepting a guilty plea, the judge must personally question the defendant, in careful detail, about every relevant aspect of the conduct and circumstances of the charged offenses. The record must reflect the defendant's accurate understanding of the governing law and possible defenses, and the judge must elicit admissions "to all elements of a formal criminal charge."[98] (For contrast, a Michigan rule reads: "the court must advise the defendant of the following and determine that each defendant understands: (1) the *name* of the offense to which the defendant is pleading; *the court is not obliged to explain the elements of the offense, or possible defenses. . . .*")[99] Even after accepting a guilty plea, the military judge must reopen the plea hearing—or providence inquiry—if a defendant subsequently makes any statement (such as in a sentencing hearing) that contradicts the conviction's factual or legal basis.[100]

The procedure is firmly planted in the adversarial tradition. Attorneys investigate the facts and negotiate a proposed disposition, summarize or introduce evidence at the court hearing, and argue at the later sentencing stage. Still, the military judge's role in guilty pleas resembles that of a European civil law jurist in another respect. The judge actively questions the defendant and bears responsibility for creating a record that documents the accuracy as well as voluntariness of the guilty plea. The unusual label for this hearing—*providence inquiry*—directs attention to the degree of prudence, foresight, and judiciousness expected before a guilty plea is accepted as valid.

The reasons for this starkly different system are many. Some are practical. The military justice system is dramatically better funded, on a per-case basis, than even the best civilian criminal justice system, and the process reflects that greater investment in every respect—in the investigation, in attorney preparation, and in judicial time. But an even more important reason is conceptual: unlike other U.S. jurisdictions, the military justice system does not have full confidence that adversarial party agreements produce convictions so accurate and reliable that they require little judicial supervision. The military justice system requires more care regarding the voluntary and knowing nature of a defendant's guilty plea, but it also puts comparatively less faith in a defendant's explicit consent as the basis for the legitimacy of convictions by guilty plea. Consequently, it requires comparatively more judicial inquiry into the factual basis for guilty pleas. Military courts "take particular care to test the validity of guilty pleas *because* the facts and the law are not tested in the crucible of the adversarial process."[101]

In large part this system responds to concerns unique to the military setting—the "subtle pressures inherent to the military environment that may influence the manner in which service members exercise (and waive) their rights."[102] Superior officers in a defendant's chain of command could improperly influence a defendant's decision to plead guilty. Yet the absence of comparable "subtle pressures" in civilian criminal justice hardly explains why civilian courts are so sanguine about the voluntariness and factual reliability of defendants' guilty pleas. Justice officials lack the same direct control over a defendant's employment and much of his private life that military officials exercise over service members' careers and lives, but the pressures defendants face in civilian criminal justice are sometimes anything but subtle. Those pressures can extend beyond the explicit guilty plea discount and a family member's legal fate tied to acceptance of a guilty plea. They often include the burdens of pretrial detention that lasts until the case is resolved and the wide range of civil consequences triggered by arrest or conviction, some of which prosecutors control—from property forfeiture and occupational licenses to public benefits eligibility and deportation of noncitizen offenders.

In sum, pressures to plead in the civilian and military justice systems differ in kind but not necessarily in degree or subtlety. The differences in how seriously the two systems take those concerns has less to do with whether undue pressures put at risk the voluntariness of guilty pleas than with the degree of responsibility that the state takes upon itself for the quality of its criminal process and the integrity of its courts' judgments. The difference is probably linked as well to how much each system cares about whether defendants themselves perceive their own process to be fair; one aim of the military system's providence inquiry is to leave defendants confident about the system's legitimacy.[103] In the military context the state takes greater responsibility for the quality of state-administered justice because defendants are service members as well as citizens. Status as a citizen is thus insufficient to trigger the same commitment, which leaves more room for the legal culture to incorporate the norms of liberal-market political economy, in which the predominant view leaves the individual to be best served by his own autonomy and initiative rather than by the state intervening (paternalistically) to safeguard those interests.

Corruption of Professional Norms

I have already noted many of the consequences of plea bargaining as typically practiced in most U.S. courts. But an additional, less-noted consequence of market-style bargaining is its corrosive effect on the professional norms of prosecution practice. Within the tradition of strongly adversarial prosecutors, the ministerial norm is weaker in part because it incorporates the instrumental norms of the market. Those norms are plainly apparent in prosecutor tactics to create trial/plea sentence disparities of the magnitude that *Bordenkircher* illustrates. That kind of disparity is detached from any plausible account of moral desert, proportionality, and consistent treatment of similar offenses, and it is indifferent to plausible concerns about coercing inaccurate pleas of guilty. The options of a five-year sentence or a life sentence are the product of a wholly instrumental calculation about a price that will induce assent to the prosecution's preferred outcome. The norms that legitimize this practice are reinforced in the body of law around plea bargaining, which overtly endorses and rationalizes such tactics in the name of efficiency, perceived necessity, and the market assumption that any two-party agreement deemed to be voluntary contains mutual gains. Beyond differences in particular procedures or sentencing laws, probably the defining distinction between plea bargaining in U.S. jurisdictions compared to criminal justice systems elsewhere is how explicitly charges and sentences are adjusted for the purpose of pressuring defendants to plead guilty without meaningful constraint from competing interests or values, and how acceptable that practice is—professionally and morally—among American prosecutors, courts, and policymakers.

Keeping in mind the usual caveat that local office and courthouse cultures vary greatly, evidence of this is not hard to find. In the federal system, U.S. attorneys routinely exercise discretion to add mandatory sentence increases—of several years or *decades*—strictly as leverage to convince defendants to plead guilty and to cooperate with law enforcement. A statute routinely used in this way is 21 U.S.C. § 851, which gives prosecutors complete control over mandatory sentence increases for drug offenders who have prior convictions. It states simply: "No person . . . shall be sentenced to increased punishment by reason of one or more prior convictions, unless . . . the United States attorney files an information . . . stating in writing the previous convictions to be relied upon." Once a prosecutor files the information, judges are required (under related statutes) to impose a significantly longer prison sentence. Depending on the drug offense, sentence severity can increase from an extra five years to life without parole. Many states have equivalent statutes that put aggravated sentences in prosecutors' control.[104]

The history of Section 851 is especially interesting, because it suggests the corrupting effect of such provisions in a regime of unregulated bargaining. The current statute, enacted in 1970, replaced an earlier law that had mandated enhanced sentences for *all* drug offenders with criminal records. The Department of Justice lobbied for reform on grounds that the law was overly harsh and unfair, because justice requires distinguishing the worst offenders who deserve enhanced sentences from those who do not. The department argued that prosecutors were in the best position to identify those who deserve longer sentences.[105]

Both the statutory design chosen by Congress and the evolution of its subsequent use reveal the influence of democratic and market norms. Of course, Congress could have given *judges* the sentencing discretion to make those distinctions after hearings that provided details of a defendant's offense and criminal record. In theory, it also could have assigned the power to prosecutors on the condition that enforceable administrative regulations apply to their decisions under the statute, although that would be far outside federal law tradition for the Justice Department. Instead, Congress fell into line with the American disposition to rely on politics rather than law: it gave prosecutors unreviewable authority to dictate sentences that judges must impose.

The subsequent history is old news. Instead of exercising their discretion to allocate sentences in proportion with offenders' culpability, prosecutors unambiguously use the statute to pressure defendants into pleading guilty. They do so without pretense. Prosecutors routinely present defendants with two choices—go to trial with a Section 851 notice or plead guilty without one. The trial penalty is commonly 100 percent or more: five years for a guilty plea or ten after a trial conviction; seven to ten years for a guilty plea versus twenty—or even life—for conviction at trial.

The instrumental use of sentence severity is not merely apparent from the charge and sentence options that prosecutors commonly present to defendants. When compelled to explain, prosecutors *tell* judges and defense attorneys that they file Section 851 notices simply to induce defendants to plead guilty and, when defendants may have useful information, to induce their cooperation. Prosecutors' letters to defense lawyers presenting such offers describe this use of Section 851 notices as standard office practice.[106] The following prosecutor said as much when the judge asked him to explain why he had filed the Section 851 notice:

> I mean, the government's goal here, as is plain from the papers, was to obtain Ms. Jones' cooperation. And I made clear to [defense counsel] from the beginning that . . . if she was not prepared to cooperate that we would file the 851 Information. . . .

> There is no constitutional impermissibility about [filing the
> information in response to the defendant's refusal to cooper-
> ate] because the Government could have done it at the beginning,
> instead [we] made the decision to try and give the defendant an *even
> bigger break*.[107]

Note the implication of leniency in the final line, conditioned on an exchange of benefits. There was no pretense that a harsher sentence is based on the nature of the defendant's crime and criminal record. One can find the same attitude in play in state justice systems, where courts can be as frank as prosecutors about the function of these statutes. According to the New Jersey Supreme Court, "[t]he primary purpose of the provision" giving prosecutors control over mandatory sentences for certain drug offenders "is to provide an *incentive* for defendants, especially low and middle level drug offenders, to cooperate with law enforcement agencies."[108] *Higher* sentences for *low-level* offenders are tools for the executive branch, not proportionate punishment.

In another federal case, when a judge asked how the prosecutor's decision to mandate a life sentence was "just," the prosecutor responded, almost literally, that the sentence enhancement was unrelated to justice. He explained that his office made "extensive efforts to try to resolve this case prior to trial," which consisted of an initial offer with a deadline for acceptance, a subsequent harsher offer with a second deadline, then a third iteration of the same tactic. But "when you're a prosecutor and you're . . . offering to make concessions that are declined . . . you lose some credibility going forward if you then make those same concessions. . . . [T]his doesn't really address your question of justness, but it gives you the background here in terms of why we are here now as opposed to this case getting resolved on a plea to a lesser sentence."[109]

There can hardly be a plainer account of the corruption that follows from combining unregulated prosecutorial discretion with unregulated bargaining in a context of expansive codes and fixed sanctions. The power to use liability and punishment as bargaining chips, with no meaningful constraints beyond partisan interest and political supervision, leads professionals inexorably to focus on the procedural utility of that power and, consequently, to the marginalization of the criminal punishment's ostensible rationales and aims. Like cases are treated alike when the similarity lies in defendants' decisions to cooperate, rather than in the defendants' wrongdoing and fault.

The more adversarial and political nature of U.S. prosecution agencies makes this corruption of ministerial norms easier, but the market's values and its instrumental rationality make the transition more intuitive and uncontroversial. The market-inspired law of plea bargaining endorses the partisan trading of criminal process and punishment as commodities with little constraint from public law principles. In turn, this body of law has altered the professional culture of prosecution agencies, the customary practice in criminal courts, and, not least, our understanding of the rule of law. Nor is the judicial role immune to a kind of corruption when everything is understood to be negotiable. A federal appellate court provides an example in its nonchalant acceptance of a prosecutor's agreement to misrepresent key facts to the sentencing judge in exchange for the defendant's appeal waiver:

> Nor is there any merit to [the defendant's] claim that he received no consideration for the waiver of his appellate rights: as the [Presentence Report's] findings about the actual loss caused by [his] conduct suggest, and as the government confirms on appeal, *in the plea agreement the government stipulated to a much lower loss amount than was actually involved in the offense of conviction, and, moreover, stood by that stipulation in the sentencing memorandum it submitted to the district court in advance of sentencing.*[110]

What should be shocking is freely tradable: the court both approves of prosecutorial misrepresentations to trial courts and affirms the practical meaningless of the statutory requirement that trial judges determine the factual basis for guilty pleas.

Public Responsibility and Rule of Law

The state has incontrovertible interests in the substantive accuracy and procedural fairness of guilty pleas. But safeguards for those interests are not found primarily in the law. They are found in the mechanisms of the market and of democracy on which criminal process is built. In this sense markets and politics reduce the role of law. This means, in practical terms, a system built around prosecutorial discretion, defense autonomy to trade away procedural entitlements, and a largely passive judiciary. The freedom granted both parties, and the strong form of private (or party) ordering in the process of criminal case settlement, represent a particular choice not only about the *role* of law but the *rule* of law, or what the criminal justice system accepts as *legality*. With its trust democratic rather than legal governance of prosecutorial discretion, which includes unfettered choice among available charges to manipulate plea bargaining incentives, this rule of law ideal encompasses action that other legal systems would view as arbitrary.[111] Guilty plea outcomes *are* arbitrary in the important sense that liability and punishment turn on party decisions and not, consistently and predominantly, on wrongdoing and fault.

American plea bargaining law instantiates this limited notion of the rule of law, because it adheres so closely to a liberal-market ideal—unusually closely compared to many non-U.S. jurisdictions, and unusually closely compared even to other, more regulated domains of ordinary private markets. That is not because keeping the state out is a practical necessity for the efficiency of criminal case settlement. It is due rather to the power of free market ideas in the law of criminal procedure, ideas that have become so intuitive they constrain imaginable alternatives. Market values give that process and its outcomes legitimacy and even normative appeal.

In this free market model of bargaining, the judge's role in party transactions looks much like the state's role in a liberal market economy. For both plea agreements and ordinary market exchanges, the law forbids little more than criminal fraud or coercion; consent given in their absence is sufficient for a valid agreement. Plea bargain terms are limited only by a large body of criminal offenses and the accompanying sentencing laws. In a significant sense, that range of autonomy is not so different from that enjoyed by typical market actors in the freest of market settings, where exchanges are restricted only by prohibitions for a small set of goods, such as human organs or sexual services. (In other markets settings such as the financial sector, exchanges are *more* regulated than plea agreements are.) For negotiated pleas as for private contracts, the law permits terms and outcomes widely condemned as unfair. In both contexts, the law does little to mitigate the effects of differences in resources, information, or other sources of advantage. In sum, the state's commitment to ensuring the substantive fairness of convictions based on guilty pleas is hardly distinguishable from its role in most private market exchanges.

CHAPTER 5

Private Responsibility for Criminal Judgments

*No procedural principle is more familiar to this Court than that a constitu-
tional right may be forfeited in criminal as well as civil cases by the failure to
make timely assertion of the right.*
—*Yakus v. United States (1944)*

*It is fair to burden the defendant with his lawyer's obligation to do what
is reasonably necessary to render the guilty plea effectual. . . . Any other
approach [would not] combat defendants' "often frivolous" attacks on the
validity of their guilty pleas.*
—*United States v. Vonn (2002)**

Introduction

In many respects, American criminal procedure is explicit and unreserved
in its embrace of democracy and markets in place of law or regulation, and
in its favor for private rather than public ordering. The prior three chapters
have considered some effects of these priorities, especially in the law related
to prosecutors, defense counsel, judicial authority, and plea bargaining. All of
this occurs within the adversarial tradition of legal process, which itself relies
more than the rival inquisitorial tradition on private ordering and market-like
mechanisms—competitive parties, passive judges, and prosecutors who are
more partisan than magistrative. By contrast, the inquisitorial tradition of
process—with its more active judges, state responsibility for accurate judgments, and quasi-judicial prosecutors—displays an inherently stronger reliance on coordination and public ordering.

Beyond these bold choices, comparable if more subtle and incremental distinctions lie in other rules and structures of criminal process, rules that specify
details of pretrial, trial, and appellate procedure. Placing the burden of proof
for some issues on defendants, for example, incrementally extends private

responsibility for proof, and it shifts from the state to the individual the risks of errors arising from some failures to carry the burden. George Fletcher characterized defense proof burdens in English and American criminal trials as evidence of a "private law style."[1] The relative ease with which a justice system permits error correction, especially post-trial, marks another set of choices about how criminal process will balance competing public and private interests, and allocate responsibility between the state and private actors for protecting those interests. The limitation of appellate review to legal errors, with a bar against the consideration of new evidence—standard in common law systems and justified by sound interests in finality and efficiency—marginally reduces the state's commitment to error correction, increasing the significance of parties' evidence production in the trial (or settlement) stage. The same is true for closely related rules that limit opportunities for new trials based on newly discovered evidence.

Much the same is true as well for rules that address a quite different problem—the inevitable "agency problems" between defendants and their counsel. Especially when they are selected and paid by the state, lawyers' interests and motivations are not always fully aligned with those of their clients. Public defender clients often suspect this, but they are poorly positioned to monitor or control the agents working on their behalf. Even when lawyers are not misled by personal interests that diverge from their clients', some of their decisions are to their clients' detriment. How much should the client pay for—and how much should court judgments be affected by—lawyers' missteps? The rough answer is, "a great deal." In these contexts and others one again finds, implicitly but unmistakably, the premises and values of markets. Subtly, modestly, or otherwise, interstitial rules of criminal process shift responsibility for the integrity of judgments further away from the judiciary and ultimately from the state. And once procedures or entitlements are well established, expectations tend to grow up around them. Rules contribute to, then reinforce, a normative vision of fair process in which defendants bear significant responsibilities for their own fate in that process, and for some portion of the errors that it produces.

Private Orientation in Public Procedure

BURDENS OF PROOF AND THE "PRIVATE LAW STYLE"

One aspect of the private orientation in American criminal procedure rules was first described by George Fletcher in his classic comparative treatise, *Rethinking Criminal Law*. Fletcher attributes Anglo American allocations of various burdens of proof in criminal trials to the influence of a lingering "private law style."[2] Fletcher uses that phrase to describe a mode of process borrowed from civil litigation to resolve private disputes, specifically one which gives parties greater responsibility for framing and proving legal issues. English courts and those in most American jurisdictions continue to place the burden of proof on *defendants* for various affirmative defenses such as claims of self-defense—that is, for issues outside the formal elements of the criminal offense, on which the state still bears the proof burden. This choice for allocating proof burdens follows the civil litigation custom of placing the burden to prove an issue on the party that raises the issue. Prosecutors must prove the elements of the offenses they charge, but if defendants raise a claim of self-defense or insanity, they bear the burden of proving it to the judge or jury, instead of the prosecutor having to prove that the defendant did not act in self-defense or was not insane. As a result, in this private law style of litigation, prosecutors do not bear the burden of proving everything relevant to culpability and liability, because the *absence* of justification or excuse is as critical to properly determining guilt as is proving the elements of the crime. Moreover, this private adjudication style extends beyond formal proof burdens, because rules that authorize an inference (or rebuttable presumption) of one fact from proof of another are functionally similar. A fact-finder can be authorized to infer that a required state of mind (such as knowledge or intent) is proven based upon proof of something else, such as conduct. Proving possession of contraband, for example, may trigger an inference that the defendant *knew* he possessed it, which the defendant would then bear the burden to refute.

In the nineteenth century, Fletcher notes, criminal courts both in common law and civil law countries employed this system, which was borrowed from private civil litigation. One rationale was that it put the burden on the party likely to have better access to evidence on an issue. Recall that in earlier eras, criminal justice had other features that also tracked private litigation. Private prosecutors were common, and criminal offenses more closely tracked the scope and subject matter of tort law or other sources of civil liability. Yet by the end of that century, Fletcher observes, Western nations had shifted to the view that criminal law is foremost an exercise through public law of state authority. As such, criminal law serves public interests, and poses risks to individual interests, not present in the private law context. (Recall that, as part of this shift, full-time police forces arose in the nineteenth century, and public prosecutors displaced private ones.) The state's greater capacity to enforce criminal law led to the need for criminal procedure reforms that provide better safeguards for the interests of individuals compelled to litigate against the state. One safeguard could be shifting the burden of proof onto the prosecution for all issues relevant to fault, liability, and punishment. As Fletcher tells the story, over time European justice systems such as Germany's did exactly that, abandoning the private law style and putting all (or nearly all) proof burdens on the state. But England and U.S. jurisdictions did not consistently follow suit. Defense-side burdens of proof remain widely used, and largely uncontroversial, in the United States.

The tradition of defense-side proof burdens is private not merely in the sense that its proof rules mimic those of litigation designed for disputes between private parties, but in the more significant respect of how it allocates public versus private responsibility for the integrity of criminal judgments and the justification for state-imposed punishment. Putting proof burdens on defendants even for defenses creates the possibility that the state may punish a defendant without having proven all the facts that bear on his culpability.[3] A defendant on trial for homicide, for example, can be held liable once the state proves that he intentionally caused the death of another, unless he successfully proves (often by preponderance of the evidence) that his conduct was a justified act of self-defense. Alternately, if the state were to bear all the burdens related to culpability, it would have to prove beyond reasonable doubt that a defendant's conduct was justified once he raised the issue with some evidence. Not every case necessarily comes out the same way under either rule.

The two options allocate differently the risks from uncertainties in available proof—or, more bluntly, risks of erroneous judgments. Putting all burdens on the prosecution increases the odds of erroneous acquittals, while putting some burdens on the defense increases the chance of erroneous convictions. The first option could be described as putting the costs of errors on the public or the state, while the second could be said to "privatize" the costs of errors by placing them on the defense. (At least primarily—public interests suffer from erroneous convictions as well.) Defense-side burdens are in some tension with the premise that punishment is justified only after the state has proven the defendant's wrongdoing and *fault*, rather than merely proving his wrongful conduct, coupled with defendant's failing to prove he was not at fault. Nothing in the nature of adversarial process requires defense-side proof burdens; a minority of U.S. jurisdictions require the prosecution to disprove defenses when defendants offer some evidence raising the defense as an issue.[4]

Defensive burdens depend on the idea that privatizing some of the responsibility for proving fault, and some of the costs of errors, is *fair*. Aside from other concerns about that premise, it becomes more defensible the more that a legal system has confidence that its prosecutors charge the right—that is, culpable—defendants in the first place. The greater that confidence, the less insistent one might be that prosecutors prove every aspect of culpability. That confidence is hardly a formal feature of adversarial criminal procedure, as the state's primary burden of proof confirms, and it hardly gains force from prosecution agencies that are less ministerial, more partisan, and more political.

In sum, burdens of proof are one example of an incremental emphasis on greater private responsibility for criminal justice. Put differently, these rules, like those considered next, reflect a choice for marginally greater private ordering; their rationales are grounded in the norms and logic of the private sphere, rather than in a capacious view of the state's responsibility for public law process.

PROCEDURAL DEFAULT RULES

Plea bargaining depends on defendants having the authority to waive procedural entitlements; those waivers are their bargaining chips (along with, for some, information useful to law enforcement).[5] But deliberate waiver is not the only way parties relinquish rights or opportunities. Parties may lose legal entitlements through forfeiture triggered by the party's wrongdoing. For example, a party that improperly makes a witness unavailable to the court (such as through bribery or intimidation) forfeits the right to use otherwise admissible hearsay evidence as a substitute for the absent witness.[6] Much more frequently, under procedural default rules parties give up entitlements by simply not taking advantage of them at the proper moment or within a permitted time frame. This might be done intentionally or not, but in any case there is no requirement that a court must find such a relinquishment to be knowing and voluntary. A party who fails during trial to call a witness, to cross-examine an opposing witness, to object to inadmissible evidence, to challenge a jury instruction, or to request a proper instruction loses the right to do these things because he passed up the chance to do them at the proper time. All these actions might affect the integrity of the judgment. Some are legal errors, such as improperly admitted evidence or erroneous instructions. Others are simply choices that affect the evidentiary record, perhaps increasing risks of inaccuracy.[7]

Among the effects of procedural default are that a party loses—in whole or in part—the right to correct specific trial errors on appeal; in some cases, that means they cannot correct wrongful *judgments* caused by those errors. That right can be lost in whole or in part. Often parties forfeit appellate review of "unpreserved" claims under the most favorable legal standard, but courts will still assess them under a much less favorable "plain error" standard.[8] Forfeiture occurs whether it followed from a counsel's well-considered tactical decision or from her negligence. Put differently, procedural default rules reduce an appellate court's obligation to correct erroneous judgments based on a party's earlier decision (or neglect) not to do something earlier that would have low-ered the risk of that error.

Procedural default follows from failures to take timely advantage of all sorts of entitlements or opportunities, including time limits on pretrial disclosure, post-trial motions, or notices of appeals. Although their requirements are more elaborate, rules of double jeopardy share a functional similarity. They bar the prosecution from a second opportunity to prove criminal charges if a defendant is acquitted at trial, or if prosecutors cause a mistrial. Prosecutors face that bar only after considerable intentional conduct, of course, but the double jeopardy rule is similar in its effect to procedural default rules in that it prevents a party from correcting errors that arose from its own lapses or miscalculations before or during trial. That bar is only modestly more than what defendants face after conviction; neither party can demand another trial simply upon realizing it made some mistakes in the first one. Defendants can appeal convictions, but only on limited grounds focused mainly on alleged errors committed by the trial judge. (That advantage is partially offset by pros-ecutors' authority to pursue pretrial appeals of trial judge rulings.)[9] Both par-ties have lost the ability to relitigate simply to make better contributions to the evidentiary record, or better legal arguments based on that record. Neither can relitigate merely because it made tactical or inadvertent mistakes that affected the judgment. Both are limited in their ability to have another trial by proving that new evidence has come to light that was not available at the first trial.

Procedural default rules (and double jeopardy rules) serve at least two broad purposes. The most obvious is finality. Finality allows parties and oth-ers to confidently rely on judgments, and by limiting relitigation strong finality rules encourage efficient use of procedural resources.[10] A second purpose is particular to adversarial systems. Default rules strengthen incentives for the parties to produce evidence, raise legal issues and bring relevant law to the court's attention. By limiting parties' abilities to correct their own misjudg-ments or inaction and by forcing them to live with the consequences of their decisions, procedural default rules increase the odds that parties will make their best efforts. These rules serve, in the Court's words, "our need to encour-age all trial participants to seek a fair and accurate trial the first time around."[11]

Procedural default rules balance finality and efficient-process interests against competing concerns about accurate outcomes and fair process. They are one way to make the trade-off between tolerating errors and the cost of correcting errors. If accurate judgments were the overriding interest, the court system would revisit judgments more readily with the ambition to reduce inac-curacies from failures to produce evidence, raise valid legal claims, or apply governing law,[12] regardless of who is at fault. All legal systems have default rules; none can relitigate indefinitely.[13] But adversarial process has a greater need for procedural default to motivate parties. Because it depends so much on parties, adversarial process must ensure each party has a self-interest not only in winning but also using the justice system efficiently. Procedural default rules add to those incentives by creating the risk that parties will have to live with *inaccurate* judgments caused by their own inaction or poor tactical judgments.

The scope and effect of procedural default rules are another context in which a justice system can calibrate public versus private responsibility for the accuracy of court orders. Procedural default puts more responsibility onto parties and less on courts (ultimately, the state) for the integrity of judgments. Making default easier to commit and harder to correct incrementally privatizes adjudication; it marginally increases the degree of private ordering that produces court judgments. This is not to say that responsibility for judgments is *fully* privatized. Appellate reversal for "plain error" is a move in the other direction, a public investment in correcting errors even after a party failed to address it at an earlier, more appropriate time. That is one safeguard against inaccurate judgments caused by a party's lapse or a trial judge's mistake. Others are discussed later. The basic point remains that, at the margin, stronger procedural default rules increase incentives on parties and decrease state responsibility for the integrity of judgments. To be clear, the discussion that follows makes no claims about how much U.S. jurisdictions privatize responsibility through default rules compared to elsewhere. The more limited aim is to draw out how an affinity for private ordering and market norms pushes judges toward stronger default doctrines and helps to rationalize the costs of doing so.

Perhaps the most common and familiar examples of procedural default rules are also those for which the default argument is strongest: decisions to call or examine witnesses, introduce or challenge evidence, and request or object to jury instructions. Even for criminal defendants, the Supreme Court has never had separate procedural default rules depending on whether a defense lawyer's decisions on these litigation choices were deliberate tactical choices or the product of negligence or inadvertence.[14] But default rules' expansive reach follow from the premises on which the doctrines are built. Default rationales rest on a concern about incentives, the motivating power of self-interest, the value of private ordering, and the fairness of adverse consequences following from voluntary choices. These are ideas related to the market, and market ideas have considerable persuasive power in U.S. criminal process. That may help explain the reach of default rules in less familiar contexts, where the argument for them is weaker. Consider briefly a couple of examples.

Objections in Guilty Plea Hearings

Judges are required to do relatively little in guilty plea hearings, but their explicit duties include eliciting defendants' informed waiver of the set of rights related to trial, including the right to legal counsel. There is little difference between state and federal rules for guilty pleas, so Federal Rule of Criminal Procedure 11 is representative. It requires the judge, before accepting a guilty plea, to advise the defendant that he would have the right to assistance of counsel if he went to trial. What if a judge neglects to do so? Should the defendant have to remind him? If a defendant later seeks to invalidate his guilty plea because of this failure, how should the effect of this procedural error be decided? Should the plea be invalidated automatically? Should the government have to prove that the failure to inform the defendant was harmless? Or should the defendant have to prove that the court's error affected his decision to plead guilty? In the 2002 case of *United States v. Vonn*, the Supreme Court held that, when a defendant fails to *object* to the judge neglecting to inform him of his right to trial counsel, the latter standard applies.[15] For that reason, lower courts must apply the plain-error standard and vacate the guilty plea only if the defendant demonstrates prejudice. Two years later, in *United States v. Dominguez Benitez*, the Court clarified that, to be granted a remedy for such an error, a defendant would have to prove he was prejudiced by it—meaning that, but for the judge's error, he probably would not have entered his guilty plea.[16]

This doctrine self-evidently reduces the state's obligation for the procedural integrity of a judgment and shifts some of the responsibility to defendants. The defendant first has the burden of objecting to the court's neglect to mention a right about which the court has a *duty* to inform him. When the defendant has a lawyer at the hearing, this merely shifts part of that duty, as a practical matter, to the private attorney. If the defendant is unrepresented at the guilty plea hearing, the burden borders on the absurd: a lay person who may not know his rights must remind the court of its duty to tell him about those rights. The obligation to object to judicial negligence, on pain of an unfavorable legal standard when the defendant later seeks to withdraw the guilty plea, privatizes responsibility. It allows judgments to stand in the wake of such irregularity, rather than allocating responsibility to the state by an automatic-reversal rule (which would force judges to bear the procedural costs of their errors) or a harmless-error rule that requires the prosecution to show the error had no effect, good or bad (which would encourage prosecutors to monitor courts' adherence to the Rule 11 checklist).

In both *Vonn* and *Dominguez Benitez*, the Court had several plausible options in constructing the doctrine for a Rule 11 error by a trial judge, based on the rule's language, the indicia of legislative intent, and precedent. Justice Stevens, dissenting in *Vonn*, stressed that the Court had, some three decades prior, interpreted an earlier version of Rule 11 to judge requests to void a guilty plea under a standard more generous to defendants—the harmless-error standard, with the prosecution bearing the burden to show that the trial court's error was harmless in this instance. In that earlier era, in fact, *prosecutors* urged that solution—perhaps a sign of how prosecution culture has shifted in a generation. The *Vonn* majority and dissent each marshalled arguments based on the text of the rules, precedent, legislative intent, and fairness. But their competing concerns about the incentives that rules create are telling. Justice Stevens was alone in seeing the virtue of "giv[ing] incentive to the judge to follow meticulously the Rule 11 requirements and to the prosecutor to correct Rule 11 errors at the time of the colloquy." *That* rule puts responsibility on public officials for the integrity of public process. Eight other Justices, by contrast, saw "only good sense" in the policy that adds to the private individual's responsibility for procedural regularity "by creating an incentive [on defendants] to file withdrawal [of plea] motions before sentence, not afterward." This risk gives them "an incentive to think through a guilty plea"—although without being fully informed of their rights by the court—"before sentence is imposed."[17]

The Rise of Instrumentalism

It is also revealing that both sides in the debate stress the language of *incentives*—an instrumental rationale—rather than the terms of public values or the state's obligation to ensure fair process. The shift toward instrumental rationales fits a larger trend. Scott Sundby has described a parallel turn in doctrines regarding the exclusion of illegally obtained evidence. Starting in the 1970s, the Supreme Court increasingly weighed the costs of excluding illegally seized evidence against exclusion's benefit as a deterrent to law enforcement illegality. For nearly a century before then, the justices had emphasized that excluding illegal evidence served core public law goals. Exclusion is important to "maintain respect for the law," "promote confidence in the administration of justice," and "preserve the judicial process from contamination."[18] Data on the broader trend are suggestive. In the thirty-three years from 1981 through 2013, the Court used the word "incentive" in relation to prosecutors or defendants seventy-seven times. In the thirty-three-year period from 1948 through 1980, it did so only a third as often—twenty-six times. In the thirty-three years from 1915 through 1947, it *never* used "incentive" in that context.[19]

Anticipatory Objections to Future Changes in the Law

In worst-case scenarios, *Vonn* requires defendants to remind judges about a right that judges know but defendants don't. Under a different rule, the defense must object to trial court decisions even though prevailing law provides no grounds for objection. *Griffith v. Kentucky* mandates that all new rules of constitutional criminal procedure must "be applied retroactively to all cases . . . pending on direct review."[20] (In *Griffith* the new rule barred prosecutors from intentionally eliminating potential jurors based on their race.) But there is a catch: defendants lose most of their entitlement to retroactive application of a new rule if they did not object to the relevant issue at trial—*before the new rule existed*, and therefore when a successful objection seemed foreclosed by existing law, which the trial court's decision followed. Nevertheless, failure to object means appellate courts are much less likely to apply the new rule; they will do so only if they find "plain error" by the trial court. The idea is to encourage defense lawyers to anticipate future changes in the law and raise these issues with trial judges—despite having no clear basis in current law—in the expectation that the current law will change between the time of the trial judgment and the time when direct appeals are exhausted.

The rule is not entirely implausible. Sometimes doctrinal changes are foreseeable, as when lower courts are divided (and especially if the Supreme Court has granted *certiorari* to resolve the split). As Toby Heytens explains, objections that are groundless under controlling law can nonetheless prompt both parties to supplement the record, or prompt the trial judge to provide reasons for decisions that otherwise would go unexplained.[21] But it is hard to see how such benefits justify a procedural default that is designed to encourage defense attorneys to make what are, at that moment, groundless objections.

The purpose of the retroactivity rule is, as the *Griffith* Court put it, to ensure "the integrity of judicial review," which requires that courts apply a new rule to all similar cases.[22] Yet in the end this doctrine hardly seems well designed to ensure similar treatment. Some prescient defense lawyers will make (groundless) objections in anticipation of a future law change; their clients will benefit from new rules. Inevitably other defense lawyers will not, and so their clients will lose that benefit.[23] Here again, as in the *Vonn* doctrine for Rule 11, a defendant loses the legal entitlement (or a large share of it) through inadvertence and inaction. Here again a portion of the responsibility for the integrity of legal process shifts from public officials to private actors. And here again the rationale is crafted by reference to incentives and practical benefits, with little reference to sustaining convictions that occurred (in light of the new rule) by unconstitutional process.

RULES ON FINALITY AND ACCURACY OF CONVICTIONS

Some criminal procedure rules calibrate the state's commitment to the integrity of judgments without an explicit focus on the parties' action or inaction. Some trade-off is inevitable between, on the one hand, the finality of judgments and the efficiency of process used to reach them, and the accuracy of judgments on the other. Every justice system must limit the time and resources devoted to reducing risks of error, and all must protect the finality of judgments sufficiently to make them meaningful and reliable enough for parties and others to act upon. Those concerns affect standards for appellate review as well as whatever other procedures provide a way to revisit convictions when subsequent developments raise real suspicions, confirmed most recently by the ever-growing list of miscarriages of justice. These rules are another indicator of how the state allocates public and private responsibility for substantive accuracy, as well as how it defines procedural fairness in criminal process. Two sets of rules illustrate the point: standards by which appellate courts confirm that evidence sufficiently supports a conviction, and rules that define when evidence discovered postjudgment justifies invalidating a conviction and either holding a new trial or letting the defendant go free.

Rules on Newly Discovered Evidence

New evidence that comes to light after a conviction has been entered and that raises doubts about guilt can sometimes justify a new trial or—when it is especially strong—a writ of actual innocence. The equivalent can be true also for new postconviction evidence that indicates guilt on a *greater* offense; within double jeopardy limits, prosecutors can sometimes charge the defendant again on the more serious offense from the same incident. All these rules balance interest in factual accuracy of criminal judgments against the costs of relitigation while defining the parameters of procedural fairness.

In some cases, the state commitment to accuracy (and to a robust notion of fairness) has been exceedingly modest. Virginia, for example, has long barred requests to the trial court for a new trial if they are made more than twenty-one days after the judgment, even if based on newly discovered evidence.[24] Rules on this deadline vary widely, from fifteen days to three years.[25] In recent years, following well-publicized wrongful convictions, nearly all jurisdictions have added opportunities at least to present new DNA evidence. Some rules distinguish opportunities to challenge convictions based on the type of new evidence that has come to light, as well as on other grounds. State rules on this point vary much more than do state rules about prosecutorial discretion or plea bargains, so generalizations only go so far. But Virginia law provides an interesting example.

Since 2004, Virginia has allowed convicted offenders to challenge convictions at any time by petitioning for a writ of actual innocence, but authorization to do so depends on the type of new evidence an offender claims to have uncovered and on whether he was convicted by a guilty plea. Only defendants who were convicted at trial can petition for a writ of innocence based on new *nonbiological* evidence; those who pled guilty cannot. Thus a core premise in the law of guilty pleas—that a defendant's consent substitutes for judicial fact-finding—reappears in the law of postconviction error correction. That means one of two things. Either the state takes consent-based convictions—even under prosecutor-created pressure to plead guilty that U.S. law permits—to be *more* reliable than those based on fact-finding at trial, so that writs of innocence (based on nonbiological evidence) are more likely to be meritorious for trial-based than plea-based convictions. Or alternately, this rule is based on the premise that defendants who have consented to conviction have forfeited on their right to have courts correct inaccurate judgments based on nonbiological evidence, regardless of the risk of inaccuracy for such convictions.

By contrast, guilty plea convictions for a subset of serious offenses *can* be revisited under Virginia law if the petition is based on new *biological* evidence. These different rules for when a state is willing to revisit the accuracy of serious convictions follow from assumptions about the greater reliability and clarity of biological (especially DNA) evidence compared to nonbiological evidence. Courts have long considered new, nonbiological evidence—such as recanting witnesses or previously unknown witnesses—to be much more suspicious and less credible, largely due to concerns about witness intimidation or collusion.[26] Those are valid concerns; presuming DNA analysis to be more reliable than most other sources of evidence is plausible, notwithstanding that DNA evidence can be ambiguous or sometimes mislead as well. Yet it is also true that a significant number of wrongful convictions—achieved by pleas as well as trial verdicts—have been uncovered and confirmed through nonbiological evidence.[27] Barriers to correcting errors in those kinds of cases reveal the limits of a state's commitment to the accuracy of its courts' judgments. Under other rules, concerns about relatively minor potential costs outweigh interests in the integrity of judgments, as does an offender blame for causing delay. Motions merely to *test* new biological evidence, for example, are limited by the probable value of the evidence and by whether the defendant's prior inaction justifies procedural default of the opportunity to test evidence. Motions to test are granted only if the evidence may prove actual innocence (rather than merely raise a reasonable doubt or reduce guilt to a lesser offense), and only if the defendant has not "unreasonably delayed" his motion.[28]

In sum, distinguishing by evidence type is one mechanism by which the state calibrates its tolerance for inaccurate convictions. Only for those cases in which biological evidence can be salient does the state create additional procedural safeguards to vindicate accuracy at the expense of finality. At bottom, that is more a cost-benefit analysis than a normative public commitment to ensuring accuracy whenever a certain quantum of evidence later comes to light that raises questions about that accuracy. The rules weigh public costs of error correction against the costs of erroneous convictions, which are borne mostly (but not wholly) by defendants. For errors in low-level offenses, the burdens imposed on the wrongly convicted do not justify procedures to correct errors based on newly available evidence. Error costs are thus left in the private realm. Restricting chances to correct errors should increase defendants' motivations to prevent errors at the pretrial and trial stage, especially by searching out all relevant evidence. That calculus is integrated into other criteria that turn on the private defendant's decisions—whether he has pled guilty and whether he was sufficiently diligent in pursuing allegations of an inaccurate conviction. Here is the same trace of market rationality recognized elsewhere: a party's own choices or failures justify rules that put the loss on him, even in the form of an accurate judgment. On that ground, the state can, if only marginally, reduce public responsibility for the integrity of judgments.

Review for Sufficiency of Evidence

The other primary means to revisit the factual accuracy of convictions is more familiar and more uniform across U.S. jurisdictions: appellate review to confirm that the trial record contains minimally sufficient evidence to support a judgment. *Jackson v. Virginia*[29] defined a minimal due process standard for whether evidence presented at trial is adequate to justify a conviction: an appellate court should overturn a trial conviction only if no reasonable fact-finder could have concluded the defendant was guilty based on the evidence presented. Appellate judges must interpret the evidence in a light most favorable to the judgment.

For present purposes, only a couple of points about this standard are important, both obvious but implicit. One is that *Jackson* provides the only basis on which appellate courts directly assess the factual accuracy of convictions, although appellate attention to facts also occurs indirectly through review for some legal errors, such as whether the trial judge wrongly excluded evidence, prosecutors failed to disclose evidence, or an ineffective defense attorney failed to investigate and find evidence. In accord with common law tradition, appellate courts do not solicit or consider new evidence and limit their focus to legal errors or abuses of judicial discretion in the trial process.[30] As *Jackson* makes clear, appellate courts consider only the evidence that the parties introduced. Except when they can do so indirectly by addressing claims of legal errors or rights violations, appellate courts cannot consider how that trial record may be deficient, or how well the parties investigated the facts and made efforts to produce evidence for the trial court, nor how well they scrutinized (such as through cross-examination) the reliability of the evidence presented.[31]

All of this is consistent with an adversarial system that relies almost wholly on the parties to compile the factual record, with virtually no back-up role played by the judicial branch. The *Jackson* standard reinforces parties' incentives to develop trial evidence and otherwise to take full advantage of the trial process. It reconfirms that responsibility for the accuracy of convictions rests largely with the parties rather than the state, which is to say it reconfirms a large role for private ordering in public judgments. It confirms as well that the rule of law conception is based not on a guarantee to defendants that the state will ensure substantively accurate outcomes along with fair process, but rather a guarantee of the opportunity to participate in a process designed to produce accurate judgments if those opportunities are leveraged and rules otherwise followed. In that sense, appellate review for factual adequacy reiterates the tolerance identified elsewhere for inaccurate outcomes attributable to defense decisions.

Adversarial Incentives and Principal-Agent Problems

Contemporary judicial analysis pays considerable attention to the incentives that criminal procedure rules create for parties. At its core, adversarial process relies on the partisan motivations of parties, which displace almost all rules that *command* parties to do things such as gather evidence. Outside of some duties to disclose evidence in their possession, adjudication rules *require* parties to do very little. Instead, adversarial process trusts that parties who are seeking to protect their own partisan interests will do everything necessary to provide the court with an adequate evidentiary record (and properly framed legal issues) to render sound judgments. But there is an elephant in this room. Incentives are created by risks to *party* interests, and a few core decisions—notably decisions whether to plead guilty—are made explicitly by the lay client.[32] As a practical matter, though, parties must rely on lawyers, and nearly all decisions on which the success of adversarial process depends are explicitly left to the attorney rather than the client. Those include decisions about how to investigate, what evidence to introduce or to challenge, and what legal rules to invoke or arguments to make. Choices about those things should be motivated by the party's interests. Yet attorneys make these decisions, and attorneys' own interests are not always the same as those of their clients. Even in the absence of formal conflicts of interest, this can be an enormous complication.

Lawyers are the agents of their clients, and this kind of problem between principals and agents is a familiar one found in a wide variety of settings and relationships.[33] (Once you look for it, it seems nearly ubiquitous.) Whenever lawyers make decisions in their own interests rather than their clients', the parties suffer agency costs. Principals can minimize those costs if they can keep a close eye on their agents. But many principals cannot do this scrupulously. Sometimes keeping track of agents is simply too costly or impractical. But often, as with lawyers and most clients, the agents have expertise that the principals lack, so principals can't tell whether agents' decisions are the right ones or not. That's why they hired specialists to assist them in the first place.

PROSECUTION-SIDE AGENCY PROBLEMS

For several reasons, the more serious agency-cost concerns are on the defense side. But the same problems plague the prosecution, even though the prosecutor's "client" is an abstract entity understood variously as the state, "the people," or some conception of the "public interest." Prosecutors (like other lawyers) might pursue their own interests over their client's interests simply by being lazy rather than diligent. Suspicions that prosecutors are merely reducing their workload—offering overly lenient deals to avoid the hard work of trial—motivate some objections to plea bargaining. Alternately, politically attuned prosecutors might make decisions that serve their personal political interests, rather than the public interest as it would be defined either by a politically disinterested official or by local constituents with enough information about policy options. Evidence indicating that prosecutors pursue harsher charges and sentences in election years is an example of this kind of agency cost. But eliminating politics doesn't necessarily eliminate agency costs. Comparable problems sometimes arise in politically insulated prosecution agencies, where officials have opportunities to do their jobs in ways that serve their personal interests in career advancement, or in simply avoiding heavier workloads.

DEFENSE-SIDE AGENCY PROBLEMS

Agency problems between defendants and attorneys are surely more significant, because the interests at stake are those of an individual facing criminal sanction and because his counsel's performance is often critical to an accurate and fair process and judgment. Agency problems on the defense side are also more complicated as a general matter, because of the variety of ways defendants obtain counsel.

When defendants personally select and finance their own attorneys, they may have more ability to align the attorney's decision making with their own interests. Private financing alone is not a panacea. Clients also need ways to closely monitor their counsel. Some private-pay arrangements afford clients more control than others, such as those in which the client approves specific investments for more investigation or evidence analysis. Some contexts align the lawyer's personal interests with the client's more closely than others. Clients who offer lawyers the prospect of repeat business or valuable referrals have this advantage, as do those whose cases can greatly affect the lawyer's professional reputation. Those scenarios do not describe most defendants who pay criminal defense lawyers. Nonetheless, personally selecting and paying for legal services provides a stronger basis than otherwise for the general rule—across civil and criminal litigation—that a party is bound by the actions of his lawyer.

Most criminal defendants, however, neither choose nor fund their own counsel. The state does. The arrangements by which this occurs—as well as the terms and conditions under which defense lawyers work—vary greatly across U.S. jurisdictions. State-funded defense counsel for indigents is variously provided by full-time public defenders; by lawyers in private firms who agree by contract to represent indigent parties in a particular jurisdiction or court; or by attorneys who are appointed by judges to individual cases and paid either a flat fee or an hourly rate. Contract terms, workloads, and pay rates vary widely. Some of these arrangements work well, as is generally the case in the federal courts. Too often they work abysmally, as documented by countless studies of "crises" in indigent defense and periodic legal challenges to inadequate defense systems in particular states or localities.[34]

Attorneys' motivations differ depending on the payment system, and consequently so do agency costs for defendants. A fixed fee per case encourages self-interested attorneys to underinvest in a client's case. High caseloads force attorneys into harder choices about how to ration their time between clients. Firms seeking to win or renew contracts to provide defense services have reasons (under typical contract terms) to invest as little as possible in cases they handle and thereby offer highly "efficient" services to the funding agency. In many cases, local trial judges choose which lawyers to appoint, leading attorneys who seek those appointments to pay attention to the judge's preferences, which might favor speedy dispositions over slower but thorough representation. Indigent clients have little leverage over all of this. Occasionally they can succeed in requesting that a judge or defender office provide another attorney, but they have no right to dismiss an appointed advocate or insist on a different one. For the most part, they can do little more than lobby their lawyers for specific investigative efforts or strategic options.

The point is that agency problems for defendants can be substantial, and those problems significantly impede the proper functioning of the adversarial criminal process. Many criminal-process rules penalize parties to spur the performance of their lawyers, yet often lawyers have personal and professional interests that significantly cut against actions that would maximize protection of their client's interests. Where agency problems are large, the market-based premises of the adversary process work poorly, precisely because of a "market failure" in the attorney-client relationship. Especially for publicly funded defense services, clients lack the tools of the market, such as control of their agent's pay, that could reduce their agency costs and optimize the defense-side adversarial efforts on which criminal process depends.

Despite the depth of defense-side agency problems, the law's first response is largely to ignore them, and in particular to deny any meaningful difference between publicly provided and privately retained counsel. The Supreme Court has been explicit on this point. In the 2009 case of *Vermont v. Brillon*, it affirmed that "the attorney is the [defendant's] agent when acting, or failing to act, in furtherance of the litigation," and "[t]he same principle applies whether counsel is privately retained or publicly assigned."[35] The Court's focus is on the formal relationship, not on a realistic account of the incentives arising from its structure, nor on the state's role in creating these incentives. The defense counsel's "duties and obligations are the same whether the lawyer is privately retained, appointed, or serving in a legal aid or defender program. *Except for the source of payment*, the relationship between a defendant and the public defender representing him is identical to that existing between any other lawyer and client."[36] For a court that gives solicitous attention to incentives in a wide range of other contexts, the absence in this setting is curious.

One can trace the Court's developing view that public defense counsel are to be taken as identical to any private principal-agent relationship, although not quite as thoroughly as the rise of private-contract and market analogies in plea bargaining law since the 1970s. A 1991 decision was the first time the Court cited the standard treatise on the private law of agency, the *Restatement (Second) of Agency*, to support the established rule that criminal defendants bear the consequences of their lawyers' procedural errors.[37] So sparse were the criminal law precedents on this point in 1991 that the Court otherwise relied mostly on civil decisions about attorney-client relationships, even though the circumstances were far removed from those of appointed defense lawyers. One such decision, for example, *Link v. Wabash R. Co.*, held that civil parties are bound by their lawyers' actions because the party "*voluntarily chose this attorney* . . . and he cannot now avoid the consequences of the acts or omissions of this *freely selected* agent."[38]

By 2009 in the *Brillon* decision, the symmetry between privately retained and publicly appointed lawyers was firm. In *Brillon*, the Court explained why delay caused by appointed attorneys counts against the defendant's speedy trial claim, even though that delay was due to the excessive caseloads imposed on appointed attorneys by the state. The only limitation the Court has hypothesized is an extreme scenario it has never encountered—"systemic breakdown in the public defender system."[39] Other doctrines similarly foreclose state responsibility for attorneys the state selects and pays; well before *Brillon*, the Court held that public defenders are not state actors for the purpose of civil rights claims brought by their former clients who allege that poor legal representation violated their constitutional rights.[40] All this seems another way in which the law strives for a particularly "private law style" of criminal process, in this instance by something close to denial of the state's unavoidable public-coordination role in providing indigent defense services.[41]

RESPONSES TO AGENCY PROBLEMS

Solutions to agency problems are not easy. One possibility is that stronger rules could dictate more specific duties for lawyers or more detailed criteria for their decision making, and enforce those obligations through judicial review or otherwise. This strategy, in fact, is what the Supreme Court implicitly counts on by its reference to "the duties and obligations of the defense lawyer" in order to erase any differences in performance between publicly appointed or privately retained lawyers. But those duties, based on rules of professional responsibility adopted by the bar of each jurisdiction, are exceedingly general and mostly precatory with regard to the kinds of lawyering discretion implicated by procedural default rules and other actions that separate skilled from mediocre lawyering. That is even truer of prosecutors' minister-of-justice duties. Lawyer discipline from bar associations addresses only the most extreme breaches of professional responsibility rules, by either prosecutors or defense attorneys. Prosecutors commonly face no bar sanctions, for example, even when courts find that they unconstitutionally failed to disclose material evidence, triggering the reversal of a conviction.[42] The same is often true for defense lawyers whom courts find to have provided constitutionally ineffective assistance of counsel.

With respect to prosecutors, one way to address these kinds of agency problems is to make more use of legal rules and judicial review, as jurisdictions outside the United States do in some form. One purpose of modestly supervising charging discretion is to reduce agency costs from prosecutorial discretion. Unsupervised discretion is precisely what enables agents to act in ways motivated by partial, private, or idiosyncratic interest. English courts' particular suspicion of prosecutors' decisions not to charge after investigations of deaths in state custody arises from a concern that prosecutors may show bias in favor of other law enforcement officials—an example of agency costs. The same kind of concern lies behind the Canadian rule—discussed more later—that allows judges to review prosecutors' decisions to disclose some pretrial evidence on grounds of security or confidentiality. Review ensures that prosecutors have sufficient public-regarding grounds for withholding evidence, and that withholding is not merely for the sake of gaining adversarial advantage. Nondisclosure for the wrong reasons (say, mere competitive advantage) rather the right ones (such as legitimate security risks for witnesses) is, like noncharging, a form of agency cost.

Across all contexts, some risk that agents won't faithfully serve the interests of their principals is inevitable, and prosecution is no exception. The standard solution, when feasible, is to closely monitor agents. Judicial review of the sort that England and Canada employ—but U.S. jurisdictions eschew—is a practical response to the prospect of prosecution agency costs. In the United States, most monitoring of prosecutors is done through the political process rather than through laws and courts. For familiar reasons, voters and political officials are ill-suited to that task.

Still, the bigger problems remain on the defense side, where the clients are mostly poorly suited to monitor their lawyers, reduce their own agency costs, and ensure adversarial process functions adequately. The evidence suggests some institutional arrangements have better track records than others. Generally speaking, it seems salaried public defenders provide better defense representation—especially if their agency is administered by an independent board—than do systems in which judges appoint private attorneys case by case.[43] (In the latter, judges often must approve defense counsel's requests for costly evidence-development efforts such as forensic analysis or expert witness testimony. That means the judge has direct control of decisions that remain in private hands when defendants have enough money to self-fund their defense.)

Much depends on whether funding levels are adequate. A few jurisdictions statutorily mandate parity or near-parity in pay or office budgets between prosecutors and defenders, which hinders one tactic by which politicized funding decisions could make the playing field less equal.[44] Other effective devices include reasonable caseload limits, training standards, and specific qualifications for handling serious offenses such as homicide.

Strategies of this sort would reduce some sources of conflicting incentives for publicly funded defenders, along with other causes—such as inadequate training or resources—that undermine adequate adversarial process. All these strategies are forms of public coordination in the "political economy" of adversarial process. But even the most bluntly "command"-style rules in this context mitigate a kind of "market failure." That is, by improving the effectiveness with which the agent acts in service of the principal's interest, these strategies improve the market-mimicking design of adversarial process. In this context in particular, the two core themes of American criminal process interact. Reducing the *political* nature of public administration and policymaking over indigent defense improves the operation of the *market-like* structure of criminal process. It strengthens the justification for procedural default rules—that attorneys serve the interests of their clients sufficiently well to justify letting the defendant's personal interests turn on his agent's discretionary decisions even when the defendant has little influence over the agent.

REVIEW FOR ADEQUATE DEFENSE REPRESENTATION

Beyond attention to the structure by which indigent defense is provided, one other body of law addresses the problem of lawyers who poorly represent their client's interests: the constitutional guarantee of effective assistance of counsel defined in *Strickland v. Washington*. That standard is explicitly—many would say notoriously—deferential to the defense attorney's poor professional performances (although that deference is not unusual among common law systems).[45] Modest effort, mediocre legal skill, tactical misjudgments, and even some degree of negligence pass judicial scrutiny. The case law includes some scandalous examples, such as lawyers who fell asleep during jury trials in homicide prosecutions, misunderstood governing law, or did woefully little factual investigation.[46] (In the last decade, the Supreme Court has reversed several death sentences after finding that defense attorneys failed to discover or utilize significant evidence that would have aided their clients.)[47] Moreover, formally under this doctrine, *reasonable* lawyer decisions (say, to skip one option for investigating facts) that are later recognized to have *prejudiced* the defendant do not justify reversing the conviction.

   The *Strickland* standard is intentionally lax; it catches only the most egregious instances of poor lawyering. The sorts of attorney decisions that trigger procedural default, such as failures to object to evidence or jury instructions, rarely amount to *Strickland* violations. If they did, *Strickland* would nullify the effect of default rules by providing an escape from the forfeiture they impose. But the price is that defendants suffer for the missteps of their attorneys. The right to effective defense counsel provides only a minimal safeguard against the risks created by the interaction of procedural default rules and agency problems. In other words, defendants pay for their lawyers' missteps that result in procedural forfeiture but that are not bad enough to violate *Strickland*. That makes procedural default rules less effective for their intended purpose of encouraging advocates' diligence in the first trial process. For this reason, the guarantee of effective defense representation does little to reduce risks inherent in adversarial procedure, which not only depends on lawyers to represent parties' interests, but depends wholly on the parties to gather all the evidence and identify all the relevant law. Put differently, agency problems in the attorney-client relationship are a kind of "market failure" in adversary process that the right to effective counsel does little to forestall. The better way to remedy those failures is to impose less procedural default—which increases overall litigation costs—or to have adequately funded indigent defense systems, which has proven impossible to do consistently in the United States, where policymaking on criminal justice is decentralized and often politicized.

Strickland review, like the *Jackson* standard for evidence sufficiency, strongly defers to party discretion over the factual record. In doing so, both doctrines limit judicial responsibility for criminal judgments. *Strickland* is the sole authority for courts to review whether the defense adequately fulfilled its adversarial role in investigating facts, producing evidence, and informing the court of relevant law. But *Strickland* is exceedingly deferential, in part because judicial review in this context is entirely *post hoc*, when everyone has incurred considerable sunk costs in the process that produced the conviction. Courts could be more proactive *before* a trial or guilty plea in confirming that the defense attorney has done her job adequately, but they rarely are. At a level of local institutions, courts could adapt the doctrine of effective assistance (as very few have) to police gross underfunding of indigent defense systems.[48] At the level of the individual case, trial judges could take steps to detect and prevent inadequate representation without overstepping the boundaries of adversarial tradition. Before trial or plea hearings, judges might require counsel to describe with some specificity their case preparation—say, that they have spoken to witnesses, reviewed key documents, and made plausible investigative efforts. Without invading attorney-client privilege or second-guessing lawyers' tactical decisions, this basic inquiry could help prevent ineffective assistance before the stage of postconviction review where concerns about finality weigh heavily. Instead of any of this, however, *Strickland* doctrine is one more manifestation of the priority for private ordering in criminal process, and private responsibility for the integrity of outcomes.

Calibrating Public Responsibilities of Prosecutors and Judges

PROSECUTION DISCLOSURE DUTIES

Most of the rules and doctrines considered so far either concern the defense side exclusively or, as a practical matter, tend to matter more for the defense. But rules that exclusively govern prosecutors reflect the same privatizing orientation—the same emphasis on party interests and discretion, and the same marginal role for public values that lead to stronger means of state responsibility for those values. An especially clear example in federal constitutional law appears when juxtaposing the U.S. rule with its counterparts in other common law systems.

Federal Due Process Doctrine

State and federal prosecutors have the same obligation, as a matter of constitutional due process, to disclose certain kinds of evidence in the government's possession. The scope of this duty has been specified over a series of Supreme Court decisions, but its key components, as defined by *Brady v. Maryland* and subsequent cases, boil down to this: prosecutors must disclose any exculpatory evidence in their possession or possessed by other state agencies such as the police, as well as any evidence that impeaches (or undermines the credibility of) the government's witnesses. Failures to disclose such evidence justify a conviction's reversal, even if prosecutors did not act in bad faith. But the duty is limited in significant ways beyond applying only to evidence that favors the defense. It applies, in effect, only to *material* evidence—evidence so significant that, in the hindsight of appellate review, there is a reasonable probability that the judgment would have been different if the evidence had come to light. (When evidence meets *that* standard, prosecutors arguably should drop the case rather than merely disclose the damning sources of proof.)[49] The *Brady* duty does not apply until *trial*, so disclosure is not constitutionally required before a guilty plea. (Nor, if the state finds such evidence in its possession after trial, does it apply postconviction.)[50] Finally—as is well known—defendants can waive prosecution disclosure. In that sense the duty is not fully mandatory. Whether the government will reveal exculpatory evidence is one more bargaining chip in party negotiations.[51]

This duty clearly contrasts with procedural rules that depend on partisan self-interest or political judgment to accomplish a crucial aspect of the adjudication process. It is a straightforward legal command. Further, it is asymmetrical—it limits only the prosecution's power to handle disclosure with solely partisan adversarial goals in mind. Yet it is hardly unusual, or unusually strong. Criminal justice systems of all advanced democracies have equivalent duties. The tradition of disclosing the state's evidentiary file to the defense has a longer history in civil law jurisdictions than in common law ones, where it has generally been adopted only in the last half century.[52] More important, the disclosure duty's significant limits are justified by the familiar rationales that undermine broadly conceived public obligations—an emphasis on prosecutors as executive law enforcement agents rather than ministers of justice; a constrained role for judges; and a preoccupation with competing interests rather than public rights and norms critical to fair criminal process.

The first clue lies in the disclosure duty's limitation to "material" evidence, under a definition of materiality that means not merely "relevant" but something that undermines confidence in a conviction.[53] That qualification leaves it to *prosecutors* to sort out, in private, what undisclosed information is meaningful enough to fall under the disclosure duty. A stronger public norm would require disclosure of *all* exculpatory evidence. Under that kind of rule, defendants rather than prosecutors would assess whether evidence is material *to the defense case.*

More telling is the form of due process analysis the Court has favored as it developed the disclosure doctrine. *Brady* justified disclosure of exculpatory evidence as essential to a fair trial, which the Court took to be a primary public interest on par with law enforcement: "Society wins not only when the guilty are convicted but when criminal trials are fair; our system of the administration of justice suffers when any accused is treated unfairly." That language, however, has never again been used by the Court. The Court moved away from such principle-based rationales for disclosure in favor of a more instrumental analysis. In *United States v. Ruiz*, it compared the relative interests at stake for each party, implicitly taking prosecutors and defendants simply as rival partisans. It found law enforcement interests to be much weightier, and concluded unanimously that prosecutors must be allowed to bargain with defendants (aggressively) to escape disclosure obligations. Otherwise, disclosure "could seriously interfere with the Government's interest in securing . . . guilty pleas," and also "disrupt ongoing investigations and expose prospective witnesses to serious harm." Barring negotiated waivers of disclosure could "could force the Government to abandon its general practice of not 'disclos[ing] to a defendant pleading guilty information that would reveal the identities of cooperating informants, undercover investigators, or other prospective witnesses'" and "could require the Government to devote substantially more resources to trial preparation prior to plea bargaining, thereby depriving the plea-bargaining process of its main resource-saving advantages."[54]

The Canadian Alternative

The Supreme Court of Canada defined the equivalent duty under the nation's Charter of Rights and Freedoms. Its decision in *R. v. Stinchcombe* makes for a startling contrast.[55] The duty in both countries rests on equivalent constitutional text. Section 7 of the Canadian Charter guarantees that no one will be deprived of life or liberty "except in accordance with the principles of fundamental justice."[56] The U.S. Constitution's due process clauses in the Fifth and Fourteenth Amendments guarantee no deprivation of life or liberty "without due process of law." Yet the Canadian rule is significantly broader. *Stinchcombe* requires prosecutors to disclose *all relevant* evidence—inculpatory or exculpatory, without the high materiality standard that limits the U.S. disclosure mandate to evidence that would probably change the trial outcome. Also, Canadian disclosure must start at a much earlier stage: "initial disclosure should occur before the accused is called upon to elect the mode of trial or to plead."[57]

More striking than its breadth are *Stinchcombe's* rationales, and the judicial intuitions that lie behind them. Justice Sopinka's opinion for the Court found it "difficult to justify the position which clings to the notion that the Crown has no legal duty to disclose all relevant information"[58]—a notion to which U.S. judges still very much cling. The U.S. and Canadian high courts assessed the same practical arguments for and against disclosure—its likely effects on guilty pleas, and on the courts' or prosecutors' efficiency, as well as the probable risks to witnesses or ongoing investigations. But their conclusions are nearly mirror images of each other. Where *Ruiz* worried that greater disclosure would impede guilty pleas so much that it would trigger "radical change in the criminal justice process" and ruin plea bargaining's "resource-saving advantages," *Stinchcombe* predicted that greater disclosure would *increase* guilty pleas, saving time and reducing delays. Where *Ruiz* assumed that the "added value" of disclosing impeachment evidence "is often limited" and provides "small benefit" compared to the heavy burdens it puts on prosecutors, *Stinchcombe* rejected that assumption, noting that undisclosed impeachment evidence has contributed in past cases to wrongful convictions.

Both courts recognized the need to protect some government witnesses, particularly confidential informants, from public disclosure. The U.S. solution postpones the entire disclosure duty until trial, and lets prosecutors negotiate their way out of disclosure. In contrast, Canadian doctrine sets the initial disclosure duty at a much earlier pretrial stage but then gives prosecutors discretion to decide the "timing and manner of disclosure" if "serious prejudice or even harm may result to a person who has supplied evidence or information" to the government or if "early disclosure may impede completion of an investigation."[59] Those qualifications sound like American-style deference to executive-branch judgment, but the Canadian Supreme Court coupled them with an admonishment never urged by the U.S. Supreme Court: "delayed disclosure on this account is not to be encouraged and should be rare." More significantly, executive leeway on these disclosure calls were joined with a checks-and-balances limit that U.S. courts shun—judicial review of prosecutorial discretion. Canadian courts double-check executive-branch assessments that nondisclosure is justified by evaluating the risks to witnesses or to ongoing investigations, or by the irrelevance of the evidence, and they do so pretrial rather than postconviction.

Implications of Contrasting Rules and Rationales
Pretrial judicial supervision strengthens the responsibility of the state—the *state* writ large, rather than as a synonym for executive-branch

enforcement—to safeguard disclosure and the constitutional principles that demand it. *Stinchcombe* accomplishes this as well by taking the prosecutor's ministerial role seriously as a core reason for disclosure. "It cannot be over-emphasized that the purpose of a criminal prosecution is not to obtain a conviction," and prosecutors "have a duty to see that *all* available legal proof of the facts is presented. . . . The role of prosecutor excludes any notion of winning or losing; his function is a matter of public duty. . . . [T]he fruits of the investigation . . . are not the property of the Crown for use in securing a conviction but the property of the public to be used to ensure that justice is done."[60] The *Brady* decision alluded to a broad conception of the state's interests in its assertion that "society wins when criminal trials are fair," but the U.S. Supreme Court has never referenced the minister-of-justice norm in any of its disclosure-duty decisions.[61] Instead the focus on the practical implications of rules for competing party interests is another marker of the more partisan (or partial) conception of the prosecutor. The greater emphasis on parties as adversaries—rather than on judges and prosecutors as officials with responsibilities for the full range of the state's interests in criminal process—contributes, if only subtly, to the sharper private law style of American criminal justice.

WEAK JUDGES AND THE MINIMAL PUBLIC NATURE OF ADJUDICATION

Brady disclosure doctrine not only limits the scope of the ministerial norm for prosecutors. It also defines an additional restriction on judicial power. The same is true of American law's limits on judicial review of prosecutor charging decisions, and in the procedural default rules canvassed earlier. All of these rules enhance party power or responsibility, but they are also, by implication, judicial-constraint rules. In various ways these rules deprive courts of the power to correct failures that arise from party decisions, including lawyers' inadvertence. *Jackson* doctrine restricts appellate courts' power to correct erroneous judgments by limiting their consideration to the factual record that the parties created. *Griffith* limits judicial power to retroactively apply new constitutional rules consistently to all cases on direct appeal. Hinging the application of evidence rules on parties' objections reinforces a norm of passivity for trial judges on top of limiting the error-correcting authority of appellate courts.

As a general matter, procedural default rules are appear in all common law adversarial systems, and in jurisdictions based in inquisitorial traditions as well.[62] Only the details and rationales of some U.S. rules are distinctly American. The same goes for duties of evidence disclosure. Although of more recent vintage, disclosure duties now appear in all common law systems, but the limits on this duty in U.S. *Brady* doctrine are not widely shared. All these policies reaffirm or strengthen the primacy of parties and the dependence of courts on them to render fair and accurate judgments. These cumulative allocations of authority also allocate responsibility. The more responsibility parties have and the less that judges have (or that prosecutors-as-ministers have), the easier it is to take the court *judgment* itself as a less *public* and more *private* product.

Default rules attribute to parties greater responsibility than courts bear for *causing* the content of the judgment. That justifies giving them the lion's share of responsibility for the integrity of the judgment as well. Default rules focus on which party *caused* a specific error—or allowed an error to go uncorrected. Their aim is to encourage parties to exercise carefully their vast discretion in the litigation process and to help prevent errors by opponents or judges. At the same time they serve these instrumental goals, procedural default rules also help to *justify* repercussions from parties' decisions (or from their passivity). At a minimum, the consequences are lost opportunities to correct errors that occurred during litigation. At worst, parties also lose any chance to correct final judgments that are partially or even wholly erroneous. If a party defaulted on a chance to offer evidence, challenge evidence, or correct a mistaken jury instruction, then the party either actively or passively *caused* that gap in evidence or legal error. That justifies making the party bear any ill effects of its lapse on the final judgment. Some risk of error is inevitable in legal process, and emphasizing this kind of causation is one way to assign responsibility for errors that the justice system tolerates.

Focusing on causal contributions of this sort, however, is not the only way to assign responsibility for errors and outcomes. Events have multiple causes; choosing one while ignoring others is a way of allocating obligations and blame. Particularly in a public law context like this, the state could be understood to carry greater responsibility for the integrity of both the process and final judgments. It already does so in some ways, most obviously through the burden and standard of proof borne by the prosecution. The prosecution duty to disclose exculpatory evidence reflects the same priority, although the Canadian disclosure doctrine shows that American law does not go as far as it might. At other stages of law enforcement administration, the state has a political if not legal obligation to prevent harm that other actors cause. That is why we blame public officials for failing to prevent acts of terrorism, or for failing to reduce crime rates.

Adversarial procedure expects less of the state in this respect. Strong finality and procedural default rules are one means to extend the private law style of adjudication and reduce the state's responsibility for errors by its courts.

To increase it, the state would have to be more proactive in ensuring that the party-compiled evidentiary record is sufficient for accurate fact-finding, and in correcting legal errors by trial judges. But that would undermine the utility of the state's weak role, which strengthens parties' incentives to play their adversarial parts in a system that depends on them to do so. The consequences of this modest state role are easier to accept on a constrained view of what are the public interests at stake in adjudication. Downplaying *Brady*'s (and *Stinchcombe*'s) emphasis on what "society wins" from fair procedures or what "our system suffers" from miscarriages of justice reinforces that private law style of adversarialism by giving primary attention to party interests.

In its fullest and unvarnished form, this understanding removes the state altogether from any responsibility for the reliability of convictions and leaves it only the role of providing the parties with a fair *opportunity* to win accurate outcomes from partisan battle. The starkest characterization of American law on this point is surely that of Justice Scalia, who has made clear he sees no grounds for change:

> This Court has never held that the Constitution forbids the execution of a convicted defendant who has had a full and fair trial but is later able to convince a habeas court that he is "actually" innocent. Quite to the contrary, we have repeatedly left that question unresolved, while expressing considerable doubt that any claim based on alleged "actual innocence" is constitutionally cognizable.[63]

It bears emphasizing that the adversarial system per se does not compel this view, nor each of the specific rules considered here. All legal systems must impose limits on litigation with finality rules and procedural defaults. But adversarialism does not necessitate, for example, severe limits on new evidence of actual innocence, or the *Brady* doctrine's constraints on prosecution disclosure. Where procedural rules go further than the adversarial procedure requires, other ideas and values are at work. Among them are assessments of how much to spend on relitigation in a world of scarce resources. But also in the mix is an aversion to active judges and restrictions on parties' autonomy;[64] a preference for more partisan prosecution norms coupled with a deference to executive discretion; and high value on access to the private legal services market but only modest concern about agency costs that defense lawyers impose on their clients.

All of this is consistent with—and a manifestation of—the liberal market's distaste for state intervention. On Justice Scalia's description, the state does not even aspire to assure substantively just outcomes in its legal system any more than it promises just outcomes in private market exchanges. The state doesn't promise to vindicate even private initiatives that produce evidence of wrongful convictions; much less does it seek out such evidence itself. And unlike ordinary markets, this is a context in which the state compels private participation. Free market norms—the preference for private ordering and disfavor of public coordinated outcomes or regulatory safeguards against the adversities of market interactions—inform criminal process through much more subtle and marginal choices about rules, well beyond those contexts such as plea bargaining in which the law's market rationality is explicit. Adversarial process and market processes have always shared a common structure in their reliance on party competition, motivated by self-interest, to produce public goods. Especially in recent decades, the norms of liberal markets have placed another thumb on the scale in favor of a more privatized conception of criminal process, one characterized by more responsibility for parties and less for judges, and by an instrumental rationality that devalues public interests independent of the parties' interests.

CHAPTER 6

The High Cost of Efficiency

Checks and balances were established in order that this should be "a govern-
ment of laws and not of men," . . . not to promote efficiency. . . . The purpose
was not to avoid friction, but by means of the inevitable friction . . . to save
the people from autocracy.
—*Myers v. United States (1926) (Brandeis, J., dissenting)**

The Ambition of Efficient Procedure

The previous four chapters traced the rationales of American criminal procedure rules to deep national faith in the virtues of democratic governance and
free markets. This chapter turns to some of the effects of those rules for the
broader criminal justice system. Both democratic and market-based rationales
worked consistently to advance an overarching ambition for criminal justice
administration: greater *efficiency*. Most obviously, the explicit goal of plea bargaining doctrines is to accomplish convictions more quickly and cheaply, and
for a larger volume of cases, than would be possible through trial. But the same
intent has influenced many of the rules developed to strengthen the finality
of judgments. By making procedural default easier and by limiting appellate
claims or other forms of relitigation, the rules have streamlined adjudication
process. Guilty plea rates increased from an already-high baseline; fewer appellate claims are litigated on their merits; fewer convictions are overturned.

Yet despite this embrace of ever more efficient process as both essential
and unquestionably desirable, efficiency is a trickier concept than courts and
policymakers acknowledge. The consequences of efficiency can be problematic in criminal process, as they sometimes are in other settings, even though
one would be hard pressed to learn of any downside from judicial opinions. To
be fair, the same goes for policy discussions in most other settings—product
manufacturing, environmental protection, health care provision, and much
else. In criminal justice thinking and far beyond, this is the power of market

rationality or—as Tony Judt described it—"the universal contemporary resort to 'economism,' the invocation of economics in all discussions of public affairs":

> For the last thirty years, in much of the English-speaking world (though less so in continental Europe and elsewhere), when asking ourselves whether we support a proposal or initiative, we have not asked, is it good or bad? Instead we inquire: Is it efficient? Is it productive?[1]

Judicial reasoning has been anything but an exception. Few claims meet less dissent than the ever-present necessity to make legal process more efficient. A rare exception is Justice Brandeis's argument—nearly a century ago—that the virtue of constitutional separation of powers is precisely its *inefficiency*: the "inevitable friction" between branches of government, he urged, serves a beneficial purpose.[2]

Scholars, on the other hand, do recognize some of efficiency's adverse consequences. Critics such as Stephanos Bibas stress overlooked costs of plea bargaining. Those who lament the rise of case settlement and the "vanishing" civil and criminal trials highlight, at least implicitly, some of the costs of efficiency.[3] Nonetheless, the general consensus is still sympathetic to the view that adjudication can ill-afford to lose much efficiency.

Although criminal adjudication is, by familiar measures, more efficient than in the past, the terms by which its efficiency is assessed leave open the question whether—even in predominantly *economic or budgetary terms*—the gains of faster, cheaper adjudication are truly desirable and really outweigh the costs. This chapter focuses on risks and consequences of efficiency in criminal process that have received less attention. It starts by considering some complications in the definition—the very nature—of "efficiency." Concluding that one process is more efficient than another is often as much a policy judgment as an objective observation. Without clear agreement on what one wants to do efficiently and on what counts, or does not count, as a "cost" in achieving that goal, "efficiency" is indeterminate. Following this, this chapter takes up some complications that stem from the *gains* that efficiency yields. How do policymakers use the savings that come from resolving criminal prosecutions more quickly and cheaply? Do they hire fewer judges and lawyers? Keep the same staff levels and take on more cases? Or do something else altogether? The first challenge involves figuring out whether a new legal process really is more efficient. The second involves figuring out whether that achievement has done (or can do) much good—or possibly, whether its effects are inadvertently harmful.

These questions are more complicated in the context of criminal process than in some other settings, because the government controls not only the *supply* of criminal process, it also has a great deal of influence over the *demand* for it. The "supply" is simply all the necessary parts of the criminal justice system, especially the number of judges and prosecutors, as well as publicly financed defense counsel, available to handle cases, along with crime labs, clerks, and the like. If the criminal justice system were overstaffed relative to demand for its services, there would be little pressure to increase its efficiency. "Demand" refers, basically, to caseloads—the criminal prosecutions that courts must adjudicate. That number is partly a function of crime rates, but also of many other things over which the state has direct control. Because the volume of cases that courts must adjudicate rise or fall for many reasons, it is hard to tell whether the supply of criminal process is merely rising to meet demand or whether it is *driving* demand. Sorting out this question of cause and effect is critical to determining whether it is really "necessary" to make criminal process more efficient, meaning that greater efficiency is needed to meet the demand placed on courts by increasing caseloads. It could be that the volume of criminal prosecutions is growing because courts can handle more cases—that is, there is more adjudication "capacity" available—rather than because of some independent factor like rising crime rates.

This fundamental ambiguity in cause and effect undermines the claims, by the Supreme Court and other policymakers, that caseload pressures compel criminal procedure to become more efficient—by which they mean maximizing (and speeding up) guilty pleas while minimizing postconviction challenges. There are good reasons to think that those claims of necessity are largely wrong, and good reasons also to conclude that the procedures adopted in the name of efficiency are problematic in ways criminal justice officials fail to appreciate. The coerciveness of some guilty plea offers, the unfairness of punishing defendants for the sins of their lawyers, the loss of juries as a democratic check on prosecutors and judges—these consequences of efficient criminal procedure are widely recognized (even if there is disagreement about whether they should be lamented). Much less acknowledged are the counterproductive—even perverse—effects of efficient adjudication on the broader criminal justice system. Put bluntly, efficient criminal process is an important cause of the contemporary carceral state. Having eliminated too much beneficial friction, hyper-efficient procedures lead the state to reduce its financial investment in adjudication, especially in courts, prosecution, and public defense. Proportionately less spending on that stage of the criminal justice system allows (even implicitly encourages) proportionately more on policing—which supplies more cases for prosecutors and courts—and on prisons, which administer the consequences of those judgments that criminal courts churn out ever more efficiently.

Efficiency and Its Consequences

DEFINING EFFICIENCY

Efficiency has different meanings in different contexts, depending on the purpose to which it is put. An example found often in legal scholarship is Pareto efficiency, which defines one standard (but not the only one) for efficiency in the allocation of goods. When there is no other way to reallocate goods that can benefit one agent without lowering the welfare of another, an allocation is said to be Pareto efficient.[4] Alternately, a definition of *efficiency* tailored to assessing production rather than allocation is closer to what courts and policymakers have in mind when they talk about efficient criminal process. Maximum production efficiency can be defined as the lowest-cost method for producing goods, or as "allocating the available resources between industries so that it would not be possible to produce more of some goods without producing less of any others."[5] Efficiency in this sense describes the ratio between the resources required for a production process (such as trials or plea negotiations) and the outputs of that process (such as convictions).[6] One production system is more efficient than another if it yields more output without using more resources, or the same output using fewer. A *gain* in productive efficiency can take the form either of more outputs or of lower production costs, compared to alternative methods of production.

EFFECTS OF EFFICIENCY GAINS

Finding ways to reap clear efficiency gains is not the end of the matter, however, because those gains have different kinds of effects in different settings, not all of them desirable. The point is easiest to see in a specific context such as energy efficiency, a field in which the problems of efficiency gains have garnered considerable research attention. Take the example of vehicle fuel efficiency. Improving fuel efficiency might enable a car to travel thirty-five miles on a gallon of fuel, when its former model could travel only thirty miles per gallon. The efficiency gain in this case can be described in at least two ways, depending on one's choice between reference points. If the baseline is a specific level of "output" or activity such as driving thirty miles, then the gain results in lower fuel consumption—from one gallon to about 0.85 of a gallon. However, by taking a fixed amount of fuel—one gallon—as the baseline, the gain results in more activity: driving thirty-five miles instead of thirty. In this latter usage, it is easier to see greater "efficiency" as synonymous with more "productivity," although the vehicle is more productive (per unit of fuel) regardless of the baseline.

This example illustrates not only the different ways that gains from more efficient production can be used (more driving or less fuel consumption) but also how those options create a central concern for energy policy. As a matter of policy, one way to make use of the gains from improved fuel efficiency is more desirable than the other. The policy goal is nearly always to reduce energy consumption while keeping activity or production steady—that is, doing the same things while using less energy to do them. But one might instead exploit those gains in efficiency by *increasing* activity levels (for example, by driving more) while using the same energy as before. When efficiency improvements are motivated by *private* goals, more activity (or production) is oftentimes the goal. A factory, for instance, might improve its energy efficiency so it can produce more goods at the same cost. The basic point is that efficiency gains frequently can be used in a variety of ways, depending on the context. Sticking with the motor vehicle example, greater efficiency might be used not to improve a car's fuel economy but to improve its *mass* per gallon: more efficient designs could allow larger, heavier vehicles to get, say, thirty miles per gallon rather than their previous rate of twenty-five miles per gallon.

In sum, figuring out a way to improve efficiency is one thing, but figuring out what to do with the gains from it is another. Depending on the context, how an individual or a company—or a justice system—will use efficiency gains can be difficult to control or even predict, because the choice depends on who is making it and what their preferences are.

A private firm that finds a way to produce goods more efficiently (which means producing them more cheaply) has some control over what it does with that gain. It might produce more goods while production costs remain unchanged, or it might keep production quantities the same and reap the lower production costs as profits. Market conditions might restrict the firm's options; there may be no demand for more of the goods. But if market demand is "price-elastic"—if people will buy more of a good when its price falls—then the firm could lower the price of its products and sell more units.[7] What will happen, however, if rival companies have improved their own production efficiency to the same degree (so that they, too, can sell each unit more cheaply)? Competition might force the firm to use its newfound efficiency to lower its unit price, merely so that it can continue to sell the same quantity of goods as before.

Whatever the possibilities in particular settings, a private firm in the end is probably seeking ways to maintain or increase its profits. Reducing its total energy usage may or may not be a means to that end. Government policy, by contrast, typically *does* have the goal of reducing total energy usage (at least, carbon-based energy) in mind, when its ultimate goal is to reduce externalities from carbon-based energy use, such as climate change. If energy reduction is the policy ambition, then facilitating private firms' energy efficiency can be a poor strategy for achieving it. Decisions about what to do with efficiency *gains* will be made by the firms, and their interests may lead them to take those gains in some manner other than reduced energy consumption.

The same is true with the fuel efficiency of automobiles. Car makers produce more efficient vehicles, partly in response to government mandated fuel standards but sometimes also in response to market demands. Private individuals buy and drive those vehicles and thus decide how they will take advantage of these efficiency gains, although market forces (such as the price of fuel) influence their decisions as well. More fuel-efficient cars make driving cheaper. As a consequence, car owners may drive more. According to a standard demand function, demand rises as prices drop, at least when all else is equal (i.e., when nonprice determinants of demand do not cut the other way).[8] As driving gets cheaper due to greater fuel efficiency, some people choose to drive more often, rather than driving the same amount as they did before while spending less on fuel thanks to their newly efficient cars. If public policy aims to reduce fuel consumption, then improving fuel efficiency is not a sure-fire way to accomplish it. For these reasons, energy and environmental economists worry that improvements in energy efficiency might not change overall energy consumption, or may even result in *greater* usage.[9] Efficiency improvements like these that boost rather than cut consumption are commonly labeled a rebound effect, or a Jevons effect.[10]

Rebound effects are a problem only when efficiency triggers more *undesirable* consumption, according to some policy criteria such as an ambition to decrease carbon emissions. In those cases, *inefficiency*—or its equivalent, a high price—is beneficial. It reduces demand, just as a higher fuel-tax discourages fuel consumption. For actors in private markets, efficiency that reduces the price of a product and thereby increases demand for it is often the goal. Boosting demand for their products is exactly what manufacturing firms and retailers hope to do. For the most part that is not the case, however, for any rebound effects that follow from improvements in the efficiency of criminal procedure.

Supply and Demand for Criminal Adjudication

There is little debate that demand for criminal adjudication has increased over time. Criminal caseloads (like civil caseloads) have grown steadily and significantly for several decades or more, despite occasional periods of slow growth or even modest declines from one year to the next.[11] To prevent backlogs, higher caseloads mean that the supply of adjudication services—the capacity of courts to process cases—must go up.

EXPANDING ADJUDICATION CAPACITY

Several options exist for responding to greater demand for adjudication. Occasionally adjudication systems have excess capacity—judges without enough work to fill each day—with which to accommodate higher caseloads. In some places, more of this kind of slack exists than officials concede.[12] Chapter 4 noted studies of local court systems that were capable of adjudicating more cases by trial than they actually did (or than officials believed they could do).[13] Nevertheless, this kind of slack in the system frequently is not available or sufficient as a response to higher caseloads.

Alternately, jurisdictions could simply add to their criminal justice infrastructure at a pace that matches their heavier caseloads. Few if any have taken this route, which the Supreme Court has long assumed is infeasible. At least as a matter of legislative policy, the justices appear to be right. Jurisdictions have not added enough new judges, courtrooms, prosecutors, and other staff to match the growth in caseloads, certainly not enough to adjudicate most criminal cases by traditional trials.

A third possibility is that jurisdictions could make *trial* process more efficient, so that existing courts could try more cases to judgment without more personnel. Over time criminal trial process has become less efficient as it has become more formal and professionalized. "Lawyerization"—having counsel representing both sides, along with increasing legal formality that requires a lawyer's skills—was a step in that evolution, as was more careful jury selection, greater pretrial disclosure, and other changes to accommodate evolving standards of fair process.[14] Even within the bounds of contemporary due process principles, it is certainly possible to reform trial practices to make trials quicker without compromising fairness and accuracy—in other words, to make trials more efficient.[15] Those kinds of reforms would enable trial courts to meet some portion of the demand from rising caseloads without adding more judges and prosecutors, although how many more is uncertain.

All of these strategies have surely played roles in responding to higher caseloads. But none are the predominant route that U.S. justice systems have taken. Instead, they have increased the supply of criminal process by substituting guilty pleas for trials, and then by making the process for negotiating and accepting guilty pleas quicker and cheaper. (The same seems to be true for justice systems elsewhere, given the worldwide trend toward plea bargaining or similar nontrial modes of disposition.) Guilty pleas are more efficient than trials because they enable courts to produce criminal convictions at a lower "unit cost," or cost per judgment.

THE AMBIGUITY OF EFFICIENT ADJUDICATION

Quantitative measures, such as judgments-per-year-per-judge, are clearly what courts and policymakers care about, but it is worth noting that efficiency on these terms comes at a cost to other functions of trial process. The guilty plea process is not more efficient than trials at ensuring victim participation or democratic supervision of judges and prosecutors, as plea-bargain critics and jury proponents point out.[16] Those trade-offs, however, have not dissuaded generations of Supreme Court Justices or other criminal justice officials from doing all they can to encourage the resolution of most prosecutions through guilty pleas. With a singular focus on caseloads, the Court has expressed much more fear about resolving fewer cases by guilty pleas than it has about the loss of jury trials to serve interests other than speedy case resolution.[17]

Even though bench trials have proven to be a practical alternative to both jury trials and guilty pleas in some U.S. jurisdictions,[18] party negotiations are surely a quicker way to reach judgments than the typical trial process. Accepting that point, however, there remain many options for how to go about the process of negotiated settlements. The U.S. military justice system's meticulous set of safeguards lies at one extreme, but courts in England, Canada, and elsewhere have achieved very high rates of guilty pleas despite stronger regulation on various aspects of plea bargaining, as chapter 4 described. The Supreme Court has been a relentless voice for the view not merely that plea bargaining is essential for U.S. criminal justice but that it needs to be as fast and efficient as possible. Courts and prosecutors are too overwhelmed to function under rules that would even marginally reduce the speed with which negotiated judgments are reached. More expansive evidence disclosure before plea negotiations, more constraints on bargaining terms or prosecutorial vindictiveness, or more rigorous judicial inquiry into the accuracy of negotiated pleas, are luxuries American courts cannot afford.

Despite the strength of this conventional wisdom, the idea that U.S. criminal courts would crumble under the weight of their caseloads if guilty pleas were governed by anything other than the prevailing free-market-style rules for plea bargaining is not only unconfirmed, it is implausible. That conventional view overlooks the ways that efficient adjudication can *contribute* to higher caseloads rather than merely respond to them. Compared to trials (or simply to a more formal, regulated plea process) quick guilty pleas push down the "unit cost" of turning a charge into a conviction, which sets the stage for rebound effects. The standard demand function suggests that reducing the "price" of criminal process will trigger increased demand for it. Improving the efficiency of adjudication not only helps courts to meet the demand placed on them by higher numbers of criminal cases, it may *encourage more cases.* Caseloads are in part a *consequence* of plea bargaining rather than simply a cause.

Oddly, given their collective affinity for market theory, courts and policy-makers never acknowledge this possibility. Instead, the universal assumption is that the quantity of criminal cases is wholly independent of (or exogenous to) the cost of criminal process.[19] Criminal prosecutions increase because criminals commit more crimes, the thinking goes, or because law enforcement has improved its abilities to arrest and charge a larger portion of the offenders out there in the world. In this understanding, caseloads are wholly exogenous to the criminal process; they rise or fall for reasons having nothing to do with the cost or availability of adjudication. Demand for adjudication is unaffected by the supply of it—or more precisely, by the price for it.

Despite its intuitive appeal, there are reasons to be skeptical of this view, not the least of which is its tension with basic principles of supply and demand. Recall from chapter 4, for example, the evidence that local court systems do not vary their rates of plea bargaining as their caseloads rise or fall, nor does a jurisdiction with lighter caseloads necessarily have more trials than a similar jurisdiction with higher caseloads; local officials in all these settings usually perceive a *need* to resolve most cases by guilty pleas rather than trials.[20] More important, the volume of criminal prosecutions is much more discretionary—that is, much more a matter of policy—than a focus on crime rates would suggest.

Law enforcement officials and policymakers have a great deal of control over the numbers of criminal prosecutions filed in courts. Their decisions can (or should) take into account changes in the price and availability of criminal process. Once the unparalleled efficiency of American criminal adjudication is seen in the broader context of the American criminal justice system, there are good reasons to conclude that the criminal process could tolerate—indeed, benefit from—a version of Justice Brandeis's beneficial "friction." Contemporary criminal caseloads, and the carceral consequences that follow from them, suggest that a little *less* efficiency in adjudication could help to guide public policymaking to better calibrations about the desirable amount of liability and punishment.

OFFICIAL DISCRETION OVER DEMAND
FOR CRIMINAL PROCESS

The reasons why criminal as well as civil caseloads have grown steadily for decades are many and complex. Various features of modernity, including urbanization, technological advances, and ever-expanding commercial activity, have led to more crime, more civil injuries, more contract disputes, more forms of risk, and thus generally greater expectations that more kinds of interests deserve legal protection. There is much more to this story, but for present purposes the basic point is that these trends contribute to increasing caseloads both because there are more incidents of harmful or risky conduct and because the state changes the kinds of conduct it defines as criminal. No reliable, long-term data exist for any crimes save for homicide,[21] so it is difficult to connect rising criminal caseloads to rising per capita rates at which various offenses are being committed.[22] Assessing the relative magnitude of the kinds of activities that states define as criminal is not much easier, but it seems a safe assumption that criminalization policies have a significant effect on the caseloads of courts and prosecutors.[23]

One reason prosecutors are filing more criminal cases is that, over the past century or more, criminal codes have steadily expanded. Legislatures can literally raise the crime rate by enacting new offenses and lower it by abolishing existing ones. (For example, in a few states, rates for certain marijuana offenses plunged to zero after new laws legalized the drug's possession and sale.)

Second, governments can adjust funding levels for law enforcement, which affects the rates at which crimes are detected or solved and offenders arrested. Those rates are also affected by better technologies and strategies for investigating crime and gathering evidence, and by choices about enforcement priorities. A dedicated drug-crime task force usually means more drug-crime arrests. (This is especially true for crimes based on consensual conduct with no direct victim or harm, such as sale of drugs or firearms, and crimes of preparation, such as conspiracy or providing material support.) All of those policy choices can affect how many criminal charges are filed in courts even if the background rate of offending does not change. Except for homicides and a few other offenses like car thefts, the background rate of offending remains murky because the data are contingent on what people choose to report to authorities, or what law enforcement has been able to discover.[24]

Finally, prosecutors have discretion over what offenses to charge, just as police have discretion over making arrests. Studies confirm that prosecutors decline to prosecute a significant portion of cases presented to them by police, though the rates vary greatly among different prosecution agencies and for types of offenses.[25] When prosecutors decline to charge more cases, criminal caseloads decline, again regardless of the background rate of criminal offending. If only for these reasons, criminal cases are not solely a function of how many thefts, assaults, and drug sales occur each week. Just like at the policing level, public policy priorities play a big role in the number and type of criminal charges filed in courts, so those policies directly affect the "demand" placed on courts. Some examples make this relationship clear.

The "war on drugs" is a large-scale example that involves a variety of enforcement strategies by federal, state, and local agencies. The federal Department of Justice has an explicit policy not to pursue certain federal marijuana offenses if the same conduct is legal under state law.[26] Some city police and prosecution agencies, such as Seattle's (before that state legalized marijuana), made marijuana possession a low-enforcement priority. Others, such as New York City's, have made the same offenses a high priority, which placed a consequently greater caseload burden on local courts.[27] Additionally, the proliferation of drug courts has led to more variation in how different jurisdictions resolve the drug cases that make it into the judicial system. Both state and federal prosecutors have experimented with strategies such as Project Safe Neighborhoods and the High Point Drug Initiative, in which officials meet with gang members or other offenders to negotiate greater law compliance. By exchanging nonprosecution and job assistance for future law-abiding behavior and help in reducing local violence, these strategies have had some success at preventing crime while also decreasing the number of prosecutions.[28]

U.S. immigration policy provides a different large-scale example. Indeed, the federal government has adopted explicit policies, as a matter of executive discretion, not to prosecute some criminal offenses and not to initiate civil enforcement actions against some classes of undocumented immigrants.[29] Meanwhile, the Justice Department has announced policies in recent years making corporate fraud, terrorism-related activity, and child pornography high-enforcement priorities. In state justice systems, prosecution policies have varied widely in the last decade on whether and how to charge "sexting" conduct (using phones to send explicit photos) committed by teenagers. State and local policies on domestic violence have also changed over time. Intrafamily violence was once shielded from prosecution by social norms and privacy doctrines and for a time addressed by civil family courts in many places; now it is commonly a high-priority prosecution. With regard to firearm offenses, state and federal officials have cooperated in many local districts to prosecute weapon offenses more harshly in federal courts, where more severe sentences apply, rather than in state courts.[30]

Examples of similar discretionary policy choices by legislatures are easy to find as well, especially looking across a longer time frame. The history of vice and moral crimes demonstrates the point quite easily. In the nineteenth and early twentieth centuries, temperance and prohibition movements convinced legislatures as well as prosecutors to criminalize alcohol production and use. For a time (especially in the 1920s), alcohol-related offenses inundated state and federal courts. A smaller-scale historical example is usury. Most U.S. jurisdictions criminalized high-interest loans until states started to repeal those statutes in the 1970s. By that time, opinions had shifted from viewing high-interest lending as immoral to seeing it as a benign extension of credit options to low-income borrowers.[31] A more recent trend to expand criminal liability in the United Kingdom and the United States, described by Lucia Zedner and others, is the adoption of new "risk prevention" or "pre-crime" offenses, which prohibit conduct that seems to be the earliest stages of crime preparation.[32]

To sum up, the point is simply that discretionary policy choices by public officials and policymakers play a big role in the caseload burdens placed on criminal courts. In all of these ways, the state creates more demand for criminal process but may not, at the same time, add to the available supply. The volume of criminal charges is not simply a function—arguably not even *primarily* a function—of the number of offenses committed.

This is not to deny that there are good reasons motivating some expansions of criminal liability and enforcement efforts. Certainly many factors are at play. Public opinion changes about whether or not a given kind of conduct is socially harmful. Perceptions and realities change about whether or not the commission of certain offenses—or a new kind of harmful activity—is increasing. Judgments shift about whether or not criminal punishment is an effective and appropriate response for certain kinds of wrongdoing. But in the mix of motivations for criminal justice policies affecting criminal caseloads, the relative cost of criminal process also affects these discretionary choices, and that is not necessarily good news.

ENFORCEMENT DISCRETION IN THE WAKE OF MORE EFFICIENT PROCESS

To see how more efficient criminal process can trigger more prosecutions, consider another motor-vehicle analogy, this time one focused on traffic congestion. One problem in which the role of rebound effects is well documented is highway traffic. As more vehicles use roadways, traffic exceeds road capacity and average vehicle speed—the pace of travel—slows. More car traffic is simply more demand for roadways. Thinking in basic terms of supply and demand, the answer to traffic jams would seem to be to increase the road "supply." Building more highways will meet drivers' demands and ease traffic congestion. Yet in real life, that solution repeatedly backfires. It fails so frequently that economists and planners conclude the reverse is true: according to "the law of highway congestion," building more highways does not reduce traffic congestion. Instead it triggers *more* demand, because adding road capacity reduces driving costs and so makes car travel more appealing. More drivers flock to the new lanes or new roads and use them more often, then traffic congestion returns.[33] Despite strong evidence for it, this effect is so counterintuitive that policymakers (and their constituents) have a hard time believing it, and they continue to build roads—making vehicle traffic more efficient—in the hope that expansion will relieve traffic.

Underlying this misguided intuition is the premise that driving decisions are based on drivers' needs and desires, not road capacity. People drive because they have places to go; building more roads does not change that. In fact, however, a lot of driving is more discretionary than that. Some trips are optional; some can be delayed or combined with others. Sometimes transportation options such as trains exist. Over the longer term, people increase or decrease their driving by factoring transportation options into choices about where to live and work.

There is good reason to worry that criminal process works much like road traffic. To be sure, caseloads can tax the limited capacity of courts and prosecution agencies. If judicial and prosecution workloads grow too large, backlogs develop, and the time grows between when a charge is filed and when a court renders judgment. When courts and prosecutors respond by replacing more trials with guilty pleas, and by making guilty pleas quicker and easier to accomplish, they do the equivalent of adding new highway lanes. If legislatures responded to rising caseloads instead by funding more judges, prosecutors, and public defenders, that too would be the equivalent of adding roadways. But that approach would keep the cost-per-case of criminal adjudication higher. Higher prices discourage demand. In a public policy setting like criminal justice, the response to higher prices would not be as straightforward as in an ordinary market. Nonetheless it would be more likely to trigger scrutiny of whether the public fisc really needs to "buy" so much adjudication—that is, whether public safety could be achieved with lower criminal caseloads.

The challenges posed by criminal caseloads and highway congestion both confirm the insight that, in public policy contexts, the demand function is not as straightforward as in ordinary private markets. Decisions about building highways are (or should be) partly about how much driving a polity wants to accommodate. Ignoring that question and paying attention only to current traffic levels, governments are likely (absent other constraints) to build too many roads. In the same way, decisions about judicial and prosecution staffs—*or about how efficient to make criminal adjudication*—should be partly about how much criminal law enforcement a polity wants. This insight, and the more general problem of rebound effects, greatly undermines the prevailing assumption of Supreme Court jurisprudence and criminal-process policymaking—that present-day caseloads compel every effort to accommodate them by making criminal procedure ever more efficient.[34] This view is more speculation than justification, and it misunderstands the problematic relationship between the supply and demand of fundamentally public goods. High criminal caseloads in the midst of widespread plea bargaining tells us nothing about which way the causal arrow runs. Do we plea bargain because we have more prosecutions, or do we prosecute more because we plea bargain?

HISTORICAL EVIDENCE

Seen in this light, the causes that explain America's long history of plea bargaining are more ambiguous. Plea bargaining in Middlesex County, Massachusetts, for example, first arose in the context of new offenses regulating alcohol production and distribution, according to George Fisher's definitive history. New social harms (or the fear of them) that emerged in the wake of the increase in alcohol production put real pressure on local officials and communities. At the same time, the new efficiencies that local prosecutors achieved (with judges' assent) in dispensing punishments through plea bargaining made criminal regulation a cheaper and thus more appealing policy option for responding to this new threat to public order. Thus Fisher concludes that plea bargaining arose largely because it served the self-interests of prosecutors, judges, and defense lawyers, not because caseload pressures and personnel limits left them no other choice.

Those officials define their own interests, as do people more generally. For prosecutors, that includes choices about what offenses must be charged or what conduct merits punishment. For core offenses such as intentional homicide, those decisions are usually easy. But those kinds of offenses don't fill most dockets, and they did not trigger the development of plea bargaining in early Middlesex County. What did was a policy to regulate alcohol through low-level criminal offenses, without adding to prosecution and judicial staffs. The scope of such policies surely turns in part on enforcement costs, which makes it hard to tell whether improved efficiency drives up caseloads or whether caseloads compel greater procedural efficiency.[35]

The same ambiguity runs through most of American criminal law history once one recognizes that (despite variations at the local level) the steady expansion of criminal law enforcement over two centuries coincided with reforms in law and practice that made enforcement more efficient. The nineteenth century saw the advent of police forces and public prosecution agencies, the proliferation of state and local regulatory offenses, and generally more ambitious public enforcement efforts, all in response to a perceived escalation in harmful or risk-creating conduct.[36] No doubt much of that perception was accurate, given the social changes and economic disruptions that accompanied expansions in commerce, rapid industrialization, and fast-growing urban populations. But reforms that made adjudication more efficient—waiver of the jury for criminal trials and, especially, plea bargaining—made criminal law cheaper and thus more appealing, both as a strategy to enforce ordinary health and safety regulation and to address various social concerns like labor unrest and alcohol abuse. The reasons for more criminal punishment run in both directions. Antisocial conduct "compels" state intervention. At the same time, the cheap "supply" of criminal process to quickly convert charges into convictions makes punishment a more appealing instrument of state policy.

The effect of subsidies provided by criminal process efficiency is surely stronger for more discretionary components of criminal enforcement agendas, meaning those that don't involve core offenses such as homicide or robbery. The aggressive temperance and anti-vice agendas of the early twentieth century are good examples. Guilty pleas skyrocketed in the 1920s as Prohibition laws flooded state and federal courts with alcohol-related prosecutions.[37] Caseload pressures thus likely forced changes in adjudicative practice. But adjudication's greater efficiency also made criminal law a more feasible policy strategy during Prohibition; efficiency gains enabled legislators to add new criminal offenses without proportionate increases in funding for courts and prosecutors.[38]

CONTEMPORARY EVIDENCE

Developments in more recent decades provide especially strong reasons to suspect that the efficiency gains in criminal process create rebound effects that have contributed to current policies of mass incarceration. Although guilty pleas have produced the vast majority of convictions for decades, prosecutors and judges nonetheless managed to push that share even higher in recent decades—the same period in which U.S. imprisonment rates began their unprecedented climb. In federal courts, convictions by guilty plea climbed from 86 percent of all convictions in 1970 to 97 percent in 2010.[39] In addition, the overall *conviction rate* (by trial or plea) for all federal cases went up steadily as well, from 84 percent in 1991 to 93 percent in 2010. These changes made federal courts more "productive" according to metrics focused on case processing such as the number of cases handled per judge. In 1982, prosecutors filed 63 criminal cases per federal judge. That number nearly doubled by 2010, to 116 cases per judge.[40] As federal courts became more efficient at producing convictions-per-judge, more of those convictions came with prison sentences.

From 1992 to 2010, the percentage of convicted defendants sentenced to prison rose from 70.8 percent to 81 percent.[41]

Other changes contributed to that efficiency surge as well. One is almost certainly a change in how quickly guilty plea agreements were reached. As conviction and incarceration rates rose, policies deliberately coaxed greater efficiencies from plea bargaining practices by shrinking the time invested in each guilty plea. In the 1990s, the federal government instituted "fast-track" plea bargaining policies, characterized by the kinds of defense waivers of disclosure and other rights approved by the Supreme Court in *United States v. Ruiz*.[42] In the category of cases for which this policy was first widely used—immigration-related crimes—plea rates hit 99.4 percent by 2010.[43] In the five years from 2006 to 2010, prosecutions for illegal entry/re-entry offenses also multiplied, with the result that immigration-related crimes rose from 25 percent to 36 percent of all federal cases.[44] During this time span, offenses involving unauthorized immigration that were actually committed *decreased*; that is, the exogenous crime rate declined.[45] This reduction recalls "the law of highway congestion" applied to a criminal justice system that gained new capacity by speeding up its adjudication process. There may be legitimate policy reasons for more aggressive enforcement even in an environment of declining crime. Yet drivers also have good independent reasons for driving more frequently when states expand their highways. It is hard to separate, even conceptually, the effect of more efficient process from other reasons in decisions about what to criminalize, to investigate, and to charge.

Many of the same innovations—especially more aggressive demands for defense waivers in early pretrial stages—are now widely used for other kinds of offenses, from drug crimes to large-scale corporate fraud. Federal prosecutors have used nonprosecution or deferred prosecution agreements against large corporations much more often in the last decade. As Brandon Garrett has studied in detail, with little formal litigation those agreements result in huge fines and other sanctions against firms. Under nonprosecution agreements, no charges are even filed with courts, and no judges approve the settlement terms.[46] In that context as well, a procedural innovation coincides with more use of the procedure and more judgments or judgment equivalents. In more routine drug and firearms offenses, particular statutes can provide the basis for increasing and speeding up guilty pleas. Federal prosecutors' use of 21 U.S.C. § 851, described in chapter 4, is an example.[47] What started out as a provision that prosecutors would reserve for the worst offenders was converted into a routine source of leverage for swiftly negotiated guilty pleas: plead guilty by *X* date and avoid an added 851 charge, or go to trial with one.

Data from state justice systems are less detailed but consistent. State courts and prosecution offices handled many more cases as well, at the same time that those systems became more efficient. As they drove down the "unit cost" of criminal judgments, the number of charges and judgments grew. From 1974 to 2005, the number of state prosecutors went up 59 percent, from about 17,000 to approximately 27,000. Over the same period, state court felony prosecutions grew more than *300 percent*, from roughly 300,000 a year to more than one million.[48] As a consequence, prison populations over that time quadrupled. These heavier caseloads do not seem to be explained by background rates of offending and population growth: violent crime rates rose during the first half of that period, then declined for the second; the U.S. population shot up by 38 percent.[49] The easier inference is an ordinary demand function at work: driving down the process costs of convictions leads the state to seek more convictions.

How might this work at the individual or local-agency level? As prosecutors internalize a new sense of the time and effort it takes to see charges through to conviction, they might simply charge more offenses than they did before. A change in charging discretion of this kind is what John Pfaff has uncovered in recent research. His analysis of data from a majority of states suggests that prosecutors in the 1990s and 2000s began to file charges for a larger portion of the criminal complaints and arrest reports they receive from police than they did in earlier years. Moreover, Pfaff's analysis suggests that much of the U.S. incarceration increase witnessed in recent decades can be attributed to these more aggressive charging policies, rather than solely to longer sentences or "drug war" priorities.[50] It is easy to see how more efficient adjudication process would only enhance the charging practices Pfaff identifies. Quicker, easier ways to resolve cases surely affects *what kind* of charges prosecutors elect to pursue. Offenses that were formerly more costly to resolve—usually the more serious or complex offenses—are more likely to be charged once they are cheaper and easier to turn into convictions.

On top of handling a larger share of crime reports from the police, judges and prosecutors operating at new levels of efficiency may also be ready to handle a larger share from *a larger pool* of police crime reports. That is especially true if—as in the past two decades—the occurrence of core crimes, most notably homicide, has declined dramatically while criminal justice staffing did not. To increase criminal court caseloads in that environment, police forces in many jurisdictions will need to provide a larger number of arrests and crime reports to prosecutors.

More arrests by police probably did not occur simply as a result of greater funding for police. Total funding for police grew at a somewhat slower rate over this period than it did for courts and prosecutors or for prisons (although it started from a larger baseline; spending on police has always been higher than for the other two components of criminal justice systems).[51] But police agencies have many options for generating more arrests without spending more money or hiring more cops. Switching to those strategies probably explains why funding did not need to grow in order for arrests and crime reports to grow.

Policing can be made more "productive" in this sense because some kinds of arrests can be increased with little cost, especially petty offenses that pedestrian or traffic patrols can easily detect. The most publicized example of this in recent years has been the New York City Police Department's ability to ratchet up charges for drug- and weapons-possession and various "quality of life" violations through street patrols and intensive stop-and-frisk searches.[52] The department multiplied charges of this type exponentially without anything close to a proportionate increase in personnel. Lots of other choices about investigative tactics and priorities present the same kinds of opportunities. Focusing on arrests of street drug *sellers* requires less police effort than sting operations targeted at buyers, and focusing on drug transactions in public spaces requires much less police investment than the same conduct in more secluded settings.[53] In sum, by adopting different enforcement tactics and priorities, police can generate more arrests in response to prosecutors' and judges' ability to handle more charges. But in doing so police also adjust the nature of offenses, and types of offenders, to whom they—and then the rest of the justice system—give the most attention.

Overenforcement and Overpunishment

SOCIAL COSTS OF OVERENFORCEMENT

There are often sound policy reasons for charging more crimes and adjusting enforcement priorities as circumstances change. When that is the case, the lower cost of adjudication achieved by greater efficiency is not the cause of the additional prosecutions. Instead, "nonprice determinants" like rising homicide rates are. (Or more precisely, policy responses to those determinants are.) Cheaper adjudication merely enables the state to process more charges without paying for more prosecutors and judges. Properly speaking, efficiency in that context does not trigger rebound effects. But the wisdom, practical necessity, and rationale of many enforcement policies are less clear. (Depending on one's point of view, zealous prosecutions of simple marijuana possession or certain regulatory violations are examples of ineffective or counterproductive policies.) And the role adjudication costs play in these policy choices is frequently unclear. Rebound effects are a concern when quick, cheap case processing tips the balance in favor of more enforcement—or, put differently, when caseload increases are partly endogenous to the lower adjudication costs. Some policymakers and enforcement officials recognize that maximum enforcement is often wasteful, unfair, and counterproductive. Across a wide range of contexts, from illicit drug use to environmental safety laws, public officials and many citizens have joined scholars in recognizing that there is such a thing as too much criminal law enforcement.[54]

Even with regard to well-established offenses (not merely marginal or controversial ones), legislatures occasionally place restrictions on enforcement powers by limiting agencies' budgets and their scope of authority. For example, Congress has constrained the executive branch's ability to pursue certain (politically salient) offenses related to firearms and tax obligations.[55] More recently it imposed a statutory bar on the Drug Enforcement Agency's and the Justice Department's authority to pursue violations of federal marijuana laws when the same conduct is legal under state law.[56] These instances add to others previously noted, in which state and federal enforcement agencies voluntarily limit their own efforts and, as a matter of policy, opt against zealous (or sometimes *any*) enforcement for certain crimes.

Another widespread approach for choosing alternatives to criminal prosecution involves the many state and federal districts that have embraced drug courts and other "problem-solving" courts, which replace traditional conviction and punishment with alternative strategies focused on treatment and other assistance. In other settings, the change comes not from law enforcement agencies or legislatures but from political leaders and legal challenges to enforcement practices. For years, New York City followed a harsh policy of stop-and-frisk searches of pedestrians—overwhelmingly nonwhite men—which precipitated an immense uptick (compared to its pre-1990 pattern and to other cities) in the number of charges for simple marijuana possession and other petty "quality-of-life" offenses. It took a federal court judgment and a new mayor to force policy changes in 2013.[57]

Debate over the benefits of enforcement policies can be contentious, but there is no dispute that these policies' costs are tremendous, encompassing more than the direct expenditures for police, courts, and prisons. Under an enforcement policy such as New York City's, the collateral costs are borne disproportionately by the city's nonwhite residents. Offenders and the larger communities to which they belong can suffer more than their fair share of long-lasting harms.[58] Offenders suffer diminished employment prospects and public-benefits eligibility; nonoffenders suffer indignities from searches and detention; and communities suffer diminished social capital and viability. Law enforcement suffers as well from policies that, by undermining state legitimacy, reduce both basic law compliance and citizens' willingness to cooperate with enforcement efforts. Even more perversely, imprisonment can have criminogenic (crime-causing) effects that offset or outweigh its deterrent effects.

THE ROLE OF CRIMINAL PROCESS EFFICIENCY
IN MASS INCARCERATION

As rebound effects of efficient criminal process help push caseloads higher and generate more convictions, an inevitable consequence is more punishment, in particular more incarceration. Prosecutors and trial courts grew more efficient at producing convictions throughout the last three or four decades, the same era in which U.S. criminal justice systems dramatically added to the numbers of people they sent to prisons. But the contribution of faster, cheaper adjudication goes beyond simply generating more judgments that send more offenders to prisons. In effect, it also provides a modest *subsidy* for prison spending.

Public spending on incarceration in the past thirty years has grown faster than for any other sector of criminal justice systems—faster, in fact, than for nearly every other program in state budgets during most of this period.[59] According to official estimates, between 1982 and 2001 total federal, state, and local government spending on corrections (prisons, jails, probation services) rose more than 400 percent.[60] The funding increase enabled the U.S. imprisonment rate (excluding those in local jails and counting only those with sentences of at least one year) to rise from 170 individuals per 100,000 population in 1982 to almost 470 in 2001; the figure exceeds 600 when including local jail inmates. (The prison rate exceeded 500 in 2006 and peaked in 2008; the jail-plus-prison figure hit about 700. Rates declined slightly in most years since, by 1 or 2 percent.)[61]

Contrast that pattern with spending on courts and prosecution agencies, which administered the postarrest process that put many more defendants in. Keep in mind that these incarceration rates are also partial measures of *caseloads* for prosecutors and trial courts. (Their total caseloads include all those sentenced to prison plus those who incurred other kinds of sanctions, and cases that ended through dismissal or acquittal.) Over the same twenty-year period, spending on "judicial and legal services" rose only 288 percent, significantly less than did spending for prisons. The same pattern holds for data available through the year 2007, especially if one looks solely at federal criminal justice spending.[62]

In short, spending on prisons and jails went up proportionately more than spending on courts and prosecutors. In other words, over this time period, total criminal justice spending shifted *within* the system. Funding for criminal process grew as an absolute matter, but it shrank *relative to* funding for punishment. Incarceration spending grew both as an absolute *and* relative to that for courts and prosecutors.

The good news for legislators, who must decide how to fund the criminal justice system, is that more efficient process enabled prosecutors and judges to convict and to sentence more offenders with fewer resources than they did in the past, and with fewer resources relative to prison funding. Policymaking surely internalizes this efficiency gain, so the new baseline expectation is to allocate a marginally smaller portion of criminal justice funding to prosecutors, courts, and defenders, while a comparatively larger share goes to prisons.[63] One way to describe this change is that criminal process efficiency subsidized higher spending on prisons, even as it also generated demand for the new prison space purchased through that increased spending. Without faster and more frequent plea bargaining, legislatures would face harder choices between spending even more to achieve the criminal justice system's growth in caseloads and prison populations, or spending at the same rate and seeing marginally fewer convictions and prison inmates.

If one looks more carefully at individual state justice systems, the institutional dynamics get a bit more complicated. Most states fund prisons from general revenues, while their local governments are responsible for funding a large portion of the budgets for judges, prosecutors, and especially police.[64] When all the funding is not coming from the same pot, the legislature does not directly reap all the savings from criminal court efficiency, which it could then perhaps shift to the prison budget. Still, politically the system can work much as if that were the case, in part because of a moral hazard problem created by these funding distinctions. When local prosecutors and courts produce more convictions without more resources, local governments can reap the benefits without all the costs, since they do not have to directly or fully pay for the higher incarceration costs that those new convictions impose. Yet the volume of convictions produced by local courts puts political pressure on state legislators to cover those sentencing costs. The evidence for that is the three-decade-long record of ever more costly incarceration budgets.

Costs to Public Values and the Quality of Justice

Overenforcement of criminal law and overuse of imprisonment are reasons enough to re-evaluate the long, relentless drive to make criminal process more efficient. But other interests, of course, are at stake as well. The transformation from a trial-based system to a lightly regulated process of negotiated guilty pleas has led to a variety of consequences across several dimensions.

JURIES

Perhaps most obviously, reliance on guilty pleas marginalizes the lay jury on which American criminal justice (like common law systems elsewhere) purports to place high value. In the constitutional structure of criminal procedure, the jury is intended to create some Brandeisian friction. The jury separates power within the adjudication process—and within the court itself—as a check on both prosecutors and judges. It provides a means of democratic participation that injects community sentiments into fact-finding and the application of law.[65] Those aspirations are sacrificed when criminal process gains efficiency by eliminating juries, rather than by different reforms that could preserve a more meaningful role for jurors, as some have proposed.[66]

ADVERSARIAL PROCESS

When negotiated pleas dominate, adjudication loses not only juries but core features of adversarial trial process. The guilty plea process not only eliminates most public presentation of evidence; as a practical matter, it diminishes adversarial scrutiny and the confrontation of opposing evidence, especially in regimes that allow waivers of evidence disclosure, or that make disclosure infeasible by imposing short time frames.[67] Perhaps more significantly, the nature of fact-finding, and the *fact-finder*, changes. In Gerard Lynch's memorable account, plea bargaining creates a kind of bastardized inquisitorial system, in which prosecutors, as a functional matter, take over most of the judicial fact-finding role.[68] This is especially true the more that plea bargaining is practiced with limited evidence disclosure, with little or no judicial sentencing power, and with judges often making only a perfunctory commitment to assuring the factual accuracy of guilty pleas. Resolving criminal cases through negotiated guilty pleas need not take that form; a wide range of possibilities exists between prevailing practices and the near ideal of the military justice system's protocol for guilty pleas. Instead, negotiated pleas occur in this manner—a mere shadow of the adversarial tradition, with scant judicial responsibility for judgments—to achieve even greater efficiency.

PRESSURE ON MINISTERIAL NORMS

This pseudo-inquisitorial practice puts tremendous demands on prosecutorial integrity. The ministerial norms of American prosecutors already face the unique challenge of resisting political influences in the absence (generally) of civil service protections. In addition, legal rules that govern charging, pretrial, and plea bargaining practice enforce only a thin conception of the prosecutorial minister-of-justice norm, and judicial rationales for the key constitutional doctrines support a still-thinner understanding. What is left is mainly the personal integrity of individual officials, nurtured by the widely varying professional local cultures of the offices in which they work, which are in turn backed by relatively lax systems of professional discipline.[69] For prosecutors in these challenging circumstances, efficiency has been the rationale for rules

that strengthen their authority by giving them more power to pressure defendants with extraordinary trial penalties, and to dictate short time frames and
discovery limitations in pre-plea process, all with minimal judicial oversight.

This system is vulnerable to a kind of corruption—a corruption of professional norms built on informal definitions of fairness, due process, and
appropriate punishment. Prosecutors now arrive at those definitions knowing
little about what others—especially judges and jurors—think. If only in this
respect, *prosecutors* lose compared to earlier decades when as many as 10 or
15 percent of cases went to trial, and compared also to non-U.S. jurisdictions
where judges have more sentencing authority. Isolated from those points of
reference, prosecutors face real challenges exercising the powers granted to
them in the name of efficiency. One is the temptation, documented earlier, to
craft plea offers on terms designed to maintain one's negotiating credibility.
Another is the tendency to let one's role as the advocate for conviction color
discretionary judgments about evidence materiality and disclosure. Both risks
are reduced elsewhere by practices of which U.S. courts would disapprove, primarily on grounds of inefficiency. The first risk is reduced under the English
practice that leaves sentencing to judges, with plea discounts adjusted primarily according to the stage at which a defendant pleads guilty. The second is
mitigated by the Canadian practice of giving judges the power to review prosecutors' reasons for not disclosing witnesses. In service of efficiency, American
practice grants prosecutors more power, but in doing so it puts a lot of pressure
on the primary remaining safeguard—their personal and professional integrity. Many prosecutors meet that challenge, but examples in which some do not
are legion. It is far from clear that the efficiency gains sought by American rules
are worth their costs. Given the high guilty plea rates in England, Canada, and
elsewhere, those gains seem quite marginal.

THE CHANGING NATURE OF CRIMINAL JUDGMENTS

By shifting so much de facto power for determining case outcomes from
juries and judges to prosecutors, American adjudication procedure changes
the nature of court judgments. The system not only processes convictions
more quickly, in some cases it produces different convictions. Adjudication,
after all, plays a constitutive role in criminal judgments. Outcomes are often
underdetermined by legal rules, both because of frequent choices about which
rule (or offense definition) applies and because of ambiguities in the "inter-
stices of the offense definition." As Kyron Huigens explains, that means there
inevitably will be "some discretion over precisely what the law will require in
specific circumstances."[70] Given this inevitability, it matters a great deal *who*
decides and *how* the decision process occurs. That reality is a central reason

why the American system supposedly (formerly?) valued juries, and why Americans still think of prosecutors, no matter how resolute their ministerial integrity, as different from judges.[71] Differences in decision makers often mean differences in judgments, even when neither is in error. For that reason, making criminal process more efficient—at least in the manner typical of U.S. jurisdictions—changes outcomes. In the main, it leads to harsher convictions and more punitive sentences.

THE ADVANTAGE OF CONCRETE INTERESTS

These interests not only compete with the goal of speeding up and lowering the cost of criminal law enforcement, they are also largely incommensurable. Interests such as these depend on value judgments, and many times disparate values cannot be assessed on the same scale. When choices must be made nonetheless, the outcome has a tragic dimension, in that a choice between two competing goods means some good is inevitably sacrificed.[72] But the focus on efficiency tilts the calculus in favor of certain kinds of interests—those that are easily measured or quantified, rather than more qualitative, explicitly valued-based ones—another echo of the logic and persuasive force of market rationality.

The problem is familiar in other domains. It is the basis for the growing criticism, for example, about using traditional measures to calculate the gross domestic product. By aggregating certain economic data, the gross domestic product provides a proxy for annual national production or income. Expressed per capita, it serves as a proxy for individual income or well-being. Yet this complex calculus excludes many nonmarket values, including assessments of human capital such as education, environmental damage, public health, and relative income inequality. On this basis, GDP increasingly is criticized as an inadequate measure of social progress or well-being. It may even work against those goals by encouraging the *measurable* activities of which it takes account while ignoring competing, hard-to-measure interests. "What we measure affects what we do; and if our measurements are flawed, decisions may be distorted."[73]

Priority for *efficient* criminal process causes the same kind of distortion. Easy-to-measure (and easy-to-*experience*) interests get the attention in judicial or policymaking analysis—caseloads, convictions, disposition times, judicial and prosecutorial staffs and budgets. Subtler versions of this problem are found outside of the law of plea bargaining, in rules such as procedural default doctrines and harmless-error review that prioritize finality over other interests. Recall the rule that tolerates grossly deficient defense representation unless there is proof that counsel's lapses affected the conviction, a standard which disregards procedural integrity for its own sake. The same kind of choice explains the bar against using judicial supervisory powers to vindicate "the strong public interest in the integrity of the judicial process" when constitutional violations that compromise that integrity did not affect the conviction. Justice Brennan once articulated the alternative view, one which never gained any traction. In this view, judges might reverse judgments affected by clear but harmless constitutional violations because, in the right circumstances, "the public's interests in preserving judicial integrity and in insuring that Government prosecutors . . . refrain from intentionally violating defendants' rights are stronger than its interest in upholding the conviction of a particular criminal defendant."[74] Brennan's view has rarely prevailed anywhere in the landscape of criminal procedure, except for the defendant's right to use his private wealth in the legal services market.

Democracy, Markets, Law, and State Interests

EFFICIENCY THROUGH LESS LAW

Stepping back for a broader perspective on criminal procedure's efficiency transformation, the relative roles played by democracy, markets, and legal regulation come into focus. The primary mechanisms for democratic governance in American criminal justice are electoral and political supervision of prosecutors and judges. Those are radically different instruments than juries for linking criminal justice administration to popular sentiments and preferences. For the most part, that difference has worked to the advantage of state authority. Likewise, mechanisms of the market—party freedom to negotiate over nearly every aspect of process and term of settlement—have turned out to serve the state's interests much more than those of defendants, even though defendants nominally control and consent to adjudication's new efficiencies. Neither mechanism is effective at protecting more diffuse, qualitative (and therefore contestable) interests in the constitutive nature of criminal judgments or the integrity of adversarial process.

What *would* be effective is the alternative that both displace—more law. One cost of efficiency that *has* had some political salience is the exclusion of victims from participating in the adjudication process. The response to that problem, inadequate though some take it to be, has not been democracy—reliance on accountable prosecutors to integrate victims into the process—but law: mandatory rules that define victims' rights to be consulted, to be present in court, and to be heard before various judicial decisions such as bail and sentencing. But that is a singular exception to the broader pattern. Criminal process achieves its new efficiencies—and its new levels of enforcement and incarceration—by replacing law with mechanisms of the deregulated, or unfettered, market. The only effective strategies for protecting the public interests that suffer from this regime of efficiency would have to take the form of law—of legal mandates and greater judicial supervision of legal standards. Those rules could include bans on waiving some components of procedure, stronger disclosure mandates before guilty pleas, stricter regulation of plea discounts and trial penalties, greater judicial authority over sentencing, or more rigorously exercised judicial responsibility for the factual basis and legal accuracy of guilty pleas.

THE PRIORITY FOR CRIMINAL LAW ENFORCEMENT

The primary gains from greater efficiency are more charges, more convictions, and more imprisonment. Efficient adjudication expands the state's enforcement power while lowering a key cost of exercising that power. Courts have pushed this transformation by relying on the language of markets—party autonomy, free choice, and mutual advantage through voluntary agreements. That language and the rules it justifies incrementally privatize criminal process. By concentrating on party freedom, interests, and preferences, the conceptual framework elides and passes over public interests that parties' tactical decision making fails to protect. Through a rationality focused on market-like freedoms, efficiency's priorities ultimately maximize the state's enforcement capacity while minimizing the cost to state budgets.

In order to do this, efficient process undercuts interests that conflict with those of the state. Less efficient adjudication would create friction for enforcement efforts. That kind of friction would come from the public trial, particularly the jury trial, and from a more active judicial role in assuring the accuracy, integrity, and substantive justice of criminal judgments. It would come as well from rules that allow more possibilities for correcting factual errors or constitutional violations, at some cost to the finality of judgments. Justice Stevens once frankly conceded how individual interests in accuracy are sacrificed in service of efficiency. (He could have added *public* interests as well.) In agreeing that procedural rules barred the correction of a defendant's unlawfully harsh sentence, Justice Stevens observed that this "is the kind of burden that the individual litigant must occasionally bear when efficient management is permitted to displace the careful administration of justice in each case."[75]

What is achieved more efficiently? Not lay citizen input, defendant or victim participation, or procedural safeguards on the discretionary power of state officials. Those interests—the diffuse public values instantiated in public trials, adversarial practice, and jury decision making—give way in the name of efficacious law enforcement. There is some irony in expanding the state's enforcement capacity with the mechanisms and rationality of the political economy of liberal markets. Liberal markets, after all, aim to minimize the role of the state, at least in private realms. It turns out, however, that criminal process built on market ideas—coupled with a preference for a particular kind of democratic governance in criminal law administration—is an especially effective means to enhance state power.

CHAPTER 7

Criminal Justice and the Security State

*Vital to . . . the stability of a democratic society is the right of each individual
to . . . security against illegal violence.*
—To Secure These Rights: Report of the President's Committee on Civil
Rights (1947)

The first civil right of every American is to be free from domestic violence.
—Richard Nixon, Speech Accepting Party Nomination for President (1968)

*It is in the public interest that the crime be solved and the suspect detained
as promptly as possible.*
—United States v. Hensley (1985)*

Paradoxes of Expansive State Authority

This book has made the case that ideological commitments to markets and democratic politics molds American criminal justice. These ideologies continue to provide the underlying rationality for many of the system's institutional choices, and they explain a great deal about the differences between American criminal justice and justice systems in other common law nations. Criminal justice administration in the American style—free market criminal justice, made democratic by electoral politics rather than direct citizen participation—has been particularly effective at expanding the state's capacity to enforce criminal law, impose criminal sanctions, and incarcerate to an unprecedented extent. To achieve this, U.S. criminal justice over time has increased executive power and diminished the roles of juries and, to a more modest degree, judges.

The question remains *why* democratic and market ideologies had these effects. Given the collective national wariness of state power, why has the dramatic expansion of the state's criminal-law authority and carceral capacity met so little resistance, from legal elites and the public alike? In the face of considerable countervailing forces, why were these rationalities so successful?

From one viewpoint, the expansion of state power through mechanisms of democracy and the market should be puzzling. Liberal markets and democratic accountability are institutions that limit state power. Prosecutors, for example, are elected because they provide a ready means to rein in officials who lack popular support; that arrangement appeals to Americans skeptical of state bureaucracies. The same basic concerns—in short, distrust of the state and a desire for checks and balances on its power—motivated the principal institutions of common law, adversarial-style process. Public trials make government action transparent. Lay-citizen juries take power from officials. Parties rather than judges control evidence production and witness examination. Defense rights to present and challenge evidence prevent state officials' monopoly over evidence. Judicial authority enables law to check executive action. Yet paradoxically, the ideologies of markets and democracy led criminal process to marginalize most of these checks and balances on coercive state power.[1] As a result, state power through criminal law and punishment—and broadly, state power in service of domestic security, safety, and social order—has grown dramatically. At the same time, the neoliberal or laissez-faire affinity for the private over the public did nothing to slow the elimination of private actors' roles in prosecution, even though private actors retain notable authority, in a variety of forms, in jurisdictions outside the United States.

As explanations for the expansion of criminal law and punishment, scholars have pointed to several forces: politics—both populist sentiments about crime and party competition on crime policy, racial dynamics, and the effects of increased drug-related and violent crime. With those explanations in mind, this chapter identifies some additional reasons for the transformations that democracy and markets have brought to American criminal justice, and why their influence took the form of enhancing rather than restraining state power.

The first section considers modern citizens' growing expectations for the state to provide "security" from an expanding list of risks and threats to which the population feels vulnerable. Public assent to the state providing security against a range of risks explains much about how democratic influences have transformed legal process to accommodate that security agenda. In the United States, the forms by which the criminal justice realm was made democratically responsive pushed this security agenda in unique directions. U.S. legislative policy is well attuned to popular sentiments on crime. In justice administration, jury verdicts were all but supplanted, as a practical matter, political supervision of prosecutors through the electoral process. Added to this, market-inspired practices gained new persuasive force across the broad spectrum of public policies with the shift toward neoliberalism in the 1970s. In this cultural-political environment, market norms gained more appeal for criminal justice administration as they did for other public institutions. And they proved immensely compatible with the growing enforcement ambitions of a security-oriented state.[2]

The next section considers additional reasons that criminal process has evolved as earlier chapters described. Those reasons lie in the changed nature of criminal offenses and the kinds of evidence used to prove crimes. As the criminal law has grown with the modern state's security agenda, the definition of crimes and the nature of evidence have changed in ways that make trials less important—and sometimes less appropriate—at least as a procedure to determine the truth. These new types of evidence and new definitions of crimes add to the discretion of police and prosecutors, and make juries and trials less appealing.

The final section of the chapter considers why market ideas have not been *more* successful in privatizing the criminal justice system. Market rationality is central to the structure of adjudication practices. Yet privatization has not touched the state actors—police and prosecutor—in that sector, despite privatization's considerable success in the administration of prisons and probation services. Why do market effects differ across various criminal justice institutions? The answer, it appears, is that market ideas prevail when they serve state power. Within adjudication, market mechanisms facilitate state power and reduce state obligations. But the effect would be different if policing and prosecution agencies were replaced by private firms and actors or, in some settings, even if public officials shared power with private actors. Where market-inspired arrangements thrive outside of adjudication, they generally do not infringe important forms of state authority. Private security services, for example, supplement rather than supplant police departments. Privately run probation services and prisons shift costs and responsibilities for those institutions away from the state without diminishing the state's carceral capacity.

Expansion of the Security State

STATE OBLIGATION FOR SECURITY

The first responsibility of a state is to provide security for its citizens, and the growth of modern states is tied to the expansion of that responsibility. Traditionally the term refers first to national security ("the common defense," which ensures "the security of a free State"), but it has long applied as well to general domestic order (including "domestic Tranquility").[3] Criminal law is central to that agenda, but so are civil courts, which protect interests in property and family relations, as well as the administrative state, which responds to the innumerable health, safety, and financial risks that are pervasive in high-tech, industrialized societies. In the last two decades or so, "security" has become a familiar rubric under which policymakers, as well as criminologists and other scholars, approach criminal justice policy.[4] Security has become a forthright rationale for new public policies and powers, in particular for criminal law, procedure, and punishment.

Although the U.S. Supreme Court has long cited "the right of the public [that] ... a criminal ... should not go scot free,"[5] federal and state governments have no affirmative *constitutional duty* to protect citizens from privately generated risks such as interpersonal violence.[6] By contrast, the European Convention on Human Rights imposes "a positive obligation on a state to provide protection through its legal system against a person suffering such ill-treatment at the hands of others."[7] Nonetheless, U.S. governments, like those of modern states elsewhere, have a judicially recognized political obligation to minimize those risks faced by their citizens, and they have evolved expansive capacities—in policing agencies, criminal justice systems, civil regulatory agencies, national security infrastructure, and otherwise—to carry out that duty.[8] The Supreme Court has long approved government investigative, adjudicative, and punishment powers on the grounds of the compelling importance of "the public interest in the prevention and detection of ... crime,"[9] "public interest in effective law enforcement,"[10] "the power of the States to repress and punish crime,"[11] and "the fundamental public interest in implementing the criminal law."[12]

To be sure, private actors play important roles against many kinds of security risks. Private police and security agencies abound, employed on behalf of public and private entities. Private surveillance in streets, stores, workplaces, and cyberspace is ubiquitous. Nonetheless, the state's responsibility for social order and disparate security interests defines the core of the public realm.[13] Indeed, the state's legitimacy is strongest when it acts to assure national security and domestic order. By contrast—and particularly in neoliberal (or liberal-market) nations—the state's legitimacy is weakest when it intervenes in the market, family life, and other private-realm domains. One ambition of neoliberalism, after all, is to place responsibility for protecting economic interests in private rather than public hands—in the market rather than with the state.

However, even in liberal market economies, public demands on the state have grown over time. Despite much ongoing debate about some specifics, the public now looks to the state to do more to minimize various risks of harm and disorder. Public policies address a broad range of risks beyond criminal law's core concerns of interpersonal violence, theft, and domestic order. Economic security is one category, including unemployment and workers' compensation insurance and old-age pensions, as well as financial regulation (such as safeguards against securities fraud and bank failures). Contemporary states take a greater role in managing health and safety risks, through health insurance subsidies and regulation, product-safety regulations, and much more. These policies have precursors in uses of the state *police* power, or general regulatory and governance authority, over the last two centuries or more.[14]

Especially in the last four decades, however—the era when American criminal process achieved new levels of efficiency—much of the security agenda has been pursued through criminal law enforcement, as well as through allied powers such as preventive detention and other restraints on those who meet criteria of dangerousness.[15] Criminal policy began a cross-national punitive turn in the 1970s, but U.S. imprisonment levels entered a league of their own. The causes are complex; rising violent crime rates, social disorder, and concern about illicit drugs were important parts of the story but not the whole story. In the United States, racially tinged politics in the wake of civil rights advances intersected with newly salient politics of crime and, by the 1970s, disruptive economic shocks.[16] David Garland described a cross-national "culture of control" that emerged in this era, in which a long-standing welfarist orientation of punishment policies was replaced by both moralistic and instrumental rationales that led to harsher sentences with little aspiration for rehabilitation or reintegration of offenders.[17]

In the United States more than elsewhere, crime became a primary lens that reshaped much of American governance. Public policy within and beyond the criminal justice system was refocused around the experience of crime and terrorism victims, or widely shared fears of becoming victimized.[18] The salience and the scope of such fears are behind quasi-civil detention for individuals deemed to pose excessive risks of future dangerousness, from sex-crime offenders to terrorism suspects.[19] To preempt and prevent harms rather than merely react to them, law enforcement and related agencies turned to new surveillance technologies and to more "actuarial" surveillance and enforcement strategies that focus on specific groups of people, or particular kinds of activities and circumstances, that signal (or are perceived to signal) dangerousness and high risks of harm.[20]

In substantive criminal law, broad-ranging anxieties about security prompted states (within and beyond the United States) to adopt new offenses and doctrines designed to allow earlier interventions before harms occur. Variously characterized as "pre-crime," "prophylactic," "preventive," or "preemptive" offenses, new crimes of this sort are defined exclusively by early-stage planning or preparation, possession of noncontraband, or modest acts of facilitation, combined (typically) with proof of intent regarding some future wrongdoing. In tandem with new kinds of surveillance and investigation tactics, these offenses enable the state to arrest and punish in the earliest stages of risk-creating conduct, or in the activities of those who fit criteria of dangerousness. They aim to prevent rather than respond to harmful wrongdoing.[21]

All of this provides the preconditions and broader context for the criminal process changes examined in earlier chapters. The political and social salience of anxieties about crime and growing expectations for the state—as well as ambitions *of* the state—to manage security risks provide an underlying urgency for criminal process to facilitate surveillance, investigation, enforcement, and punishment. Criminal process efficiency became critical to law enforcement efficacy, which in turn was taken as critical to protecting the public from omnipresent threats of harm and disorder. Procedural efficiency required transforming the core institutions of Anglo American criminal adjudication. Both the lay jury and adversarial trial process were designed to supervise, and at times frustrate, state enforcement efforts, a function that conflicts with an expansive system with a premium on efficiency. American criminal procedure overcame those hindrances in effect by substituting prosecutors' political accountability and market-style negotiation between parties, rather than by developing legal standards and a checks-and-balances regime with a meaningful judicial role for nontrial adjudication.

LONG HISTORY OF STATE SECURITY RESPONSIBILITIES

Unprecedented incarceration, prevention-oriented crimes, ever-more-efficient guilty plea processes—these are distinctive innovations of the last generation, and they follow from the era's preoccupation with crime and security. But they occurred after a long history of growing popular expectations that the state would ensure order and *prevention* of calamitous harms. Blackstone in his *Commentaries* stressed that the state's ambition of "*preventive* justice is . . . in all respects preferable to *punishing* justice." To that end he endorsed control of identifiably dangerous persons—those for whom "there is a probable ground to suspect of future misbehavior." Until the late twentieth century, the law described those people with such colorful terms as "night-walkers, common drunkards, idle vagabonds, persons not of good fame," and the like.[22]

Precursors to the modern regulatory state were well established in the first half of the nineteenth century, by which time England's and America's largest cities had their first professional police forces, public prosecutors' offices in their modern form became more common, and several states had built the first modern prisons.[23] At the same time, state and local governments exercised considerable regulatory authority, often by means of "public welfare" offenses. To promote the general safety and welfare, these minor criminal provisions regulated everything from weights and measures, food safety, alcohol sales, and building codes to road maintenance and wharf sizes.[24]

Governments' criminal justice capacity grew in response to disruptive social changes brought by urbanization, industrialization, and—in the United States—immigration. Transformation of cities, social customs, and economic relationships provoked widespread concerns of disorder. In the United States these concerns were multiplied by the nation's new and unprecedented experiment with republican government. This degree of democratic governance came earlier in the United States than elsewhere, and its success was far from certain. America's experiment in democracy—expanded to universal white male franchise in the 1830s—also transformed social relations in ways that produced widespread anxieties about social order. American democracy quickly undermined traditional social hierarchies and customs that had long provided predictable social structure and stability.[25] This tumultuous development triggered anxieties about deteriorating morals and manners, and it coincided with the nation's highest-ever levels of alcohol consumption.[26]

The other major source of disruptive social change in the same era came not from democracy but from markets—the "market revolution." More people participated in expanding commercial markets, and those markets suffered frequent recessions. This economic dynamism aggravated inequality, economic insecurities, and dislocation at the same time that it provided new opportunities and rewards. Risks of disorder were greatest in rapidly growing cities—where police and prosecutor agencies first arose. These challenges increased with the new waves of immigration; increased ethnic diversity contributed another basis for tension and conflict, particularly during economic contractions.[27] Randolph Roth has documented that U.S. homicide rates "exploded across the nation" in the 1840s and 1850s and for the first time "truly diverged from rates elsewhere in the Western world," with the result that the "least homicidal places in the world suddenly became the most homicidal."[28]

In short, the first half of the nineteenth century brought a "crisis of confidence in the social organization of the new republic," as David Rothman put it in his history of the rise of prisons and mental hospitals during this era. Although homicide rates through the 1830s were as low as anywhere in the world,[29] to Americans of the time nonetheless "[t]he safety and security of their social order seemed to them in far greater danger than that of their fathers." The risk of "social disorganization appeared imminent," and those "fears were confirmed and exacerbated by the extent of crime, poverty, delinquency, and insanity" that Jacksonian-era Americans saw around them. Rothman identifies this sense of social crisis as central to the explanation for why nearly all American states by 1850 had, for the first time, built institutions for long-term incarceration. "The felt need for order and discipline . . . in a society deeply apprehensive about the prospect of disorder" motivated legislatures and administrators.[30]

Those fears transformed policing, prosecutors, and criminal courts as well. Mary Vogel's study of Boston criminal courts before 1850 described a context in which "concern abounded in Boston about crime, rioting and unrest." As conflict among social groups increased throughout the urban Northeast, "a sense of massive change, social transformation, and crisis" challenged traditional political arrangements and courts in particular, from which Vogel interprets the advent of plea bargaining as one response.[31] The same social disruptions—riots, worker strikes, ethnic conflict, growing street violence, economic crashes—magnified social disorder in other cities including Philadelphia, which created its full-time public police force and public prosecutor office as a strategy to improve domestic order and security.[32] McConville and Mirsky documented similar transformations of New York City's criminal justice institutions, triggered by the same concerns about rising crime associated with ethnic diversity, economic growth and instability, and rapid increases in population.[33]

In sum, the security challenges of modernizing nations led states to expand their capacity to maintain domestic order and reduce or prevent widely perceived risks. *Executive* officials in particular gained the most responsibility—as police, prosecutors, and prison administrators. Private prosecutors and other forms of private ordering came to seem increasingly inadequate. For consensual offenses such as alcohol sales, there may be no private parties with a motivation to report violations. For other kinds of offenses—both public welfare regulations and those that arose from riots or other public events—victims were often poorly positioned to report or prosecute violations, much less prevent them. Preventive security instead required police, public inspectors, and other public officials. That need only grew with the creation of new crimes to prevent mail and wire fraud, and when alcohol regulation evolved into alcohol (and narcotics) prohibition.

Motivated by security anxieties, majority sentiment generally supported this expansion of state authority in the nineteenth century. The same was true in the twentieth century, although to be sure there was dissent on many policies. Sanctions against worker protests or union strikes, expansive alcohol and social regulation pushed by Temperance groups, and racially disparate enforcement patterns all met with notable dissent.[34] Still, the long progress of the security state is built on a basic level of majoritarian assent. With important differences in detail, this seems true throughout developed nations. Especially in the United States, where criminal justice policy is tightly bound to democratic politics, it could hardly be otherwise. In that light, the populist punitive turn in crime policy after the 1960s is a notably acute episode, but one consistent with a much larger pattern of support for state criminal justice authority. Support for "the public interest in effective law enforcement" put relentless pressure on traditional, "inefficient" law and structure of criminal adjudication.

STATE BUILDING

The growth of the criminal justice security state was a central component in the larger project of modern state building. In all advanced nations, governments grew increasingly bureaucratic and "rationalized" over the nineteenth and twentieth centuries. They expanded their capacities to govern in diverse ways so as to meet the new challenges from industrialization, technological advances, urbanization, and population growth—in general, new forms of risk, and new potential sources of discord. Some nations adapted to these challenges of domestic security while also facing others caused by ambitions to expand their borders and unify diverse populations into one nation with a central government broadly accepted as legitimate. The United States vastly expanded its territory throughout the nineteenth century, and the Civil War in the 1860s was fundamentally a war about unification and national government legitimacy. Other nations had comparable histories. Germany and Italy, for example, also consolidated diverse states into a single nation through wars of unification in the 1860s and 1870s. France had the advantage of more stable borders and state identity, but it went through a series of difficult changes in governance and constitutional forms. These nationalizing agendas added to governments' burdens of maintaining domestic safety and order. Compared to these European states, however, the United States was unique in its relative *lack* of success at legitimizing the authority of its national government by the late nineteenth century. The Civil War preserved the Union and subsequent constitutional amendments strengthened federal authority over states, but pervasive and violent white resistance throughout the South to racial equality and the federal government's Reconstruction policies reinforced the long tradition of skepticism about the national government's authority. Skepticism of national authority was also long reflected in the nation's aversion to a standing army; U.S. military capacity was comparatively modest until the approach of World War II. That skepticism is embedded in the federal constitutional structure, which preserves significant sovereign powers for the states.[35]

Recent historical research suggests that the comparatively weak legitimacy of government in the United States has an unexpected, and ironic, effect. Historians have constructed sound estimates for much of America's and Europe's homicide rates going back over two hundred years. Their laborious archival research provides increasingly solid evidence that the U.S. homicide rate, which was lower than Europe's in the nation's earliest decades, departed upward from Europe's in the 1840s and 1850s and has remained higher ever since. More interesting is the explanation for this American anomaly, developed by Randolph Roth along with others. The factors that correlate most strongly and consistently with homicide rates, Roth argues, are not the most familiar forces thought to affect crime rates, such as unemployment, poverty, ethnic conflict, prevalence of guns, or policing tactics. They are instead the depth of shared feelings about the legitimacy of government, socio-economic order, and social solidarity expressed through patriotism and civil society institutions, along with sufficient state capacity—especially policing and criminal law enforcement—to make the rule of law credible.[36] The irony, then, is that American distrust of government has contributed to the conditions of insecurity and disorder that lead a polity to embrace a particularly coercive form of government power: criminal law enforcement. To make that power more effective, U.S. criminal justice systems minimize rule of law constraints and enhance executive officials' enforcement discretion, including de facto adjudicative and sentencing power. A deficit of state authority contributes to conditions of insecurity and the prevalence of violence that, in turn, generate support for stronger state security infrastructure.

Even if one is unpersuaded by this explanation for patterns of violence, the incontrovertibly high U.S. homicide *rates*, compared to Europe, surely play a role in collective perceptions of insecurity and the salience of fears about victimization that underlie penal populism and democratic support for harsh and efficient criminal justice. This is in a sense a striking departure from the American tradition of skepticism of government power. The contrast is most apparent from a constitutional perspective. Although the federal Constitution aimed to—and did—increase national government power compared to its predecessor, and did so at the expense of the states, the founding generation was nonetheless skeptical of many aspects of government power. The founders held a dim view of excessively *democratic*, or populist, institutions, a description which characterized many early state legislatures. More important here, they worried about the government's criminal law enforcement authority.* For that reason the Bill of Rights placed substantial limits on the state's power to search, to compel testimony, to control trial location and process, and to impose excessive punishment. The powers it *ensured* went to those who could frustrate state authority. The criminal jury can impede prosecutors,

---

* The founders likewise worried about government's military authority and disfavored a standing army. For modern generations, security concerns eventually outweighed reasons for disapproving strong state capacity in both the military and criminal law enforcement realms.

legislatures, and judges. The defense can marshal and challenge evidence with the aid of skilled counsel.[37]

The Constitution's criminal procedure regime, in short, reflects a notable distrust of criminal enforcement authority. But the expanding need and support for the state to provide security through criminal law conflicts with that vision and has played a key role in growing majoritarian trust of that authority. Personal and domestic security concerns prompt less worry about government overreach in criminal enforcement. Most of the time, the greater worry has been threats posed by private actors—wrongdoing for which the state's police, prosecutors, and prisons provide the response.

Both of those sets of concerns always coexist, and their balance varies across times and places. Government surveillance practices are one prominent site for contemporary debates about the line between legitimate security needs and government overreach.[38] And *majority* support for various criminal enforcement policies is often accompanied by some level of minority disaffection, and in U.S. criminal justice that difference commonly falls in good part along racial and ethnic lines.[39] Nonetheless, the popular support for expansive criminal law and punishment has had significant implications for criminal *process*. As primary concerns shifted from state *abuse* of power to the *ineffectiveness* of that power (and the financial cost of its administration), criminal procedure transformed. To say the least, processes designed as safeguards against government overreach are not the same as those that facilitate enforcement or lower its cost. Again the most obvious example is the jury. Where the *grand* jury has survived, it has done so either by becoming a useful investigative body for prosecutors (as in the federal system) or an efficient alternative to judicial scrutiny of prosecutors' proposed charges (as in state systems). The *trial* jury—and the trial *process*, for that matter—experienced no similar transformation. Empanelling a trial jury grew more cumbersome (it was once common for a single jury to decide several cases per day).[40] Trial jurors remained a hurdle rather than help to prosecutors; their function remained second-guessing officials. As a consequence, criminal process evolved to marginalize the trial jury.

In short, changing circumstances have steadily increased the state's responsibility for public security, which has transformed the scope of criminal law and punishment, and in turn criminal procedure as well. Very broadly speaking—and again acknowledging some dissent, particularly along racial and ethnic divides—the expansion of criminal enforcement capacity occurred with sustained popular support, as studies of penal populism suggest.[41] In contrast to a general skepticism of government power, that popular endorsement reflects a strong, basic *trust* in the state's criminal justice administration, and especially in its strong version of executive enforcement discretion. Popular accountability is important to that level of trust, and political control is the preferred U.S. mode of monitoring—and legitimizing—state officials. But the real and felt demands for security are also essential to explaining democratic assent to the broad reach of the state's contemporary law enforcement and carceral capacity.

Needless to say, a politically responsive criminal justice system has proven quite compatible with expansive criminal law and punishment.[42] Political responsiveness drives much of that expansion because, in the typical conditions of advanced capitalist democracies, concerns about crime victimization exceed fears of law enforcement and state punishment. "Penal populism" describes policies that are overly harsh precisely because they too closely track unmediated majoritarian views.[43] Additionally, majorities sometimes embrace policies that are wrong in principle. Examples, racial segregation laws, are easy to find. Constitutional law defines what policies and practices a nation preserves or forbids as matters of principle and takes them off the table for democratic decision making. One account of European democracies since World War II is that they have adopted stronger constitutional restraints on democratic policymaking through human rights law, including criminal justice rights.[44] In their policing infrastructures as well as substantive laws, criminal justice regimes in all advanced democracies reflect the modern consensus on the state's central obligation for security and social order. But the sharply political structure of American criminal justice is at the core of its uniquely harsh carceral response to the security challenges and fears of the last half century.

Democratic Facilitation of the Carceral State

If there are popular expectations for the state to address a wide range of contemporary security threats, then it is no surprise that criminal justice systems characterized by a high degree of political responsiveness facilitate state capacities to carry out those responsibilities. But that does not mean that democratic justice systems necessarily lead to expansive state authority throughout criminal justice policies and procedures. Advanced nations have adapted their criminal justice systems to this security role in distinct ways. Some differences are relatively small, such as how procedural rules balance pretrial evidence disclosure against witness safety or the executive's enforcement interests. Others, such as differences in incarceration policies, are much larger. The options that a justice system chooses turn, in some part, on its *forms* of democratic practice—on *how* it is democratic, as well as *how democratic* it is. Some democratic processes foster better deliberation and compromise than others; some systems of democratic governance integrate expertise and reliable information sources into policymaking to a greater degree than others.[45] Changes in American criminal process can be traced in part to the dramatic changes over time in how citizens have influenced or governed criminal justice.

FROM JURIES TO BALLOTS

Democratic governance of American criminal justice has shifted over time from the level of the criminal case to the level of state policy, because its primary site shifted from the jury box to the ballot box. Citizens once routinely played direct roles in individual criminal cases, as jurors but also as private prosecutors. Before modern media, much "democratic monitoring" of justice administration was done by courtroom spectators; before the rise of the prison, many also observed hangings and other forms of public punishment. The advent of elected (or politically appointed) prosecutors was followed by the demise of private prosecutors and the steady growth of procedural substitutes for the jury trial. Political officials shifted democratic input from the courtroom to the voting booth, and from a focus on the outcome in individual cases to broad assessments of criminal justice administration. Lay jurors as *adjudicators* were gradually displaced by a negotiation process managed by professional lawyers in private. Elections for prosecutors and judges gradually took the place of juries as *democratic monitors* of those officials. As a consequence, if prosecutors and judges respond to popular sentiments about criminal justice, it is as those views are collectively expressed through the electoral process, rather than from jurors who render verdicts in individual cases.

Changes in democratic practice lead to changes in democratic outcomes. Judgments after trials are often based on better information—more detailed factual accounts—than settlements negotiated by lawyers, at least in many state court systems dominated by routine criminal cases.[46] Moreover, peoples' judgments tend to differ depending on the amount of information they possess. Paul Robinson's extensive work on lay preferences about criminal liability and sentencing has stressed this point. His studies suggest that, when well informed on specific cases, people often favor more moderate outcomes than sentencing laws dictate or real-life criminal procedure produces.[47] When the primary vehicle for public input on criminal justice is voting in elections, voters rarely have information about particular criminal cases, save for occasional high-profile prosecutions. At best, decisions are based mostly on some sense of crime trends and enforcement practices. On top of that, voting for office holders allows citizens to express only crude or "muddy" signals about their preferences for criminal justice policy.

The literature on electoral accountability has identified several weaknesses in the link between voters' preferences and elected officials' policy decisions. A core difficulty is that even when both voters and officials act rationally, officials nonetheless are often inclined to pursue actions that depart from voters' interests. Officials will prefer policies or actions that provide voters with clear, memorable information, even when those choices conflict with actions that better accommodate voters' preferences for policy outcomes.[48] That is why prosecutors worry about conviction rates and sentences, which might lead them to discount concerns about accuracy or seek disproportionately severe punishments. Voters may desire strong enforcement but without compromising accurate and proportionate outcomes. Yet voter information about the accuracy and proportionality of judgments in particular will almost always be low, while information about conviction rates is highly salient and easily conveyed.[49] Low voter information, and the feedback distortion it triggers, is a form of agency problem—the challenge principals face in monitoring agents. This has implications for prosecutors' democratic legitimacy. If elected agents cannot be adequately monitored, there is less reason to trust their autonomy and good reasons to seek other ways to supervise prosecutors' performance. As noted previously, one way is through more *law*—legal standards monitored modestly by judicial review of prosecutor actions. Precisely the mechanisms, in short, that the U.S. Supreme Court has weakened to the point of irrelevance.

The particular criminal justice outcomes that follow from these politically based institutions vary across time and locality. Although harsh penal policies are a familiar outcome now of electoral influence on criminal justice, in a few jurisdictions local preferences can cut the other way. A Bronx prosecutor won easy re-election after announcing his refusal to seek the death penalty even against defendants accused of killing police officers; San Francisco twice elected a liberal defense attorney as its prosecutor, and many state and local electorates have supported decriminalization or minimal-enforcement policies on marijuana.[50] In the early decades of the American republic, leading politicians could serve as prominent criminal defense lawyers without damage to their careers—a reminder of the shift from an era more worried about government excess than ineffectiveness in criminal adjudication.[51] McConville and Mirsky's study of adjudication in nineteenth-century New York City found that the district attorney office, under the influence of the Tammany Hall political machine, used its discretion to increase leniency through plea bargaining and *nolle prosequi* dismissals; criminal defendants came from the political bosses' base of popular support and were rewarded with favoritism.[52]

Nonetheless, there is no disputing that in recent decades America's particular forms of criminal justice institutions, in the context of the era's political and social dynamics, have produced uniquely severe punishment practices, and played a role also in its dispiriting record of wrongful convictions.[53] Prosecutors' political accountability has contributed to courts' deference to their authority, and it encouraged a less ministerial, more partisan model of the prosecutor's role. In addition, prosecutors' political status has made it accept the marginalization of juries while still maintaining a version of democratic criminal justice, even—or especially—one that makes aggressive use of state enforcement power.

Contemporary Crimes and Evidence

Another set of developments has aided the expanded security agenda and helps to explain how criminal process has evolved in now-familiar ways. The character of crimes has changed, and so has the nature of evidence. Both changes augment executive control in criminal process, and both work against the trial process.

CHANGING NATURE OF CRIMINAL OFFENSES

Over several decades, the kinds of crimes that make up a significant portion of enforcement efforts have changed in three broad, somewhat overlapping ways. First, some offense definitions became simpler and easier to prove. Bill Stuntz developed the insight that American legislatures responded to judicial expansion of criminal procedure rights, and to the invalidation of some long-standing offenses as excessively vague,[54] by adopting simpler, clearer offense definitions that continued to give police wide enforcement discretion and at the same time made violations easier to prove. By creating lots of specific offenses that police can selectively enforce, legislatures, as Bill Stuntz observed, "reduce the cost of prosecution [and] . . . make criminal litigation cheaper." Narrowly defined offenses enable "law enforcers to evade costly procedural rules, to turn questionable searches and arrests into clearly legal ones, and to turn expensive trials into cheap guilty pleas," all of which encourages more enforcement.[55]

A second, overlapping change is the one several scholars have noted as characteristic of the contemporary security orientation—the expansion of preventive offenses, or crimes of early-stage preparatory conduct. The proliferation of possession crimes, and their centrality to contemporary law enforcement, are an important example.[56] Possession per se is not harmful conduct; it is the later *use* of the weapon or drug that is the law's real concern. But criminalizing possession is easy to prove and also allows for preemptive intervention long before the moment of use. Criminal codes in the United States and elsewhere have added inchoate offenses of this sort in recent decades. Examples range from conspiracy statutes to offenses of providing otherwise-legal goods as early-stage "material support" for future terrorist acts, to crimes against deliberately structuring bank deposits in increments under $10,000 to avoid bank reporting requirements.[57]

The final change contrasts with the first: the increased number of offenses that govern complicated forms of wrongdoing. Prime examples are offenses in the financial sector and racketeering activity by organized criminal networks. The complexity of regulation—by criminal and civil laws—of securities markets, banking, and other large sectors of commercial activity, for example, is an inevitable byproduct of the size and complexity of modern economies. Unlike possession crimes and many other preemptive offenses that fill state and federal criminal dockets, these offenses are not easy to prove. The large volume and complex nature of evidence, as well as complicated elements of offense definitions, make the common law jury trial an unappealing mode of adjudication. Juries evolved when trials typically dealt with a very different kind of case: one defendant, a discrete act or incident of alleged wrongdoing, with most evidence in testimonial rather than documentary form. The jury trial has adapted fairly well to handle multiple defendants, multiple offenses, and larger-scale wrongdoing, but it remains less than ideal for cases that arise from complex patterns of conduct with voluminous, specialized documentary evidence. For those reasons, especially with respect to large-scale corporate crime, negotiated civil or criminal settlements have become the predominant means to resolve such cases, sometimes without ever filing criminal charges in a court.[58] And resolving prosecutions through negotiated settlements rather than trials gives executive-branch officials greater control and reduces the roles of judges and judicial process.[59]

For different reasons, the expansion of specific, clearly defined crimes and crimes of preparatory conduct work to make trials, all else equal, marginally less appealing. Simple, clear offense elements improve the odds that the state will have ample evidence of a violation at the time of arrest or charging. Consider that, in federal courts, the two largest categories of offenses are immigration crimes and drug crimes. Most immigration violations are for entry without authorization or re-entry after deportation, both of which require, basically, proof of the defendant's presence in the United States plus some proof of unauthorized status. Most drug crimes require simply proof of the drug's identity and weight, defendant's possession, and (usually) intent to distribute, which can be inferred from the quantity of drugs. Once law enforcement arrests an undocumented resident within the United States, or someone in possession of drugs, proof usually seems clear, and there usually seems little need for trial as a fact-finding process. To be sure, errors and evidentiary disputes occur even in the simplest of cases—identities are mistaken, public records are wrong, law enforcement prevaricate, drug analysis is flawed. But many of those mistakes, if noticed at all, are recognized by the lawyers before trial and charges are dismissed. At least from the point of view of state officials, who have tremendous influence over defendants' decisions to go to trial through the rules for plea bargaining, there seems little genuine need for trial to settle uncertainties or demonstrate the requisite level of proof. That is less true for more complicated, vague, or harder-to-prove offenses, which include petty crimes such as "wandering or strolling around from place to place without any lawful purpose," to serious crimes such as rape (when lack of consent is at issue) or a "scheme to defraud."[60]

CHANGING NATURE OF EVIDENCE

The second set of developments that push against traditional trial adjudication—and help to push decision making from judges and juries to police and prosecutors—has to do with the changing nature of investigation methods and contemporary forms of evidence. Changes in both follow from advancements in science and technology. Gradually over the last century and rapidly in recent decades, evidence has increasingly appeared in new recorded, scientific, or documentary forms. Examples are well known. One category is audio and video recordings (wiretaps, surveillance cameras and microphones, video of police traffic stops or suspect interrogations). Related kinds of evidence are drawn from electronic searches and records related to digital communications and databases (phone and email metadata or actual text content, cell phone tower data, transactions traced through debit and credit cards). The volume of documentary sources has grown exponentially and become immensely more accessible for everything from financial transactions to records of car or gun ownership. Personal identity records and other means to establish identity were less extensive, available, and reliable a century or two ago. On top of all this is the advent of scientific and forensic evidence. Much evidence in that category has proven to be woefully unreliable despite courts' wide acceptance of it.[61] But some is well grounded in science and, properly developed, has a high degree of reliability. DNA evidence is the best example, but less glamorous examples, such as blood alcohol/drug-content analysis, have immense practical importance. The same is true of longer-established techniques such as drug-chemistry analysis, and to varying degrees identification practices developed specifically for criminal investigations, such as ballistics and fingerprint analysis.

These technology-driven developments in evidence forms have two related effects worth noting here. First, they reduce the need for the trial as an *evidence-gathering* device, which was a primary function that the common law trial evolved to perform.[62] For cases in which the most critical evidence takes testimonial form, the trial may be the first time anyone (prosecutors included) learns what all critical witnesses have to say. That is most likely to be true for prosecutions that respond to completed acts of wrongdoing, as in a traditional theft, assault, or homicide offense. Second, new technologies put more of the critical information in the hands of the parties—especially prosecutors—well before trial. With preemptive-style offenses (including possession crimes) as well as complex organization crimes, officials usually have most if not all of the critical evidence in hand early on, because those offenses mostly arise from proactive, often elaborate investigations that provide officials with most of the critical evidence even before charges are filed.

New, technology-based evidence has recognized vulnerabilities. Police interrogations produce a small but significant percentage of false confessions, yet selective or partial recordings can obscure rather than reveal error. Crime-scene evidence such as partial fingerprints can be unclear; samples sent for lab analysis can be contaminated; forensic analyses can err due to incompetence, fraud, or methodological limits. Databases may contain errors, and electronic-records evidence (such as phone tower data) can be ambiguous or require interpretation. Nonetheless, those flaws have not precipitated a revival of trials as evidence-development events. This kind of evidence, in the hands of parties, often *seems* reliable. It seems to (and often does) provide an adequate, unambiguous evidentiary file compared to past eras, or compared to present-day cases based largely on witness testimony. (Consider rape prosecutions. When the offender's identity is at issue, DNA analysis now can be dispositive where good evidence formerly was unavailable. But when identity is undisputed and *consent* is disputed, new evidentiary sources rarely help, which leaves courts mostly with conflicting testimony.) With evidence that seems, and often is, unambiguous and highly reliable, the professionals with pretrial access to it—prosecutors and police, but also defense attorneys and eventually judges—perceive less need for trial. They are confident in their conclusions about guilt or innocence based on such information, and confident also about the decisions juries or judges would (or should) make at trial. In a larger portion of cases than in earlier eras, a trial is not needed to *produce* evidence. Arguably, it is also needed to *evaluate* evidence less often than in earlier eras, when many cases turned wholly on witness testimony, some heard for the first time at trial. Moreover, the public often can have the same confidence (and too much confidence) about case outcomes without trial, either because so much evidence is recounted in media coverage or simply because of a general awareness of the kinds of technology-based evidence that are increasingly available. The pretrial presence of seemingly strong evidence makes guilty pleas rather than trials seem like the sensible procedural route. Such evidence may also bolster trust in law enforcement decisions about who to charge with what offenses. Those views, combined with broad preferences for an active state security role through criminal law enforcement, undermine traditional trial process.

These anti-trial, pro-settlement effects gain support from other developments as well. Modern discovery rules give parties better pretrial evidentiary access than was true in earlier eras. John Langbein has described this with respect to federal civil procedure: discovery rules allow parties to inspect opponents' evidence to a degree they formerly could not. That makes settlement more likely; trials are less critical for discovering and examining evidence.[63] The same is true in criminal practice, despite stricter limits on pretrial information exchange. Even in jurisdictions with the most restrictive regimes, such as the federal courts, disclosure is broader now than it was a generation or two earlier. Pretrial information exchange by parties is *relatively* greater nearly everywhere than in the past. And what discovery rules do not provide to parties before trial is partly offset—much more so for prosecutors than the defense—by contemporary investigative capacities.

This picture is painted in broad strokes. A lot of evidence in ordinary cases remains in traditional forms—witness testimony, paper documents, and objects such as weapons or contraband. Given the record of miscarriages of justice, it is hard to conclude that new evidence sources have made criminal justice dramatically more accurate than in the past. But it is not hard to see the advent of new evidentiary sources as a contributing cause in the decline of the trial and the rise of the guilty plea. Like the reform of criminal offense definitions, this evidentiary change strengthens executive authority in justice administration.

That transformation affects enforcement patterns and the scope of punishment. Judgments for the same cases will differ depending on the adjudicative procedures employed to reach them. Process is, in that sense, constitutive of legal judgments. Evidence is assessed and judgments are made differently in one setting (such as the trial) from another (such as a prosecutor's office).[64] Reallocating power between prosecutors and judges has the same effects. Decision makers often must apply concepts such as recklessness, reasonableness, or complicity, and their judgments rest on myriad choices about evidence credibility and persuasiveness.[65] It matters *who* makes those choices, and how. That's why common law systems preferred juries over judges. In a criminal justice system inclined for other reasons to elevate prosecutors and plea bargains over judges and trials, new kinds of evidence and offenses have made these transitions easier.

The Forms and Limits of Markets in Criminal Justice

Beyond adjudication, liberal market ideas have taken different forms and had different effects across criminal justice institutions—from policing and surveillance through administration of punishment. To oversimplify a bit, market ideas are usually integrated into public institutions in one of two ways. First, institutions can incorporate market premises and mechanisms while they remain under public ownership and control. This describes traditional adversarial process. Like markets, adversarialism depends on party autonomy, competition, and self-interested motivations; it produces public goods through pursuit of private ends. The American version of adversarial process is deeply committed to this kind of market rationality.

The second way markets are integrated into public institutions is privatization, meaning that private entities control formerly public assets or private actors handle tasks formerly done by public officials. Privatization has had not the least inkling of success with courts and prosecution agencies, the central agencies of criminal adjudication. Nor has it had success with police departments and related law enforcement agencies. They remain staffed and administered by government officials, despite the prevalence of private security firms with expertise in the same functions. (That stands in contrast to the inroads that private firms have made in displacing government security forces in military and diplomatic contexts.)[66] On the other hand, privatization has had considerable success at the punishment end of the process, where private firms own and administer prisons and run probation services under contracts with governments. Private entities also provide some services ancillary to policing. For example, state officials sometimes rely on private labs for forensic analysis and traffic enforcement surveillance cameras may be privately operated under contracts with governments.[67]

What accounts for varied forms of success—as well as the limits—of market mechanisms across criminal justice? The answer again lies in the firm, expansive commitment to state responsibility for domestic security and social order. Market ideas succeed where they can enhance state security power. They take the particular institutional forms that serve the state's security capacity and that, consistent with that capacity, reduce public expenditures.

PROSECUTION AND ADJUDICATION

From earlier chapters, this explanation is most apparent in the context of prosecution services. All U.S. jurisdictions abolished the authority of private prosecutors by the late nineteenth century. Since then, the monopoly control of public prosecutors has never been seriously questioned. Even more than in the criminal justice systems elsewhere, where public prosecutors also control charging and litigation, the U.S. prosecution administration incorporates probably the *least* amount of private ordering. Private actors no longer play even modest, supplemental roles in criminal charging and litigation, although other nations' justice systems demonstrate the feasibility of allowing private individuals to share some of the public prosecutor's authority. Recall that other nations with strong public prosecution agencies, notably England, still permit privately initiated criminal charges (subject to public prosecutors' takeover or veto), much like private rights of action in U.S. law that enlist "private attorneys general" to supplement public enforcement of civil statutes. As noted earlier, nations such as Germany, Spain, France, and Italy give victims a right to veto certain criminal charges or allow their attorneys to take ancillary roles in the trial process alongside public prosecutors. Private influence in public prosecution need not take the form of wholesale privatization, although that is probably a fair description of the New Zealand model in which the government selects solicitors in private law firms to carry out prosecution duties (a model England employed until the 1980s).[68]

The immunity of U.S. criminal justice to privatization of any aspect of public prosecution authority is puzzling in light of the confluence since the 1970s of two important policy trends that seem to favor such an approach. The first is the considerable success of neoliberal ideologies, which spurred governments in the United States, the United Kingdom, and elsewhere to privatize any number of formerly public services. The other, which gained notable political influence at the same time, is the crime victims' rights movement, through which aggrieved persons won considerable rights of notice, access, and participation as witnesses but no formal authority to file or veto charges, or to participate in trials as litigants. Even together, these two trends never changed the terms of debate about the public monopoly over prosecution discretion.

Instead, the market model of adjudication makes public prosecutors adversarial competitors to the defense. Both parties act *like* market rivals and compete to produce evidence and legal arguments (unless they negotiate an agreement to settle). In doing so they produce public goods—starting with the factual record—that the state needs to render judgments and punishment orders. Here too choices exist for mechanisms that could temper some of the market-style structure in relatively modest ways—less severe procedural default rules, broader prosecution disclosure duties, better indigent defense funding. Or, departing a bit further from market structure, the judiciary could take more active responsibility to ensure that the parties generate sufficient factual records, as a backstop against failures from agency problems or other lapses of partisan diligence.

Why does the market's influence take the form of (1) adversarial process combined with public prosecution monopolies, rather than (2) some degree of privatized prosecution authority, or (3) a more "regulated-market" form of process? One answer is tradition. Beyond that, the structural affinities between adversarialism and markets support the role of market mechanisms in legal process. Common law countries tend to favor liberal market economies, so they more readily see advantages (and virtues) in market-like structures. The public prosecution monopoly is harder to explain, because

it runs against liberal market ideas. In England, private prosecution authority breaches that monopoly, and judicial review holds prosecutors to modest rule of law parameters. Neither is true in the United States. Instead, faith
in political accountability is to the overt justification for public monopoly
power. But an additional, unstated rationale is to reinforce the state's power to
ensure general security. Any diminution in public prosecution power would
weaken the state's—specifically, the executive's—control over law enforcement.[69] Even private prosecution, which adds private resources to enforcement efforts, undercuts public authority to determine enforcement policy
as well as control individual cases. With that public monopoly in place, the
American adversarial process then entrenches strongly market-based rules for
adversarial practice that serve the state interests without such explicit executive control. Limits on error-correction opportunities, for example, favor
the state's interests in efficiency and finality. And the law of defense counsel
ensures that only wealth gained from the market—significant in only a small
portion of cases—is likely to provide equality of arms between prosecution
and defense teams.

POLICING ADMINISTRATION

The state maintains largely the same monopoly over policing. It is possible
for governments to privatize policing tasks through contracts with private
security firms to replace public police departments, as they do now for probation services, prison administration, and other government functions.[70]
Although the federal government has increasingly relied on private contractors for armed security services in diplomatic and military contexts,[71] rarely
do private firms take the place of ordinary state and federal law enforcement
agencies. The primary reason for privatizing public services in this way is usually to reduce public expenditures on the theory that private firms provide the
same services more efficiently. Even if savings were possible in the policing
context, one ground to resist is that policing probably would become less democratically accountable.[72] That is not an indisputable argument. Public officials
would still be held to account for how they monitored and regulated contract
police forces even if they did not directly run them, as they are (or should be)
in innumerable other privatization contexts. Nonetheless, policing is an unusually salient public endeavor, and one that by its nature requires public policy choices about enforcement priorities and trade-offs with competing public
interests. Running prisons or probation agencies are policy-rich endeavors as
well, but with generally lower public salience. Moreover, privately contracted
police forces would entail some loss (or at least risk of loss) of direct, immediate state control over policing that is critical to state public-order and security

policies. Those are probably reasons enough why privatized local police agencies has never held much appeal.

Given that, it is unimaginable that governments would dramatically shrink public police forces and rely on the private sector to fill the void with privately hired security services, robust "neighborhood watch" programs, evidence gathering motivated by offers of rewards, and the like.[73] That roughly describes the world of the early nineteenth century, which relied mostly on private citizens to deter and report crime, supplemented by a thin public staff of sheriffs, constables, and night watchmen, as well as—in some places—a general duty to report knowledge of crimes.[74] Such a system would share with markets and adversarial process a reliance on self-interested motivation to produce public goods, rather than on public control and hierarchies that characterize police forces.

Contemporary security ambitions, however, are beyond the private sector's capacity to meet. A good portion of policing goes toward conduct without direct victims. Considerable investment also goes toward detecting wrongdoing before any harm—even much more conduct that would cause harm—occurs. Individuals and groups won't expend much effort against wrongdoing that does not directly threaten them; the "free rider" problem would leave many offenses underpoliced. (In the adjudication stage, by contrast, the state *can* align private incentives with public ends; defendants risk an adverse judgment if they fail to generate evidence, invoke applicable law, or take advantage of process.) Again, contemporary security expectations put responsibility for criminal law enforcement on the state.

PUNISHMENT INSTITUTIONS

By contrast, private administration of prisons and related services of criminal justice supervision have had some success, for reasons noted earlier.[75] States expect to save money, and public awareness of those services is much lower than it is with policing. Likewise, there is less public concern about whether those services are provided well and fairly. Still, it is worth noting an obvious limit of the market in this context as well: by its nature, criminal punishment is a state act that cannot be privatized. Certainly private actors have innumerable ways to "punish" each other in a practical sense. In many circumstances, private sanctions can be quite effective to deter antisocial conduct and maintain order; they provide "order without law," as the title of Robert Ellickson's seminal book put it.[76] But *criminal punishment*, by definition, can be imposed only by the state. Even when private firms *administer* punishment on behalf of the state, the state always dictates who is punished and the nature and duration of punishment. Despite privatizing its prisons, the state retains control of, and responsibility for, the terms of punishment, if not every detail of its daily conditions and practices.

This is consistent with the account of neoliberal penality developed by Bernard Harcourt in *The Illusion of Free Markets*, which explains the resilience and pervasiveness of state authority in a strongly free market society. Though skepticism of state regulation is a signature feature of neoliberalism and free market ideology, the state's coercive punishment power nonetheless has a critical role to play. Criminal law not only ensures security as a precondition for market exchange. At its core, much of criminal law's function is to prevent private actors from *bypassing the market*—obtaining others' property not by consensual exchange but through force or fraud.[77] On that view, it is easier to see why a strong turn toward markets since the 1970s has been accompanied by dramatic expansions of state-imposed incarceration. This parallel rise of markets and carceral power is not unprecedented. America's first era of "market revolution" in the nineteenth century was characterized by both laissez-faire ideology and the first prisons, full-time public prosecutors, and police forces.

Conclusion

American criminal justice shares so much with criminal justice systems elsewhere. Strong expectations that the state will ensure security, ever more broadly understood, are characteristic of modernity rather than particular national cultures. The same is true of modern capacities for evidence gathering and production, whether through surveillance or science. National criminal codes vary in ways that matter, but American criminal law is not, on the whole, uniquely expansive. Like U.S. jurisdictions, other nations rely on public prosecution and police monopolies even as they privatize various other state functions, including prisons. Other common law systems rely on adversarial processes that are built on market-like premises of party competition. Like the United States, most of their convictions come through guilty pleas while juries are marginalized to only a small fraction of cases. Like the United States, other nations reconcile strong state criminal law authority with liberal market political economies.

American criminal justice stands out, notoriously, for the severity of its punishment practices.[78] It is more forthright about how much it privatizes responsibility for criminal process and conviction integrity, and about the instrumental rationales on which its rules and institutions are built. The earlier and less hesitant embrace of plea bargaining is evidence of that, as are the anything-goes rules for plea bargaining, the acceptance of guilty pleas without either an admission of actual guilt or rigorous fact-finding, and much else.

Beyond the international comparisons, American criminal justice is striking on its own terms for its resort to exceptional carceral force and robust executive authority, in light of powerful national traditions that distrust state authority. American criminal justice institutions have managed to reconcile a singular capacity for criminal law enforcement with the nation's deep, durable political commitments to democracy and private markets. Indeed, they have built their authority *through* those commitments rather than in spite of them. That is a remarkable achievement when compared simply to other public agencies, programs, and institutions in American state and federal governance. Rarely do legislatures delegate broad authority to agencies with few strings attached; rarely can state officials exercise such blunt authority with so little transparency and so few meaningful checks and balances.

CHAPTER 8

Epilogue

THE AMERICAN WAY OF CRIMINAL PROCESS

The Special Status of Criminal Justice in the American State

In the story of American political development, criminal justice administration is an almost bizarre outlier. The unusual pattern of American political development left its mark on the design of U.S. agencies and regulatory schemes. In most European countries, central government authority and the rule of law were established well before democratic institutions. In the United States, broad-based democracy, along with strong common law courts, preceded a strong central government, and preceded in particular a strong executive and administrative capacity. The legacy was a distrust of executive power and a "state of courts and parties." Judges and legislatures played greater roles in policymaking and administration than in European or Asian nations. Executive agencies developed relatively late, in the late nineteenth century; traditions of patronage appointments were slowly displaced by civil service regimes. The federal Department of Justice, created only after the Civil War, is a good example.[1]

The first administrative agencies reflected this political history in their designs. The Interstate Commerce Commission (ICC), generally described as the first federal regulatory body, became a cautionary tale in how the "courts and parties" model and fear of executive bureaucracy led to an ineffective agency. The ICC was headed by a board appointees balanced between the political parties and independent of the president. Congress gave it unclear policy mandates and inadequate enforcement powers. A series of restrictive Supreme Court decisions left it with insufficient policy*making* authority.[2] Subsequent agencies often have been more effective.[3] But most still operate under significant legislative oversight or control imposed through the appointments process, control over agency budgets, or other mechanisms of influence. Courts typically have power to review rulemaking and to supervise administrative action through complaints filed by private litigants. In some regulatory regimes, such as civil rights statutes, private parties—"private attorneys general"—rather than agency staff most enforcement activity. Despite the size of and need for the contemporary administrative state, regulatory bureaucracies still reflect suspicions of executive power in ways that can impair their effectiveness.

As a consequence, U.S. regulatory agencies fare poorly in many comparisons with their counterparts in Western Europe or Japan.[4] As Francis Fukuyama has summarized, the common critique is that "the courts and legislature have usurped many of the proper functions of the executive. . . . Distrust of executive agencies leads to demands for more legal checks on administration, which reduces the quality and effectiveness of government [and] . . . reduction of bureaucratic autonomy, which in turn leads to rigid, rule-bound, uninnovative, and incoherent government."[5] The characteristic problem of American governance "is an imbalance between the strength and competence of the state on the one hand, and the institutions that were originally designed to constrain it on the other." By that Fukuyama means state executive capacity is too *weak*, and the constraints on it are too strong. There is "too much law and too much 'democracy.'"[6]

What is striking is how much of this critique is irrelevant to U.S. criminal justice institutions. More than that, it is simply wrong. The last ailment from which criminal justice suffers is weak executive capacity. Far from usurping authority, legislatures and courts have given executive officials autonomy they enjoy in few other spheres of governance. One can debate how useful criminal law is for responding to the social problems it targets, and there are certainly places that law enforcement cannot reduce violence or catch all offenders.[7] But by most plausible measures and in light of their resources, police and prosecutors are exceedingly effective at enforcing criminal law and meting out sanctions. The United States is unrivaled in administration of punishment. Whatever other hurdles they face, criminal justice agencies are not hindered by courts and legislatures from accomplishing their core mandate.

With enthusiasm rather than hesitation, legislatures delegate enforcement discretion to prosecutors free of statutory guidelines. Prosecution agencies do not share authority with private attorneys general, and they need not promulgate nor abide by formal regulations regarding their enforcement actions or policies. When they choose to issue nonbinding policies, they face no formal public comment or consultation period. (By contrast, as this book goes to press, a private party in England won judicial approval to challenge the

Crown Prosecution Service charging guidelines in cases of assisted suicide.)[8] Courts follow the same course; they affirm and facilitate rather than supervise executive discretion. The common complaint is that U.S. regulatory regimes suffer from excessive "judicialization." That criticism is debatable for police investigation practices; it is wholly implausible for prosecution-led grand jury investigations and the adjudication process, where the problem is too *little* law rather than too much. From Fukuyama's account, only the allegation of "too much democracy" holds in the criminal process context. Thin insulation from politics and majority sentiment is the only institutional feature prosecution agencies share with other bureaucracies. Yet even on this point, the effect of "too much democracy" is distinct. In the criminal justice setting, democratic accountability strengthened rather than constrained executive capacity.

Too Little Law

The idea that American criminal process suffers from too little law may seem to conflict with the familiar story about the "Warren Court revolution" in criminal procedure. In the 1960s, the Supreme Court developed a large body of constitutional doctrine for criminal justice administration. The story is now often told critically, as a cautionary tale of excessive judicial lawmaking with unintended consequences. *Miranda* warnings, exclusion of illegally seized evidence, and new prohibitions on vaguely worded offenses constrained the ability of police to investigate, gather evidence, and make arrests. Trials became more costly to administer with new rights to counsel and new rules related to juries. In reaction, legislatures added new, more specific criminal offenses—often drafted in ways that made proving violations easy—which gave police more bases to stop, search, and arrest. That is true, as far as it goes, but the details matter. Most of the criminal procedure revolution focused on police practices and trial practices. Save for the right to counsel, the revolution left the real adjudication system, from charging through sentencing, largely untouched. *Real* adjudication, of course, is *nontrial* adjudication—the procedure for 95 percent of prosecutions. Even the *Brady v. Maryland* duty of prosecutors to disclose exculpatory evidence is defined a *trial*, rather than *pretrial*, right. Charging and sentencing decisions matter in every case; plea negotiations matter in almost all. Yet neither constitutional law nor statutes speak meaningfully to charging or bargaining.[9] The U.S. Constitution is nearly irrelevant for sentencing as well (outside of capital punishment and juvenile life terms). Sentencing statutes' most important effect is to shift power from judges to prosecutors. Rules for pretrial evidence disclosure, on the other hand, have genuinely improved over the last half century (in some jurisdictions much more than others), although not consistently in ways that affect plea bargaining. And constitutional doctrine has never had much to say about the structure of the core criminal justice institutions—prosecution agencies, public defenders, or state courts.[10] The real adjudication system continues to have too little law rather than too much.

The law of criminal procedure developed in this way because of the pull of democratic and market ideology. The effect is easiest to see in the Supreme Court's decisions, but the same forces—strengthened by the Court's endorsement—have affected policymakers and state judges as well. Democratic and market-based rationales can be so influential in part because constitutional law typically requires so much specification. Properly understood, constitutional law itself contains relatively little "law" that is distinct from the moral and political judgments that specify its content. In other words, constitutional law is accepted as legally valid even when it is explicitly based on political or moral norms. This is the notion of *law* in the sense that legal positivists, notably H. L. A. Hart, define it. Under Hart's "rule of recognition," law is whatever a particular legal system recognizes as law, by whatever criteria and conventions that system has chosen.[11]

One criterion for federal constitutional law in the United States is a decision by the Supreme Court. Among other criteria are the kinds of reasons that courts provide for decisions. "Due process requires X because in my opinion that's the best thing to do" is never taken as a valid basis for law. Other reasons are acceptable bases for constitutional meaning. The "original public meaning" of a constitutional provision, for example, is an accepted basis by some. So are "fundamental conceptions of justice which lie at the base of our civil and political institutions," "the community's sense of fair play and decency," and "the evolving standards of decency that mark the progress of a maturing society."[12] Judges specify constitutional meaning, although they draw on the political and moral views made plausible in the broader culture and that now exist in a national political culture polarized on important issues with constitutional implications.[13] The political processes by which most judges are selected are a tacit recognition of this political dimension.

Particularly for unspecified obligations such as "due process" (or even "assistance of counsel"), under which courts have specified large bodies of constitutional doctrine including criminal procedure rules, the political norms and policy judgments that judges use to define specific constitutional rules are critical and often explicit. Due process analysis forthrightly rests on judicial assessments of "the private interest at stake" weighed against "the adverse impact"—that is, the anticipated practical effect—"upon the Government's interests."[14] Law defined on these grounds is uncontroversially recognized as valid, which makes it *law* by Hart's definition, even if openly built on political or moral norms and policy judgments.

This need for (and acceptance of) normative content in constitutional law creates the opening for democratic and market ideologies. In the U.S. legal tradition, among the norms recognized as playing a legitimate role in specifying constitutional doctrine—particularly for criminal procedure, and particularly in the last forty years—are democratic and market norms. Over and over, "the law" of criminal adjudication takes the form of rules or practices that prize democratic governance and political discretion, as well as market-like private motivations and interactions. The law of prosecutorial charging discretion is that there is no law, in the sense of criteria or standards that confine that discretion as a matter of constitutional due process; "the law" is basically that politics governs discretion. Similarly, the law of criminal process—even though widely criticized as a prolix code—actually *mandates* very little; most restrictions and entitlements can be deliberately waived or inadvertently forfeited. There are a lot of procedural rights and opportunities, but party self-interest (or negligence) determines, case by case, which ones are employed and which are ignored. The law of plea bargaining is that no rules—beyond the law of crimes, such as extortion or bribery—limit negotiating tactics. No overriding public interests—in substantive fairness, procedural transparency, or judicial fact-finding—trump party preferences; partisan interests and savvy have free rein. Constitutional and statutory laws create some duties of evidence disclosure, but here too parties, not legal rules, decide whether disclosure will actually take place. The constitutional law of prosecution disclosure has been crafted from instrumental rationales with a deference to political judgment—the approach that the Supreme Court has assumed will best balance cost-effective procedure with the executive branch's ability to maximize enforcement as it sees fit.[15]

These same political norms guide most of the statutory law of criminal procedure. Democratic and market norms are powerful influences on American legislators as well as on judges. In addition, constitutional law built around those norms has some influence on statutory law. There are plenty of exceptions to be sure. The law of pretrial discovery is broader than the Constitution requires—much broader in some states. But constitutional norms nonetheless have significant "gravitational pull" on statutory policymaking. That is especially likely when constitutional doctrine is built on arguments about why a specific rule is good *policy* rather than, say, why it is compelled by the Constitution's plain meaning. The law of plea bargaining stands out in this respect.

In short, democratic and market norms leave the law of criminal procedure exceedingly thin. Democratic and market procedures take the place of legal rules and judicial review. U.S. criminal process has less public law but more political judgment and private ordering. Democracy and markets can substitute for law because both are fundamentally procedural institutions. Both are practices for aggregating information, choosing between options, and allocating resources. They share something else as well: without more, both democracy and markets are indifferent to the outcomes they produce. It is the *liberal* half of the term *liberal democracy*—the principles of political liberalism—that defines a polity's substantive values, including the limits on democratic decision making. It is social welfare and regulatory policy that limit the outcomes of markets, by barring some market exchanges, facilitating some, defining terms for others, and moderating some undesirable market effects with non-market-based public policies.

The power of democratic and market norms explains why, on so many fundamental points, we can speak accurately about *American* criminal justice. The fifty state criminal justice systems and the federal system show remarkable uniformity in many of their core institutions and practices, despite a system of federalism that permits diversity and preserves their autonomy from each other, save for basic parameters set by constitutional law. "It is one of the happy incidents of the federal system," Justice Brandeis famously observed, "that a single courageous State may, if its citizens choose, serve as a laboratory; and try novel social and economic experiments."[16] Certainly there are important differences in the fifty state criminal justice systems. Jury sizes, disclosure rules, and sentencing policies (including capital punishment) vary, as do incarceration rates, methods of selecting judges, and more. Nonetheless, it is striking how much uniformity prevails on central components of U.S. criminal justice systems, especially regarding features about which the federal Constitution has nothing to say and about which non-U.S. systems—with the same traditions of English common law and adversarial trial procedure—have coalesced around a different alternative. Nonpolitical prosecution agencies may be the most obvious example; they are the norm in other common law countries but the exception in the United States. (The federal Constitution mentions judges, juries, and defense counsel but not prosecutors.) From that difference, others follow, such as the norm permitting U.S. prosecutors' partisan advocacy (and through statutory law, explicit control) on sentencing.

Perhaps this distinctiveness and internal uniformity, despite states' autonomy to follow separate paths, reflects an insularity in American governance and national culture, an attribute of a large country insulated by oceans from most others. (While English authorities in recent years have consulted with American officials on possibilities for reform of certain practices,[17] one is hard pressed to find a federal or state justice department or judiciary looking for inspiration in the practices of foreign systems.) In any case, the uniformity across U.S. jurisdictions speaks to the dominance of American political and economic traditions to shape the institutional choices. The influence of democratic and market norms that have long shaped U.S. governments and policies far exceed influences from the basic common law tradition or from the successful practices of other nations.

Incarceration, Inequality, and Polarized Politics

Over the last forty years, the United States has experienced three broad transformations in public policy and political life. Criminal justice administration has been marked by unprecedented incarceration levels, far beyond historical precedents or the practices of other nations. In the economic realm, inequality as measured by personal income and wealth sharply increased, a consequence in part of the turn toward neoliberal social and economic policies.[18] Finally, the sphere of democratic politics has seen a stark rise in political polarization and partisanship among both elected officials and the American electorate generally.[19] All three of these trends began in the 1970s, and all three are related. Some of the primary causes of inequality and partisanship have also transformed criminal justice policy.

INEQUALITY AND CRIMINAL JUSTICE

Liberal market economies not only favor weaker social safety nets and less regulated markets, they also tend to rely more on imprisonment as an instrument of social order. The governments of coordinated and social-democratic economies, by contrast, intervene more in private markets—resulting in more egalitarian wealth distributions—and on the whole they incarcerate fewer people.[20] The patterns in those economic, social policy, and carceral realms draw from deeper conceptual ideas about the proper roles of the market and the state.[21] Faith in markets and private ordering reduces the state's role in most endeavors beyond providing basic order and security. Confidence in state capacity and wariness of unregulated markets, on the other hand, leads to different, more expansive understandings of social and economic security, and more generous social welfare policies and less punitive criminal justice policies.

The United States is the exemplar of liberal market political economies, of carceral severity, and of a market-inspired moral and logical infrastructure for criminal justice rules and institutions. The constitutional rules for plea bargaining are only the most unabashed and forthright example of public law doctrines built on analogies to the law of private contract and free market exchange. It is hardly surprising that this plea bargaining regime leads to more criminal punishment, efficiency its singular ambition. Neoliberal faith in the market that started to transform U.S. economic and social policy in the 1970s—and contributed to the "great divergence" of income and wealth[22]—had some of its earliest success in the law of criminal procedure.

The same market logic facilitates an inequality in criminal justice administration much like that which characterizes strongly market-oriented economies. The law's extraordinary protection of a defendant's ability to leverage private resources in the market for legal services likewise rests frankly on market rationality.[23] In this instance the law does all it can to assure that the inequities from the private realm will carry into public adjudication. Defendants similarly situated under the criminal law are more likely to have distinct procedural experiences, and perhaps outcomes, because the law recognizes noninstrumental value in freedom to spend private funds for legal assistance. More subtly, adversarialism's market-inspired emphasizes each party's responsibility to protect its own interests and concomitantly minimizes the judicial role. That emphasis grows under the particulars of procedural default and forfeiture rules. The consequences of this party responsibility model are made deeply problematic by agency problems, the price defendants pay for their lawyers' mistakes. And inequities in the quality of defense representation mean that the agency costs suffered by parties will be spread unequally as well. Both parties and lawyers come to litigation with different levels of ability. The more that judgments depend on litigants' actions, the more that relative skill levels affect outcomes, much as in the private realm.

The Constitution's drafters, in fact, were plain on this point. *Federalist No. 10* observed that from "different and unequal faculties of acquiring property, the possession of different degrees and kinds of property immediately results."[24] In other words, inequality of market outcomes follow inevitably from disparities in talents (and from unequal wealth, the *Federalist* added, different "interests" and "sentiments"). American political economy has been unusually accepting of inequity. So has American criminal justice.

Market rationalities—and markets' implicit morality—work against strong rule of law norms dedicated to robust notions of fairness, or even of public interests distinct from party interests. Fairness in the market realm, at bottom, is the opportunity to pursue one's own interests, which no guarantees about the fairness of proportionality of outcomes. That market idea of fairness, transferred to the criminal adjudication context, leads to the view, bluntly articulated by Justice Scalia, that the criminal process does not guarantee any particular outcome to—nor even forbid the execution of—an innocent defendant "who has had a full and fair trial."[25] In adjudication as in the free market, one is entitled to freely participate in a fair process, not to the outcome one deserves. This market rationality would seem to explain why the meaning of "due process" in the criminal litigation context remains largely literal—that is, *procedural*, despite the substantive content courts have given it in other contexts.[26] But elsewhere, market values can push constitutional meaning far from literalist moorings. Efficiency, after all, coupled with the high value on giving parties control, led the Court to reject the unambiguously plain meaning of Article III's command that "The Trial of all Crimes . . . *shall be by Jury.*"[27]

The market narrative in criminal procedure has diminished the social and public and elevated the private and the economic. Like its source, the classical economic account, this narrative combines a claim about improvement through private markets with an assumption of inevitability: the exigencies that compel ever more efficient administration is a natural process, not a product of human decisions or official policies. This course of events is assumed to be a matter of necessity.[28]

The transformation in criminal adjudication resounds with echoes of another emblematic policy reform in this neoliberal era: welfare reform. Both are marked by a move away from a foundation of public rights and state obligations. Both have shifted attention to incentives for individual effort. Both stress personal over public responsibility. Both insist that market-attentive transformations are morally exemplary as well as economically efficient.

Policy can have real civic costs, however, even if it is sound sensible economic policy. At bottom, criminal procedure defines and guarantees fair process for those compelled into litigate against the state. The law makes that process conditional on individual skill and diligence through an array of rules and practices that diminish state obligations for just outcomes. Criminal judgments are contingent on each party's contribution to producing it and, in no small part, to their resources. Like welfare policy in liberal market economies, the law demands initiative and a good deal of self-sufficiency from the accused, while offering only a modicum of public assistance.

In reality, neither a system of robust criminal procedure entitlements nor robust social welfare provision is market-based. That is precisely the point. In both domains, as T. H. Marshall wrote in reference to the latter, the public role is intentionally to "supersede the market by taking goods and services out of it, or in some way to control and modify its operations so as to produce a result it would not have produced itself."[29] The expansion of criminal procedure rights in the twentieth century—perhaps foremost the positive right to effective counsel—were acknowledgments that certain public rights are essential to fair and accurate adjudication. In the half century since the right to counsel gained constitutional status, it should be clear that other components of criminal process are also critical to just outcomes but not adequately provided by the private realm or personal initiative, making them properly obligations of public regulation or provision. But the orientation of policies in a strongly liberal market economy points, across many domains, in the other direction.

POLITICAL PARTISANSHIP AND CRIMINAL JUSTICE

The realignment of two main U.S. political parties began in the same decade that economic inequality and incarceration rates began to rise. Criminal justice policy was an early, significant, and sustained topic in the political process of this period. Violent crime and property crime rates began to rise in the 1960s, and crime quickly became a salient political topic. Crime rates peaked and began to decline in the early 1990s, but incarceration rates continued to climb for fifteen years. In some large part the popular concern about crime was due also to general social disorder of the late 1960s. All of this occurred in the immediate aftermath of contentious changes in the social customs and legal order surrounding race in America, marked by the 1964 Civil Rights Act and the 1965 Voting Rights Act. Reform of American racial order was critical in initiating a new era in partisan politics; crime remained a key electoral issue for decades. The best studies of American party politics in this era emphasize the intersecting dynamics of race and crime, which politicians explicitly leveraged to potent effect in state and national elections. Beginning with the presidential contests of the 1960s and continuing for at least the next quarter century, punitive criminal justice policies were the politically successful ones in increasingly hard-fought party competition. Political polarization increases the prospects of politicized policymaking that are already inherent in American political process. Winner-take-all, first-past-the-post elections already keep political competition sharp, and nonparliamentary legislative systems put less value on compromise. Political competition over crime policy abated only when the Democrats joined the Republicans to make punitive policies the consensus approach into the early twenty-first century. Nonpolitical commissions, think tanks, experts, and bureaucracies, always weaker than in other advanced democracies, had no real hope of influencing criminal justice policy until two decades of falling crime rates finally had an effect on public and politicians' consciousness, roughly sometime around Barack Obama's election in 2008. But in the political context of the preceding forty years, criminal justice enforcement became vastly more punitive, and more racially disproportionate.

Throughout this period, changes in the law of criminal adjudication frequently tilted toward more partisan and political modes as well. When criminal process can choose between operating by legal standards or political judgment, the latter most often prevailed. Prosecutorial power is fundamentally political in U.S. systems—firmly executive in its nature, democratically accountable, and adversarial. Kenneth Culp Davis's observation nearly a half century ago remains true: prosecutors' power is "almost completely uncontrolled" by legal standards or judicial review, despite the trend toward accountability and due process limits for other types of officials with discretionary authority.[30] And in the last forty years, prosecutor power has grown and judicial power has waned in criminal justice administration.

This is most apparent in the law of sentencing. Mandatory sentencing provisions and strict guidelines reduced *judicial* discretion while giving prosecutors more leverage and control. Beyond this shift, state and federal legislation has transferred other, related powers from judicial to prosecutorial hands. In many jurisdictions, prosecutors have the exclusive power to declare a defendant eligible for a sentencing discount or for a repeat-offender enhancement, to charge some youthful offenders as adults rather than as juveniles, or to determine which first offenders (or drug offenders) can take advantage of nonpenal diversion programs rather than face ordinary prosecution.[31] In these ways, authority in the criminal process moves to more partisan actors. That is the *aim* of transferring power from the judicial to the executive branch. U.S. policymakers trust political officials more than judicial officials; they trust politics more than law. Even though most American judges are elected or politically appointed, the judicial identity remains too much of a counterweight for those who want criminal justice administered by politically attuned officials.

Somewhat more modestly, the *Brady* requirement for the state to disclose exculpatory evidence expresses the same preference for political over judicial judgment. Disclosure is not required by the Constitution—or the federal rules and those of some states—until trial. That leaves disclosure when it matters in most cases—before a negotiated guilty plea—to prosecutors' discretion. A rule that requires judicial approval for *non*disclosure before trial, by contrast, puts higher value on judicial review according to legal standards. The same favor for political over legal judgment can be inferred from prosecutorial immunity for civil liability. No matter how egregious a prosecutor's breach of constitutional rules, nor how grave the miscarriage of justice that follows from it, any sanction or remedy must come from the political process.[32]

These rules, strengthened over the last few decades, reinforce much longer patterns of the deference to political decision making throughout other aspects of criminal procedure. U.S. judges declined to make use of their statutory power to review prosecutors' dismissal of criminal charges, and they never developed a meaningful abuse-of-discretion standard to police extreme prosecutorial actions. And U.S. legislators never imposed on prosecutors administrative regulations comparable to those on most other executive agencies.

In his classic account *Two Models of the Criminal Process*, Herbert Packer identified a trend toward the "crime control model" in American procedure.[33] Half a century later, that trend has proven remarkably durable, and U.S. criminal justice systems still instantiate the model's defining features. Packer's crime control model relies on guilty pleas and executive administration, while "adjudicative fact-finding is reduced to a minimum." It is focused on security—as Packer put it, "crime repression"—and tolerates error in order to put a "premium on speed and finality." In Packer's view, the alternative "due process model"—committed to greater procedural formality, judicial responsibility, and error prevention—prevailed more in rhetoric than reality. "The legal norms today tend strongly toward the Due Process Model while the factual situation tends even more strongly toward the Crime Control Model."[34] What the subsequent five decades have clarified is the means by which the crime control model has prevailed. The state has directly asserted its carceral capacity, but at the adjudication stage the law facilitates crime control ambitions by a strategic retreat of the state and an elevation of the private, coupled with a retreat of legal regulation and an elevation of the political. Part of this trajectory is a contraction of what counts as due process, which now takes more of its content from political and market norms than it did in Packer's time. Process defined by legal mandates rather than a party's choice or two parties' mutual agreement smacks of "arbitrary limits" rather than the rule of law.[35] On that view, of course, no such process is due.

Conclusion: Law, Politics, and Reform

Things might have been different. Both England and the United States experienced sustained surges in crime from the 1970s into the 1990s, and both responded with waves of tough-on-crime legislation under conservative and then "third way" Democratic or Labour governments. English law, among other reforms, abolished peremptory strikes for jury selection and forced defendants to make pretrial disclosure of their defenses far broader than any U.S. jurisdictions demand. England, like many U.S. jurisdictions, also adopted sentencing guidelines, along with an array of new offenses and enforcement tactics, and as a result its incarceration rates rose substantially after 1990. But English criminal procedure left sentencing power in the hands of judges, relied much less on mandatory sentences, and limited sentence discounts for plea bargains. The large category of "triable either way" offenses encourages defendants to waive jury trials in exchange for bench trials with a much lower maximum sentence. And Parliament in 1987 created the Crown Prosecution Service as a politically insulated and regulated agency. A similar reform path for U.S. prosecutors is hard to imagine, save perhaps at the federal level, where similar models exist in most agencies outside the Justice Department. But it is not inconceivable that U.S. reforms otherwise might have taken forms closer to those in England, instead of choosing to emphasize mandatory sentences, deregulated plea bargaining, and other expansions of prosecutor power. The difference might have been substantial. While U.S. imprisonment rates quintupled since the 1970s, England's incarceration rates "merely" doubled (from a lower baseline) between 1993 and 2012.[36]

There is little reason to expect that U.S. criminal adjudication will retreat from its embrace of markets and democracy anytime soon. But change is nonetheless possible within the constraints of those commitments, and politically attuned criminal justice does not lead inevitably to harsher criminal justice, if only because elements of chance always play a role in policymaking and institutional design. Carol Steiker has persuasively argued that U.S. incarceration rates are "not the unfolding of a longstanding cultural predisposition to impose degrading discipline, but the result of the confluence of many factors and many different kinds of factors, some of them quite contingent."[37] Politics—the strong "populist influence" on U.S. criminal justice—is only one element. In the last half century, crime rates and racial dynamics have been among the others. But the policies these elements triggered were not inevitable, and their consequences were neither inevitable nor wholly foreseen.

In a justice system heavily invested in market mechanisms, inequality, and the role that fortune plays in case outcomes, will likely always be greater. But American criminal justice was once much more moderate, and there are indications in just the last few years that it one day could become so again. U.S. sentencing practices were not sharply different from Europe's until the 1970s. Into the 1960s, state governors often granted clemency, even to murderers, with little controversy. In the last decade several state legislatures have abolished capital punishment in their jurisdictions. A larger number have moderated other sentencing laws, decriminalized marijuana to some degree, and increased access to DNA evidence as a means to correct erroneous convictions.[38] The U.S. Department of Justice has told federal prosecutors not to interfere with state regulation of legalized marijuana and to charge less often offenses that carry mandatory prison terms.[39] For juvenile offenders, the Supreme Court in the last decade has barred sentences of death and life-without-parole.[40] Late in the second Obama administration, politicians on the left and on the right profess interest reducing incarceration and its collateral consequences in private and civil life.

A politically responsive justice system will follow the politics of the era, and over the last half century American criminal justice politics have been harsh indeed. But perhaps U.S. crime policy, after this long turn toward the extreme, may be finally entering again an era of comparative moderation and common sense. Whether that turn continues for long also will depend on politics. Because unlike its counterparts in the community of advanced democracies, the United States does little to insulate the administration of criminal justice from politics—or from the market.

NOTES

Chapter 1

1. Roy Walmsley, International Centre for Prison Studies, World Prison Population List (10th ed. 2013).
2. *Death Penalty Information Center, Executions by Year Since 1976*, at http://www.deathpen-altyinfo.org (updated May 2015).
3. *See generally* National Registry of Exonerations at https://www.law.umich.edu/special/exoneration/Pages/about.aspx (maintained by Univ. of Michigan Law School). On May 19, 2015, the Registry listed more than 1,600 exonerations, including five in the first eighteen days of May 2015, the most recent of which was exoneration of Michael McAlister, who served thirty-five years in a Virginia prison for a wrongful conviction on attempted rape. *See generally* Brandon Garrett, Convicting the Innocent: Where Criminal Prosecutions Go Wrong (2011).
4. Lafler v. Cooper, 132 S. Ct. 1376, 1397 (2012) (plea bargaining "is no longer a somewhat embarrassing adjunct to our criminal justice system; rather . . . 'it is the criminal justice system.'") (*quoting* Robert E. Scott & William J. Stuntz, *Plea Bargaining as Contract*, 101 Yale L.J. 1909, 1912 (1992)).

    The data are better for federal courts than state justice systems, but the dominance of plea bargaining is similar in all jurisdictions. In U.S. federal courts in the fiscal years 2007–2011, guilty plea rates increased from 95.8 to 96.9 percent of all convictions; percentage of convictions following trial declined from 4.2 to 3.1 percent. U.S. Sent. Comm'n, *Sourcebook for Federal Sentencing Statistics* (2011), figure C, *available at* http://www.ussc.gov/research-and-publications/annual-reports-sourcebooks/annual-reports-sourcebooks-archives. Guilty plea rates within each of the twelve federal circuits showed little variation, ranging from 93.8 to 98.3 percent in FY2011. *Id.* at Table 10.

    In state courts, 3 percent of criminal cases were resolved by either bench or jury trial; the remainder were resolved by guilty pleas, dismissals, or other disposition, according to a study with data from twenty-two states in the year 2000. Hawaii had the highest trial rate at 12.8 percent; Vermont's rate of 0.9 percent was lowest. Brian J. Ostrom, Neal Kauder, & Robert LaFountain eds., *Examining the Work of State Courts, 2001: A National Perspective from the Court Statistics Project* 63–64 (National Center for State Courts 2001), *available at* https://www.ncjrs.gov/pdffiles1/Digitization/195881NCJRS.pdf; *see also* National Center for State Courts, *State-of-the-States Survey of Jury Improvement Efforts* (2007) (reporting similar, more recent data, although in different terms, e.g., trials per 100,000 population).
5. *See* David Garland, Peculiar Institution: America's Death Penalty in an Age of Abolition (2012) (describing how American federalism and structures of democratic governance contribute to continuing use of capital punishment).

6. *See* Charities Aid Foundation, *World Giving Index 2014: A Global View of Giving* Trends (Nov. 2014) (ranking the United States tied for first among nations on three measures of charitable giving). For an influential account of diminished social solidarity in the United States, see ROBERT D. PUTNAM, BOWLING ALONE: THE COLLAPSE AND REVIVAL OF AMERICAN COMMUNITY (2000).

7. *In re* Davis, 557 U.S. 952, 955 (2009) (Scalia, J., dissenting) ("This Court has never held that the Constitution forbids the execution of a convicted defendant who has had a full and fair trial but is later able to convince a habeas court that he is 'actually' innocent.").

8. 5 JOHN WIGMORE, EVIDENCE § 1367, p. 32 (J. Chadbourn rev. 1974), *quoted in* United States v. Salerno, 505 U.S. 317 (1992) (Stevens, dissenting) (asserting more modestly that "in the Anglo American legal system cross examination is the principal means of undermining the credibility of a witness whose testimony is false or inaccurate.").

9. *See generally* JOHN H. LANGBEIN, THE ORIGINS OF THE ADVERSARY CRIMINAL TRIAL (2003).

10. AKHIL AMAR, THE BILL OF RIGHTS 95–104 (1998) (discussing the jury's structural role in the judiciary and the analogy of the judge and jury as a "bicameral" judiciary).

11. On the weakness of separation of powers in criminal justice, see Rachel E. Barkow, *Separation of Powers and the Criminal Law*, 58 STAN. L. REV. 989 (2006). The three provisions regarding the criminal jury in the U.S. Constitution are found in section 2 of Article III, the Fifth Amendment (grand juries), and in the Sixth Amendment. (The Seventh Amendment guarantees jury trials for some civil cases.) On the structural separation of power in the Bill of Rights criminal justice provisions, see AMAR, *supra* note 10, at 81–117.

12. JONATHAN SIMON, GOVERNING THROUGH CRIME: HOW THE WAR ON CRIME TRANSFORMED AMERICAN DEMOCRACY AND CREATED A CULTURE OF FEAR (2009); IAN LOADER & NEIL WALKER, CIVILIZING SECURITY (2007) (examining meaning of individual security and the relationship between security and modern state practices); Ian Loader, Benjamin J. Goold, & Angélica Thumala, *The Moral Economy of Security*, 18 THEORETICAL CRIMINOLOGY No. 3 (2014) (discussing under what conditions people experience the buying and selling of security goods and services as morally troubling), *available at* http://ssrn.com/abstract=2431339; PETER RAMSAY, THE INSECURITY STATE: VULNERABLE AUTONOMY AND THE RIGHT TO SECURITY IN THE CRIMINAL LAW (2012); Lucia Zedner, *Pre-Crime and Post-Criminology?*, 11 THEORETICAL CRIMINOLOGY 261 (2007); Lucia Zedner, *Securing Liberty in the Face of Terror: Reflections from Criminal Justice*, 32 J.L. & SOC'Y 507 (2005).

13. The jury's democratic role is an implicit them in the U.S. Supreme Court line of decisions that require jury fact-finding for certain sentencing factors. *See* Apprendi v. New Jersey, 530 U.S. 466, 477 (2000) (approving the jury's role as a "guard against a spirit of oppression and tyranny on the part of rulers" and to serve "as the great bulwark of [our] civil and political liberties") (brackets in original; internal quotation marks omitted); Blakely v. Washington, 542 U.S. 296, 306–07 (2004) ("The jury could not function as circuit-breaker in the State's machinery of justice if it were relegated to making a determination that the defendant at some point did something wrong, a mere preliminary to a judicial inquisition into the facts of the crime the State actually seeks to punish.").

14. MIRJAN R. DAMASKA, THE FACES OF JUSTICE AND STATE AUTHORITY: A COMPARATIVE APPROACH TO THE LEGAL PROCESS (1986).

15. Attorneys may have professional obligation to diligently investigate facts and produce evidence in order to adequately serve their client's interests, but the parties themselves have no legal obligation to do so. In practice that professional obligation is lightly enforced (if at all) on the defense side by effective-assistance-of-counsel doctrine. On the side of the prosecution, where the "client" is the state itself, decisions about evidence production fall under the broader rubric of unregulated prosecutorial discretion.

16. ALEXIS DE TOCQUEVILLE, DEMOCRACY IN AMERICA 270 (1841; 1969) (George Lawrence transl.; J. P. Mayer ed.).

17. Seymour Lipset, American Exceptionalism: A Double-Edged Sword 20–21, 40 (1996). *See also* Gerald Rosenberg, The Hollow Hope: Can Courts Bring About Social Change? (1991).

18. Robert Kagan, Adversarial Legalism (2001).

19. *Id.* at 4.

20. William J. Stuntz, The Collapse of American Criminal Justice (2011); Stephanos Bibas, The Machinery of Criminal Justice (2012).

21. Stuntz, *supra* note 20, at 31, 39; Bibas, *supra* note 20, at 92, 116, & 126–27.

22. *See* George Fisher, Plea Bargaining's Triumph: A History of Plea Bargaining in America (2004); Mike McConville & Chester Mirsky, Jury Trials and Plea Bargaining: A True History (2005); Mary E. Vogel, Coercion to Compromise (2007) (social and political context of early plea bargaining in the United States); Mary E. Vogel, *The Social Origins of Plea Bargaining: An Approach to the Empirical Study of Discretionary Leniency?*, 35 J.L. & Soc'y 201 (2008); Mary E. Vogel, *The Social Origins of Plea Bargaining: Conflict and the Law in the Process of State Formation*, 33 Law & Soc'y Rev. 161 (1999); Lawrence Friedman & Robert V. Percival, The Roots of Justice: Crime and Punishment in Alameda County, California, 1870–1910 (1981).

23. Two themes are common to all accounts. One is that the rise of plea bargaining is associated to some degree with rising caseloads, or more precisely to caseloads that grow faster than trial court capacity—thus more cases *per* prosecutor and judge. The second theme is that plea bargaining served the interests of the trial court actors who created it. Bargaining served the interests of the professionals with the most power over adjudication practice, prosecutors and trial judges. Scholars disagree about how important caseload pressure is to bargaining practice and about how precisely to describe the interests that trial court officials pursue through bargaining. Some stress pressure to resolve cases and clear docket backlogs, to minimize workloads, to gain certainty over case outcomes through negotiated settlements rather than face the uncertain outcome of trials. Others suggest that a key interest is expanding the state's criminal enforcement capacity within existing resources. But caseloads and some mix of professional self-interest are central to every account of plea bargaining. Bibas, Fisher, and Mirsky and McConville all stress in various ways the self-interests of trial court professionals.

24. *See* Maximo Langer, *Rethinking Plea Bargaining: The Practice and Reform of Prosecutorial Adjudication in American Criminal Procedure*, 33 Am. J. Crim. L. 223 (2006).

25. Fifty-one jurisdictions accounts for the fifty states and the federal courts. One can raise the number by adding the District of Columbia and other nonstate jurisdictions such as Puerto Rico.

26. The leading argument on this point is William J. Stuntz, *The Pathological Politics of Criminal Law*, 100 Mich. L. Rev. 505 (2001).

Chapter 2

* *Epigraphs:* Taylor v. Louisiana, 419 U.S. 522, 530 (1975); Atkins v. Virginia, 536 U.S. 304, 323–24 (2002) (Rehnquist, C.J., dissenting).

1. For a brief overview linked to capital punishment in the United States, see David Garland, Peculiar Institution: America's Death Penalty in an Age of Abolition 152–57 (2012). For more sweeping overviews, see Peter Schuck & James Wilson, Understanding America: The Anatomy of an Exceptional *Nation* (2008); Russell Duncan & Joseph Goddard, Contemporary America (2005); Seymour Lipset, Continental Divide: The Values and Institutions of the United States and Canada (1990); John L. Campbell & Ove K. Pedersen, *Knowledge Regimes and Comparative Political Economy, in* Ideas and Politics in Social Science Research 167–90 (Daniel Béland & Robert Cox eds., 2011) (discussing evidence that expertise and information sources influencing public policymaking in the United States

more often come from partisan political sources than is true in the United Kingdom or European nations); JOHN L. CAMPBELL & OVE K. PEDERSEN, THE NATIONAL ORIGINS OF POLICY IDEAS: KNOWLEDGE REGIMES IN THE UNITED STATES, FRANCE, GERMANY AND DENMARK (2014) (book-length study of the same).

2. *See* SANFORD LEVINSON, OUR UNDEMOCRATIC CONSTITUTION (2006).

3. THE DEMOCRATIC EXPERIMENT: NEW DIRECTIONS IN AMERICAN POLITICAL HISTORY (Meg Jacobs, William J. Novak, & Julian E. Zelizer eds., 2003). On localism, see Thomas J. Sugrue, *All Politics Is Local: The Persistence of Localism in Twentieth Century America*, in *id.* at 301.

4. BERNARD GROFMAN & LISA HANDLEY, REDISTRICTING IN COMPARATIVE PERSPECTIVE (2008) (United States is one of only fourteen countries—out of sixty studied—that uses legislatures to redraw electoral districts, and twelve of the other thirteen have proportional representation requirements).

5. Ballard v. United States, 329 U.S. 187, 193, 195 (1946), *quoting* Thiel v. Southern Pacific Co., 328 U.S. 217, 220 (1946).

6. In 2006 state courts produced 1,132,290 convictions, compared to 79,725 convictions in federal district courts the same year—about 7 percent of the state-court volume. *See* Bureau of Justice Statistics, U.S. Dep't of Justice, Bureau of Justice Statistics, *Sourcebook of Criminal Justice Statistics—2014*, tbls. 5.44 & 5.24. Federal prisons held about 8 percent of all U.S. prison and jail inmates in 2003: 165,800 federal inmates compared to 1,912,800 inmates in state custody. *Id.* at tbl. 6.2.

7. For examples from Indiana, Maryland, Michigan, New York, Pennsylvania, and Virginia of state constitutions in this era making local prosecutors into elected positions, see: IND. CONST. 1851 (art. 7, sec. 11); MD. CONST. 1851 (art. 5; see also art. 3, forbidding creation of state attorney general office); 11. MICH. CONST. 1850 (arts. 8 and 10); N.C. CONST. 1868 (art. 29); N.Y. CONST. 1846 (art. 10); VA. CONST. 1851 (art. 16, sec. 19). *See also* MIKE MCCONVILLE & CHESTER MIRSKY, JURY TRIALS AND PLEA BARGAINING: A TRUE HISTORY 25–42 (2005) (describing early systems in New York of judicial or gubernatorial appointment of prosecutors, until elections election of prosecutors began in 1847); ALLEN STEINBERG, TRANSFORMATION OF AMERICAN CRIMINAL JUSTICE: PHILADELPHIA, 1800–80, at 152–57 (1989) (Philadelphia's judges were shifted to elective office in 1851; the district attorney followed in 1852).

8. JED HANDELSMAN SHUGERMAN, THE PEOPLE'S COURTS 6, 57–102 (2012); *id.* at 101 (describing hope that elected judges would have power to check corrupt legislatures); *see also* Caleb Nelson, *A Re-Evaluation of Scholarly Explanations for the Rise of the Elective Judiciary in Antebellum America*, 37 AM. J. LEGAL HIST. 190 (1993) (same).

   Prosecutors, like police agencies and judges, nonetheless grew more professionalized in the decades after the shift to elections, at least in the sense that more were full-time positions. On prosecutors' professionalization, see Jed Handelsman Shugerman, *The Creation of the Department of Justice*, 66 STAN. L. REV. 121 (2014) (hereafter *Dep't of Justice*). Some historians point to their gradual control over criminal justice administration as an explanation for plea bargaining's rise. Full-time status of these officials made bargaining easier and changed their professional self-interests in ways well served by bargaining. Leading scholarship on the professionalization/plea bargaining thesis includes LAWRENCE M. FRIEDMAN & ROBERT V. PERCIVAL, THE ROOTS OF JUSTICE: CRIME AND PUNISHMENT IN ALAMEDA COUNTY, CALIFORNIA, 1870–1910, at 194 (1981); Malcolm M. Feeley, *Plea Bargaining and the Structure of the Criminal Process*, 7 JUSTICE SYSTEM J. 338, 349–50 (1982); Lawrence M. Friedman, *Plea Bargaining in Historical Perspective*, 12 LAW &. SOC'Y REV. 247 (1979); John Langbein, *Understanding the Short History of Plea Bargaining*, 12 LAW & SOC'Y REV. 261, 262–64 (1979); *see also* MCCONVILLE & MIRSKY, *supra* note 7, at 6–9 (discussing competing theories of plea bargaining and the relevance of professionalization). For federal prosecutors, professionalization, and anti-patronage reforms (though not civil service protection) began in the 1870s. Shugerman, *Dep't of Justice, supra* note 8.

9. *See* McConville & Mirsky, *supra* note 7, at 198, 217, 310–14 (describing politicized judges in nineteenth New York); Carolyn B. Ramsey, *The Discretionary Power of "Public" Prosecutors in Historical Perspective*, 39 Am. Crim. L. Rev. 1309 (2002) (describing New York City); Steinberg, *supra* note 7, at 92–96 & 119 (describing courts in nineteenth-century Philadelphia); Pound, Criminal Justice in America 183 (1924) (criticizing "intimate connection of the prosecutor's office with politics."); Raymond Moley, Politics and Criminal Prosecution (1927) (similar).

10. Alaska, Connecticut, and New Jersey (and the federal district, Washington, D.C.) do not elect prosecutors. *See* Steven W. Perry, *Prosecutors in State Courts, 2005*, at 2 (Bureau of Justice Statistics, Bulletin No. NCJ No. 213799, July 2006), *available at* http://www.ojp.usdoj.gov/bjs/pub/pdf/psc05.pdf. *See also* Ronald F. Wright, *How Prosecutor Elections Fail Us*, 6 Ohio St. J. Crim. L. 581, 589 (2008–2009). On the federal system, see 28 U.S.C. § 541-46 (specifying chief federal prosecutors are appointed by the president to four-year terms subject to Senate confirmation and—like their assistant prosecutors—serve at the pleasure of the president); Michael J. Ellis, *The Origins of the Elected Prosecutor*, 121 Yale L.J. 1528, 1528 n.1 (2012) (documenting uniqueness of U.S election of prosecutors). For Connecticut, whose prosecutors are appointed through an independent commission, see website of Criminal Justice Commission, http://www.ct.gov/cjc/site/default.asp (noting state Constitution art. XXIII establishes the Commission and its power to appoint prosecutors).

11. *See* Perry, *supra* note 10, at 11 (appendix).

12. Some state attorneys general have formal authority to supervise or take over local prosecutions, but they exercise it only rarely; others lack even formal power save in special circumstances, such as authorization by the governor. Legislation often authorizes local prosecutors within a state to independently devise prosecution policies, although statewide prosecutor associations can exert some influence toward more uniform practices. *See, e.g.,* Fla. Stat. §775.08401 (2014) (requiring "the state attorney in each judicial circuit" to adopt "uniform criteria" for charging under certain sentence-enhancement statutes, and requiring each circuit's policy to be on file with the state prosecutor association, but prohibiting judicial enforcement of such policies); Fla. Stat. § 741.2901 (2010) and Wisc. Stat. § 968.075 (2012) (both requiring local prosecutors to devise policies regarding domestic violence prosecutions).

    Many states vest the duty to prosecute expressly with local prosecutors rather than the attorney general. *See* 7 Am. Jur.2d Attorney General §§ 15, 34 (2012); 7A C.J.S. Attorney General § 67 (2012). For statutes limiting attorney general power to intervene in local prosecution, see, e.g., Colo. Rev. Stat. § 24-31-101(1)(a) (2010); N.Y. Exec. L. § 63(2) (2010). For examples of statutes authorizing general or supervisory power to the attorney general, see, e.g., Cal. Gov't Code § 12550 (2010); Wash. Rev. Code § 43.10.090 (2010). For decisions describing limits on powers of the attorney general under state law, see People v. Knippenberg, 325 Ill. App. 3d 251, 757 N.E.2d 667 (Ill. App. 2001); Com. v. Mulholland, 702 A.2d 1027 (Pa. 1997); Johnson v. Pataki, 691 N.E.2d 1002 (N.Y. 1997) (describing governor's statutory authority to replace locally elected prosecutors, and the state attorney general's power to take over local prosecutions only after authorization from the governor). For an overview of U.S. prosecutorial power and the lack of judicial supervision, see Abby L. Dennis, *Reining in the Minister of Justice: Prosecutorial Oversight and the Superseder Power*, 57 Duke L.J. 131 (2007).

13. Elected attorney generals or justice ministers have ultimate authority prosecutors in many countries, as discussed later in this chapter. In Switzerland, the closest analogue to prosecutors, investigating judges, are elected in a few localities (cantons), though not in most. *See* Steven P. Croley, *The Majoritarian Difficulty: Elective Judiciaries and the Rule of Law*, 62 U. Chi. L. Rev. 689, 691 n.3 (1995); The Training of Judges and Public Prosecutors in Europe, vol. 68, p. 147 (Council of Europe & Centre for Judicial Studies 1995).

    For discussions of political accountability and influence in federal prosecution, see Daniel C. Richman, *Political Control of Federal Prosecutions: Looking Back and Looking*

Forward, 58 Duke L.J. 2087 (2009); Daniel C. Richman, *"Project Exile" and the Allocation of Federal Law Enforcement Authority*, 43 Ariz. L. Rev. 369 (2001); Daniel C. Richman, *Criminal Law, Congressional Delegation and Enforcement Discretion*, 46 UCLA L. Rev. 757 (1999); Cornell W. Clayton, The Politics of Justice: The Attorney General and the Making of Legal Policy (1992).

In the Police Reform and Social Responsibility Act 2011, England and Wales switched to a system of locally elected Police and Crime Commissioners with the power to supervise local police agencies and dismiss local Chief Constables. *See* House of Commons Home Affairs Committee, *Police and Crime Commissioners: Power to Remove Chief Constables* (July 17, 2013), at http://www.publications.parliament.uk/pa/cm201314/cmselect/cmhaff/487/487.pdf.

14. For an overview of differences in approaches to prosecution, see Jacqueline Hodgson & Andrew Roberts, *Criminal Process and Prosecution, in* The Oxford Handbook of Empirical Legal Research 64 (Peter Cane & Herbert M. Kritzer eds., 2010).

15. Smedleys Ltd. v. Breed [1974] AC 839, 856 (Viscount Dilhorne) ("It has never been the rule in this country . . . that criminal offences must automatically be the subject of prosecution.").

16. On differing civil law and common law understandings of the legality principle and trust in judges and prosecutors, see James Q. Whitman, *No Right Answer?, in* Criminal Procedure and Evidence in a Comparative and International Context 371, 377–87 (John T. Jackson, Maximo Langer, & Peter Tillers eds., 2008). *See also* Isabel Kessler, *A Comparative Analysis of Prosecution in Germany and the United Kingdom: Searching for Truth or Getting a Conviction?, in* Ronald Huff & Martin Killias, Wrongful Convictions: International Perspectives on Miscarriages of Justice 213, 216 (2008); Julia Fionda, Public Prosecutors and Discretion: A Comparative Study (1995) (describing German prosecutors' opportunity principle as granting wide discretion for low-level crimes but less discretion for more serious offenses).

17. *See* Fionda, *supra* note 16, at 11 (describing historical reasons for Germany's restrictions on prosecutorial power).

18. On a classic analysis of American prosecutorial discretion to charge and to decline to charge, compared to other officials, see Kenneth Culp Davis, Discretionary Justice: A Preliminary Inquiry 188, 207–08 (1969) ("The affirmative power to prosecute is enormous, but the negative power to withhold prosecution may be even greater, because it is less protected against abuse. . . . The plain fact is that nine-tenths of local prosecutors' decisions are supervised or reviewed by no one.").

19. Charles Winfield, *Nolle Prosequi*, 5 Crim. L. Mag. 1 (1884); James Fitzjames Stephen, 1 History of Criminal Law of England (1st ed. 1872); Commonwealth v. Tuck, 20 Pick. 356, 37 Mass. 356 (1838). The only traditional limit on *nolle prosequi* power comes at a late stage; once a jury is sworn, jeopardy attaches and a prosecution-initiated dismissal can bar re-prosecution. States since the nineteenth century have varied their statutory rules on whether a judge must approve dismissal or the prosecutor's *nolle pros* power is unilateral, but that distinction has little practical effect. Judges cannot command prosecutors to prosecute; refusal to dismiss amounts only to the power to bar the prosecutor's authority to re-file the same charge later.

For a representative modern statement of prosecutor's *nolle pros* power, see State v. Vixamar, 687 So.2d 300 (Fla. App. 4th Dist. 1997) (noting "the prosecutor's exclusive discretion to decide whether a criminal case should be discontinued and in the absence of a procedural rule authorizing judicial intervention," *citing* State v. Matos, 589 So.2d 1022 (Fla. 3d Dist. 1991)).

20. On weaknesses of grand juries, see Andrew D. Leipold, *Why Grand Juries Do Not (And Cannot) Protect the Accused*, 80 Cornell L. Rev. 260 (1995). For an argument that juries have little indirect effect on bargaining, see Stephanos Bibas, *Plea Bargaining Outside the Shadow of Trial*, 117 Harv. L. Rev. 2463 (2004).

21. R. (FB) v. DPP [2009] Cr. App. R. 38, at ¶52.
22. R. v. DPP Ex p. Manning [2001] Q.B. 330, at ¶23.
23. *R. (FB)* [2009] Cr. App. R. 38, at ¶52.
24. Leading decisions include R. v. Director of Public Prosecutions Ex p. Manning [2001] Q.B. 330, R. (Da Silva) v. Director of Public Prosecutions [2006] EWHC 3204 (Admin); Sharma v. Brown-Antoine [2006] UKPC 57; [2007] W.L.R. 780; Marshall v. Director of Public Prosecutions [2007] UKPC 4; R. v. Metropolitan Police Commissioner, ex p. Blackburn [1968] 2 Q.B. 118; R. v. DPP (Kebiline) [2000] 2 A.C. 326.

   England created its prosecution agency, the Crown Prosecution Service (CPS), only in 1985. *See* Prosecution Offences Act of 1985, No. 1800, c.23, § 1 (England and Wales); Andrew Ashworth & Mike Redmayne, The Criminal Process 222–23 (4th ed. 2010). The Director of Public Prosecutions was created in 1879 but did not handle most prosecutions until the creation of the CPS. In the intervening century, police came to dominate filing of criminal charges, supplemented by private prosecutions, a system that eventually was viewed as providing insufficient supervision of charging decisions by police. *See* Glanville Williams, *The Power to Prosecute*, (1955) Crim. L. Rev. 596, 601–03.

25. *R (Da Silva)* [2006] EWHC 3204 (Admin) (summarizing three grounds for review at ¶24) and *citing* R. v. DPP, ex p. C [1995] Cr. App. R. 136); R (on application of Guest) v. DPP [2009] 2 Cr. App. R. 26, Crim. L.R. 730; R. v. General Council of the Bar, *ex parte* Percival [1990] 3 All ER 137. For an overview, see C. Hilson, *"Discretion to Prosecute and Judicial Review,"* [1993] Crim. L. Rev. 739; Ashworth & Redmayne, *supra* note 24, at 222; Crown Prosecution Service, *Legal Guidance: Appeals: Judicial Review of Prosecutorial Decisions*, at http://www.cps.gov.uk/legal/a_to_c/ appeals_judicial_review_of_prosecution_decisions/.

   English courts have noted that the European Convention on Human Rights may impose affirmative obligations on member states that certain instances *require* prosecutions, or that more generally require a state to maintain criminal justice system that provides sufficient protection to citizens. So far, English standards of review of noncharging decisions, based in domestic law, have been held sufficient to meet any such obligation. *See* R. (FB) v. DPP [2009] Cr. App. R. 38 [2009] EWHC 106 (discussing state obligations under Articles 2 and 3). But the adequacy of English law suggests that its standards of judicial review operate in effect to impose a modest affirmative duty on prosecutors that has no American parallel.

   Separately, because the English judiciary lacks authority equivalent to American judges' power to invalidate statutes as unconstitutional, a court will not stay a prosecution under a statute simply because the court concludes the statute is in conflict with the European Convention on Human Rights. *But see* R. v. DPP (Kebiline) [2000] 2 A.C. 326 (noting that in exceptional cases, defense arguments that a charged offense is incompatible with the ECHR (or that evidence gathering violated the ECHR) may be raised as abuse of process on the basis that it is unfair for the prosecution to proceed).

26. *R (Da Silva)* [2006] EWHC 3204 (Admin) at ¶60 (noting use of redacted investigative report and case notes from CPS but disavowing evaluation of evidence).

27. Jordan v. United Kingdom (2003) 37 EHRR 52 ¶¶ 82–86, 122–23, 142–45 (under ECHR art. 2, prosecutors should give reasons explaining a decision not to bring criminal charges after an investigation into a death caused by police shooting for not charging to victim's family when deceased is killed by police). *See also* the view of Bingham C.J., in R. v. DPP Ex p. Manning [2001] Q.B. 330 ("In the absence of compelling grounds for not giving reasons, we would expect the Director to give reasons in such a case [of nonprosecution]: to meet the reasonable expectation of interested parties that either a prosecution will follow or a reasonable explanation for not prosecuting be given. . . .").

   For rare examples of U.S. rules requiring prosecutors to give reasons for not charging, see Colo. Rev. Stat. § 16-5-209; Pa. R. Crim. Pro. 506 (both requiring prosecutor's reasons upon private complaint objecting to nonprosecution).

For a description of Irish law that insulates prosecutor decisions from victim challenges and judicial review to a greater degree than England and Wales, see Barry Donoghue, *Explaining Prosecution Decisions in Ireland* (July 2008), *available at* http://www.isrcl. org/Conference_Papers.htm (International Society of Criminal Law Reform; visited Dec. 6, 2012).

28. *R (Da Silva)* [2006] EWHC 3204 (Admin) at ¶20.

29. *See* R. v. DPP Ex p. Manning [2001] Q.B. 330; R. v. Metropolitan Police Commissioner ex p Blackburn [1958] 2 QB 118; Ashworth & Redmayne, *supra* note 24, at 221–22.

30. For an example of a court finding wrongful a decision to discontinue prosecution, see R (FB) v. DPP [2009] Cr. App. R. 38 [2009] EWHC 106 (Admin). On prosecutor's *nolle pros* authority, see R. v. B(F) [2010] 2 Cr. App. R. 35, at ¶13; R(Gujra) v. Crown Prosecution Service [2013] A.C. 484. *See also* R. v. DPP, ex p. C [1995] Cr. App. R. 136.

31. R. v. Inland Revenue Commissioners, *ex parte* Mead [1993] All ER 772. On general standard of unreasonableness that justifies a judicial decision to quash a public agency's decision, see Associated Provincial Picture Houses Ltd. v. Wednesbury Corporation [1948] KB 223 (*Wednesbury*-unreasonableness); *see also* Ashworth & Redmayne, *supra* note 24, at 221. On practice elsewhere in the Commonwealth, see Dana S. Seetahal, Commonwealth Caribbean Criminal Practice and Procedure 22–23 (3d ed. 2011). For an example of contrasting American rule that bars courts from instructing juries on lesser offenses over a prosecutor's objection, see People v. Birks, 960 P.2d 1073 (Cal. 1998).

32. On abuse of process standards, including pursuit of charges after agreeing not to do so, see, Nembhard v. DPP [2009] EWHC 194 (court's authority to stay prosecutions for abuse of process); R. v. Bloomfield [1997] Cr. App. R. 135 (staying prosecution under abuse of process standard from continuing with drug prosecution after announcing that that intended to not to); R. (on the application of Smith) v. CPS [2010] EWHC 3593 (same in domestic violence case). *See generally* Andrew Choo, Abuse of Process (2d ed. 2008).

33. R. v. Adaway [2004] EWCA Crim 283; (2004) 168 J.P. 645.

34. In extreme cases U.S. courts also dismiss prosecutions for police misconduct. *See, e.g.*, United States v. Broward, 459 F. Supp. 321 (W.D. N.Y. 1978) (government agents deliberate misrepresentation in affidavit of facts relating to informant identity, made to magistrate, and related false statements to district judge, required dismissal of drug prosecution for governmental misconduct).

35. R v. Horseferry Road Magistrates' Court, *ex parte* Bennett [1994] AC 42, 150.

36. R. v. B(F) [2010] 2 Cr. App. R. 35 (trial judge had no power to quash a valid indictment on grounds that resources are limited). For a similar American decision, see People v. Stewart, 217 N.W.2d 894 (Mich. 1974); *see also* Czajka v. Koweek, 953 N.Y.S.2d 394, 397 (App. Div. 2012) (district attorney has wide discretion over public resources to discharge duties and quoting Matter of Soares v. Herrick, 928 N.Y.S.2d 386, 390 (App. Div. 2011)).

37. *See, e.g.*, McArthur v. State, 597 So.2d 406 (Fla. App. 1st Dist. 1992) (victim has no authority over decisions to prosecute; that power rests with the state's attorney). Scanlon v. State Bar of Georgia, 443 S.E.2d 830 (Ga. 1994) (private citizens have no *judicially cognizable* interests in prosecutions or decisions not to prosecute) State v. Winne, 12 N.J. 152, 96 A.2d 63 (N.J. 1953) (prosecutor's exclusive authority).

For a more subtle example of U.S. disfavor of restrictions on prosecutorial authority based on prior notice to defendants, consider judicial interpretation of the following federal statute:

Hearing before report of criminal violation. Before any violation of this chapter is reported by the Secretary to any United States attorney for institution of a criminal proceeding, the person against whom such proceeding is contemplated shall be given appropriate notice and an opportunity to present his views, either orally or in writing, with regard to such contemplated proceeding.

21 U.S.C.A. § 335. The Supreme Court has concluded that failure of officials to meet this obligation is not a prerequisite to prosecution. United States v. Dotterweich, 320 U.S. 277, 278–79 (1943).

A few states have rarely-used provisions giving courts or private parties some ability to check public prosecutors. Two states require prosecutors to file reasons for nonprosecution decision with the court in certain serious cases. *See* MICH. COMP. LAWS § 767.41 (in certain cases, prosecutors must file reasons with court for not charging, and court upon review can order prosecutor to file charge); NEB. REV. STAT. § 29-1606 (same). Additionally, Pennsylvania requires prosecutors to give reasons, which courts may review, only for nonprosecution after receiving a *private* complaint. PA. R. CRIM. PRO. 506.

38. *See* ALA. CODE § 12-17-186 (1975) (presiding judge may appoint an attorney to act as public prosecutor in cases of conflict of interest "or when the district attorney refuses to act"; no appellate decisions document that this power has ever been used); MINN. STAT. § 388.12 (same, but whenever public prosecutor "is present," requiring his consent for any payment to court-appointed prosecutor); COLO. REV. STAT. § 16-5-209 (upon private complaint alleging "unjustified" refusal to charge, judge may require public prosecutor to explain reasons; if "arbitrary and capricious," judge may order prosecution or appoint special prosecutor); N.D. CENT. CODE § 11-16-06 (authorizing court to appoint special prosecutor if "the state's attorney has refused or neglected to perform any" duties). Additionally, Pennsylvania allows courts to authorize private prosecutors to take over cases from public prosecutors. 16 PA. CONST. STAT. ANN. § 1409 (authorizing private prosecutors). And Texas alone retains a unique "court of inquiry" procedure, also rarely deployed, that empowers judges to investigate suspected crimes and issue arrest warrants. *See* TEX. CODE CRIM. PRO. arts. 52.01-52.08.

39. Wayte v. United States, 470 U.S. 598, 607 (1985); Bordenkircher v. Hayes, 434 U.S. 357, 364 (1978). *See also* United States v. Giannattasio, 979 F.2d 98, 100 (7th Cir. 1992) ("Prosecutorial discretion resides in the executive, not in the judicial, branch, and that discretion, though subject of course to judicial review to protect constitutional rights, is not reviewable for a simple abuse of discretion."); Linda R. S. v. Richard D., 410 U.S. 614, 619 (1973) (holding that a crime victim lacks standing in federal court to seek an injunction against a state prosecutor's unconstitutionally discriminatory enforcement policy for crime of failure to pay child support, because "a private citizen lacks a judicially cognizable interest in the prosecution or non-prosecution of another").

40. *Wayte*, 470 U.S. at 607; *quoted in* United States v. Armstrong, 517 U.S. 456, 463–65 (1996). *See also* United States v. Giannattasio, 979 F.2d 98, 100 (7th Cir. 1992) (Posner, J.) ("Prosecutorial discretion resides in the executive, not in the judicial, branch, and that discretion, though subject of course to judicial review to protect constitutional rights, is not reviewable for a simple abuse of discretion.").

41. *See generally* 27 C.J.S. District and Prosecuting Attorneys § 28 (2012) (collecting and summarizing cases that affirm wide prosecutorial discretion subject to judicial review generally only under deferential constitutional rules). U.S. courts commonly emphasize the limits of judicial capacity to interfere with prosecutors' decisions, especially if the remedy would be dismissal of criminal charges. *See, e.g.,* United States v. Smith, 231 F.3d 800 (11th Cir. 2000); State v. Perleberg, 736 N.W.2d 703 (Minn. Ct. App. 2007), *review denied*, (Oct. 16, 2007). Dismissal is an "extraordinary remedy" that must meet high standards for "outrageous" government misconduct. United States v. Dyke, 718 F.3d 1282 (10th Cir. 2013); United States v. Smith, 924 F.2d 889, 897 (9th Cir.1991) ("[T]o dismiss on the basis of outrageous government conduct, the court must find the

government's conduct 'so grossly shocking and so outrageous as to violate the universal sense of justice.'"); United States v. Garza-Juarez, 992 F.2d 896, 903–04 (9th Cir. 1993) ("government's conduct may warrant a dismissal of the indictment if that conduct is so excessive, flagrant, scandalous, intolerable and offensive as to violate due process") *citing* United States v. Luttrell, 889 F.2d 806, 811 (9th Cir.1989), amended, 923 F.2d 764 (9th Cir.1991) (en banc). For published federal prosecutorial standards that are not judicially enforceable, see Dep't of Justice, *U.S. Attorney's Manual, available at* http://www.justice.gov/usao/eousa/foia_reading_room/usam/. *See also* United States v. Williams, 504 U.S. 36 (1992) (federal courts' supervisory powers over grand jury does not include power to make a rule allowing dismissal of an otherwise valid indictment where the prosecutor failed to introduce substantial exculpatory evidence to a grand jury).

42. United States v. Nixon, 418 U.S. 683, 693, 707 (1974), *citing* Confiscation Cases, 74 U.S. (Wall.) 454 (1869).

43. *Nixon*, 418 U.S. at 707.

44. Blackledge v. Perry, 417 U.S. 21 (1974).

45. *See* U. S. v. Goodwin, 457 U.S. 368 (1982) (imposed an insuperable requirement "actual evidence" of prosecutorial vindictiveness claims); Bordenkircher v. Hayes, 434 U.S. 357 (1978) (approving prosecutor's increase in charge severity as a means to encourage plea bargaining).

46. *Bordenkircher*, 434 U.S. at 364–65; *quoted in* Wayte v. United States, 470 U.S. 598, 607 (1985); *see also* United States v. Armstrong, 517 U.S. 456, 463–65 (1996) (same, quoting *Wayte*). For a comparable faith in prosecutorial rectitude, see Purkett v. Elem, 514 U.S. 765, 767–68 (1995), which establishes a presumption against prosecutors' racial bias in striking potential jurors from the jury.

47. *See* Wayte v. United States, 470 U.S. 598 (1985); *Bordenkircher*, 434 U.S. 357; United States v. Giannattasio, 979 F.2d 98, 100 (7th Cir. 1992); United States v. Armstrong, 517 U.S. 456 (1996).

48. Heckler v. Chaney, 470 U.S. 821, 832 (1985). The Take Care Clause is U.S. Const., art. II, § 3.

49. *Wayte*, 470 U.S. at 607; *quoted in* United States v. Armstrong, 517 U.S. 456, 463–65 (1996).

50. *See, e.g.,* Confiscation Cases, 74 U.S. (Wall.) 454 (1869) ("The prosecutive decision traditionally has been exercised by the executive department"); United States v. Armstrong, 517 U.S. 456, 464 (1996) ("A selective-prosecution claim asks a court to exercise judicial power over a 'special province' of the Executive. . . . They have this latitude because they are designated by statute as the President's delegates to help him discharge his constitutional responsibility to 'take Care that the Laws be faithfully executed.'") (*citing* Heckler v. Chaney, 470 U.S. 821, 832 (1985)) Morrison v. Olson, 487 U.S. 654 (1988) (affirming independent prosecutor statute, inter alia because the prosecutor remained in the executive branch, despite president's lack of control, and judges did not exercise "supervise" prosecutor); United States v. Ferreira, 54 U.S. 40 (1851). For examples of lower court decisions addressing distinctions of judicial and executive powers and defining prosecution as part of the latter, see United States v. Scott, 631 F.3d 401, 405 (7th Cir. 2011) ("Under our system of separation of powers, prosecutors retain broad discretion to enforce criminal laws because they are required to help the President 'take Care that the Laws be faithfully executed.'"); United States v. Woods, 576 F.3d 400, 409 (7th Cir. 2009) (explaining that "[t]here is nothing that this court either could or should do about the prosecutorial discretion that is exercised at the charging state"); United States v. Moore, 543 F.3d 891, 899–900 (7th Cir.2008); *In re* United States, 503 F.3d 638, 641 (7th Cir. 2007); United States v. Roberson, 474 F.3d 432, 434 (7th Cir. 2007); Nader v. Bork, 366 F. Supp. 104, 109 (D.D.C. 1973) ("The suggestion that the Judiciary be given responsibility for the appointment and supervision of a . . . [p]rosecutor . . . . is most unfortunate. . . . The Courts must remain neutral. Their duties are not prosecutorial.").

For example of state courts on this point, see, e.g., People v. Birks, 960 P.2d 1073, 1089–90 (Cal. 1998) ("prosecuting authorities, exercising executive functions, ordinarily have the sole discretion to determine whom to charge. . . . The prosecution's authority in this regard is founded, among other things, on the principle of separation of powers, and generally is not subject to supervision by the judicial branch. . . . [T]he power to dispose of charges is judicial in nature, but . . . it is ordinarily the prosecution's function to select and propose the charges."); *In re* Padget, 678 P.2d 870, 873 (Wyo. 1984). *More generally, see* James Madison, THE FEDERALIST NOS. 47 & 51 (C. Rossiter ed., 1961); Rachel E. Barkow, *Separation of Powers and the Criminal Law*, 58 STAN. L. REV. 989 (2006); Stuart P. Green, *Private Challenges to Prosecutorial Inaction: A Model Declaratory Judgment Statute*, 97 YALE L.J. 488, 494–98 (1988). This deference to prosecutors extends to a range of issues beyond charging, including disclosure of prosecutors' files and plea bargaining tactics. *See* Connick v. Thompson, 563 U.S. 51, 131 S. Ct. 1350, 1356 (2011); United States v. Armstrong, 517 U.S. 456 (1996); United States v. Ruiz, 536 U.S. 622 (2002).

51. Pugach v. Klein, 193 F. Supp. 630, 635 (S.D.N.Y. 1961).

    While federal criminal law in its earliest decades evidenced no significant judicial supervision in prosecution powers, the federal executive hardly maintained close or exclusive control over enforcement. Federal crimes were sometimes prosecuted by state rather than federal officials and occasionally by private parties, who could pursue close analogs to criminal prosecutions in private qui tam actions. *See* Harold J. Krent, *Executive Control over Criminal Law Enforcement: Some Lessons from History*, 38 AM. UNIV. L. REV. 275 (1989).

52. *See* Krent, *supra* note 51. Even today federal courts have power to make interim appointments for federal prosecution vacancies, and to appoint special prosecutors to handle criminal contempt charges. *See* 28 U.S.C. § 546(d); *see also* 153 Cong. Rec. 6599, 6600 (2007) (statement of Sen. Diane Feinstein explaining that federal district courts have had authority to make interim appointments to unfilled U.S. Attorney offices since at least 1863). On federal judicial appointment of prosecutors for criminal contempt, see Young v. United States *ex rel*. Vuitton et Fils, 481 U.S. 787, 810, 814 (1987).

53. For one of the earliest state decisions describing a prosecutor's wide discretion, see People v. Wabash, St. L. & P. Ry. Co., 12 Ill. App. 263 (1882) (the prosecutor "is charged by law with large discretion in prosecuting offenders against the law. He may commence public prosecutions, in his official capacity by information and he may discontinue them when, in his judgment, the ends of justice are satisfied.").

54. *Birks*, 960 P.2d at 1075.

55. State *ex rel*. Holmes v. Denson, 671 S.W.2d 896, 899 (Tex. Crim. App. 1984); *In re* State, 390 S.W.3d 439 (2012). *See also* State *ex rel*. Holmes v. Salinas, 784 S.W.2d 421, 427–28 (Tex. Crim. App. 1990) (restrain them from presenting evidence to a grand jury); State v. Perleberg, 736 N.W.2d 703 (Minn. Ct. App. 2007), *review denied*, (Oct. 16, 2007) ("'a prosecutor has broad discretion in the exercise of the charging function and ordinarily, under the separation-of-powers doctrine, a court should not interfere with the prosecutor's exercise of that discretion' absent special circumstances").

56. *In re* Padget, 678 P.2d 870, 873 (Wyo. 1984).

57. *See generally* Heckler v. Chaney, 470 U.S. 821, 830–34 (1985). *For an example, see* Dunlop v. Bachowski, 421 U.S. 560 (1975) holds that, under Section 482 of the Labor-Management Reporting and Disclosure Act, 29 U.S.C. § 481, union members may seek judicial review of the secretary of labor's decision not to initiate civil enforcement action regarding certain labor law violations. Section 482 provides that, upon filing of a complaint by a union member, "[t]he Secretary shall investigate such complaint and, if he finds probable cause to believe that a violation . . . has occurred . . . he shall . . . bring a civil action. . . ."

58. *See* CAL. PENAL CODE § 1385 ("The judge or magistrate may, either of his or her own motion or upon the application of the prosecuting attorney, and in the furtherance of

justice, order an action to be dismissed."); People v. Superior Court (Romero), 917 P.2d 628 (Cal. 1998) (concluding that in California disposition of pending charges is a judicial function and a statute that gave prosecutors control over judicial dismissal of allegations affecting sentencing would violate separation of powers). *See also* discussion of California separation-of-powers doctrine *infra*, with citations to earlier decisions such as People v. Tenorio, 473 P.2d 993, 3 Cal.3d 89 (1970). For other states that give judges unusual power over dismissals, see Iowa Code Ann. Rule 2.33 ("The court, upon its own motion or the application of the prosecuting attorney, in the furtherance of justice, may order the dismissal of any pending criminal prosecution, the reasons therefor being stated in the order and entered of record."); Or. Rev. Stat. § 135.755 (2011) (similar); State v. McDonald, 10 Okla. Crim. Rep. 413, 137 P. 362 (1914) (noting court's statutory authority to dismiss charges over prosecutor's objection).

59. *See* Mich. Comp. Laws § 767.41 (in certain cases, prosecutors must file reasons for not charging, and court upon review can order prosecutor to file charge); Neb. Rev. Stat. § 29-1606 (same). *See* People v. Stewart, 217 N.W.2d 894 (Mich. 1974) (trial judge lacks supervisory power and may reverse only for abuse of discretion, so as not to substitute his judgment for the prosecutor's); *compare* State v. Sanchell, 216 N.W.2d 504, *on reargument*, 220 N.W.2d 562 (Neb. 1974) (statute requiring prosecutor to file information after preliminary examination unless court approves not doing do so requires court's approval before a charge can be dismissed). *See also* Pa. R. Crim. Pro. 506 (requiring prosecutors to give reasons for decisions not to prosecute upon a private complaint, which courts may review).

60. Calif. Penal Code § 1192.7; N.Y. Crim. Proc. L. § 220.10.

61. Robert F. Williams, The Law of American State Constitutions 235–45 (2009) (overview of differences in state separation-of-powers law); *id.* at 237 (noting that forty state constitutions have explicit separation-of-powers provisions, unlike the federal Constitution); *cf.* Prentis v. Atlantic Coast Line Co., 211 U.S. 210, 255 (1908) (Holmes, J.) ("when, as here, a state Constitution sees fit to unite legislative and judicial powers in a single hand, there is nothing to hinder, so far as the Constitution of the United States is concerned.").

62. Williams, *supra* note 61, at 241; Gary J. Greco, *Standards or Safeguards: A Survey of the Delegation Doctrine in the States*, 8 Ad. L.J. Am. U. 567 (1994).

63. Williams, *supra* note 61, at 291 & 296; *see, e.g.*, In re Advisory Opinion to the Governor, 732 A.2d 55 (R.I. 1999) (describing differences in state and federal separation of powers). One implication of the nonunitary executive structure is that state courts may have a different approach to issues of whether judicial supervision powers over prosecutors "are of such a nature that they impede the President's"—in the case of states, a governor's— "ability to perform his constitutional duty," as did the Supreme Court in Morrison v. Olson, 487 U.S. 654, 691 (1988).

64. *See generally* Michael J. Ellis, *The Origins of the Elected Prosecutor*, 121 Yale L.J. 1529 (2012). For detailed histories of specific jurisdictions, see McConville & Mirsky, *supra* note 7, at 25–42 (describing early systems of judicial or gubernatorial appointment of prosecutors, until elections were added in 1847); Steinberg, *supra* note 7, at 152–57 (describing the same in Philadelphia, before elections were adopted in 1852). For a jurisdiction that continues to formally place prosecutors in the judicial branch, see Florida Const. art. V § 17 (state attorneys in the "Judiciary" article that also creates courts and judges); Louisiana Const. art. V § 26 (district attorneys in the article that creates the "Judicial Branch"); *see also* State v. Hayes, 75 So.3d 8 (La. App. 4th Cir. 2011) (unlike federal law, prosecutorial power under the Louisiana constitution is in the judicial, not the executive, branch).

65. Only in the 1980s did Connecticut amend its constitution to follow the federal model more closely and locate prosecutors in the executive branch. Until then, prosecutors were appointed by judges. *See* Conn. Const. amend. XXIII; Transcript of Connecticut

Legislative Hearings on Proposed Amendment, March 5, 1984 (statement of Austin McGuigan, Chief State's Attorney, opposing the amendment). Louisiana's constitution still defines prosecutors within the judicial branch. *See* LA. CONST. art. 2, § 2; State v. Hayes, 75 So.3d 8 (La. App. 4. Cir. 2011) (*citing* Section 2 and noting that unlike federal law, prosecutorial power in Louisiana is in the judicial, not the executive, branch).

66. *See* State v. Brimage, 706 A.2d 1096 (N.J. 1998) (in context of a plea bargain, review of prosecutor's decision to invoke statutory provision for mandatory sentence); State v. Baynes, 690 A.2d 594 (N.J. 1997) (review of prosecutor's reasons for charging instead of diverting defendant into drug program). *See also* Comm'n Workers of America, AFL-CIO v. Florio, 617 A.2d 223, 23–32 (N.J. 1992) (describing N.J. governor as an unusually strong model for the state executive, and noting courts scrutinize "encroachment" on power of one branch by another more closely than abdications of power). New Jersey is one of very few states with a unitary executive similar to the federal model, including appointed prosecutors under the authority of an appointed attorney general.

67. People v. Navarro, 7 Cal.3d 248 (1972) (invalidating statute giving prosecutor the ability to veto a judicial decision to commit a convicted defendant to a drug treatment program in lieu of prison); People v. Tenorio, 473 P.2d 993, 3 Cal.3d 89 (1970) (statutory provision giving prosecutor the power to preclude the court from exercising its discretion to strike a prior conviction for purposes of sentencing violated separation of powers doctrine); Esteybar v. Municipal Court, 485 P.2d 1140 (Cal. 1971) (statutory scheme granting magistrate the authority to reduce a "wobbler" offenses to a misdemeanor but conditioning the exercise of this power on the approval of the prosecutor violated separation of powers).

68. *See* Crown Prosecution Service, *The Code for Crown Prosecutors* 2 (2013); Prosecution of Offences Act 1985 s 10. For a brief account, see Regina (Gujra) v. Crown Prosecution Service [2013] A.C. 484, 510 (Lord Mance).

69. *See* CPS website on Code Consultations, at http://www.cps.gov.uk/consultations/index.html.

70. *See, e.g.,* FLA. STAT. § 775.08401 (2014) (local prosecutor authority on sentencing policies); FLA. STAT. § 741.2901(2014) (legislative guidance on local prosecutors' domestic violence charging policy); WIS. STAT. § 968.075(7) (2014) (same).

71. *See* John C. Jeffries Jr., *The Liability Rule for Constitutional Torts*, 99 VA. L. REV. 207, 221–30 (2013); Connick v. Thompson, 563 U.S. 51, 131 S. Ct. 1350, 1356 (2011).

72. A rare exception of prosecutors facing criminal charges for work-related conduct proves the rule. In 1996, Chicago three prosecutors (and four sheriff's deputies) who were indicted for conspiracy, obstruction of justice, and perjury that contributed to wrongful murder convictions. Charges against two of the prosecutors were dismissed before trial; the other was acquitted in a 1999, as were the deputies. Note that the allegations of evidence fabrication were far beyond equivalents of biased charging decisions or violation of a mandatory-prosecution duty. Although the local government paid a $3.5 million dollar settlement to the wrongly convicted men, all prosecutors continued to practice law—one as a chief judge of a state circuit court, one as a federal prosecutor, one as a defense attorney. *See* Andrew Bluth, *Prosecutor and 4 Sheriff's Deputies Are Acquitted of Wrongfully Accusing a Man of Murder*, N.Y. TIMES, June 5, 1999; Northwestern Law School Center for Wrongful Convictions, http://www.law.northwestern.edu/legalclinic/wrongfulconvictions/exonerations/il/rolando-cruz.html (describing civil settlement).

73. StGB § 339 (German Penal Code) (*Rechtsbeugung*, or perversion of justice, punishable by one to five years in prison); *see also* StGB § 258, 258a (punishment for police or prosecutor's failure to investigate or prosecute colorable offenses). *See* Kessler, *supra* note 16, at 216; Markus Dubber, *Criminal Law Between Public and Private Law*, in THE BOUNDARIES OF CRIMINAL LAW 191, 204–05 (R. A. Duff et al. eds.) (2010). English practice remains closer to the American in related respects. For example, English prosecutors face no sanctions for failing to meet requirements to disclose evidence to defendants. *See* Jacqueline

Hodgson, *The Future of Adversarial Criminal Justice in Twenty-First Century Britain*, 35 N.C.J. Int'l L. & Comm'l Reg. 319, 330–40 (2010).

74. On presumption of regularity, which the Court sometimes notes is assured by legal education, bar oversight and internal supervision within prosecutors' offices, see Connick v. Thompson, 563 U.S. 51, 131 S. Ct. 1350, 1356 (2011); Hartman v. Moore, 457 U.S. 250, 263 (2006); United States v. Ruiz, 536 U.S. 622 (2002); United States v. Armstrong, 517 U.S. 456, 464 (1996); *see also* Town of Newton v. Rumery, 480 U.S. 386, 388 (1987); Wayte v. United States, 470 U.S. 598, 607–08 (1985). On sufficiency of informal regulation, see Malley v. Briggs, 475 U.S. 335, 342–43 & n.5 (1986); Imbler v. Pachtman, 424 U.S. 409, 428–30 (1976). *See generally* on this point, Jennifer Laurin, *The Legacy of* Connick v. Thompson, *in* 27 Civil Rights Litigation and Attorney Fees Handbook 29, 51–58 (Steven Saltzman ed., West 2011).

75. On judicial review of prosecutors' evidence disclosure decisions in Canada, see R. v. Stinchcombe [1991] 3 SCR 326.

76. *In re* Padget, 678 P.2d 870, 873–74 (Wyo. 1984) (first quoted passage); *In re* Hickson, 765 A.2d 372, 380 (Pa. Super. 2000) (second quoted passage, offered to justify denying standing to a private complainant seeking to challenge district attorney's decision not to prosecute based on a private complaint). *See also* Czajka v. Koweek, 2012 N.Y. Slip Op. 07365 (N.Y. App. Div. 3. 2012) (district attorney is a constitutional officer, chosen by county voters to prosecute all crimes, with wide discretion over public resources to discharge duties as he judges most effective).

77. Milliken v. Stone, 7 F.2d 397 (S.D.N.Y. 1925), *aff'd*, 16 F.2d 981 (2d Cir. 1927), *certiorari denied*, 274 U.S. 748 (1927), *cited in* Pugach v. Klein, 193 F. Supp. 630, 635 (S.D.N.Y. 1961) ("The remedy for any dereliction of his duty lies, not with the courts, but, with the executive branch of our government and ultimately with the people."); *see also* United States v. Woody, 2 F.2d 262 (D. Mont. 1924) (similar). The Supreme Court, much more recently, continues to endorse the same idea. *See* Cheney v. U.S. District Court, 542 U.S. 367 (2004) ("The decision to prosecute a criminal case, for example, is made by a publicly accountable prosecutor subject to budgetary considerations. . . ."). For another, recent example emphasizing the limits of judicial capacity to interfere with prosecutors' decisions, especially if the remedy would be dismissal of criminal charges, United States v. Smith, 231 F.3d 800, 807 (11th Cir. 2000). *See also* cases collected in West Keynotes 110k36.5.

78. Scholarly views of this faith in democratic process has been mixed at best. Nearly a century ago, leading scholars such as Roscoe Pound kicked off an ongoing tradition of lamenting the political nature of American prosecutors' offices. Roscoe Pound, Criminal Justice in America 183 (1924) (urging civil service reform and concluding that "the bane of prosecution in the United States today is the intimate connection of the prosecutor's office with politics."). Raymond Moley, a prominent Columbia law professor, made the same criticism in the same era. Moley, *supra* note 9. Scholarly criticism of prosecutorial discretion has continued in succeeding generations. *See, e.g.*, Herbert Packer, The Limits of Criminal Sanctions 290 (1968) (criticizing prosecutorial discretion as "simply that it is lawless, in the literal sense of that term"); Davis, *supra* note 18; Jack M. Kress, *Progress and Prosecution*, 423 Annals AAPSS 99, 105 (1976). Interestingly, the American Bar Association formerly endorsed "the check of periodic elections—a direct accountability of stewardship—as a mechanism exemplifying the power of the people over their servant." *See* ABA *Criminal Justice Standards: Prosecution and Defense Functions*, at 19 (1971 draft). Its current position, found in Standard 3-2.3, is more ambivalent: "Opinion has long been divided on the question of whether the office of prosecutor should be appointive or elective. These Standards take no position on this subject. The National District Attorneys Association, however, expressly favors local election of the chief prosecutor with a term of office of no less than four years." On the other hand, contemporary critics such as Bill Stuntz and Stephanos Bibas mostly direct

their criticisms elsewhere, and influential scholars such a Dan Richman stress that the efficacy of political checks in the form of legislatures that monitor prosecutors through oversight hearings and budget allocations. *See also* Daniel C. Richman, *Federal Criminal Law, Congressional Delegation, and Enforcement Discretion*, 46 UCLA L. REV. 757 (1999); Daniel C. Richman, *Political Control of Federal Prosecutions—Looking Back and Looking Forward*, 58 DUKE L.J. 2087 (2009).

79. R. (Da Silva) v. DPP [2006] EWHC 3204 at ¶23.

80. *Sharma* [2006] UKPC 57, 1 WLR 780 [32] (Privy Council).

81. *See generally* Hodgson, *supra* note 73, at 330; ASHWORTH & REDMAYNE, *supra* note 24, at 221–23. For examples, see Prosecution of Offences Act 1974, § 2(5) (Republic of Ireland) (the "Director [of Public Prosecutions] shall be independent in the performance of his functions"); Australia's Office of the Commonwealth Director of Public Prosecutions, whose director is appointed for a seven-year term, "is an independent prosecuting agency . . . [that] is within the portfolio of the Commonwealth Attorney-General, but the Office operates independently of the Attorney-General and of the political process." OCDPP website at http://www.cdpp.gov.au/AboutUs/ (Dec. 2012); Director of Public Prosecutions Act 1983, Act No. 113 (as amended 2012); *see also* MARK FINDLEY, STEPHEN ODGERS, & STANLEY YEO, AUSTRALIAN CRIMINAL JUSTICE 125–26 (1994) (describing "the development of prosecutorial independence from the executive"). Canada's Public Prosecution Service describes itself as "an independent prosecution authority," see http://www.ppsc-sppc.gc.ca/eng/bas/dpp-dpp.html, and the Canadian Supreme Court affirms the prosecutor's wide discretion with reference to his political independence. *See* Krieger v. Law Society (Alta.), 217 D.L.R. (4th) 513, 527 (2002) ("the independence of the Attorney-General, in deciding fairly who should be prosecuted, is . . . a hallmark of a free society"). For Caribbean systems, see SEETAHAL, *supra* note 31, at 48–49.

82. CLAYTON, *supra* note 13, at 40 (comparing more political U.S. Attorney General to less political attorney general in England). For other insightful accounts of the U.S. approach to political insulation versus accountability of U.S. prosecutors, see Rachel K. Barkow, *Insulating Agencies: Using Institutional Design to Limit Agency Capture*, 89 TEX. L. REV. 15 (2010); Rachel K. Barkow, *Institutional Design and the Policing of Prosecutors: Lessons from Administrative Law*, 61 STAN. L. REV. 869 (2009).

It bears stressing that the federal Department of Justice is widely credited with a generally professional prosecution staff. Shugerman, *Dep't of Justice*, *supra* note 8 (history of federal civil service reform and Justice Department's professionalization). Strong tradition disfavors presidents removing U.S. attorneys during a four-year term, and the attorney general's power is mediated by bureaucratic procedures for attorney misconduct. *See* Kevin M. Scott, *U.S. Attorneys Who Have Served Less than Full Four-year Terms, 1981–2006* (Cong. Res. Service Report Feb. 22, 2007) (noting rarity of presidents dismissing U.S. attorneys midterm). Occasional scandals reveal federal prosecutors with politically motivated agendas, but it not clear that those lapses are different from the lapses seen occasionally in the prosecution agencies of other nations as well. On investigation of federal prosecutor misconduct that could lead to dismissal, see *U.S. Dept. of Justice Office of Professional Responsibility*, http://www.justice.gov/opr/. For accounts of the Justice Department more recently including episodes of political influence on prosecutions, see Dep't of Justice Inspector General & Office of Prof'l Responsibility, *An Investigation into the Removal of Nine U.S. Attorneys in 2006* (Sept. 2008), at http://www.justice.gov/oig/special/s0809a/final.pdf; JAMES MCGEE & BRIAN DUFFY, MAIN JUSTICE: THE MEN AND WOMEN WHO ENFORCE THE NATION'S CRIMINAL LAWS AND GUARD ITS LIBERTIES (1997).

83. See Philip C. Stenning, *Prosecutions, Politics and the Public Interest: Some Recent Developments in the United Kingdom, Canada and Elsewhere*, 55 CRIM. L.Q. 449, 456 (2010) (describing efforts across several nations to depoliticize prosecution).

In England, the trend of recent reforms altered the potential for political influence on the judiciary. The Lord Chancellor is a cabinet member with administrative power over the courts, but lost his former role as a member of the judiciary in 2005. His role in selecting judges is also limited to candidates identified by a commission. On the other hand, combining the roles of Lord Chancellor and justice secretary has met with criticism. *See* UK Joint Committee on Human Rights, *The Implications for Access to Justice of the Government's Proposals to Reform Judicial Review* (2014) (HL 174; HC 868), at pp.10–12 ¶¶18–23 (criticizing "the conflict inherent in the combined roles" since 2005 of justice secretary, a political minister, and Lord Chancellor, head of the judiciary with a duty to uphold judicial independence).

84. Police Reform and Social Responsibility Act 2011. *See* House of Commons Home Affairs Committee, *Police and Crime Commissioners: Power to Remove Chief Constables* (July 17, 2013), at http://www.publications.parliament.uk/pa/cm201314/cmselect/cmhaff/487/487.pdf; Ian Loader & Richard Sparks, *Beyond Lamentation: Towards a Democratic Egalitarian Politics of Crime and Justice* (2012), *available at* SSRN: http://ssrn.com/abstract=2158171 or http://dx.doi.org/10.2139/ssrn.2158171.

85. The New York governor's power over local prosecutors led to a politically controversial, case-specific intervention during an era of high public concern about crime. After a locally elected prosecutor in the Bronx decided not to seek the death penalty for a defendant charged with killing a police officer, the New York governor used his statutory authority to order the attorney general to take over the prosecution in order to seek the death penalty. *See* Johnson v. Pataki, 691 N.E.2d 1002 (N.Y. 1997) (*citing* N.Y. CONST. art. 4, § 3 and N.Y. EXEC. L. § 63, subd. 2). It is worth noting that Robert Johnson, the elected district attorney who was removed from the case, was re-elected in wake his refusal to seek the death penalty.

For a comparison in the Irish context: one of the few grounds on which Irish courts will review prosecutor charging decisions is when an initial charging decision has been reversed, after a victim's request, by a higher-level official. *See* Donoghue, *supra* note 27, at text accompanying notes 6–11.

86. Director of Public Prosecutions Act, S.C. 2006, c. 9, s. 121. For a good discussion, see Kent Roach, *Prosecutorial Independence and Accountability in Terrorism Prosecutions*, 55 CRIM. L.Q. 486, 495–97 (2010). Similar legislation aims to increase the political independence of Canada's provincial prosecution services. *See* Public Prosecutions Act, 1990, S.N.S. 1990, c. 21 (Novia Scotia); *see* the Director of Criminal and Penal Prosecutions Act, 2005, R.S.Q., c. D-9.1.1 (Quebec); both noted in Stenning, *supra* note 83, at 452–53.

87. New Zealand's chief law officer is the attorney general, a member of the government who appoints the solicitor general, a senior civil servant in charge of the crown prosecution service. The Crown Solicitors Network consists of sixteen Crown Solicitors who are partners in private firms and are appointed for prosecution duties in regional districts. *See* website of New Zealand Crown Law Office, http://www.crownlaw.govt.nz/ (visited May 29, 2015); New Zealand Law Commission, *Report 66: Criminal Prosecution* (Oct. 2000). Australia's Director of Public Prosecutions appointed in 2007, Christopher Craige, SC, as a career public defense attorney before the appointment, http://www.cdpp.gov.au/Director/, a career path unlikely in the United States. For other evidence of professional norms in political appointments of chief prosecutors, see *Silbert Appointed Chief Crown Prosecutor*, SYDNEY MORNING HERALD, Mar. 4, 2008 (Victoria, Australia), http://news.smh.com.au/national/silbert-appointed-chief-crown-prosecutor-20080304-1wqg.html.

88. Duncan v. Louisiana, 391 U.S. 145 (1968). That phrase—which also cautioned against the "biased or eccentric judge"—has been subsequently quoted twenty-three times by the Court since *Duncan* and more than one hundred times by lower courts.

89. *See* Young v. United States *ex rel.* Vuitton et Fils, 481 U.S. 787, 810, 814 (1987) (establishing "a categorical rule against the appointment [by a federal judge] of an interested

prosecutor" to prosecute violation of a court order as criminal contempt; prosecutor's interest arose from business interests that benefited from the underlying court order); 18 U.S.C. § 208(a) (federal prosecutors prohibited from representing the government in any matter in which they, their family, or their business associates have any interest). For a typical state law defining "interested" prosecutors, see COLO. REV. STAT. § 20-1-107. For state decisions holding that private prosecutors are not sufficiently disinterested, see State v. Harrington, 534 S.W.2d 44, 48–49 (Mo. 1976) (private prosecution "inherently and fundamentally unfair" despite its long history in the state); People v. Municipal Court, 27 Cal. App. 3d 193, 206, 103 CAL. RPTR. 645, 654–55 (1972) (rejecting trial court authorization for a private prosecutor because due process requires that "any criminal proceeding be authorized and approved by the district attorney"). *Private* prosecutors routinely had such motivations, and courts looked on them with increasing disfavor even in the few jurisdictions in which they retained residual statutory authority.

90. Williams, *supra* note 24, at 601–03 (also noting creation of the office of the DPP in 1879).
91. McCONVILLE & MIRSKY, *supra* note 7, at 23–24 (describing private prosecution in New York City, circa 1800–1840); STEINBERG, *supra* note 7, at 24–69 (private prosecution in Philadelphia through most of the nineteenth century); See Goldstein, *Prosecution: History of the Public Prosecutor, in* 3 ENCYCLOPEDIA OF CRIME AND JUSTICE 1242–46 (Joshua Dressler ed., 2d ed. 2002); John Langbein, *The Origins of Public Prosecution at Common Law*, 17 AM. J. LEGAL HIST. 313 (1973). *See also* Margaret Z. Johns, *Reconsidering Absolute Prosecutorial Immunity*, 2005 BYU L. REV. 53, 111–14 (*citing and discussing* nineteenth-century decisions of private prosecutors, whose misconduct provided grounds for tort claims of malicious prosecution).
92. Ramsey, *supra* note 9, at 1323–27 (documenting demise of private prosecution in New York City). On the demise of private prosecutors elsewhere, see STEINBERG, *supra* note 7, at 119 (describing Philadelphia); Biemel v. State, 37 N.W. 244, 247 (Wis. 1888) (discussing 1887 Wisconsin statute barring private prosecutors); Meister v. People, 31 Mich. 99, 103–04 (Mich. 1875) (describing Michigan statute barring private prosecution as "designed to secure impartiality from all persons connected with criminal trials"); *see also* People v. Cahoon, 50 N.W. 384, 385 (Mich. 1891); United States v. Stone, 8 F. 232 (C.C.Tenn.1881) (describing the common law rule, and Tennessee state law at the time, as authorizing private prosecution and contrasting federal courts where they are prohibited).
93. McCONVILLE & MIRSKY, *supra* note 7, at 28–29, 34, 38, 42 (noting at p.28 that private prosecutors initiated "the overwhelming majority of complaints" in New York City through at least 1850; and at p.35, noting private prosecutors appearing alongside, or in place of, public prosecutors).
94. NICOLAS R. PARRILLO, AGAINST THE PROFIT MOTIVE: THE SALARY REVOLUTION IN AMERICAN GOVERNMENT, 1780–1940, at 255–94 & 363–65 (Yale 2013).
95. *See* Linda R. S. v. Richard D., 410 U.S. 614 (1972) (denying a crime victim's right to compel a criminal prosecution because "a private citizen lacks a judicially cognizable interest in the prosecution or non-prosecution of another"); State v. Casey, 44 P.3d 756 (Utah (2002)) (*citing* UTAH CONST. art. I § 28(2) and noting victims' rights provisions cannot lead to "relief from any criminal judgment" even if victims' rights were violated in process leading to judgment); McArthur v. State, 597 So.2d 406 (Fla. App. 1st Dist. 1992) (victim has no authority over decisions to prosecute; that power rests with the state's attorney); Scanlon v. State Bar of Georgia, 443 S.E.2d 830 (Ga. 1994) (private citizens have no judicially cognizable interests in prosecutions or decisions not to prosecute); State v. Winne, 96 A.2d 63 (N.J. 1953) (prosecutor's exclusive authority); Stuart P. Green, *Private Challenges to Prosecutorial Inaction: A Model Declaratory Judgment Statute*, 97 YALE L.J. 488, 493–96 (1988).
96. For an example of a statute common in many states, see N.C. GEN. STAT. § 15A-304 (authorizing judges to issue arrest warrants upon testimony of private individuals).

Pennsylvania and Rhode Island may the only states in which statutes still authorize a limited power of private prosecutions. In Pennsylvania, courts may approve a private prosecutor's request to take over prosecution from a district attorney who "neglect[s] or refuse[s]" to pursue a properly grounded charge. *See* 16 PA. CONST. STAT. ANN. § 1409 (2012) (authorizing victims dissatisfied with public prosecutor to petition the court, and granting courts the power to allow victim's attorney to take over as private prosecutor). Pennsylvania courts are the rare U.S. example in which private prosecutors are recognized as part of the "checks and balances" on public prosecutors. *See In re* Hickson, 765 A.2d 372, 377 (Pa. Super. 2000) (but denying private standing to seek judicial review of decision not to prosecute). For Rhode Island, which authorizes private misdemeanor prosecutions only, see R.I. GEN. LAWS §§ 12-4-1, 12-4-2, 12-4-6, 12-12-1.3 (2013); Cronan *ex rel.* State v. Cronan, 774 A.2d 866 (R.I. 2001) (approving private misdemeanor prosecution for assault under state statutes). New Hampshire might permit private prosecution of misdemeanors under state common law; *see* State v. Martineau, 148 N.H. 259, 808 A.2d 51 (2002). *See also* 63C Am. Jur. 2d Prosecuting Attorneys § 12 (2013) (citing authority in at least three states permitting private attorneys to assist public prosecutors).

97. On private prosecution in England, see Prosecution of Offences Act 1985 § 6; R. (Gujra) v. Crown Prosecution Service [2012] UKSC 52; [2013] Cr. App. R. 12 (p.169) (Lord Wilson and Lord Mance); R. v. DPP Ex p. Duckenfield [2000] W.L.R. 55; ASHWORTH & REDMAYNE, *supra* note 24, at 222. For an account of Commonwealth law, see SEETAHAL, *supra* note 31, at 53 (describing private prosecution authority in Caribbean systems).

98. *See* STEPHEN C. THAMAN, COMPARATIVE CRIMINAL PROCEDURE 23–30 (2d ed. 2008), summarizing and citing European code provisions on private or "popular" prosecution, including LECr. §§ 100-105 (Spanish Code of Criminal Procedure) CPP §§ 191, 192 (Italian Code of Criminal Procedure); StPO §§ 374-406 (German criminal procedure code on private and "accessory" prosecutors).

99. StPO § 374 (Germany). If citizens prosecute the charge themselves rather than filing a complaint and requesting public prosecution, various restrictions apply, including mandatory mediation for some offenses and, for the nonindigent, posting a bond to cover defendant's litigation expenses if he prevails. All these serve to reduce private prosecutions.

100. StPO § 390 (German code; appellate remedies for private prosecutors after dismissal); StPO §§ 395-401 (accessory prosecutors); StPO § 403 (civil claims of aggrieved persons in connection with criminal prosecutions).

101. *See* 392(1) & 394 CPP (Italy) (aggrieved party can request prosecutor and judge to preserve evidence; prosecutor must provide written reasons for any refusal); *see also* 401 CPP (Italy) (right of aggrieved parties to participate in evidence hearings); for a discussion of these provisions, see THAMAN, *supra* note 98, at 38–39.

102. Art. 125 Const. (Spain) ("citizens may initiate popular prosecutions"); *see* discussion in THAMAN, *supra* note 98, at 28–30.

103. JACQUELINE HODGSON, FRENCH CRIMINAL JUSTICE: A COMPARATIVE ACCOUNT OF THE INVESTIGATION AND PROSECUTION OF CRIME IN FRANCE 31–42 (2005).

104. For a rare U.S. court description of private prosecutors as part of the "checks and balances" on public prosecutor power, see *In re* Hickson, 765 A.2d 372, 377–80 (Pa. Super. 2000).

105. *See* website of New Zealand Crown Law Office, http://www.crownlaw.govt.nz/ (visited May 29, 2015); New Zealand Law Commission, *Report 66: Criminal Prosecution* (Oct. 2000). Private contracting for prosecution in the United States is marginal. An apparently small number of localities that cannot justify employing a full-time prosecutor contract with private attorneys to handle prosecution duties, usually only for low-level offenses not handled by the elected prosecutor. *See* Roger A. Fairfax Jr., *Delegation of the Prosecution Function to Private Actors*, 43 U.C. DAVIS L. REV. 411, 416–18 (2009) (citing

examples of contracts for misdemeanor prosecutions in Washington and Minnesota, both of which elect most prosecutors, and criticizing private contracts for prosecution services).

106. On private probation, see Sarah Stillman, *Get Out of Jail, Inc.*, New Yorker, June 23, 2014. On private prisons, see Sharon Dolovich, *How Privatization Thinks: The Case of Prisons, in* Government by Contract: Outsourcing and American Democracy 128 (Jody Freeman & Martha Minow eds., 2009).

107. Marie Gottschalk, The Prison and the Gallows: The Politics of Mass Incarceration in America 83–92 (2006). For an overview of victims' rights laws, see Douglas E. Beloof, Paul G. Cassell, & Steven J. Twist, Victims in Criminal Procedure (3d ed. 2010) (including discussions of orders for financial restitution to victims).

108. U.K. Ministry of Justice, *Code of Practice for Victims of Crime* (2013); Andrew Ashworth, *Victims' Views and the Public Interest*, 2014 Crim. L. Rev. 775. The U.K. system includes a Victim Commissioner who monitors and reports on agencies' compliance with victims' rights regulations.

   A distinction in U.K. law that is largely absent in U.S. law is the limitation that victims may be heard on the crime's impact but may not express views to the court on what they think the sentence ought to be for an offender, on the premise that sentences are set by judges on the basis of legal guidelines, not victim preferences. U.S. courts are generally open to victims' views on the sentence. This difference could be taken as another example of the greater English inclination for decision making by legal criteria, while the U.S. system is more open to—depending on how on characterizes it—democratic or private-actor influence.

109. American statements of the norm are common. *See* Model Rules of Prof'l Conduct, R. 3.8 cmt. 1 (2003) ("minister of justice"); Model Code of Prof'l Responsibility EC 7-13 (1983) (prosecutor's "duty is to seek justice, not merely to convict"); ABA Standards for Criminal Justice, Prosecution Function 3-1.2(c) (same); ABA Canons of Prof'l Ethics, Canon 5 (1908) ("The primary duty of a lawyer engaged in public prosecution is not to convict, but to see that justice is done."). For state sources, see, e.g., State v. Fields, 730 N.W.2d 777 (Minn. 2007) (prosecutor is an officer of the court with an obligation to achieve justice and fair adjudication rather than merely convictions); State v. Ramey, 721 N.W.2d 294 (Minn. 2006) (prosecutor is a minister of justice with a duty to guard the rights of the accused as well as to represent public interests); State v. Fisher, 202 P.3d 937 (Wash. 2009) (prosecutors represent the state and are presumed to act with impartiality in the interest of justice; they are quasi-judicial officers with a duty to moderate adversary zeal to ensure fair trials for defendants); State v. Smith, 671 N.W.2d 854 (Wis. App. 2003) (prosecutor's duty is to ensure justice prevails and not merely to achieve convictions); Hardy v. State, 962 A.2d 244 (Del. 2008); People v. Alvarado, 47 Cal. Rptr. 3d 289 (Cal. App. 2d Dist. 2006). The U.S. Supreme Court's classic statement on this point is found in Berger v. United States, 295 U.S. 78, 88 (1935) ("[W]hile [the prosecutor] may strike hard blows, he is not at liberty to strike foul ones. It is as much his duty to refrain from improper methods calculated to produce a wrongful conviction as it is to use every legitimate means to bring about a just one."). On the weakness of these rules and of courts' weak interpretation of them, see Bruce Green, *Prosecutors and Professional Regulation*, 25 Geo. J. Legal Ethics 873 (2012).

110. On the English minister-of-justice conception of the prosecutor's office, see Andrew Ashworth, *Prosecution and Procedure in Criminal Justice*, [1979] Crim. L. Rev. 481, 482 (describing and endorsing ministerial role); Ashworth & Redmayne, *supra* note 24, at 65–68. Regarding the norm in Canada, see R. v. Stinchcombe [1991] 3 SCR 326. On the Scottish system, see Fionda, *supra* note 16, at 65–66 (describing Scottish prosecutors' strong tradition of a neutral ministerial norm rather than an adversarial norm). For an account of German prosecutors, see Shawn Marie Boyne, *The Cultural Limits on*

Uniformity and Formalism in the German Penal Code, 59 Crime Law & Social Change 371, 374–82 (2013) (describing legal structure and professional norms of German prosecutors, who have job security to insulate them from political influence). For a description of French prosecutors, see Jacqueline Hodgson, *Conceptions of the Trial in Inquisitorial and Adversarial Procedure, in* 11 The Trial on Trial: Judgment and Calling to Account 223, 230–32 (R. A. Duff, Lindsay Farmer, Sandra Marshall, & Victor Tadros eds., 2006).

111. *See generally* Maximo Langer, *From Legal Transplants to Legal Translations: The Globalization of Plea Bargaining and the Americanization Thesis in Criminal Procedure,* 45 Harv. Int'l L.J. 1 (2004) (describing differences in conceptions of prosecutors across inquisitorial and adversarial systems including in France, and the challenges of comparisons).

112. Justice Marshall captured the difficulty of the prosecutor's conflicting role:

> [T]he dual role that the prosecutor must play poses a serious obstacle to implementing [the duty to disclose exculpatory evidence to the defense]. The prosecutor is by trade, if not necessity, a zealous advocate. He is a trained attorney who must aggressively seek convictions in court on behalf of a victimized public. At the same time, as a representative of the state, he must place foremost in his hierarchy of interests the determination of truth. Thus, for purposes of *Brady* [disclosure], the prosecutor must abandon his role as an advocate and pore through his files, as objectively as possible, to identify the material that could undermine his case. Given this obviously unharmonious role, it is not surprising that these advocates oftentimes overlook or downplay potentially favorable evidence, often in cases in which there is no doubt that the failure to disclose was a result of absolute good faith.

United States v. Bagley, 473 U.S. 667, 696–97 (1985). *See also* Jeffries, *supra* note 71, at 227–30 (describing incapability of serving both as "officer of the court" and "hard-charging, competitive lawyers whose reputations and satisfactions depend on obtaining convictions," especially given the challenges of cognitive phenomena such as selective information processing and belief perseverance); Daniel S. Medwed, *The Prosecutor as Minister of Justice: Preaching to the Unconverted from the Post-Conviction Pulpit,* 84 Wash. L. Rev. 35 (2009).

113. Though not necessarily everywhere, of course. France, a civil law jurisdiction, has some recent history of government interference in the investigative and charging priorities of its career prosecutors. *See* Hodgson, *supra* note 103, at 75–79; Jacqueline Hodgson, *Guilty Pleas and the Changing Role of the Prosecutor in French Criminal Justice, in* The Prosecutor in Transnational Perspective 116 (Erik Luna & Marianne Wade eds., 2012).

114. *See, e.g.,* Michael Tonry, Thinking about Crime: Sense and Sensibility in American Penal Culture 9–10, 206–10 (2004); Michael Tonry, *Why Aren't German Penal Policies Harsher and Imprisonment Rates Higher?,* 5 German L.J. 1187 (2004); William T. Pizzi, *Understanding Prosecutorial Discretion in the United States: The Limits of Comparative Criminal Procedure as an Instrument of Reform,* 54 Ohio St. L.J. 1325, 1331–36 (1993); Richard S. Frase, *Comparative Criminal Justice as a Guide to American Law Reform: How Do the French Do It, How Can We Find Out, and Why Should We Care?,* 78 Cal. L. Rev. 539 (1990).

115. For a good general discussion of prosecutors and local politics, see Daniel S. Medwed, *The Zeal Deal: Prosecutorial Resistance to Post-Conviction Claims of Innocence,* 84 B.U. L. Rev. 125, 150 (2004) ("the institutional culture of prosecutorial agencies is determined, to some extent, by the political landscape of the particular community").

116. *See generally* Abraham S. Goldstein, *Prosecution: History of the Public Prosecutor, in* 3 Encyclopedia of Crime and Justice 1242 (2d ed. 2002).

117. Argument of Respondent, represented by California Attorney General, in Mooney v. Holohan, 294 U.S. 103, 108 (1935). *See* discussion in Colin Starger, *50 Years Before Brady*, THE CHAMPION 34, 36 (May 2013).

118. For an analysis of many recent examples of state and federal prosecutor offices, and prosecutor associations, opposing ethical rules governing their conduct, see Bruce Green, *Prosecutors and Professional Regulation*, 25 GEO. J. LEGAL ETHICS 873 (2012). For a discussion of the effects of prosecutorial office culture on professional conduct, see Ellen Yaroshefsky, *New Orleans Prosecutorial Disclosure in Practice After* Connick v. Thompson, 25 GEO. J. LEGAL ETHICS 913 (2012).

119. Smith v. Cain, 132 S. Ct. 627 (2012) (overturning murder conviction because prosecutor unconstitutionally withheld evidence favorable to defendant); *Connick*, 131 S. Ct. 1350 (documenting prosecutor misconduct in wrongful armed robbery conviction but overturning civil damages award); *see, e.g.*, KATHLEEN M. RIDOLF & MAURICE POSSLEY, PREVENTABLE ERROR: A REPORT ON PROSECUTORIAL MISCONDUCT IN CALIFORNIA 1997–2009 (2010); BRANDON GARRETT, CONVICTING THE INNOCENT: WHEN CRIMINAL PROSECUTIONS GO WRONG (2011); Peter A. Joy, *The Relationship Between Prosecutorial Misconduct and Wrongful Convictions: Shaping Remedies for a Broken System*, 2006 WIS. L. REV. 399. On use of dubious "snitch" informant-witnesses, see ALEXANDRA NATAPOFF, SNITCHING: CRIMINAL INFORMANTS AND THE EROSION OF AMERICAN JUSTICE (2011); James S. Liebman, Jeffrey Fagan, Andrew Gelman, Valerie West, Garth Davies, & Alexander Kiss, *A Broken System, Part II: Why There Is So Much Error in Capital Cases and What Can Be Done About It*, http://www2.law.columbia. edu/brokensystem2/index2.html (Feb. 11, 2002) (in a ten-state study covering a twenty-three-year period, documenting prosecutors withholding evidence of one of several causes for erroneous capital murder convictions); James S. Liebman, Jeffrey Fagan, & Valerie West, *A Broken System: Error Rates in Capital Cases, 1973–1995*, http://papers.ssrn.com/papers.taf?abstract_id=232712 (June 12, 2000) (same); Ken Armstrong & Maurice Possley, *Trial and Error—The Verdict: Dishonor*, CHICAGO TRIBUNE, Jan. 11, 1999 (reporting on widespread, documented examples of prosecutors withholding exculpatory evidence).

120. The United States is hardly the only jurisdiction with a record of wrongful convictions in which prosecutors played a responsible role—England, Belgium, and France have all had their own examples. C. RONALD HUFF & MARTIN KILLIAS EDS., WRONGFUL CONVICTIONS AND MISCARRIAGES OF JUSTICE: CAUSES AND REMEDIES IN NORTH AMERICAN AND EUROPEAN CRIMINAL JUSTICE SYSTEMS (2013); C. RONALD HUFF & MARTIN KILLIAS EDS., WRONGFUL CONVICTION: INTERNATIONAL PERSPECTIVES ON MISCARRIAGES OF JUSTICE (2008).

121. *See* Sara Sun Beale, *Rethinking the Identity and Role of United States*, 6 OHIO ST. J. CRIM. L. 369 (2009) (discussing the Bush administration's political pressure on U.S. attorneys and politically motivated firings of U.S. attorneys who resisted pressure); U.S. Department of Justice Inspector General Report, *An Investigation into the Removal of Nine U.S. Attorneys in 2006* (2008), http://www.usdoj.gov/oig/special/s0809a/final.pdf.

122. Jeffrey Ulmer & Christopher Bader, *Do Moral Communities Play a Role in Criminal Sentencing? Evidence from Pennsylvania*, 49 SOC. Q. 737 (2008) (finding in county-level data that "Christian religious homogeneity" increases the likelihood of incarceration, especially when Christian denominations are civically engaged, partially through the effect of local Republican Party dominance via the election of judges and prosecutors). Carlos Berdejó & Noam Yuchtman, *Crime, Punishment, and Politics: An Analysis of Political Cycles in Criminal Sentencing*, 95 REV. ECON. & STAT. 741 (2013) (finding that elected judges in Washington State assign longer sentences in years closest to elections); Sanford C. Gordon & Gregory A. Huber, *The Effect of Electoral Competitiveness on Incumbent Behavior*, 2 Q.J. POL. SCI. 107 (2007) (hereafter *Electoral Competiveness*) (comparing partisan and nonpartisan judicial elections in Kansas and finding strong effects on

sentencing when judges in partisan elections expect or face challengers); Andrew Dyke, *Electoral Cycles and the Administration of Criminal Justice*, 133 Pub. Choice 417 (2007) (using data on North Carolina prosecutors); *see also* Sanford C. Gordon & Gregory A. Huber, *Oversight and the Electoral Incentives of Criminal Prosecutors*, 46 Am. J. Pol. Sci. 334 (2002); *cf.* Sanford C. Gordon, *Assessing Partisan Bias in Federal Public Corruption Prosecutions*, 103 Am. Pol. Sci. Rev. 534 (2009) (evidence of political party bias among federal prosecutors); Scott Ashworth, *Electoral Accountability: Recent Theoretical and Empirical Work*, 15 Ann. Rev. Pol. Sci. 183–201 (2012).

123. John F. Pfaff, *The Causes of Growth in Prison Admissions and Populations* (Jan. 2012) (especially Figure 3B and accompanying text) (unpublished manuscript), *available at* http://papers.ssrn.com/sol3/papers.cfm?abstract_id=1990508; John F. Pfaff, *The Micro and Macro Causes of Prison Growth*, 28 Ga. St. U. L. Rev. 1239 (2012); John F. Pfaff, *The Myths and Realities of Correctional Severity: Evidence from the National Corrections Reporting Program on Sentencing Practices*, 13 Am. L. & Econ. Rev. 491 (2011) (arguing that admission practices rather than longer sentences are driving prison growth).

124. Ramsey, *supra* note 9, at 1340–47.

125. *See* U.S. Attorney General, *Memorandum: Department Policy on Charging Mandatory Minimum Sentences and Recidivist Enhancements in Certain Drug Cases, Aug. 12, 2013* (reserving mandatory drug sentences for "high-level or violent traffickers" and noting their use in the past for "low-level, non-violent drug offenses" has been "unduly harsh").

126. Sari Horwitz, *Some Prosecutors Fighting Effort to Eliminate Mandatory Minimum Prison Sentences*, Wash. Post, Mar. 13, 2014. *See also* the website of the National Association of U.S. Attorneys, at http://www.naausa.org/2013/.

127. Key statutes on assistant U.S. Attorneys' appointments and job security include 5 U.S.C. §§ 2103 & 2302; 5 U.S.C. § 542 (2014).

128. U.S. Attorney General, *Memorandum of Aug. 12, 2013, supra* note 125.

129. *See* Michael C. Dorf & Charles F. Sabel, *A Constitution of Democratic Experimentalism*, 98 Colum. L. Rev. 267, 401–02 (1998) (hereafter *Experimentalism*); Allegra M. McLeod, *Decarceration Courts: Possibilities and Perils of a Shifting Criminal Law*, 100 Geo. L.J. 1587 (2012); Josh Bowers, *Contraindicated Drug Courts*, 55 UCLA L. Rev. 783 (2008); Michael C. Dorf & Charles F. Sabel, *Drug Treatment Courts and Emergent Experimentalist Government*, 53 Vand. L. Rev. 831 (2000) (hereafter *Drug Treatment Courts*). Drug courts are not without critics. *See* Justice Policy Institute, *Drug Courts: How a Growing Dependence on Drug Courts Impacts People and Communities* (Mar. 2011) (arguing that drug courts result in more people who need drug treatment being shifted into the criminal justice system instead of alternative routes to treatment), *available at* http://www. justicepolicy.org.

130. *See* Fionda, *supra* note 16, at 155–58, *citing* J. Graham, *Decarceration in the Federal Republic of Germany: How Practitioners Are Succeeding where Policy-Makers Have Failed*, 30 Brit. J. Criminology 150–70 (1990). The German imprisonment rate that prosecutors sought to lower, it bears noting, was always low by U.S. standards—roughly one-fifth of the American rate, depending on the years in which one makes the comparison. German prosecutors' ability to pursue to this policy suggests that they exercise more discretion than the traditional mandatory-prosecution rule implies.

    Canada made comparable reforms in the 1990s through legislation. The Canadian Sentencing Reform Act of 1996 authorized a new punishment option, conditional sentencing or community custody, as a means to reduce prison rates. Offenders may receive community supervision (and remain employed) in lieu of prison. *See generally* Julian V. Roberts et al., Penal Populism and Public Opinion: Lessons from Five Countries (2002); Julian V. Roberts & Jane B. Sprott, *Exploring the Differences Between Punitive and Moderate Penal Policies in the United States and Canada*, in 4 Crime and Crime Policy: International Perspectives on Punitivity 55, 71–72 (Helmut Kury & Theodore N. Ferdinand eds., 2008).

131. Hold aside the long-standing English norm in which the Crown's barrister would refrain from attempts to influence the judge's sentencing decision; that has never been the American approach, and statutes such as Section 851 confirm legislators' embrace a dominant prosecutorial role in sentencing.
132. United States v. Talafierro, 2009 WL 3644114 (D.N.H. 2009) (No. 08–CR–7).
133. *See* R. v. Atkinson [1978] 2 All ER 460 (Lord Scarman stating, "In our law the prosecution is not heard on sentence. This is a matter for the court, after considering whatever has to be said on behalf of an accused man."); John May, *The Responsibility of the Prosecutor to the Court* 90, 94, *in* J. E. Hall ed., THE ROLE OF THE PROSECUTOR (1987) (author was a Lord Justice of Appeal). Since the 1980s, English prosecutors have been called on to assist the court by bringing attention to governing sentencing law and relevant facts, but they still avoid the strong sentencing advocacy that is ubiquitous among U.S. prosecutors. ASHWORTH, SENTENCING AND CRIMINAL JUSTICE 377–78 (5th ed. 2010).

  For a discussion of opposing views and subsequent developments as well Australian practice, see FIONDA, *supra* note 16, at 41–45; *see also id.* at 70–71, 87–88, & 93–94 (describing Scottish practice and noting many Scottish prosecutors *resist* proposals that they should make sentence recommendations). On current Australian practice, see CDPP, *Guidelines and Directions Manual* 1–2 (Sept. 2012) (describing criteria for prosecutors' sentencing input), at http://www.cdpp.gov.au/Publications/Guidelines-and-Directions/CDPP-GDM-Sentencing.pdf; *cf.* Chow v. Director of Public Prosecutions (NSW) (1992) 28 NSWLR 593 ("The judge's sentencing discretion is to be exercised in the public interest. Even where the prosecution and the accused are agreed [on facts], they cannot fetter the judge's performance of the judicial function. ..."). On Caribbean Commonwealth practices, see SEETAHAL, *supra* note 31, at 325.

  Current English rules restrict victim input on sentencing in a manner similar to the traditional bar on prosecutorial recommendations. Courts should consider victim personal statements regarding the impact of the crime, but victims' views on what the sentence should be are not relevant, because judges determine sentences on the basis of applicable guidelines. *See* Criminal Practice Directions 2013 Pt. VII.F; Perkins [2013] EWCA Crim 323; [2013] Cr. App. R. (S.) 72; Andrew Ashworth, *Victims' Views and the Public Interest*, 2014 CRIM. L. REV. 775.
134. 18 U.S.C.A. § 3742 (emphasis added). An implicit rationale for the statute might be that prosecutors who would want to a sentence revised because it exceeded the agreed-upon term could normally achieve that by bring the matter to the trial court's attention, saving appellate resources. But that does not seem to fully explain why prosecutors should be *prohibited* by statute from appealing to vindicate a valid claim of sentencing error, given the state's ministerial interest in lawful sentencing.
135. Nick Vamos, *Please Don't Call It Plea-Bargaining*, [2009] CRIM. L. REV. 617, 623–29; *see generally* ASHWORTH & REDMAYNE, *supra* note 24, at 257–70. For an example of a disclosure doctrine by the Canadian Supreme Court that is broader than its U.S. counterpart, see R. v. Stinchcombe [1991] 3 S.C.R. 326 (discussed further in chapter 5).
136. Yerby v. State, 997 A.2d 144, 153 (Md. 2010); United States v. Bagley, 473 U.S. 667, 675 (1985). For other cases limiting *Brady* by the defendant's duty to investigate available information, see Porter v. Warden of Sussex I State Prison, 722 S.E.2d 534, 540 (Va. 2012); Storey v. Vasbinder, 657 F.3d 372, 375 (6th Cir. 2011) *cert. denied*, 132 S. Ct. 1760 (U.S. 2012); State v. Rooney, 19 A.3d 92 (Vt. 2011); United States v. Cottage, 307 F.3d 494 (6th Cir. 2002); Hoke v. Netherland, 92 F.3d 1350, 1355–56 (4th Cir.1996); United States v. Payne, 63 F.3d 1200, 1208 (2d Cir. 1995); United States v. Clark, 928 F.2d 733, 738 (6th Cir. 1991).
137. For an excellent discussion of reasons that prosecutor discretion may operate differently in practice, see Hodgson & Roberts, *supra* note 14, at 64–94.
138. On French prosecutors and judges, see D. Boccon-Gibod, *The Judicial Officers and the Judges: The Public Prosecutor*, HENRI CAPITANT L. REV. (No. 4 June 2012); Hodgson, *supra* note 110, at 223–40; HODGSON, *supra* note 103.

139. *See* Jenia Iontcheva Turner, *Judicial Participation in Plea Negotiations: A Comparative View*, 54 AM. J. COMP. L. 199, 215, 227–31 (2006) (describing the "stark" contrast between German prosecutors' obligation to fully disclose evidence to the defense "at all stages of the investigation," with U.S. federal criminal process, where disclosure is "much more limited"); *id.* at 230 (noting "German police and prosecutors have a duty to investigate and gather exculpatory, as well as inculpatory evidence"); THAMAN, *supra* note 98, at 32–35; *see generally* MICHAEL BOHLANDER, PRINCIPLES OF GERMAN CRIMINAL PROCEDURE (2012).

140. United States v. Olsen, 737 F.3d 625. 626 (9th Cir. 2013) (Kozinski, J., dissenting from petition for rehearing en banc, joined by three other judges). Decentralized criminal justice systems inevitably mean a lot of variation. Local professional cultures vary widely even within states, as does the competitiveness of chief prosecutor elections. In practice, prosecutors avoid electoral and media scrutiny in low-profile cases. *See* Ramsey, *supra* note 9, 1360–62, 1383–90 (describing New York prosecutors' greater leeway to plea bargain outside of prominent murder cases).

141. For background on *Brady* violations in Orange County, Calif., see Radley Balko, *Calif. Prosecutors Opt for Freeing Accused Murderers instead of Transparency*, WASH. POST, Oct. 15, 2014; Rex Dalton, *More Murder Charges Dropped in Wake of DA Informants Case*, VOICE OF ORANGE COUNTY (newspaper), Sept. 30, 2014. *See also* Orange County District Attorney Tony Rackauckas's official website at http://orangecountyda.org/office/ocda.asp (first elected in 1998 and re-elected every four years through 2014).

142. STEINBERG, *supra* note 7, at 132–39.

143. On New York, see MCCONVILLE & MIRSKY, *supra* note 7, at 35. For contemporary outliers, see ALA. CODE § 12-17-186 (1975); MINN. STAT. § 388.12; COLO. REV. STAT. § 16-5-209; N.D. CENT. CODE § 11-16-06, all cited *supra* note 38. *See also* 16 PA. CONST. STAT. ANN. § 1409 (courts may authorize private prosecutors to take over cases from public prosecutors).

144. According to Jed Shugerman's leading account, reformers hoped direct election would give judges autonomy from legislatures and governors and thereby enable them to restrain some of the corruption and excesses of those political actors. SHUGERMAN, *supra* note 8, at 103–22; *see also* Nelson, *supra* note 8.

145. WILLIAMS, *supra* note 61, at 290 (describing judicial selection and noting estimates that 87 percent of state judges face voters at some point). For one attempt to assess differences in elected and appointed judges, see Stephen J. Choi, G. Mitu Gulati, & Eric Posner, *Professionals or Politicians: The Uncertain Empirical Case for an Elected Rather than Appointed Judiciary*, 26 J.L. ECON. & ORGANIZATIONS 290 (2010) (describing differences between elected and appointed judges based on measures for three aspects of judicial performance—effort, skill, and independence).

146. SHUGERMAN, *supra* note 8, 177–206 (describing state adoption of judicial appointment systems). *See also* Gordon & Huber, *Electoral Competitiveness*, *supra* note 122 (noting thirty-nine states elect at least some judges). Polling data suggest strong popular support in the U.S. for electing judges. A 2011 survey found 65 percent of Americans support electing judges and only 22 percent favored appointment. *See Rasmussen Report*, at http://www.rasmussenreports.com/index.php/public_content/politics/general_politics/april_2011/65_say_most_judges_should_be_elected_political_class_disagrees (May 12, 2011 poll). On debates about judicial constitutional interpretation and democratic legitimacy is LARRY D. KRAMER, THE PEOPLE THEMSELVES: POPULAR CONSTITUTIONALISM AND JUDICIAL REVIEW (2004). For an account of U.S. federal agencies gaining bureaucratic autonomy from political officials with formal control over them by developing popular and interest-group support independently, see DANIEL P. CARPENTER, FORGING OF BUREAUCRATIC AUTONOMY: REPUTATIONS, NETWORKS, AND POLICY INNOVATION IN EXECUTIVE AGENCIES, 1862–1928 (2001).

147. Constitutional Reform Act 2005 (U.K.). Japan and France elects some lower court judges. *See* Amalia D. Kessler, *Marginalization and Myth: The Corporatist Roots of France's Forgotten Elective Judiciary*, 58 AM. J. OF COMP. L. 679 (2010); Croley, *supra* note 13, at 691 n.3. Of course, political pressures or affiliations might affect judiciaries even in jurisdictions in which they gain appointments through nominally nonpolitical systems, although institutional design and tradition seem to reduce those risks in many contexts. For a sample of the growing body of research on this point for various national courts, see, e.g., Nuno Garoupa, Fernando Gomez-Pomar, & Veronica Grembi, *Judging under Political Pressure: An Empirical Analysis of Constitutional Review Voting in the Spanish Constitutional Court*, 29 J.L. ECON. & ORG. 513 (2013) (assessing political variables in decisions of the Spanish Constitutional Court, describing limits on ideology imposed the civil law tradition of consensual courts, and concluding that political influence in the court cannot be simply described as a reflection of political alignment); Chris Hanretty, *The Decisions and Ideal Points of British Law Lords*, 43 BRIT. J. POL. SCI. 703 (2013) (studying thirty years of decisions by British Law Lords and finding no basis for describing individual judges' decisions in political terms, based on a standard method for assessing judicial ideology); Raphael Franck, *Judicial Independence under a Divided Polity: A Study of the Rulings of the French Constitutional Court, 1959–2006*, 25 J.L. ECON. & ORG. 262 (2009) (concluding that judges on the French Constitutional Court rendered primarily independent rulings in periods when left-wing and right-wing parties were sharply divided).

148. *See* Gordon & Huber, *Electoral Competitiveness, supra* note 122 (using Kansas data, judges elected in partisan elections sentence more harshly than judges who face nonpartisan retention elections); Gregory A. Huber & Sanford C. Gordon, *Accountability and Coercion: Is Justice Blind When It Runs for Office?*, 48 AM. POL. SCI. REV. 247 (2004) (similar finding using dataset of elected Pennsylvania judges' sentencing decisions). For general, comparative discussions of elected and appointed judges focused on sentencing, see Richard S. Frase, *Comparative Perspectives on Sentencing Policy and Research, in* SENTENCING AND SANCTIONS 259, 276–77 (Michael Tonry & Richard S. Frase eds., 2001); JULIAN V. ROBERTS ET AL., PENAL POPULISM AND PUBLIC OPINION: LESSONS FROM FIVE COUNTRIES (2002).

149. James M. Anderson & Paul Heaton, *How Much Difference Does the Lawyer Make? The Effect of Defense Counsel on Murder Case Outcomes*, 122 YALE L.J. 154, 190–92 (2012) (reporting lawyers' claims that judges' appointments of defense counsel constitutes "largely a patronage system" through which judges "pay back supporters for their political help," and that judges "appoint the next guy on the list they get from [their political] party").

150. WILLIAMS, *supra* note 61, at 291.

151. New York granted courts *nolle prosequi* authority in 1829, during its era of private and judicially appointed prosecutors. MCCONVILLE & MIRSKY, *supra* note 7, at 35 (*citing* 1829 Revised Statutes of the State of New York, Title IV, Sec. 68, p.730 & Sec. 54. p.726). For a broad overview of state *nolle pros* laws, see *Power of Court to Enter Nolle Prosequi or Dismiss Prosecution*, 69 A.L.R. 240 (1930 & supp. 2012); the federal rule is Fed. R. Crim. Pro. 48(a). Control over dismissal of charges effectively gives judges the power to compel prosecutors to litigate charges at trial or lose by forfeiture. Yet the overwhelming trend has been for state and federal courts to interpret such statutes as not giving courts power to dismiss over a prosecutor's objection or based on their own policy judgments, and as requiring deference to prosecutorial judgments. *See, e.g.*, Genesee Prosecutor v. Genesee Circuit Judge, 215 N.W.2d 147 (Mich. 1974). For federal cases, see, e.g., Dawsey v. Government of Virgin Islands, 34 V.I. 174, 931 F. Supp. 397 (D.V.I. 1996); United States v. Smith, 55 F.3d 157 (4th Cir. 1995); United States v. Smith, 853 F. Supp. 179 (M.D. N.C. 1994); United States v. Perate, 719 F.2d 706 (4th Cir. 1983).

A standard explanation for deference is that judges lack means to compel prosecutors to litigate charges at trial. *See, e.g.,* United States v. Greater Blouse, Skirt & Neckwear Contractors Ass'n, 228 F. Supp. 483, 489–90 (S.D.N.Y. 1964) ("Even were leave of Court to the dismissal of the indictment denied, the Attorney General would still have the right to . . . , in the exercise of his discretion, decline to move the case for trial. The Court in that circumstance would be without power to issue a mandamus or other order to compel prosecution of the indictment, since such a direction would invade the traditional separation of powers doctrine."). But judges have options short of mandamus. Presumably they could hold prosecutors in contempt for failures to appear, as they could for all other attorneys. And whenever prosecutors retain an interest charges they seek to dismiss, judges could incentivize them by ruling that failure to litigate charges results (as for civil parties) in forfeiture of the claim, or dismissal with prejudice.

152. *See* Dorf & Sabel, *Experimentalism, supra* note 129, at 401–02; Dorf & Sabel, *Drug Treatment Courts, supra* note 129; McLeod, *supra* note 129; Bowers, *Contraindicated Drug Courts, supra* note 129.

153. Renee Lettow-Lerner, *The Transformation of the American Civil Trial: The Silent Judge,* 42 WM. & MARY L. REV. 195, 245–48, 261 (2000) (describing nineteenth-century legislation to restrict the judicial practice of commenting on evidence in criminal as well as civil cases). *See also* McCONVILLE & MIRSKY, *supra* note 7, at 152 (documenting judges' comments on evidence to juries in New York courts and describing its influence on juries). Federal judges retain the power to comment on evidence. *See* Quercia v. United States, 289 U.S. 466, 469 (1933) (noting federal trial judges have power to explain and comment on evidence); United States v. Murdock, 290 U.S. 389, 394 (1933) (urging caution in judicial comments to juries relating to guilt in criminal cases). But the power seems to be disfavored today. *See* Kern v. Levolor Lorentzen, Inc., 899 F.2d 772, 780 (9th Cir. 1990) ("Comments by the judge require reversal if the judge expresses his opinion on an ultimate issue of fact in front of the jury. . . .")

154. *See* Renee Lettow Lerner, *New Trial for Verdict against Law: Judge-Jury Relations in Early Nineteenth-Century America,* 71 NOTRE DAME L. REV. 505 (1996) (describing various means of judicial influence over jury decisions in eighteenth and nineteenth centuries).

155. Harris v. United States, 536 U.S. 545, 571 (2002) (Breyer, J., concurring) (mandatory minimum statutes "transfer sentencing power to prosecutors, who can determine sentences through the charges they decide to bring."). For an early example of a statute increasing prosecutor authority, see People v. Tenorio, 473 P.2d 993 (Cal. 1970). In the wake of changes in federal sentencing rules that give judges greater discretion, prosecutors forthrightly responded strategically by more often charging offenses with mandatory minimums to restrict that discretion. *See* Testimony of Patrick J. Fitzgerald, U.S. Attorney, Northern District of Illinois, to the United States Sentencing Commission, at 252 (Sept. 2009) ("[A] prosecutor is far less willing to forgo charging a mandatory minimum sentence when prior experience shows that the defendant will ultimately be sentenced to a mere fraction of what the guidelines range is."). *See generally* Ronald Wright, *Charging and Plea Bargaining as Forms of Sentencing Discretion, in* THE OXFORD HANDBOOK OF SENTENCING AND CORRECTIONS 247–69 (Kevin Reitz & Joan Peterselia eds., 2012); Erik Luna & Paul G. Cassell, *Mandatory Minimalism,* 32 CARDOZO L. REV. 1 (2010) (history of mandatory minimum sentencing, especially in the federal system, offering reasons for their resilience); KATE STITH & JOSE CABRANES, FEAR OF JUDGING (1998); *Sentencing Symposium,* 105 COLUM. L. REV. 933–1415 (2005). For examples of sentencing statutes that increase prosecutor power, see, e.g., FLA. STAT. §§775.084 & §775.08401 (2014) (recidivist sentencing provisions; authorization for prosecutors to define policies on use of recidivist sentences); 21 U.S.C. § 841 (mandatory minimum sentences for drug offenses).

Judges (or juries) enjoyed wide sentencing discretion for much of the twentieth century until sentencing reforms after the 1970s, but that was not always the case. *See* JOHN

LANGBEIN, THE ORIGINS OF ADVERSARY CRIMINAL TRIAL (2003) (noting English judges had relatively little sentencing discretion into the early nineteenth century, because of mandatory death penalty). The era of judicial sentencing discretion—which prevailed for most of the twentieth century, in the era of "penal modernism"—did much to affirm the idea of sentencing as a core judicial function. On penal modernism, see James Q. Whitman, *The Case for Penal Modernism: Beyond Utility and Desert*, 1 CRITICAL LEGAL ANALYSIS 144 (2014); DAVID GARLAND, CULTURE OF CONTROL (2001).

156. *See* Alleyne v. United States, 133 S. Ct. 2151 (2013) (*quoting* inter alia 2 J. STORY, COMMENTARIES ON THE CONSTITUTION OF THE UNITED STATES 540–41 (4th ed. 1873)); Williams v. Florida, 399 U.S. 78, 100 (1970) (jury "prevent[s] oppression by the government"); Duncan v. Louisiana, 391 U.S. 145, 156 (1968) (stating that the right to a criminal jury trial was intended to "prevent oppression by the Government" including "judges too responsive to the voice of higher authority . . . [or] the compliant, biased, or eccentric judge." The jury right reflects "a reluctance to entrust plenary powers over the life and liberty of the citizen to one judge or to a group of judges."). In this the Court was echoing Blackstone from two centuries earlier. WILLIAM BLACKSTONE, 2 COMMENTARIES ON THE LAWS OF ENGLAND 380 (William Carey Jones ed., 1916) (describing judges' "involuntary bias toward those of their own rank and dignity"). For a leading account of the jury's structural role in the U.S. Constitution, see AKHIL REED AMAR, THE BILL OF RIGHTS 81–118 (1998). For a basic statement of functions of criminal juries, see John Baldwin & Mike McConville, *Criminal Juries*, 2 CRIME & JUSTICE 269 (1980). Literature on "legal origins" largely by economists also stresses the jury's original core function has a decision maker less susceptible to coercion from the sovereign than government judges. *See* Edward L. Glaeser & Andrei Shleifer, *Legal Origins*, 117 Q. J. ECON. 1193 (2002).

157. *See, e.g.,* GEORGIA CONST. art. I, para. 11 (2009) ("In criminal cases, . . . the jury shall be the judges of the law and the facts."); Georgia v. Brailsford, 3 U.S. 1 (1794) (instruction to jury on their power to "determine" the law as well as facts); Fisher v. People of Ill., 23 Ill. 283 (1859) (*quoting* the "emphatic language" of ILL. CRIM. CODE § 188 that "[j]uries, in all cases, shall be judges of the law and the fact" and concluding it puts "no limits" on power of jurors, who "are not bound by the law, as given to them by the court, but can assume the responsibility of deciding, each juror for himself, what the law is"); *see also* Renee Lettow Lerner, *New Trial for Verdict against Law: Judge-Jury Relations in Early Nineteenth-Century America*, 71 NOTRE DAME L. REV. 505, 516–17 (1996) (noting many English and American jurists in the eighteenth and nineteenth centuries who affirmed jurors' power to determine law as well as facts); MCCONVILLE & MIRSKY, *supra*, note 7 at 141 (describing jury's law power in nineteenth-century New York courts).

158. *Cf.* G. EDWARD WHITE, THE CONSTITUTION AND THE NEW DEAL 11–61, 165–97 (2000) (describing transition from classical to modernist understanding of law, from something found by judges to something created by judges).

159. Sparf v. United States, 156 U.S. 51 (1895) (holding that federal judges need not tell jurors of their ability "judge" the law or engage in nullification).

160. In contrast to common law systems, civil law systems give judges responsibility for ensuring *factual* accuracy but place much less trust in judges to make or define *law*. James Whitman has described the original ambition of civil codes to constrain judges by specifying as much of the law as possible in legislation, which ideally would reduce or eliminate judicial discretion over law. Civil codes in this sense reflect an anxiety about judges' power that is much weaker in the common law tradition, which also includes a deep skepticism about the possibility and desirability of legislation that specifies much of law's detail in advance of its application. The common law tradition trusts judges to develop law incrementally in the context of cases and is relatively comfortable with acknowledging that common lawmaking and statutory interpretation can amount to interstitial lawmaking. Whitman, *supra* note 16, at 375–79.

161. U.S.Const.art.III,§2;*see*Akhil Reed Amar,America's Constitution:A Biography 240–42 (2005).

162. State v. Carmen, 5 Crim. L. Mag. 560 (Iowa S. Ct. 1884). The Iowa court's reasoning reflects the worry that replacing the jury with a judge may undermine *accuracy* of criminal judgments. On this view, the prohibition on waiving the jury placed a priority on truth determination at some cost to both honoring party preferences and to the efficiency of public courts. For other examples, see Harris v. People, 21 N.E. 585, 591 (Ill. 1889); Morgan v. People, 26 N.E. 651 (Ill. 1891) (both holding jury not waivable; not overturned until Swanson v. Fisher, 172 N.E. 722, 728 (Ill. 1930)). For a similar position taken by the U.S. Supreme Court, see Thompson v. Utah, 170 U.S. 343, 353–54 (1898). *See also* W. F. Elliot, *Waiver of Constitutional Rights in Criminal Cases*, 6 Crim. L. Mag. 182 (1885) (discussing how the public nature of criminal trial rights limits the parties' abilities to waive them and citing cases limiting waiver of criminal jury).

163. Tex. Code Crim. Proc. art. 23 (1886); *see also id*. arts. 518, 519, & 534 (allowing defendants to plead guilty to felonies "in open court" if a jury is impanelled to assess punishment), *cited in* Moore v. State, 2 S.W. 634, 635 (Tex. App. 1886). For another example, see State v. Carmen, 63 Iowa 130, 18 N.W. 691 (Iowa S.Ct. 1884) (holding defendant's waiver of jury and judgment by bench trial invalid on charge of assault).

164. *See* Joel Prentiss Bishop, 1 Bishop's Criminal Procedure § 893 (3d ed. 1880); Francis Wharton, A Treatise on Criminal Pleading and Practice § 733 (8th ed. 1880) (both cited in Moore v. State, 2 S.W. 634 (Tex. App. 1886)). *See also* Merritt A. Thompson, *The Right to Trial by Jury*, 5 Crim. L. Mag. 771, 776 (1884) ("the decisions are at variance as to whether a legislative authorization is necessary to enable a party to waive a trial by jury in a criminal cause.").

165. Federal law affirmed the same view. Patton v. United States, 281 U.S. 276, 277, 293–98, 308–309, 312 (1930) (federal constitutional rights in Article III and the Sixth Amendment are not part of the "frame of government" but rather rights that defendant may waive; jury waiver in federal trials requires consent of the prosecutor and judge).

166. *See In Re* Staff, 23 N.W. 587 (Wis. 1885) (holding statute is constitutional that permits waiver of jury in municipal court); State v. Lockwood, 43 Wis. 403 (1877) (in absence of a statute addressing waiver, holds jury cannot be waived in felony or misdemeanor cases); State v. Carmen, 18 N.W. 691 (Iowa 1884) (in absence of a statute addressing waiver, defendant charged with attempted murder cannot consent to bench trial and citing decisions in other states holding same; dissenter, Seevers, J., would infer party power to waive constitutional jury right but concedes "the great weight of authority is against" this view); Cancemi v. People, 4 E.P. Smith 128, 18 N.Y. 128 (N.Y. 1858) (holding Constitution bars parties and trial court from consenting to a jury of 11, and strongly implying that parties may not waive jury trial and agree to bench trial); Elliot, *supra* note 162 (commentary citing and summarizing numerous state statutes and court decisions that authorize parties to waive criminal jury and submit to bench trial and noting most exclude some class of serious offenses from this waiver, either capital cases or all felonies).

167. Examples of long-standing statutes that prohibit guilty pleas when the punishment is death include La. Rev. Stat. Ann. § 15:262 (1951) (current version at La. Code Crim. Proc. Ann. art. 557 (2003)) ("No court has authority to receive an unqualified plea of guilty in any capital case, and if any defendant so plead, the court shall refuse to receive the plea and shall order the plea of not guilty entered for him."); N.Y. Code Crim. Proc. § 332 (McKinney 1958) (current version at N.Y. Crim. Proc. Law § 220.10(5)(e) (McKinney 2014)) ("A conviction shall not be had upon a plea of guilty where the crime charged is or may be punishable by death." New York, however, no longer uses capital punishment).

168. New Jersey's statute after 1893 read: "if, upon arraignment [for murder], such plea of guilty shall be offered, it shall be disregarded and a plea of not guilty entered, and a jury impaneled shall try the case in manner aforesaid." *See* N.J. Stat. sec. 68 (1893) (revised

from 1874 statute), *cited in* Valentina v. Mercer, 201 U.S. 131 (1906). For other examples, see Iowa Code § 690.4 (1977) (enacted in 1851 and codified under varying section numbers through 1977), *cited in, e.g.,* State v. Kelley, 115 N.W.2d 184 (Iowa 1962) and State v. Brown, 44 N.W.2d 409 (Iowa 1950); State v. Blackwell, 198 P.2d 280 (Nev. 1948); People v. Quicksall, 33 N.W.2d 904 (Mich. 1948); State v. Frohner, 80 N.E.2d 868 (Ohio 1948); Commonwealth v. Kramer, 22 A.2d 46 (Pa. Super. 1941); People v. Bellon, 182 P. 420 (Cal. 1919). Wash. Code § 229 (1859) and Tex. Code art. 609 (1857) required juries to determine the degree of murder liability after a plea of guilty.

169. Tex. Code tit. 18, sec. 1, art. 609 (1857) ("[I]f any person shall plead guilty to an indictment for murder, a jury shall be summoned to find of what degree of murder he is guilty, and in either case, if they shall find the offence of murder to be of the second degree, they shall also find the punishment."); Wash. Code tit. XX, sec. 230 (1859) (same). *Available at* http://heinonline.org.

170. Utah Code chap. 32, tit. 2, sec. 7 (1855). States with this rule included California, Iowa, Maryland, Michigan, Nebraska, Nevada, Ohio, Oklahoma, and Pennsylvania. For similar statutes, see Neb. Code sec. 7, p.226 (1855); Ohio Code vol. 33, sec. 39 (1834); Okla. Code chap. 25, sec. 13 (1890); Pa. Code chap. CIX, sec. II (1794, 1846). All available at http://heinonline.org.

171. Halsbury's Laws of England, vol. 61 (2010 & 2014 supp.). The Criminal Justice Act 2003 authorized for the first time trials on indictment without jury in serious fraud cases, upon application of the prosecution rather than waiver of the defendant. The Court of Appeal has stressed that this option is a "last resort." *See* J, S, M v. R. [2010] EWCA Crim 1755 ("We must emphasise as unequivocally as we can that, notwithstanding the statutory arrangements introduced in the 2003 Act which permit the court to order the trial of a serious criminal offence without a jury, this remains and must remain the decision of last resort."). *See also* R. v. Canterbury et al [1982] Q.B. 389, 411–12, 414–15 (discussing judicial review of prosecutor's decision to charge an "either-way" offense as lesser offense with a summary trial in Magistrate's Court rather than a greater offense entitled to jury trial).

172. For an overview and sources, see John D. Jackson & Sean Doran, *The Case for Jury Waiver*, 1997 Crim. L. Rev. 155 (notes 9, 10, and 11 summarize sources for Canada, New Zealand, and Australia, respectively). On Canadian law, see *R. v. Turpin* (1989) 48 C.C.C. (3d) 8 (Supreme Court of Canada). On Australian law, see *Brown v. The Queen* (1986) 160 C.L.R. 171 (High Court of Australia) (summarizing law of jury waivers in Australian states and elsewhere). New South Wales Law Reform Commission, Vol. I, Criminal Procedure from Charge to Trial: Specific Problems and Proposals 214–15 (Disc. Paper 1987) (indictable offenses first became "triable either way" in New South Wales in 1883).

173. Nathan T. Elliff, *Notes on the Abolition of the English Grand Jury*, 29 Am. Inst. Crim. L. & Criminology 3 (1938–1939).

174. For an overview of state grand juries, see Sara Sun Beale & William C. Bryson, Grand Jury Law and Practice §1.7 (1986); Ric Simmons, *Re-Examining the Grand Jury: Is there Room for Democracy in our Criminal Justice System?*, 82 Boston Univ. L. Rev. 1 (2002). For another favorable account of grand juries, see Roger Fairfax, *Grand Jury Discretion and Constitutional Design*, 93 Cornell L. Rev. 703 (2008).

175. Simmons, *supra* note 174, at 10–15.

176. *Id.*, at 20–25. There is a modest trend in grand jury states toward requiring that prosecutors produce exculpatory evidence. *See, e.g.,* Schuster v. Eighth Judicial District Court, 160 P.3d 873 (Nev. 2007); *also* Dep't of Justice, *U.S. Attorney's Manual* § 9-11.233 (recommending disclosure).

177. Ronald Wright, *How Prosecutor Elections Fail Us*, 6 Ohio St. J. Crim. Law 581 (2009). *Cf.* Gregory A. Huber & Sanford C. Gordon, *Directing Retribution: On Political Control of Lower Court Judges*, 23 J.L. Econ. & Org. 386 (2007) (modeling influence of legislators and voters on judges' sentencing behavior and noting difficulties in monitoring judges). *See also* other studies by Gordon & Huber, *supra* note 122.

178. For an example of current politicians condemning unaccountable bureaucracies, see Donald Lambro, *DeLay Slams Court Activism as Autocracy*, WASH. TIMES, Aug. 14, 2005, at http://www.washtimes.com/national/20050814-115425-3341r.htm. For skepticism of that view, see Croley, *supra* note 13.

179. In addition to STUNTZ, COLLAPSE OF AMERICAN CRIMINAL JUSTICE (2011), and STEPHANOS BIBAS, THE MACHINERY OF CRIMINAL JUSTICE (2012), for scholars who make the case in various ways that lay decision making should lead to more moderate criminal justice outcomes, see Josh Bowers, *The Normative Case for Normative Grand Juries*, 47 WAKE FOREST L. REV. 319 (2012) (hereafter *Grand Juries*); Josh Bowers, *Legal Guilt, Normative Innocence, and the Equitable Discretion Not to Prosecute*, 110 COLUM. L. REV. 1655 (2010); PAUL H. ROBINSON, INTUITIONS OF JUSTICE AND THE UTILITY OF DESERT (2013); PAUL ROBINSON & JOHN M. DARLEY, JUSTICE, LIABILITY AND BLAME: COMMUNITY VIEWS AND THE CRIMINAL LAW (1996).

180. For examples in a compelling narrative, see MARIANNE WESSON, A DEATH AT CROOKED CREEK: THE CASE OF THE COWBOY, THE CIGARMAKER, AND THE LOVE LETTER (2013). *See also* Roderick M. Hills, *Federalism and Corruption: (When) Do Federal Criminal Prosecutions Improve Non-Federal Democracy?*, 6 THEORETICAL INQUIRIES IN LAW 113 (Jan. 2005) (describing differences in state and federal conceptions of corruption and conflicts).

181. *See* Mooney v. Holohan, 294 U.S. 103 (1935); *also* Colin Starger, *50 Years Before* Brady, THE CHAMPION 34 (May 2013).

182. DAVID SKLANSKY, DEMOCRACY AND THE POLICE (2008) (political democratic theory for policing); Bowers, *Grand Juries, supra* note 179 (grand jury charging discretion); BIBAS, *supra* 179, at 156–66 (sentencing juries). *Cf.* Rachel Harmon, *Federal Programs and the Real Costs of Policing*, 90 NYU L. REV. 870 (2015) (assessing how federal funding interferes with local-level accountability for police); Dan M. Kahan & Tracey L. Meares, *The Coming Crisis of Criminal Procedure*, 86 GEO. L.J. 1153 (1998) (local accountability of police).

183. Recognizing the benefits of bureaucracies need not deny ongoing debates about accountability of politically insulated agencies is an ongoing concern in nations that rely on them. Ronald Wright & Marc Miller, *The Worldwide Accountability Deficit for Criminal Prosecutors*, 67 WASH. & LEE L. REV. 1587 (2010).

Chapter 3

* *Epigraph:* United States v. Mezzanatto, 513 U.S. 196, 208 (1995).

1. *See* Sarah Stillman, *Get Out of Jail, Inc.*, NEW YORKER, June 23, 2014, at 49. For the United Kingdom, see Alan Travis, *Two Companies to Run more than Half of Privatised Probation Services*, GUARDIAN.CO.UK (Oct. 29, 2014). On privatization of public functions more generally in the United States, see Jon D. Michaels, *Privatization's Progeny*, 101 GEO. L.J. 1023 (2013); *Privatization's Pretensions*, 77 U. CHI. L. REV. 717 (2010). On nineteenth-century leasing of state prisoners, see DAVID M. OSHINSKY, WORSE THAN SLAVERY: PARCHMAN FARM AND THE ORDEAL OF JIM CROW JUSTICE (1997). For a U.K. focus, see articles in 97 CRIMINAL JUSTICE MATTERS No. 1 (2014) (special issue on "Criminal Justice Marketisation"); MINISTRY OF JUSTICE, TRANSFORMING REHABILITATION: A STRATEGY FOR REFORM (2013); Angélica Thumala, Benjamin Goold, & Ian Loader, *A Tainted Trade? Moral Ambivalence and Legitimation Work in the Private Security Industry*, 62 BRIT. J. SOC. 283 (2011).

2. A few rural jurisdictions do the same for prosecutors in certain courts that generally are limited low-level offenses. *See* Roger Fairfax, *Delegation of the Criminal Prosecution Function to Private Actors*, 43 U.C. DAVIS L. REV. 411 (2009).

3. NICOLA LACEY, THE PRISONERS' DILEMMA: POLITICAL ECONOMY AND PUNISHMENT IN CONTEMPORARY DEMOCRACIES (2008); John R. Sutton, *The Political Economy of*

Imprisonment in Affluent Western Democracies, 1960–90, 69 AM. Soc. REV. 170 (2004) (finding imprisonment rates correlate with national political economy features such as the strength of unions and corporatist versus liberal economic interventions). Sutton finds imprisonment rates are lower in corporatist economies. On the same correlations between welfare spending and incarceration policies among U.S. states, see Katherine Beckett & Bruce Western, *Governing Social Marginality: Welfare, Incarceration, and the Transformation of State Policy*, 3 PUNISHMENT & SOCIETY 43–59 (2001), *reprinted in* MASS IMPRISONMENT: ITS CAUSES AND CONSEQUENCES 35–51 (David Garland ed., 2001). Katherine Beckett & Bruce Western, *Crime Control, American Style: From Social Welfare to Social Control, in* CRIMINAL POLICY IN TRANSITION: CRIMINAL POLICY TRENDS INTO THE NEW MILLENNIUM (Penny Green & Andrew Rutherford eds., 2001), also published in CRIME, INEQUALITY AND THE STATE: CRIMINAL JUSTICE IN LATE MODERNITY (ch. 9) (Mary Vogel ed., 2007); Bruce Western & Katherine Beckett, *How Unregulated Is the U.S. Labor Market? The Penal System as a Labor Market Institution*, 104 AM. J. Soc. 1030 (1999). Other studies have found similar correlations between high imprisonment rates and high levels of economic inequality, more market-oriented economies, and even the common law as opposed to civil law basis of a nation's legal system. Holger Spamann, *The U.S. Crime Puzzle: A Comparative Perspective on US Crime & Punishment*, Harvard John M. Olin Discussion Papers, No. 778 (2014), available on http://ssrn.com.

4. BERNARD HARCOURT, THE ILLUSION OF FREE MARKETS: PUNISHMENT AND THE MYTH OF NATURAL ORDER (2011). In his influential book *The Culture of Control* (2002), David Garland examined deep cultural-political changes that affected criminal justice policy in the late twentieth century, when Anglo American policy turned from "penal welfarism" to punitive retributivism. There is also a substantial international literature, much of it empirically based on the forms and effects of "penal populism." *See* JULIAN V. ROBERTS ET AL., PENAL POPULISM AND PUBLIC OPINION: LESSONS FROM FIVE COUNTRIES (2002). *See also* LOIC WACQUANT, PUNISHING THE POOR: THE NEOLIBERAL GOVERNMENT OF SOCIAL INSECURITY (2009).

5. United States v. Mezzanatto, 513 U.S. 196, 208 (1995); Puckett v. United States, 556 U.S. 129, 137 (2009).

6. Search in Westlaw database of U.S. Supreme Court decisions conducted August 2014. Searched for "incentive /s (defendant prosecutor prosecution)" within three date ranges: DA(aft 12-31-1980 & bef 01-01-2014); DA(aft 12-31-1947 & bef 01-01-1981); and DA(aft 12-31-1914 & bef 01-01-1948). On the rise in usage of "incentive" or "incentivize" in books and political officials' speech since 1950, see MICHAEL SANDEL, WHAT MONEY CAN'T BUY: THE MORAL LIMITS OF MARKETS 86–87 (2012) (use of "incentivize" in newspaper reports rose 1400% since the 1980s).

7. On the "marketplace of ideas" in U.S. free speech law, see Frederick Schauer, *Facts and the First Amendment*, 57 UCLA L. REV. 897 (2010); United States v. Alvarez, 567 U.S. __, 132 S. Ct. 2537 (2012) ("The theory of our Constitution is 'that the best test of truth is the power of the thought to get itself accepted in the competition of the market,'" *citing* Abrams v. United States, 250 U.S. 616, 630 (1919) (Holmes, J., dissenting)). On the *Lochner* era and "liberty of contract," see BARRY CUSHMAN, RETHINKING THE NEW DEAL COURT (1998); Jedediah Purdy, *Neoliberal Constitutionalism: Lochnerism for a New Economy*, 77 LAW & CONTEMP. PROBS. 195 (2015).

8. Regarding Smith's "invisible hand" metaphor, see ADAM SMITH, THE WEALTH OF NATIONS 354 (1776; 1872) ("[B]y directing [domestic] industry in such a manner as its produce may be of the greatest value, [the individual] intends only his own gain, and he is in this, as in many other cases, led by an invisible hand to promote an end which was no part of his intention."); *id.* at 57–64 (without using the phrase, describing the process by which markets harness self-interest that would later be central to the meaning of the "invisible hand" metaphor).

9. *See* Crawford v. Washington, 541 U.S. 36 (2004).

10. *Mezzanatto*, 513 U.S. 196, 208.

11. *See* DOUGLAS N. HUSAK, OVERCRIMINALIZATION: THE LIMITS OF CRIMINAL LAW (2008). On strict liability, see Darryl K. Brown, *Criminal Law Reform and the Persistence of Strict Liability*, DUKE L.J. (2012). The growth of federal power in the twentieth century included a vast expansion of federal criminal law and enforcement agencies. Federal influence over state enforcement systems has grown as well with federal funding for state criminal justice programs, and coordinated state-federal enforcement policies. *See generally* Rachel Harmon, *Federal Programs and the Real Costs of Policing*, 90 NYU L. REV. No. 3 (2015).

12. RONALD COASE, THE FIRM, THE MARKET, AND THE LAW 7, 9 (1988).

13. *See* HARCOURT, *supra* note 4; COASE, *supra* note 12, at 9.

14. *See, e.g.,* Labor Management Relations Act of 1947 (a.k.a. Taft-Hartley Act), 29 U.S.C. § 401-531, 80 H.R. 3020, Pub. L. 80–101, 61 Stat. 136, enacted June 23, 1947; RAYMOND L. HOGLER, THE END OF AMERICAN LABOR UNIONS: THE RIGHT-TO-WORK MOVEMENT AND THE EROSION OF COLLECTIVE BARGAINING (2015). History seems to be part of the story, too. Unions in the United States and United Kingdom were traditionally craft-based rather than industry-based, which put them at disadvantage in taking on a stronger, more coordinating role with employers. *See* Torben Iversen & David Soskice, *Distribution and Redistribution: The Shadow of the Nineteenth Century*, 61 WORLD POLITICS 438, 459–64 (2009).

15. Thomas R. Cusack, Torben Iversen, & David Soskice, *Economic Origins of Political Systems*, 101 AM. POL. SCI. REV. 373 (2007).

16. *See* Neil Fligstein, *Markets as Politics: A Political-Cultural Approach to Market Institutions*, 61 AM. SOC. REV. 656 (1996) (discussing incumbent firms' advantages over challenger firms in various markets). A historical example is laws that favor large exchanges over small "bucket shops" as authorized markets for commodities or futures trading. *See* HARCOURT, *supra* note 4, at 183. Contemporary examples are the pervasive state laws in the United States that require automobiles to be sold exclusively through dealer franchises, which hinders new auto manufacturing firms that seek to sell directly to consumers. *See* Amy Wilson, *Dealers Call Tesla Factory Stores Illegal*, AUTOMOTIVE NEWS, Oct. 8, 2012, *available at* http://www.autonews.com/apps/pbcs.dll/article?AID=/20121008/RETAIL07/310089952/dealers-call-tesla-factory-stores-illegal#.

17. Elizabeth Anderson, *Values, Risks and Norms*, 17 PHIL. & PUB. AFF. 54 (1988).

18. *See generally* MARK J. ROE, STRONG MANAGERS, WEAK OWNERS: THE POLITICAL ROOTS OF AMERICAN CORPORATE FINANCE (1994); Lucian A. Bebchuk & Mark J. Roe, *A Theory of Path Dependence in Corporate Ownership and Governance*, 52 STAN. L. REV. 127 (1999).

19. *See* FRIEDRICH VON HAYEK, THE ROAD TO SERFDOM (1944); ANGUS BURGIN, THE GREAT PERSUASION 44–45, 130–31 (2012); Yuval Levin, *Putting Parents First*, WEEKLY STANDARD, Dec. 4, 2006 (discussing tensions between traditional values central to family life and market values); JOSEPH SCHUMPETER, CAPITALISM, SOCIALISM AND DEMOCRACY 139–64 (1943; 2003); IRVING KRISTOL, TWO CHEERS FOR CAPITALISM (1978); DANIEL BELL, THE CULTURAL CONTRADICTIONS OF CAPITALISM (1976); FRANK H. KNIGHT, THE ETHICS OF COMPETITION 49 (1935; 1997); *see also* Lynn A. Stout, *Killing Conscience: The Unintended Behavioral Consequences of "Pay For Performance,"* 39 J. CORP. L. 525 (2014) (incentive contracts for firm employees undermine prosocial behavior and encourage opportunistic behavior that increases unethical and illegal conduct).

20. *See* PETER A. HALL & DAVID SOSKICE, VARIETIES OF CAPITALISM: THE INSTITUTIONAL FOUNDATIONS OF COMPARATIVE ADVANTAGE (2001); Peter A. Hall & Kathleen Thelen, *Institutional Change in Varieties of Capitalism*, 7 SOCIO-ECON. REV. 7 (2009); MATTHEW M.C. ALLEN, THE VARIETIES OF CAPITALISM PARADIGM: EXPLAINING GERMANY'S COMPARATIVE ADVANTAGE? (2006).

21. Anna Sauerbrey, *Why Germans Are Afraid of Google*, N.Y. TIMES, Oct. 10, 2014 ("The German voter-consumer will always trust the state more than he will any private company" and "Germans regularly report much higher levels of trust in the leading state institutions.").

22. Mark J. Roe, *Can Culture Constrain the Economic Model of Corporate Law?*, 69 U. CHI. L. REV. 1251 (2002).

23. For a critical view that emphasizes the hybrid forms and heterogeneity within these models, see Colin Crouch, *Models of Capitalism*, 10:4 NEW POL. ECON. 439–56 (2005). On defense funding of research, see *Report of the Defense Science Board Task Force on Basic Research* (Jan. 2012), *available at* http://www.fas.org/irp/agency/dod/dsb/basic.pdf.

24. HALL & SOSKICE, *supra* note 20 at 12–13.

25. John L. Campbell & Ove K. Pedersen, *Knowledge Regimes and Comparative Political Economy, in* IDEAS AND POLITICS IN SOCIAL SCIENCE RESEARCH 167–90 (Daniel Béland & Robert Cox eds., 2011). For a description of the diminished role for non-political expertise in recent British crime policy, see Ian Loader, *Fall of the "Platonic Guardians": Liberalism, Criminology and Political Responses to Crime in England and Wales*, 46 BRIT. J. CRIMINOLOGY 561, 579–81 (2006).

26. William D. Adler, *State Capacity and Bureaucratic Autonomy in the Early United States: The Case of the Army Corps of Topographical Engineers*, 26 STUDIES IN AM. POL. DEV'T 107, 109–10 (2012). A seminal work in American political development is STEPHEN SKOWRONEK, BUILDING A NEW AMERICAN STATE: THE EXPANSION OF NATIONAL ADMINISTRATIVE CAPACITIES, 1877–1920 (1982). *See also* KAREN ORREN & STEPHEN SKOWRONEK, THE SEARCH FOR AMERICAN POLITICAL DEVELOPMENT (2004); Elisabeth S. Clemens, *Lineages of the Rube Goldberg State: Building and Blurring Public Programs, 1900–1940, in* RETHINKING POLITICAL INSTITUTIONS: THE ART OF THE STATE 187, 189 (Ian Shapiro et al. eds., 2006) ("[T]he problem of indirect or delegated governance is addressed from the vantage point of state governments during an era when many political actors favored construction of the 'monocratic bureaucracies' analyzed by Weber. . . ."); William J. Novak, *The Myth of the "Weak" American State*, 113 AM. HIST. REV. 752 (2008) (critiquing the use of exclusively European models of state development and asserting that the American state structure is not "weak" in comparison to the centralized bureaucracies of Europe).

27. JACOB S. HACKER, THE DIVIDED WELFARE STATE: THE BATTLE OVER PUBLIC AND PRIVATE SOCIAL BENEFITS IN THE UNITED STATES (2002).

28. SEYMOUR M. LIPSET, AMERICAN EXCEPTIONALISM: A DOUBLE-EDGED SWORD (1997); DAVID RUNCIMAN, THE CONFIDENCE TRAP: A HISTORY OF DEMOCRACY IN CRISIS FROM WORLD WAR I TO THE PRESENT 1–36 (2013) (both discussing Tocqueville's *Democracy in America*); JOHN LAURITZ LARSON, THE MARKET REVOLUTION IN AMERICA: LIBERTY, AMBITION, AND THE ECLIPSE OF THE COMMON GOOD (2009).

29. On the "free trade constitution," see H.P. Hood & Sons v. Du Mond, 336 U.S. 525, 538 (1949) ("The material success that has come to inhabitants of the states which make up this federal free trade unit has been the most impressive in the history of commerce, but the established interdependence of the states only emphasizes the necessity of protecting interstate movement of goods against local burdens and repressions."); Richard Schragger, *Cities, Economic Development, and the Free Trade Constitution*, 94 VA. L. REV. 1091 (2008); LAURENCE H. TRIBE, 1 AMERICAN CONSTITUTIONAL LAW 1057–58 (3d ed. 2000); Jim Chen, *Pax Mercatoria: Globalization as a Second Chance at "Peace for Our Time,"* 24 FORDHAM INT'L L.J. 217, 230–33 (2000).

30. For much of the nineteenth century, this led to a system that Harry Scheiber influentially termed "rivalistic state mercantilism." Harry N. Scheiber, *Federalism and the American Economic Order, 1789–1910*, 10 LAW & SOC'Y REV. 57 (1975).

31. BRIAN BALOGH, A GOVERNMENT OUT OF SIGHT: THE MYSTERY OF NATIONAL AUTHORITY IN NINETEEN CENTURY AMERICA 11, 42 (2009).

32. Charles Sellers, The Market Revolution: Jacksonian America 1815–46 (1991). Larson, *supra* note 28. Much about the historical interpretation of that era is contested. Debates about the national government's role in facilitating economic growth were heated, although states regulated private property and enterprise pervasively to benefit public welfare. For alternate accounts of the era, see Daniel Walker Howe, What Hath God Wrought: The Transformation of America, 1815–1848 (2007); William J. Novak, The People's Welfare: Law and Regulation in Nineteenth Century America (1996).

33. Balogh, *supra* note 31 at 248–49 (citing sources).

34. *Id.*, at 242; Harry N. Scheiber, *Public Rights and the Rule of Law in American Legal History*, 72 Calif. L. Rev. 217 (1984); Scheiber, *supra* note 30.

35. *Criminal Justice Matters* vol. 97 No. 1 (2014) ("Criminal Justice Marketisation"); Ministry of Justice, *Transforming Rehabilitation: A Strategy for Reform*; Thumala, Goold, & Loader, *supra* note 1.

    Kevin Albertson & Chris Fox, *Justice for the Elephant: The Role of Moral Sentiments in Reducing Criminality*, Policy Eval. Res. Unit Briefing 14/1 (2014), *available at* http://www.mmu.peru.co.uk.

36. Bernard Harcourt makes this point especially well in his genealogy of free market ideology. Harcourt, *supra* note 4. Ronald Coase pressed this point. Commodity and stock exchanges, he noted, "regulate in great detail the activities of those who trade in these markets" despite the view that they are paramount examples of competitive free markets. Exchanges confirmed for Coase that "for anything approaching perfect competition to exist, an intricate system of rules and regulations would normally be needed." Coase, *supra* note 12, at 9.

37. The choice between markets and corporate hierarchies is a standard theme of theories of private firms; *see* George Geis, *The Space Between Markets and Hierarchies*, 95 Va. L. Rev. 99, 106–10 (2009). For a classic argument of markets' virtues compared to centralized state planning, see Hayek, *supra* note 19.

38. Securities Act of 1933; Regulation D §§ 230.505 &.506; http://www.sec.gov/answers/accred.htm. Harcourt described in trenchant detail the analogous, complex rules of a paradigmatic free market, Chicago Mercantile Exchange. *See* Harcourt, *supra* note 4.

39. For a sample of large economic literature on auctions, see, e.g., James Bergin, Microeconomic Theory: A Concise Course 101–46 (2005); Flavio Menezes, An Introduction to Auction Theory (2005); Paul Milgrom, Putting Auction Theory to Work (2004); Charles A. Holt & R. Sherman, *Waiting-Line Auctions*, 90 J. Pol. Econ. 280 (1982).

40. For an example of a cap-and-trade program, see EPA v. EME Homer City Generation, 134 S. Ct. 1584 (2014) (affirming Cross-State Air Pollution Rule, 76 Fed. Reg. 48271, 48284-48287, a cap-and-trade sulfur dioxide regulation promulgated under Clean Air Act, 42 U. S. C. §§7407-7410); U.S. EPA, Acid Rain Program 2007 Progress Report: Clean Air Markets—Air & Radiation (Jan. 2009); Curtis Carlson et al., *Sulfur Dioxide Control by Electric Utilities: What are the Gains from Trade?*, 108 J. Pol. Econ. 1292 (2000).

41. Two random examples of information-forcing rules are 15 U.S.C. § 1681a (2012) (Fair Credit Reporting Act) and 12 C.F.R. § 16.3 (2014) (prospectus disclosure prior to sale of securities). A voluminous literature debates the merits of rules mandating disclosure in a wide range of settings. *See, e.g.*, Ian Ayres, *Ya-HUH: There Are and Should Be Penalty Defaults*, 33 Fla. St. U. L. Rev. 589, 600–11 (2006) (surveying dozens of applications of information-forcing rules in scholarly accounts and the law); Omri Ben-Shahar & Carl E. Schneider, *The Failure of Mandated Disclosure*, 159 U. Pa. L. Rev. 647 (2011); Alan Schwartz & Louis L. Wilde, *Intervening in Markets on the Basis of Imperfect Information: A Legal and Economic Analysis*, 127 U. Pa. L. Rev. 630 (1979); William C. Whitford, *The Functions of Disclosure Regulation in Consumer Transactions*, 1973 Wis. L. Rev. 400.

42. For an insightful analysis of information control in criminal process, see Alexandra Natapoff, *The Information Culture of the Criminal System*, 30 CARDOZO L. REV. 965 (2012).

43. *See* the discussion of this topic in chapter 2, and see generally CRIMINAL PROCEDURE AND EVIDENCE IN A COMPARATIVE AND INTERNATIONAL CONTEXT (John T. Jackson & Maximo Langer & Peter Tillers eds., 2008); JACQUELINE HODGSON, FRENCH CRIMINAL JUSTICE: A COMPARATIVE ACCOUNT OF THE INVESTIGATION AND PROSECUTION OF CRIME IN FRANCE 66–72 (2005); Jenia Iontcheva Turner, *Judicial Participation in Plea Negotiations: A Comparative View*, 54 AM. J. COMP. L. 199 (2006).

44. *In re* Davis, 557 U.S. 952, 955 (2009) (Scalia, J., dissenting) ("This Court has never held that the Constitution forbids the execution of a convicted defendant who has had a full and fair trial but is later able to convince a habeas court that he is 'actually' innocent."). The position Scalia summarizes holds regardless of whether the defendant or the state is the cause of the "full and fair trial" nonetheless convicting an innocent man.

45. ROBERT A. KAGAN, ADVERSARIAL LEGALISM: THE AMERICAN WAY OF LAW (2001). *See also* MONICA PRASAD, THE POLITICS OF FREE MARKETS: THE RISE OF NEOLIBERAL ECONOMIC POLICIES IN BRITAIN, FRANCE, GERMANY AND THE UNITED STATES (2006) (describing how "adversarial politics" facilitated neoliberal reforms and "adversarial state structures" in the United States that "led to a greater need for politicians to mobilize populist appeals to acquire or maintain power").

46. To be sure, liberal market economies significantly intervene in some markets to address wealth and resource disparities, providing analogies to litigation rules counteract differences in litigants' relative capacities. Regulation of health insurance contract terms, minimum wage laws, and workplace safety rules can all be understood in part as addressing imbalances in bargaining power from wealth, sophistication, or information deficits. Many antidiscrimination laws in workplaces and other settings can be understood to do much the same. Market prohibitions, such as those for sexual services or human organs, are motivated in part by concerns for the weaker status of one party. Overall, however, liberal market economies have fewer and more modest versions of these market regulations than is common in coordinated economies.

47. *Gonzalez-Lopez*, 548 U.S. 140, 147 (2006).

48. Powell v. Alabama, 287 U.S. 45, 68–69 (1932).

49. Gideon v. Wainwright, 372 U.S. 335 (1963); Strickland v. Washington, 466 U.S. 668 (1984); MIRJAN R. DAMASKA, THE FACES OF JUSTICE AND STATE AUTHORITY: A COMPARATIVE APPROACH TO THE LEGAL PROCESS 235 (1986).

50. MORRIS M. KLEINER, LICENSING OCCUPATIONS: ENSURING QUALITY OR RESTRICTING COMPETITION? (2006), discussed in Alan B. Kreuger, *Do You Need a License to Earn a Living? You Might Be Surprised at the Answer*, N.Y. TIMES, Mar. 2, 2006.

51. *See* SAMUEL WALKER, TAMING THE SYSTEM (1993) (recounting evidence of insufficient defense counsel funding over several decades); American Bar Ass'n Report, *Gideon's Broken Promise: America's Continuing Quest for Equal Justice* (2004).

52. For a rare exception, see State v. Peart, 621 So.2d 780 (La. 1993).

53. *Strickland*, 466 U.S. 668; *Gideon*, 372 U.S. 335. Other right-to-counsel decisions for poor defendants include Betts v. Brady, 316 U.S. 455 (1942); Powell v. Alabama, 287 U.S. 45 (1932) (due process right to counsel in capital cases). Subsequent elaborations of the right to appointed counsel are found in Alabama v. Shelton, 535 U.S. 654 (2002) and Argersinger v. Hamlin, 407 U.S. 25 (1972).

54. Powell v. Alabama, 287 U.S. 45, 53 (1932).

55. United States v. Gonzalez-Lopez, 548 U.S. 140, 144 (2006). For a more recent summary and endorsement of this right from a justice who dissented in *Gonzalez-Lopez*, see Kaley et vir v. United States, 134 S. Ct. 1090 (2014) (Roberts, C.J., dissenting).

56. *Gonzalez-Lopez*, 548 U.S. at 148.

57. *Id.* at 146.

58. Wheat v. United States, 486 U.S. 153 (1988).
59. *Wheat*, 486 U.S. at 159.
60. Caplin & Drysdale v. United States, 491 U.S. 617, 624–25 (1989) (emphasis added).
61. Kaley et vir v. United States, 134 S. Ct. 1090 (2014) (Roberts, C.J., dissenting).
62. Morris v. Slappy, 461 U.S. 1, 14 (1983) ("[W]e reject the claim that the Sixth Amendment guarantees a 'meaningful relationship' between an accused and his counsel").
63. *Gonzalez-Lopez*, 548 U.S. at 150; *see also id.* (Consequences of "erroneous deprivation of the right to counsel of choice . . . are necessarily unquantifiable and indeterminate. . . .").
64. *Id.* at 147–48.
65. *Id.* at 147.
66. *Id.* at 147.
67. *Id.* at 147.
68. *Id.* at 146.
69. *Id.* at 147–48.
70. *See* Scott E. Sundby, *The Majestic and the Mundane: The Two Creation Stories of the Exclusionary Rule*, 43 Tex. Tech L. Rev. 391 (2010) (interest balancing in criminal procedure exclusionary rules).
71. Pamela S. Karlan, *Discrete and Relational Criminal Representation: The Changing Vision of the Right to Counsel*, 105 Harv. L. Rev. 670, 709–10 (1992); *Caplin & Drysdale*, 491 U.S. 617 (1989); Cuyler v. Sullivan, 446 U.S. 335 (1980).
72. *Gonzalez-Lopez*, 548 U.S. 140 (5–4 decision).

Chapter 4

* *Epigraphs:* Puckett v. United States, 556 U.S. 129, 137 (2009); Bordenkircher v. Hayes, 434 U.S. 357, 364 (1978).
1. *See* Stephen Thaman ed., World Plea Bargaining: Consensual Procedures and the Avoidance of the Full Criminal Trial (2010); Jenia I. Turner, Plea Bargaining Across Borders (2009) (descriptions of bargaining Germany, Russian, Bulgaria, China, and Japan); David Nelkin, *Comparative Criminal Justice: Beyond Ethnocentrism and Relativism*, 6 Euro. J. Criminology 291 (2009) (half of all criminal cases diverted from courts in Germany with prosecutor-controlled sentencing or settlement practices); Arie Freiberg, *Non-Adversarial Approaches to Criminal Justice*, 17 J. Judicial Admin. 205–22 (2007) (90 percent plea bargaining rate in Australia); Bron McKillop, *What Can We Learn from the French Criminal Justice System?*, 76 Australian L.J. 49, 51–55 (2002) (99 percent of French criminal cases adjudicated in lower courts with expedited process); Thomas Weigend, *Lay Participation and Consensual Disposition Mechanisms*, 72 Revue Internationale de Droit Penal 595 (2001) (describing trend toward plea bargaining or similar nontrial adjudication in many countries). In 1987, the Council of Europe Committee of Ministers' Recommendation R (87) 18 urged member states to use discretionary prosecution and develop simplified, out-of-court procedures for minor offences as a means to reduce delay in criminal justice systems. Interestingly, across national contexts bargaining usually seems to develop from the bottom up—it starts out in trial courts and later gains statutory or appellate courts' endorsement.
2. Superb archival studies have documented bargaining in some places back to the early nineteenth century. *See* George Fisher, Plea Bargaining's Triumph: A History of Plea Bargaining in America (2004); Mike McConville & Chester Mirsky, Jury Trials and Plea Bargaining: A True History (2005); Mary E. Vogel, Coercion to Compromise (2007) (social and political context of early plea bargaining in the U.S.); Mary E. Vogel, *The Social Origins of Plea Bargaining: An Approach to the Empirical Study of Discretionary Leniency*, 35 J.L. & Soc'y 201 (2008); Mary E. Vogel, *The Social Origins of Plea Bargaining: Conflict and the Law in the Process of State*

Formation 1830–1860, 33 LAW & SOC'Y REV. 161 (1999) (hereafter *State Formation*); LAWRENCE FRIEDMAN & ROBERT V. PERCIVAL, THE ROOTS OF JUSTICE: CRIME AND PUNISHMENT IN ALAMEDA COUNTY, CALIFORNIA, 1870–1910 (1981); ABRAHAM S. BLUMBERG, CRIMINAL JUSTICE (1967). For an earlier generation of plea bargaining studies, see Raymond Moley, *The Vanishing Jury*, 2 SO. CALIF. L. REV. 97 (1928); Missouri Ass'n for Crim. Justice Survey Committee, *The Missouri Crime Survey* (1926); N.Y. State Crime Comm'n, *Report to the Commission of the Sub-Committee on Statistics* (1927). English studies include: JOHN BALDWIN & MICHAEL MCCONVILLE, NEGOTIATED JUSTICE (1977), and Aogan Mulcahy, *The Justification of "Justice": Legal Practitioners' Accounts of Negotiated Case Settlement in Magistrates' Courts*, 34 BRIT. J. CRIMINOLOGY 411 (1994).

3. Now-classic contemporary observational studies include: Albert Alschuler, *Implementing the Defendant's Right to Trial: Alternatives to the Plea Bargaining System*, 50 U. CHI. L. REV. 931 (1983) (hereafter *Implementing the Right to Trial*) (including a challenge to claims of significant cost savings from plea bargaining); Albert Alschuler, *The Changing Plea Bargaining Debate*, 69 CALIF. L. REV. 652 (1981); *Plea Bargaining and Its History*, 79 COLUM. L. REV. 1 (1979); Albert Alschuler, *The Trial Judge's Role in Plea Bargaining* (pt. 1), 76 COLUM. L. REV. 1059 (1976); Albert Alschuler, *The Supreme Court, the Defense Attorney, and the Guilty Plea*, 47 U. COLO. L. REV. 1 (1975); Albert Alschuler, *Sentencing Reform and Prosecutorial Power: A Critique of Recent Proposals for "Fixed" and "Presumptive" Sentencing*, 126 U. PA. L. REV. 550 (1978); Albert Alschuler, *The Defense Attorney's Role in Plea Bargaining*, 84 YALE L.J. 1179 (1975); Albert Alschuler, *The Prosecutor's Role in Plea Bargaining*, 36 U. CHI. L. REV. 50 (1968); Stephen J. Schulhofer, *Plea Bargaining as Disaster*, 101 YALE L.J. 1979 (1992); Stephen J. Schulhofer, *Is Plea Bargaining Inevitable?*, 97 HARV. L. REV. 1037 (1984); MALCOLM FEELEY, THE PROCESS IS THE PUNISHMENT: HANDLING CASES IN A LOWER CRIMINAL COURT (1979); MILTON HEUMANN, PLEA BARGAINING: THE EXPERIENCES OF PROSECUTORS, JUDGES, AND DEFENSE ATTORNEYS (1978).

4. MCCONVILLE & MIRSKY, *supra* note 2 (attributing bargaining to changes in macro-political economy and emerging state interests in social control); FISHER, *supra* note 2 (attributing bargaining to civil and criminal caseload pressures and the self-interests of prosecutors and judges); HEUMANN, *supra* note 3 (arguing against caseload pressure as explanation for bargaining); FEELEY, *supra* note 3 (arguing against caseload pressure as explanation for bargaining); Vogel, *State Formation*, *supra* note 2 (explaining bargaining through changes in political economy); FRIEDMAN & PERCIVAL, *supra* note 2 (attributing bargaining to caseloads and the increased involvement of lawyers in adjudication).

5. *See, e.g.*, Oren Bar-Gill & Omri Ben-Shahar, *The Prisoners' (Plea Bargain) Dilemma*, 1 J. LEGAL ANALYSIS 737 (2009); Oren Bar-Gill & O. Gazal-Ayal, *Plea Bargains Only for the Guilty*, 49 J. L. & ECONOMICS 353 (2006). For other arguments about plea bargaining's costs, risks, and adverse effects, see STEPHANOS BIBAS, THE MACHINERY OF CRIMINAL JUSTICE (2012); Stephanos Bibas, *Plea Bargaining Outside the Shadow of Trial*, 117 HARV. L. REV. 2463 (2004); Michael M. O'Hear, *Plea Bargaining and Procedural Justice*, 42 GA. L. REV. 407 (2008) (hereafter *Procedural Justice*); Michael M. O'Hear, *Plea Bargaining and Victims: From Consultation to Guidelines*, 91 MARQUETTE L. REV. 323 (2007); Gerard Lynch, *Our Administrative System of Criminal Justice*, 66 FORDHAM L. REV. 2117 (1998).

6. For the leading account of wrongful convictions through guilty pleas or otherwise, see BRANDON GARRETT, CONVICTING THE INNOCENT (2011). The leading U.S. database on miscarriages of justice is the National Registry of Exonerations at https://www.law. umich.edu/special/exoneration/Pages/about.aspx (maintained by Univ. of Michigan Law School) (on May 19, 2015, the Registry listed more than 1,600 exonerations). For examples from the United Kingdom, see Criminal Cases Review Commission, *Annual Report and Accounts 2011/12*, at 15–16, 19 (2012) (describing wrongful convictions from

guilty pleas). *See also* Josh Bowers *Punishing the Innocent*, 156 U. Pa. L. Rev. 1117 (2008) (describing reasons for innocent misdemeanor defendants to plead guilty).

7. For an excellent account of weakness in trial process fact-finding, see Dan Simon, In Doubt: The Psychology of the Criminal Justice Process (2012). On government informants as a source of fraudulent evidence, see Alexandra Natapoff, Snitching: Criminal Informants and the Erosion of American Justice (2011).

8. On plea bargaining practices that shortchange victim interests, see Bibas, The Machinery of Criminal Justice, *supra* note 5.

9. Brady v. United States, 397 U.S. 742 (1970); McMann v. Richardson, 397 U.S. 759 (1970) (affirming validity of guilty pleas by three defendants to lesser charges than they would have faced at trial); *see also* Boykin v. Alabama, 395 U.S. 238, 242 (1969) (voluntariness standard for guilty pleas).

10. *Compare* R. v. Turner [1970] 2 QB 321 *with* Brady v. United States, 397 U.S. 742 (1970); North Carolina v. Alford, 400 U.S. 25 (1970); McMann, 397 U.S. 759 (1970). *See also* Santobello v. New York, 404 U.S. 257 (1971). Disobedience of *Turner* drew periodic criticism the Court of Appeal and elsewhere. *See, e.g.,* Pitman [1991]1 All ER 468; Attorney General's Reference No. 44 of 2000 (Peverett) [2001] 1 Cr App R 416; Andrew Ashworth & Mike Redmayne, Criminal Process 311 (4th ed. 2012). *Turner* was eventually overturned by R. v. Goodyear [2006] 1 Cr App R (S) 23 (authorizing judges to provide defendants with advance notice of the sentence to follow a plea).

11. Bordenkircher v. Hayes, 434 U.S. 357 (1978) ("clandestine practice"); Blackledge v. Allison, 431 U.S. 63, 68–71 (1977) ("atmosphere of secrecy"); *id.* at 76 ("Only recently has plea bargaining become a visible practice accepted as a legitimate component in the administration of criminal justice. For decades it was a *sub rosa* process shrouded in secrecy and deliberately concealed by participating defendants, defense lawyers, prosecutors, and even judges." But now "the fact is that the guilty plea and the often concomitant plea bargain are important components of this country's criminal justice system.").

12. Santobello v. New York, 404 U.S. 257 (1971).

13. Kercheval v. United States, 274 U.S. 220, 223 (1927).

14. North Carolina v. Alford, 400 U.S. 25 (1970).

15. Wayne LaFave et al., Criminal Procedure § 21.4 at 1050 (5th ed. 2009) (Except in the case of *Alford* pleas, "as a general matter the determination of a factual basis for the plea is not constitutionally required").

16. *Santobello,* 404 U.S. 257, 266 (Douglas, J., concurring).

17. Brady v. United States, 397 U.S. at 750.

18. Bordenkircher v. Hayes, 434 U.S. 357 (1978).

19. United States v. Batchelder, 442 U.S. 114 (1979) (approving prosecutor's power to choose between two identical statutes that carry different punishment ranges as long as the choice is not based on invidious grounds such as racial bias); *Bordenkircher,* 434 U.S. at 364. There is some irony in the fact that one of the Court's few forthright admissions of the risk of plea bargain offers leading the innocent to plead guilty came in a dissent by Justice Scalia in which he opposed a rule expanding defense counsel's obligations during plea negotiations. *See Lafler,* 132 S. Ct. 1376, 1397 (Scalia, J., dissenting) (plea bargaining "presents grave risks of prosecutorial overcharging that effectively compels an innocent defendant to avoid massive risk by pleading guilty to a lesser offense.").

20. Corbitt v. New Jersey, 439 U.S. 212, 218–20 & n.9 (1978).

21. *See* ACLU, A Living Death: Life Without Parole for Non-Violent Offenses 60–110 (Nov. 2013) (describing plea bargain offers and post-trial sentences in federal and state prosecutions including United States v. Douglas, 4:92-CR-141-Y (N.D. Texas Aug. 30, 1993) (four-year plea offer); United States v. Martinez, No. 91 CR 53-2 (N.D. Ill. Mar. 27, 1992) (eight-year plea offer); Saltzman v. State of Florida, No. 4D07-1143 (Fla. 4th Dist. Ct. July 2011) (five-year plea offer)), *available at* https://www.aclu.org/

files/assets/111813-lwop-complete-report.pdf. Travion Blount, who participated in an armed robbery at age fifteen with two older co-defendants, declined plea bargain offers from Virginia prosecutors with an eighteen-year sentence. After conviction at trial in 2008, he was sentenced to six life terms plus 118 years. *See* Louis Hansen, *Life Times Six,* VIRGINIAN-PILOT, Nov. 4, 2013, at https://www.aclu.org/blog/criminal-law-reform-hu man-rights/15-year-old-gets-six-life-sentences. *See also* Richard A. Oppel Jr., *Sentencing Shift Gives New Leverage to Prosecutors,* N.Y. TIMES, Sept. 25, 2011 (describing Florida prosecutors' offer of two-year prison sentence to Shane Guthrie in exchange for pleading guilty to assault charges; after Guthrie declined, prosecutors filed a charge carrying a mandatory life term).

22. *Corbitt,* 439 U.S. at 225.
23. United States v. Bennett, 332 F.3d 1094 (7th Cir. 2003) (defendant's guilty plea conditioned on co-defendant also pleading guilty); Miles v. Dorsey, 61 F.3d 1459 (10th Cir. 1995) (plea voluntary despite threats to charge defendant's parents); United States v. Pollard, 959 F.2d 1011 (D.C. Cir. 1992) (plea to life sentence voluntary despite threats to charge defendant's wife).
24. *See, e.g.,* Stephen J. Schulhofer, *Assessing the Federal Sentencing Process: The Problem Is Uniformity, Not Disparity,* 29 AM. CRIM. L. REV. 833 (1992) (describing perverse effects of determinate sentencing mixed with plea bargaining, including prosecutor's increased control and weaker connection between nature of wrongdoing and amount of punishment); Erik Luna & Paul G. Cassell, *Mandatory Minimalism,* 32 CARDOZO L. REV. 1 (2010) (critical history of mandatory minimum sentencing and reasons for their resilience); *see also* BALDWIN & MCCONVILLE, *supra* note 2 at 18–24 (summarizing studies).
    Legislatures have granted prosecutors related powers as well—to determine whether sentencing guideline discounts apply, whether habitual offender sentence enhancements apply, or whether a defendant will get pretrial diversion in lieu of prosecution. *See* FLA. STAT. §§ 775.084 & .0843 (2014) (habitual offender criteria and policies); State v. Brimage, 706 A.2d 1096, 1099 (N.J. 1998); State v. Baynes, 690 A.2d 594 (N.J. 1997) (review of prosecutor's reasons for charging instead of diverting defendant into drug program); U.S. SENT. GUIDELINES § 3E1.1 ("acceptance of responsibility"); *id.* § 5K1.1 (discount for cooperation).
25. United States v. Tunning, 69 F.3d 107, 111–12 (6th Cir. 1995) ("strong evidence of actual guilt is not necessary to satisfy Rule 11(f), even where a defendant protests his innocence").
26. United States v. Ruiz, 536 U.S. 622 (2002); Brady v. Maryland, 373 U.S. 83 (1963). Canada, by contrast, has the opposite rule: prosecutors must disclose relevant evidence *before* defendants choose between trial and guilty plea. R. v. Stinchcombe, [1991] 3 SCR 326.
27. For a definitive overview of recent waiver practices, see Susan Klein, Donna Elm, & Aleza Remis, *Waiving the Criminal Justice System* (unpublished manuscript 2014 on http:// ssrn.com). Many courts have approved waivers that defendants from subsequent claims that they entered pleas only on advice from ineffective counsel, although a few state bar associations have recently declared such waivers to constitute unethical practices, and the U.S. Attorney General has ordered federal prosecutors (against the wishes of many) not to seek such waivers. Joe Palazzolo, *Government Rethinks Waivers with Guilty Pleas Defense Lawyers Say Giving Up Right to Appeal Presents Conflicts of Interest,* WALL ST. J., Sept. 26, 2014.
28. Puckett v. United States, 556 U.S. 129 (2009); Santobello v. New York, 404 U.S. 257.
29. JAMES BRADLEY THAYER, JOHN MARSHALL 102–08 (1901).
30. To be sure, there are examples of statutes, regulations or policies that relinquish powers that the Constitution permits officials to exercise. One example is the federal Justice Department's *Petit* policy. The Constitution places no double jeopardy limit federal and state governments prosecuting an offer for the same offense. But the *Petit* policy specifies

U.S. Justice Department criteria for cases in which federal prosecutors will charge offenders who were previously prosecuted in a state court for the same conduct.

31. National Commission on Criminal Justice Standards and Goals, *Courts* 46–49 (1973) ("plea negotiation is inherently undesirable and . . . within five years no such bargaining should take place").

32. Santobello v. New York, 404 U.S. 257, 260–61 (1971); *see also* Ludwig v. Massachusetts, 427 U.S. 618, 627–28 n.4 (1976) (bargaining is the most important means of achieving "the interest of the State in efficient criminal procedure"), *quoted in* Corbitt v. New Jersey, 439 U.S. 212, 219 n.9 (1978); Bordenkircher v. Hayes, 434 U.S. 357, 372 (1978) (Powell, J., dissenting) ("plea-bargaining process . . . is essential to the functioning of the criminal-justice system"). *Contrast* Alschuler, *Implementing the Right to Trial, supra* note 3 (noting and rebutting claims of plea bargaining's practical necessity).

33. Missouri v. Frye, 132 S. Ct. 1399, 1407 (2012) (*quoting* Lafler v. Cooper, 132 S. Ct. 1376 (2012) and Robert Scott & William Stuntz, *Plea Bargaining as Contract*, 101 YALE L.J. 1909, 1912 (1992)).

34. *Lafler*, 132 S. Ct. at 1397 (Scalia, J., dissenting).

35. The quotations are, in order, from Ludwig v. Massachusetts, 427 U.S. 618, 627–28 n.4 (1976), and *Bordenkircher*, 434 U.S. at 364; *see also* United States v. Ruiz, 536 U.S. 622 (2002) ("the government's interest [is] in securing guilty pleas").

36. *Ruiz*, 536 U.S. at 631.

37. R. v. Stinchcombe, [1991] 3 SCR 326.

38. *See, e.g.*, EINER ELHAUGE, STATUTORY DEFAULT RULES: HOW TO INTERPRET UNCLEAR LEGISLATION (2008); Ian Ayres, *Valuing Modern Contract Scholarship*, 112 YALE L.J. 881, 890–92 (2003) (overview of economic analysis regarding default rules); Ian Ayres & Robert Gertner, *Filling Gaps in Incomplete Contracts: An Economic Theory of Default Rules*, 99 YALE L.J. 87, 91 (1989) (arguing default rules create incentives to draft explicit contract terms); Mark Roe, *Can Culture Constrain the Economic Model of Corporate Law*, 69 U. CHI. L. REV. 1251, 1251–52 (2002) (describing corporate law is a set of default rules that parties can contract around).

39. *See* United States v. Pollard, 959 F.2d 1011 (D.C. Cir. 1992).

40. *Bordenkircher*, 434 U.S. at 364, *quoted in* United States v. Mezzanatto, 513 U.S. 196, 210 (1995).

41. *Ruiz*, 536 U.S. at 631.

42. *Id.*, at 631.

43. Corbitt v. New Jersey, 439 U.S. 212, 219, 222 (1978); Brady v. United States, 397 U.S. 742, 752–53 (1970).

44. *Mezzanatto*, 513 U.S. at 208. There is nothing in the Court's body of plea bargaining law to suggest, as Justice Scalia wrote in a 2012 dissent, that "until today it has been regarded as a necessary evil." *Lafler*, 132 S. Ct. at 1397.

45. *See* O'Hear, *Procedural Justice, supra* note 5 (proposing plea bargain reforms focused on procedural justice).

46. Significant plea bargaining decisions decided by 5–4 votes include *Bordenkircher*, 434 U.S. 357; Ricketts v. Adamson, 483 U.S. 2 (1987); Newton v. Rumery, 480 U.S. 386 (1987); *Lafler*, 132 S. Ct. 1376; *Frye*, 132 S. Ct. 1399. *See also* Santobello v. New York, 404 U.S. 257 (1971) (6–3 plus Douglas, J., concurring); *Corbitt*, 439 U.S. 212 (6–3 plus Stewart, J., concurring only in the judgment); McMann v. Richardson, 397 U.S. 759, 766 (1970) (6–3); North Carolina v. Alford, 400 U.S. 25 (1970) (6–3).

47. *Santobello*, 404 U.S. 257, 261–64 (*citing* Kercheval v. United States, 274 U.S. 220, 224 (1927)).

48. United States v. Bowler, 585 F.2d 851, 854 (7th Cir. 1978).

49. *Bowler*, 585 F.2d at 854–55.

50. Hayes v. Cowan, 547 F.2d 42 (6th Cir. 1976), *overturned*, Bordenkircher v. Hayes, 434 U.S. 357 (1978).

51. *Bowler*, 585 F.2d at 854–55.

52. United States v. Brown, 500 F.2d 375 (4th Cir. 1974) (holding that where the prosecutor promised to recommend a particular sentence, the mere half-hearted recitation of the recommended sentence without reasons for supporting it breached the plea agreement); Correale v. United States, 479 F.2d 944, 947 (1st Cir. 1973) ("most meticulous standards of both promise and performance must be met by prosecutors engaging in plea bargaining"); Palermo v. Warden, Green Haven State Prison, 545 F.2d 286, 296 (2d Cir. 1976) ("fundamental fairness and public confidence in government officials require that prosecutors be held to 'meticulous standards of both promise and performance'"), *cert. denied*, 431 U.S. 911 (1976); Geisser v. United States, 513 F.2d 862 (5th Cir. 1975) (ordering prosecutors to make "strong recommendations" to Parole Board as well as to Department of State against defendant's extradition to fulfill promises made in plea bargain); Hayes v. Cowan, 547 F.2d 42 (6th Cir. 1976), *overturned*, Bordenkircher v. Hayes, 434 U.S. 357 (1978).

53. Cooper v. United States, 594 F.2d 12 (4th Cir. 1979). In *Cooper*, the prosecutor offered to dismiss three of four charges in exchange for defendant's guilty plea and cooperation in other cases. The defense quickly met with his client and called to accept the offer four hours after it was extended, but during that time a supervising prosecutor had vetoed the offer and so the office refused to abide it. The court held that the offer was enforceable. Private contract law generally would not enforce an offer before acceptance, absent defendant's detrimental reliance on the agreement.

54. Among the most prominent examples in American scholarship aside from that written by economists are: Robert E. Scott & William J. Stuntz, *Plea Bargaining as Contract*, 101 YALE L.J. 1909 (1992); Frank H. Easterbrook, *Plea Bargaining as Compromise*, 101 YALE L.J. 1906 (1992). To be sure, dissenting scholarly voices continue; *see* Stephen J. Schulhofer, *Plea Bargaining as Disaster*, 101 YALE L.J. 1979 (1992).

55. *See Bordenkircher*, 434 U.S. at 372 (Powell, J., dissenting). Powell added that prosecutors' discretion must be exercised "within constitutional constraints," which amount to little more than that charges be grounded in probable cause and the toothless equal protection doctrine against racially motivated charging decisions. *See* United States v. Armstrong, 517 U.S. 456 (1996).

56. Mabry v. Johnson, 467 U.S. 504, 507–09 (1984).

57. United States v. Hyde, 520 U.S. 670, 677–78 (1997) ("[I]f the court rejects the Government's promised performance, then the agreement is terminated and the defendant has the right to back out of his promised performance (the guilty plea), just as a binding contractual duty may be extinguished by the nonoccurrence of a condition subsequent," *citing* J. CALAMARI & J. PERILLO, LAW OF CONTRACTS and A. CORBIN, CORBIN ON CONTRACTS.). Puckett v. United States, 556 U.S. 129, 137 (2009) ("[P]lea bargains are essentially contracts."). Court similarly base remedies for breaches of plea agreements on those developed in private contract law. *See Frye*, 132 S. Ct. 1399; *Lafler*, 132 S. Ct. 1376. *See generally* Nancy J. King, *Judicial Oversight of Negotiated Sentences in a World of Bargained Punishment*, 58 STAN. L. REV. 293 (2005).

58. Agreements between prosecutors and defendants are only enforceable after a court has approved the agreement in a formal judgment. *See, e.g.*, FLA. R. CRIM. PROC. 3.172(f) (agreement not binding on either party until approved by court). Limited exceptions apply primarily if the defendant performed his part of an agreement to his potential detriment, often by voluntarily submitting to forensic testing. For representative decisions taking this view and citing other courts adopting this approach, see State v. Vixamar, 687 So.2d 300 (Fla. App. 4th Dist. 1997); Comm. v. Scuilli, 621 A.2d 620 (Pa. Super. 1993).

    For examples of states' commitment to the rule of broad prosecutorial discretion, see, e.g., *In re* State, 390 S.W.3d 439, 443 (2012) ("An obvious corollary to a district attorney's duty to prosecute criminal cases is the utilization of his own discretion in the preparation of those cases for trial."). For comparable state court principles, see, e.g., People

v. Cortes, 71 Cal. App. 4th 62, 79, 83 CAL. RPTR. 2d 519, 351 (Cal. App. 6 Dist. 1999); Ebron v. Commissioner of Correction, 992 A.2d 1200 (Conn. App. 2010); State *ex rel.* Thomas v. Rayes, 213 Ariz. 326, 141 P.3d 806 (2006).

    State rules have varied from the federal model in some relatively modest ways. Some states permit the parties to consult the trial judge during plea negotiations, so that the judge can express a view about the acceptability of a proposed agreement. And many states required defendants to be informed about immigration consequences and other civil or collateral consequences of pleading guilty before the Supreme Court held that competent defense counsel must provide defendants with those warnings.

59. Corbitt v. New Jersey, 439 U.S. 212, 225 (1978) (*quoting* Bordenkircher v. Hayes, 434 U.S. 357, 363 (1978)) (emphasis added); *see also* Boykin v. Alabama, 395 U.S. 238, 242 (1969) (emphasis on voluntariness of guilty plea). On the weak role of judges with regard to prosecutorial discretion and plea bargaining, see generally ABRAHAM GOLDSTEIN, THE PASSIVE JUDICIARY: PROSECUTORIAL DISCRETION AND THE GUILTY PLEA (1981).

60. Courts continue to supervise disputes over whether either party breached a plea agreement. A representative decision is U.S. v. Ataya, 864 F.2d 1324 (7th Cir. 1988). More recently, the Court's only meaningful constitutional constraints on plea bargaining take the form of more specific rules for minimally effective assistance of defense counsel. *Frye*, 132 S. Ct. 1399; *Lafler*, 132 S. Ct. 1376; Padilla v. Kentucky, 559 U.S. 356 (2010). Notably, that approach aims to strengthen defendants' knowing engagement in the bargaining process without restricting prosecutors' negotiation tactics or giving courts a meaningful role in supervising bargaining practices or terms. State law overwhelmingly takes this approach as well.

61. National Center for State Courts survey of nine states found the percentage of felonies taken to trial was 2.3 percent in 2009, compared to 8 percent in 1976. Summarized in Oppel, *supra* note 21.

62. Most of the data on low guilty plea rates are at least twenty-five years old. *See* Donald McIntyre & David Lippman, *Prosecutors and Early Disposition of Felony Cases*, 56 A.B.A. J. 1154, 1156 (1970) (reporting guilty plea rates of 47 percent in Los Angeles and 17 percent in Baltimore, in part due to common use of nonjury trials; figures exclude dismissals and *nolle prosequi* cases); *see* MARTIN LEVIN, URBAN POLITICS AND THE CRIMINAL COURTS 80 (1977) (35 percent guilty plea rate in Pittsburgh in 1966, not including dismissals); *1972 Annual Report of the Philadelphia Common Pleas and Municipal Courts* (1973) (guilty pleas resolved 36 percent of felony cases in Philadelphia in 1972, not including dismissals); Welsh White, *A Proposal for Reform of the Plea Bargaining Process*, 119 U. PA. L. REV. 439, 441–42 (1971); Lynn Mather, *Some Determinants of the Method of Case Disposition: Decision-Making by Public Defenders in Los Angeles*, 8 LAW & SOC'Y REV. 187, 195 (1973) (48 percent of cases in Los Angeles courts ended with guilty plea in 1970).

63. *See, e.g.,* Stephen Schulhofer, *Is Plea Bargaining Inevitable?*, 97 HARV. L. REV. 1037, 1057–60 (1984) (describing Philadelphia prosecutors' policy against offering concessions for pleas and its relative success; in particular, finding a rate in 1982 of 45 percent guilty pleas and 55 percent trials, with most pleas occurring without any charge or sentence inducement); *see also* Thomas Uhlman & Darlene Walker, *"He Takes Some of My Time; I Take Some of His": An Analysis of Judicial Sentencing Patterns in Jury Cases*, 14 LAW & SOC'Y REV. 323 (1980) (study concluding that sentencing by Philadelphia judges from 1968 to 1972 revealed no discount for guilty pleas). For a more recent study of an unnamed locality that reduced plea bargaining rates, see David Lynch, *A Tale of Two Counties*, 19 LAW & SOC. INQUIRY 115 (1994) (also interpreting findings to conclude that claims of necessity of plea bargaining are overstated).

64. Alschuler, *Implementing the Right to Trial, supra* note 3, at 943–44 (describing El Paso at 943–44 and Philadelphia and Pittsburgh studies at 1024).

65. Ronald Wright & Marc L. Miller, *The Screening/Bargaining Trade-Off*, 55 STAN. L. REV. 29 (2002). For other evidence of guilty pleas without bargaining, see Thomas Uhlman & Darlene Walker, *"He Takes Some of My Time; I Take Some of His": An Analysis of Judicial Sentencing Patterns in Jury Cases*, 14 LAW & SOC'Y REV. 323 (1980) (study concluding that sentencing by Philadelphia judges from 1968 to 1972 revealed no discount for guilty pleas) (Uhlman & Walker did not identify the city studied as Philadelphia, but Schulhofer did, at 97 HARV. L. REV. at 1061 n.88.) An early, groundbreaking English study is BALDWIN & MCCONVILLE, *supra* note 2 (finding, in a study of Birmingham courts in 1975–1976, that 29 percent of defendants who pled guilty did so without any bargain or pressure from their defense lawyer; another 40 percent did so without a bargain but under perceived pressure from the defense lawyer).

66. The same New Orleans District Attorney office subsequently was revealed to have a range of other serious problems during the same period, including illegal suppression of exculpatory evidence in cases of factually innocent defendants. *See* Smith v. Cain, 132 S. Ct. 627 (2012); Connick v. Thompson, 563 U.S. 51, 131 S. Ct. 1350 (2011).

67. State v. Buckalew, 561 P.2d 289 (Alaska 1977) (barring judges from participation in plea bargaining and noting attorney general's directive banning plea bargaining statewide); M. RUBINSTEIN, S. CLARKE, & T. WHITE, ALASKA BANS PLEA BARGAINING (1980), and Rubinstein & White, *Alaska's Ban on Plea Bargaining*, 13 LAW & SOC'Y REV. 367, 373–74 (1979) (both describing Alaska plea bargaining ban). For other accounts of limits on bargaining, see NAT'L ACAD. SCIENCES, 1 RESEARCH ON SENTENCING 28 (A. Blumstein, J. Cohen, S. Martin, & M. Tonry eds., 1983) (noting prosecutors largely refrained from bargaining when rules prohibited it).

68. FEELEY, *supra* note 3, at 244–77; HEUMANN, *supra* note 3; Milton Heumann, *A Note on Plea Bargaining and Case Pressure*, 9 LAW & SOC'Y REV. 515 (1975). For a similar, more recent finding, see Mulcahy, *supra* note 2; *see also* David Lynch, *A Tale of Two Counties*, 19 LAW & SOC. INQUIRY 115 (1994) (finding evidence from study of two local court systems that claims of necessity of plea bargaining can be overstated).

69. *See* CALIF. PENAL CODE § 1192.7 (purporting to ban plea bargaining for certain serious offenses); N.Y. CRIM. PROC. LAW § 220.10 (purporting to limit guilty plea charge discounts). Several states have rules forbidding plea bargains for a small number of specific crimes, often traffic offenses. *See* COLO. REV. STAT. §§ 18-6-801(3), 42-4-1301 (2013); KAN. STAT. ANN. §§ 8-1567(n), 8-2144(l); NEV. REV. STAT. §§ 212.189, 483.560, 484C.420 to 484C.470 (2013); 47 OKLA. STAT. ANN. § 172 (F) & (K). For a state statute endorsing plea bargaining, see REV. CODE. WASH. §§ 9.94A.450.

70. Blackledge v. Perry, 417 U.S. 21 (1974). Later Supreme Court restricting *Blackledge* vindictiveness doctrine include Bordenkircher v. Hayes, 434 U.S. 357 (1978) and United States v. Goodwin, 457 U.S. 368 (1982). For examples of the doctrine as applied in lower courts, see United States v. Goodwin, 637 F.2d 250 (4th Cir. 1981), *reversed*, 457 U.S. 368 (1982) (holding the Due Process Clause prohibits the government from bringing more serious charges against the defendant after he has invoked his right to a jury trial, unless it comes forward with objective evidence that the increased charges could not have been brought before defendant exercised his right); Hayes v. Cowan, 547 F.2d 42 (6th Cir. 1976), *reversed*, Bordenkircher v. Hayes, 434 U.S. 357 (1978); United States v. Ruesga-Martinez, 534 F.2d 1367, 1369–70 (9th Cir. 1976). For other examples of good-faith standards, see United States v. Lanoue, 137 F.3d 656 (1st Cir. 1998); United States v. Nell, 570 F.2d 1251, 1254–55 (5th Cir. 1978). *See generally* Note, *Breathing New Life into Prosecutorial Vindictiveness Doctrine*, 114 HARV. L. REV. 2074 (2001). An equivalent doctrine restricting judicial vindictiveness in sentencing, defined in North Carolina v. Pearce, 395 U.S. 711 (1969), has been largely defanged as well. *See* Alabama v. Smith, 490 U.S. 794 (1989); Texas v. McCullough, 475 U.S. 134 (1986); Wasman v. United States, 468 US 559 (1984).

71. *See* the discussion of information-forcing disclosure rules in chapter 3.

72. *See* Maximo Langer, *From Legal Transplants to Legal Translations: The Globalization of Plea Bargaining and the Americanization Thesis in Criminal Procedure*, 45 HARV. INT'L L.J. 1 (2004) (examining U.S. influence on adoption of plea bargaining in four nations and exploring why the practice has taken notably different forms elsewhere).

73. English courts and the English bar did not acknowledge openly the existence of plea bargaining until at least the late 1970s, in the wake of Baldwin and McConville's controversial study documenting its practice. BALDWIN & MCCONVILLE, *supra* note 2 (reporting rates of guilty pleas and plea bargains based on investigation of Birmingham courts in 1975–1976); *see id.* Preface at vii–xii (recounting controversy surrounding the study's publication, including calls for nonpublication from prominent lawyers and officials).

74. McKinnon v. United States of America [2008] UKHL 59 (suggesting than an extreme plea bargain discount could constitute unlawful pressure, but describing a U.S. plea bargain offer of 50–70 percent as "very marked" but insufficient to constitute abuse of process under extradition treaty); Nick Vamos, *Please Don't Call It Plea-Bargaining*, [2009] CRIM. L.R. 617.

75. Criminal Justice Act of 2003, §§ 144, 172 (England); Sentencing Guidelines Council, *Reduction in Sentence for a Guilty Plea* (2004); Attorney General's Reference No. 14 and No. 15 (2006) (noting guidelines "do no more than provide guidance" to judges and "there may well be circumstances which justify awarding less than a discount of one third where a plea of guilty has been made at the first opportunity"). England's sentence-discount limit is a dramatic by U.S. standards, but some English critics still worry it is too large. *See* ASHWORTH & REDMAYNE, *supra* note 10, at 302 (authorized authority for plea bargain discounts "is likely to exert a considerable pressure toward pleading guilty").

76. *See* §444(1, 2) CPP (Italy) (Appendix, 255). On Spanish discounts for guilty pleas, see STEPHEN C. THAMAN, COMPARATIVE CRIMINAL PROCEDURE 23–30 (2d ed. 2008), and Jacqueline Hodgson, *Plea Bargaining: A Comparative Analysis*, in INTERNATIONAL ENCYCLOPEDIA OF THE SOCIAL AND BEHAVIORAL SCIENCES 226 (James Wright ed., 2014). Russia adopted a similar procedure in 2001 that (since 2003) applies to offenses punishable by a sentence of no more than ten years. §§ 314-317 UPK (Russia). On French plea bargaining, see JACQUELINE HODGSON, FRENCH CRIMINAL JUSTICE: A COMPARATIVE ACCOUNT OF THE INVESTIGATION AND PROSECUTION OF CRIME IN FRANCE (2005).

    For another contrast, consider Australia, which like the United States is a federal state with multiple criminal justice systems. No state has a rule imposing a firm cap on plea bargain discounts equivalent to English law. Yet every state jurisdiction has a strong—and apparently effective—precatory limit for plea discounts defined either by statute, state common law, or a sentencing council. All recommend that plea discounts not exceed 30 percent of the expected post-trial sentence. Australian states generally limit plea discounts to a 30 percent discount or less, although their policies are less formal and precise and leave more to judicial sentencing discretion. *See* Australian Sent. Council, Sentencing Indications and Specified Sentencing Discounts: Discussion Paper 17-19 (2007), *available at* https://sentencingcouncil.vic. gov.au/sites/sentencingcouncil.vic.gov.au (viewed Nov. 25, 2012); R. v. Thomson; R. v. Houlton [2000] NSW CCA 309, revised 6 October 2000 (plea discount policy of New South Wales Court of Criminal Appeal, which "not binding in any formal sense" but "operates by way of encouragement and not by way of prescription," recommending plea discounts of 10–25 percent). For similar guidelines in other Australian states, see Heferen v. R (1999) 106 A Crim R 89, Vershuren v. R (1996) 17 WAR 467 (Western Australia policy); R. v. Sharma (2002) 54 NSWLR 300 (New South Wales); R. v. Place (2002) 81 SASR 395 (policy of South Australian Court of Criminal Appeal). *See also* Crimes (Sentencing) Act 2005 (ACT), s 35 (statutory criteria for plea sentencing discounts in Australian Capital Territory).

Evidence indicates that Australian plea bargain sentences average no more than 30 percent reduction from trial sentences. Arie Freiberg, *Australia: Exercising Discretion in Sentencing Policy and Practice*, 22 FED. SENT. RPTR. 204 (2010). But that data leave much unanswered, especially for comparative purposes. U.S. plea discounts may well not exceed a 30 percent *on average*, but the question is remains how often much greater discounts are employed and for what reasons.

While the United States does not forbid plea bargaining for any offense category, it's "lowest" guilty plea rate is for homicide charges. For federal courts in 2011, the 74.3 percent of homicide convictions resulted from guilty pleas. For all other core serious crimes, the rate was over 87 percent. U.S. Sent. Comm'n, *Sourcebook for Federal Sentencing Statistics* (2011), Table 11.

77. BGH Aug. 14, 2007: Case 3 StR 266/07 (*Bundesgerichtshof*—Federal Court of Justice, for nonconstitutional issues); Karstan Gaede, *Plea Bargaining: Defense Rights*, 72 J. CRIM. L. 109–12 (2008). *See also* Thomas Weigend & Jenia Iontcheva Turner, *The Constitutionality of Negotiated Criminal Judgments in Germany*, 15 GERMAN L.J. 81 (2014), *available at* http://www.germanlawjournal.com/index.php?pageID=11&artID=1611

    As is true in England, German sentencing law remains less determinate than in much of the United States, and thus sentences are judges retain substantial control over sanctions. Karstan Gaede, *Plea Bargaining: Defense Rights*, 72 J. CRIM. L. 109–12 (2008) (noting German courts' sentencing discretion).

78. [2008] UKHL 59; [2008] 1 W.L.R. 1739; [2008] 4 All E.R. 1012; [2008] U.K.H.R.R. 1103. *See also* Vamos, *supra* note 74, at 625.

79. R. (on the application of Smith) v. CPS, [2010] EWHC 3593. For other decisions defining judicial power to bar prosecutions for prosecutorial abuse of process, see, e.g., Nembhard v. Director of Public Prosecutions [2009] EWHC 194 (describing court's authority to bar prosecutions for abuse of process); R. v. Bloomfield, [1997] 1 Cr. App. R. 135 (barring prosecution under abuse of process standard from continuing with drug prosecution after announcing that that intended to not to).

80. *See* CROWN PROSECUTION SERVICE, CODE FOR CROWN PROSECUTORS § 6.3 ("Crown Prosecutors should never go ahead with more charges than are necessary just to encourage a defendant to plead guilty to a few"); *see also id.* §§ 4.5-4.9 & 5.9 (requirement that charges have a "realistic prospect" of conviction). For an argument that CPS Code's "strict, enforceable" rules on charging "forbid[ ] a prosecutor from using [the charging] decision as a bargaining tool," see Vamos, *supra* note 74, at 622.

    U.S. Department of Justice policies on plea bargaining are more restrictive than constitutional or statutory law requires, but they are not judicially enforceable. Plea bargains with sentences that are far outside the ranges defined by federal sentencing guidelines are common. Discounts for defendants who cooperate with prosecutors in other cases are often 50 to 100 percent below the minimum guideline range. *See* U.S. SENTENCING COM'N, SOURCEBOOK OF FEDERAL SENTENCING STATISTICS, tbl. 30 (2010) (summarizing sentence discounts in exchange for cooperation with prosecutors).

81. *See* Criminal Procedure and Investigations Act 1996 (the principal disclosure duties, which apply only after defendant is charged); R. v. DPP, ex p. Lee [1999] 2 Cr. App. R. 304, DC (common law disclosure duties for prosecutors, which require pre-charge disclosure in some circumstances); *also* Attorney General's Office (England & Wales), *The Introduction of a Plea Negotiation Framework for Fraud Cases in England and Wales: A Consultation* at 15 (Apr. 2008) (noting the effect of these disclosure duties in giving defendants reasons to delay guilty pleas). Yet English prosecutors face no sanctions for failing to meet requirements to disclose evidence to defendants, for example. *See* Hodgson, 35 N.C.J. Int'l L. & Comm. Reg. at 330. In Canada, the prosecutorial disclosure duty is stronger than in the United States in that it applies before guilty pleas. *Compare* R v. Stinchcombe, [1991] 3 SCR 326 (disclosure duty applies with defendant chooses either trial or guilty plea) *with Ruiz*, 536 U.S. 622 (disclosure duty does not apply until trial).

Disclosure rules, of course, impose costs on the government and may therefore reduce bargaining; the question is whether those costs are justified in terms of fairness. *See* Jessica de Grazia, Review of the Serious Fraud Office: Final Report at 63–64 (June 2008) (noting substantial costs to disclosure duties in serious fraud cases, and the value of disclosure in preventing wrongful convictions).

82. *See generally* World Plea Bargaining, *supra* note 1 (studies of plea bargain practices in the U.S., European, and international courts); Turner, *supra* note 1 (accounts of bargaining in U.S., European, and Asian systems); Nelkin, *supra* note 1; Freiberg, *supra* note 1.

83. Criminal Cases Review Commission, *Annual Report and Accounts 2011/12*, at 15–16, 19 (2012) (for England, Wales, and Northern Ireland, describing cases of "people who have been wrongfully convicted" after pleading guilty on advice of defense attorneys, despite having valid defenses); *see also* R. v. O [2008] EWCA Crim 2835 (quashing an unlawful guilty plea conviction for failures by prosecutors, defense counsel and the trial court characterized as a "shameful set of circumstances").

84. For 2009 federal data, see Mark Motivans, *Bureau of Justice Statistics, Federal Justice Statistics 2009—Statistical Tables*, at tbl. 4.2 (Dec. 2011), http://www.bjs.ojp.usdoj.gov/content/pub/pdf/fjs09st.pdf (96.7 percent of convictions from guilty pleas). In U.S. federal courts in the years 2007–2011, guilty plea rates increased from 95.8 to 96.9 percent of all convictions; percentage of convictions following trial declined from 4.2 to 3.1 percent. U.S. Sent. Comm'n, *Sourcebook for Federal Sentencing Statistics* (2011), figure C, *available at* http://www.ussc.gov/Data_and_Statistics/Annual_Reports_and_Sourcebooks/2011/SBTOC11.htm. Guilty plea rates within each of the twelve federal circuits showed little variation, ranging from 93.8 to 98.3 percent in 2011. *Id.* at Table 10.

In 2000, data from twenty-two states found 3 percent of state criminal cases were resolved by either bench or jury trial, the remainder by guilty pleas, dismissals, or other disposition. Hawaii had the highest trial rate at 12.8 percent; Vermont's rate of 0.9 percent was lowest. Brian J. Ostrom, Neal Kauder, & Robert LaFountain eds., *Examining the Work of State Courts, 2001: A National Perspective from the Court Statistics Project* 63–64 (National Center for State Courts 2001), *available at* https://www.ncjrs.gov/pdffiles1/Digitization/195881NCJRS.pdf; *see also* National Center for State Courts, *State-of-the-States Survey of Jury Improvement Efforts* (2007) (reporting similar, more recent data, although in different terms, e.g., trials per 100,000 population).

85. CPS, *Annual Report and Resource Accounts 2011–12*, Annex B, at 85 tbl. 7 (data for years 2009 through 2012), http://www.cps.gov.uk/publications/docs/cps_annual_report_and_accounts_2012.pdf. Of the 27.5 percent of charged defendants who did not plead guilty, 13 percent went to trial (where 7.2 were convicted), and the remainder earned dismissal or judge acquittal.

86. Fed. R. Crim. Pro. 11. State courts have equivalent requirements. *See, e.g.,* N.C. Code § 15A-1022(c) (2012). Many state rules go beyond Federal Rule 11 and require that judges also confirm that defendants are aware of an additional certain collateral consequences that follow a criminal conviction from other, civil bodies of law, such as the prospect of deportation for noncitizens. *See, e.g.,* N.C. Code § 15A-1022(a)(7); Padilla v. Kentucky, 559 U.S. 356 374 n.15 (2010) (listing more than twenty state statutes). For a leading analysis of collateral consequences to criminal punishment, see Gabriel J. Chin, *The New Civil Death: Rethinking Punishment in the Era of Mass Conviction*, 160 U. Pa. L. Rev. 1789 (2012).

87. Nev. Rev. Stat. § 174.061 (plea bargains that include defendant's testimony for the prosecution must be in writing); N.J. Rule 3:9(b) ("Any plea offer to be made by the prosecutor shall be in writing and forwarded to the defendant's attorney."). In the federal system, plea agreements are often reduced to writing, sometimes by requirement of local rules or Justice Department policy. *See* U.S. Attorneys' Manual § 9-27.450 (2009) ("All negotiated plea agreements . . . shall be in writing and filed with the court.").

88. *See* Nancy J. King, *Judicial Oversight of Negotiated Sentences in a World of Bargained Punishment*, 58 STAN. L. REV. 293, 295–300 (2005) (discussing judges' inability to ensure the factual accuracy of federal sentences).

89. The constitutionally required standard of proof for criminal for trial judgments defined in *In re* Winship, 397 U.S. 358 (1970) has never been held to apply guilty pleas. *See, e.g.,* United States v. Fountain, 777 F.2d 351, 357 (7th Cir. 1985) (describing the standard as "some factual basis). TURNER, *supra* note 1, at 41 (summarizing cases and concluding "inquiry into the factual basis has become a mere formality").

90. Not all procedural entitlements must be waived knowingly; defendants may unknowingly forfeit, for example, the right to challenge an earlier confession as involuntary and coerced, the right against double jeopardy, or the right against racial bias in selection of grand jurors. *See* Brady v. United States, 397 U.S. 742, 746 (1970) (plea not involuntary because defendant believed he could face the death penalty if convicted at trial); McMann v. Richardson, 397 U.S. 759, 766 (1970) (challenge to voluntary confession waived with guilty plea); United States v. Broce, 488 U.S. 563, 569 (1989) (double jeopardy claims waived with guilty plea); *contrast* Menna v. New York, 423 U.S. 61 (1975) (allowing habeas corpus petitioner to raise double jeopardy claim despite plea of guilty); Tollett v. Henderson, 411 U.S. 258 (1973) (forfeiture of claim regarding racial bias in grand jury selection).

91. For an example, see North Carolina v. Alford, 400 U.S. 25 (1970).

92. R. v. Newton [1982] 4 Cr App R (S) 388; and R v. Beswick, [1996] 1 Cr App R (S) 343 (approval of trial judge's decision to require a *Newton* hearing to determine facts even when prosecutor's account of facts matched defendant's and those stated in agreement). Published reports confirm that they do so in some cases, although this does not mean that they consistently take more care with factual accuracy of pleas than U.S. courts. Elicin and Moore [2009] 1 Cr App R (S) 561; R. v. Underwood [2004] EWCA Crim 2256, [2005] 1 Cr. App. R.(S.) (judge is not bound by parties' agreement on facts and may on his or her own motion to insist on calling any evidence relevant to the facts in dispute); Criminal Proc. Rules IV.45.5 – IV.45.22 (England); *see also* Attorney-General's Reference No. 44 of 2000 (Peverett) [2001] 1 Cr App R 416, 418–19 (where part of agreement was that that defendant's less serious account of facts should be accepted).

93. 10 U.S.C. §§ 801–946 (2006). The Military Justice Act of 1968, Pub. L. No. 90-632, 82 Stat. 1335, and the Military Justice Act of 1983, Pub. L. No. 98-209, 97 Stat. 1393, both codified as amended in scattered sections of 10 U.S.C. and 28 U.S.C., added provisions such as appellate courts intended to improve the quality and legitimacy of military justice. For an overview, see Note, *Prosecutorial Power and the Legitimacy of the Military Justice System*, 123 HARV. L. REV. 937, 940–41 (2010) (hereafter *Prosecutorial Power*); H. F. Gierke, *The Thirty-Fifth Kenneth J. Hodson Lecture on Criminal Law: Reflections of the Past: Continuing to Grow, Willing to Change, Always Striving to Serve*, 193 MIL. L. REV. 178, 183 (2007). *See also* Joint Serv. Comm. On Military Justice, *Manual for Courts-Martial, United States* (2008 ed.) (hereafter *MCM*).

94. *See* UNIFORM CODE OF MILITARY JUSTICE art. 45(b), 10 U.S.C. § 845(b) (2006).

95. *See Annual Report of the Code Committee on Military Justice* § 3 app. at 20 (2008) (indicating that approximately 95 percent of general courts-martial ended in convictions); Edye U. Moran, *The Guilty Plea—Traps for New Counsel*, ARMY LAW., at 62 n.7 (Nov. 2008) (reporting that approximately 75 percent of Army courts-martial ended in guilty pleas in 2006).

96. *See MCM, supra* 93, at pt. II, R. 705(c)(1)(B) (banning sentence agreements); *cf.* U.C.M.J. art. 30(a), 10 U.S.C. § 830(a) (2006). On appellate review, see *MCM, supra* note 93, at pt. II, R. 705(c)(1)(B). Defendants also cannot waive a full adversarial hearing on sentencing. *See MCM, supra* note 93, at pt. II, R. 705(c)(1)(B). *See also* United States v. Coffman, 62 M.J. 676 (N-M Ct. Crim. App. 2006); *see also* United States v. Pinero, 60 M.J. 31, 33 (C.A.A.F. 2004); United States v. Care, 18 C.M.A. 535, 539 (1961).

97. UNIFORM CODE OF MILITARY JUSTICE art. 32, 10 U.S.C. § 832 (2006). The Article 32 investigation is comparable in formality to a civilian grand jury—e.g., witnesses testify under oath—but defendants are present, represented by counsel, and may cross-examine witnesses. *See id.*

98. United States v. Pinero, 60 M.J. 31, 33 (C.A.A.F. 2004); *see also MCM, supra* note 93, at pt. II, R. 910(c)-(e) & discussion.

99. Mich. Rule 6.302(B) (emphasis added).

100. *MCM, supra* note 93, at pt. II, R. 910(h)(2). For an example, see United States v. Phillippe, 63 M.J. 307 308–11 (C.A.A.F. 2006) (setting aside conviction when trial judge failed to re-open providence inquiry in the wake of defendant's statement at post-plea sentencing suggesting facts that could constitute a defense).

101. *Pinero,* 60 M.J. at 33 (emphasis added).

102. *Pinero,* 60 M.J. at 33 (emphasis added) (*citing* United States v. Chancelor, 16 C.M.A. 297, 299 (1966) and United States v. Care, 18 C.M.A. 535, 539 (1961)).

103. Note, *Prosecutorial Power, supra* note 93, at 954.

104. *See, e.g.,* N.J.S.A. 2C:35-6 & 35-12 (mandatory minimum sentence for drug offenses in a school zone, which prosecutor has discretionary authority to waive); FLA. STAT. §§ 775.084 (increased sentences for repeat offenders; requires that "if the state attorney pursues a three-time violent felony offender sanction against the defendant ..., the court must sentence the defendant as a three-time violent felony offender"); *see also* Bordenkircher v. Hayes, 434 U.S. 357, 358 (1978) (describing KY. REV. STAT. § 431.190, repealed 1975).

105. For a good account of this history, see United States v. Kupa, 976 F. Supp.2d 417 (E.D.N.Y. 2013).

106. United States v. Jones, 2009 WL 2912535 (N.D. Cal. 2009) ("These letters were part of an office-wide policy of the U.S. Attorney, as described by the Assistant U.S. Attorney in charge of the case to defense counsel."); *see Kupa,* 976 F. Supp.2d 417 (citing other evidence of this prosecution policy).

107. Transcript of Proceedings at 15, 23, United States v. Jones, No. 08–CR–887 (N.D. Cal. July 29, 2009), ECF No. 138; *cited in Kupa,* 976 F. Supp.2d 417 (emphasis added). For a study documents this sentencing practice and that surveyed prosecutors and defense attorneys, see U.S. Sentencing Comm'n, *Mandatory Minimum Penalties in the Federal Criminal Justice System* 112, 255 (2011). Many courts note (and complain about) prosecutors' explicit use of sentencing provisions to induce guilty pleas or cooperation. *See, e.g.,* United States v. Dotson, 513 Fed. Appx. 221, 223 (3d Cir. 2013) (noting that the government agreed to "withdraw one of the convictions from the [prior felony] information to reduce Dotson's sentencing exposure from a mandatory life sentence to a mandatory minimum sentence of twenty years' imprisonment"); Gilbert v. United States, 640 F.3d 1293, 1298 (6th Cir. 2011) (observing the "non-application of [the prior felony information] obviously was part of the [plea] agreement"); United States v. Espinal, 634 F.3d 655, 659 (2d Cir. 2011) (describing that, in 2006, the government advised the defendant that, "if he did not plead guilty by September 15, it would file a prior felony information. ... Filing such an information would, among other things, enhance the applicable mandatory minimum sentence from ten years in prison to twenty."); United States v. Shaw, 426 Fed. Appx. 810, 812 (11th Cir. 2011) (describing how the prosecutor informed the defendant that, "if [he] went forward with the suppression hearing, [the prosecutor] would file the § 851 notice seeking the mandatory-minimum life sentence"); United States v. Harris, 394 Fed. Appx. 676, 679–80 (11th Cir. 2010) (mentioning that the government agreed to withdraw the notice of two prior felonies—thereby taking a mandatory life sentence off the table—only if the defendant pleaded guilty); United States v. Forrester, 616 F.3d 929 (9th Cir. 2010) (referencing how, five days before trial, the government "extended a plea offer ... [and] told [the defendant] that if both he and [his co-defendant] accepted the 'package deal,' [the defendant] could limit his exposure

to 20 years. The government stated that if the plea offer was not accepted by 2:00 pm that same day, it would file a sentence enhancement pursuant to 21 U.S.C. § 851. The offer was not accepted by either [defendant] . . . and the government filed the § 851 enhancement."); Coleman v. United States, 339 Fed. Appx. 643 (7th Cir. 2009) (denying a 28 U.S.C. § 2255 motion for ineffective of counsel; the attorney had advised the defendant that the government would file a prior felony information unless he pleaded guilty); United States v. Jenkins, 537 F.3d 1, 4 (1st Cir. 2008) (no presumption of prosecutorial vindictiveness where government decided to file a prior felony information because the defendant refused to plead guilty); Vadas v. United States, 527 F.3d 16, 19 (2d Cir. 2007) (observing that the written plea agreement with the U.S. Attorney for the District of Connecticut provided that, "[i]n exchange for the plea, . . . *[t]he government also agrees to withdraw the Amended Second Notice Information filed March 15, 2001 pursuant to . . . Section 851.*") (emphasis in original).

108. State v. Thomas, 920 A.2d 142 (N.J. Super. 2007); State v. Brimage, 706 A.2d 1096, 1099 (N.J. 1998). Evidence of legislative intent in New Jersey suggests the same purpose. *See id.* at 1099 (*quoting* N.J. Legislature's Judiciary Committee, Commentary to the Comprehensive Drug Reform Act, at 26 (Nov. 23, 1987) that "[o]ne of the key objectives of this section and the act is to provide persons engaged in illicit drug activities with strong incentives to cooperate with law enforcement"). *See also* Taylor v. District of Columbia, 49 A.3d 1259 (D.C. 2012) (noting city council enacted a lesser offense as a "tool for plea bargaining" so that prosecutors "could offer [it] as an incentive" to those charged with greater offense to plead guilty).

109. Transcript of Sentencing at 4–5, United States v. Doutre, 08–CR–10215 (D. Mass. Mar. 22, 2010), ECF No. 168, *cited in* Kupa, 976 F. Supp.2d 417. *See generally* DANIEL S. MEDWED, PROSECUTION COMPLEX: AMERICA'S RACE TO CONVICT, AND ITS IMPACT ON THE INNOCENT 52–75 (2012) (prosecutor plea bargaining practices and motivations).

110. United States v. Coston, 737 F.3d 235, 237 (2d Cir. 2013) (emphasis added).

111. *See, e.g.,* Camilleri v. Malta, ECHR (22 Jan. 2013) (finding violation of ECHR Article 7 in a statute that gives prosecutors the choice between two courts in which to file a criminal charge, consequently which punishment range will apply; "Article 7 . . . provide[s] effective safeguards against arbitrary prosecution . . . and punishment" and requires that "only the law [not prosecutors' discretion] can define a crime and prescribe a penalty").

Chapter 5

* *Epigraphs:* Yakus v. United States, 321 U.S. 414, 444 (1944); United States v. Vonn, 535 U.S. 55, 73 n.10 (2002).

1. GEORGE P. FLETCHER, RETHINKING CRIMINAL LAW 524–49 (1978).

2. *Id.,* at 524–49.

3. *See* John C. Jeffries Jr. & Paul B. Stephan III, *Defenses, Presumptions, and Burden of Proof in the Criminal Law,* 88 YALE L.J. 1325 (1979).

4. *Id.* (surveying such rules); George Fletcher, *Two Kinds of Legal Rules: A Comparative Study of Burden-of-Persuasion Practices,* 77 YALE L.J. 880 (1968) (same); RICHARD J. BONNIE ET AL., CRIMINAL LAW 230 (3d ed. 2010) (estimating that "[p]erhaps as many as half the states" place the burden of persuasion on defendants to disprove specific intent with intoxication evidence). Where a defendant does not bear the burden of persuasion on a defense, he may nonetheless bear the burden of production (or "going forward" with some evidence) to raise the issue as a factual dispute. *Cf.* People v. Cleaves, 229 Cal. App. 3d 367; 280 CAL. RPTR. 146 (4th App. Dist. 1991) (in homicide trial, defendant has burden to produce evidence providing "some basis" for a jury instruction on lesser charge of assisting a suicide).

5. Peretz v. United States, 501 U.S. 923 (1991) ("The most basic rights of criminal defendants are similarly subject to waiver," including right to have Article III judge supervise jury selection). *See, e.g.,* United States v. Gagnon, 470 U.S. 522, 528 (1985) (absence of objection constitutes waiver of right to be present at all stages of criminal trial); Levine v. United States, 362 U.S. 610, 619 (1960) (failure to object to closing of courtroom is waiver of right to public trial); Yakus v. United States, 321 U.S. 414, 444 (1944) ("No procedural principle is more familiar to this Court than that a constitutional right may be forfeited in criminal as well as civil cases by the failure to make timely assertion of the right"); Segurola v. United States, 275 U.S. 106, 111 (1927) (failure to object constitutes waiver of Fourth Amendment right against unlawful search and seizure).

6. *See* Fed. R. Evid. 804; United States v. Gray, 405 F.3d 227 (4th Cir. 2005), *cert. denied,* 546 U.S. 912 (2005).

7. Default works against prosecutors as well as defendants. Thus if the prosecution neglects to seek jury instructions on facts necessary for an increased sentence, authority for a higher sentence is lost because "the government bears the obligation to request the jury instruction necessary to support the penalty it seeks." United States v. Southern Union Co., 942 F. Supp. 2d 235, 241 (D. R.I. 2013). Enforcing party responsibility through procedural default rules trumps any interest what may be a more accurate sentence. *Southern Union* also illustrates the view that more severe sentencing is a partisan interest of the prosecution. For another example, see United States v. Nelson–Rodriguez, 319 F.3d 12, 47 (1st Cir. 2003) ("The government . . . does have an interest in going above the maximum [sentence], so it should bear the burden of requesting submission of the issue to the jury.").

8. *See* FED. R. CRIM. PRO. 52(b) (plain error standard); Rule 30 ("Failure to object [to a jury instruction] in accordance with this rule precludes appellate review, except as permitted under Rule 52(b)."); United States v. Olano, 507 U.S. 725 (1993) (describing differences between waiver and forfeiture and review standard for forfeited claims).

9. For prosecutors, see Brown v. Ohio 432 U.S. 161, 169 n.7 (1977) ("An exception [to the Double Jeopardy bar against subsequent prosecutions] may exist where the State is unable to proceed on the more serious charge at the outset because the additional facts necessary to sustain that charge have not occurred or have not been discovered despite the exercise of due diligence."); United States v. Southern Union Co., 942 F. Supp. 2d 235 (D. R.I. 2013) (prosecution waived jury finding as to sentencing facts and thereby opportunity to seek a sentence above the statutory maximum).

   Regarding new evidence, see VA. CODE § 19.2-327.1 (motion for postconviction forensic testing of new evidence to prove innocence authorized if "the evidence was not known or available at the time the conviction" and "the person convicted . . . has not unreasonably delayed the filing of the petition"). In the context of collateral review by federal courts of state court convictions, the standard for claims based on newly discovered evidence is especially restrictive. *See* 28 U.S.C. § 2244(b)(2)(B) (2012). Before any appeal, federal trial judges must correct any "clear errors" in calculating a sentence within fourteen days. FED. R. CRIM. PRO. 35(a).

10. Flanagan v. United States, 465 U.S. 259, 263–64 (1984) ("The final judgment rule serves several important interests. It helps preserve the respect due trial judges by minimizing appellate-court interference. . . . It reduces the ability of litigants to harass opponents and to clog the courts through a succession of costly and time-consuming appeals. It is crucial to the efficient administration of justice.").

11. Johnson v. United States, 520 U.S. 461, 466 (1997).

12. FEDERAL RULE OF CRIMINAL PROCEDURE 52(b) formally allows courts to correct plain errors even if parties do not raise the error, although as a practical matter it seems parties always initiate the issues. *See Olano,* 507 U.S. at 741 (Kennedy, J., concurring) (discussing a court's power under 52(b) to correct errors "on its own initiative," *citing* Silber v. United States, 370 U.S. 717, 718 (1962)).

13. *Cf.* Thomas Weigend, *Throw It All Out? Judicial Discretion in Dealing with Procedural Faults, in* Discretionary Criminal Justice in a Contemporary Perspective 185 (Michele Caianiello & Jacqueline S. Hodgson eds., 2015) ("No procedural system is immune from faults, and the range of such faults is broad."). Weigend defines "procedural faults" differently and more narrowly than "procedural *default*" is used here; his term refers to "procedural acts (or omissions) that violate a binding legal rule." *Id.* at 187.

14. For decisions attributing attorney's procedural default of claims to defendants, see, e.g., Coleman v. Thompson, 501 U.S. 722, 752–54 (1991); Murray v. Carrier, 477 U.S. 478, 492 (1986) (both involved procedural default of habeas claims). For a contrary view, see Carrier v. Hutto, 724 F.2d 396 (4th Cir. 1985), overturned by *Carrier*, 477 U.S. 478; *also Carrier*, 477 U.S. at 524–25 (Brennan, J., dissenting) ("[T]o say that the petitioner should be bound to his lawyer's tactical decisions is one thing; to say that he must also bear the burden of his lawyer's inadvertent mistakes is quite another. . . . [W]here a petitioner's constitutional rights have been violated and that violation may have affected the verdict, a federal court should not decline to entertain a habeas petition solely out of deference to the State's weak interest in punishing lawyers' inadvertent failures to comply with state procedures.").

    On the textual reference to *Link*, see Link v. Wabash R. Co., 370 U.S. 626, 633–34 (1962), *cited in* Coleman v. Thompson, 501 U.S. 722, 753 (1991), which was in turn cited in Vermont v. Brillon, 556 U.S. 81, 91 (2009).

15. United States v. Vonn, 535 U.S. 55 (2002).

16. United States v. Dominguez Benitez, 542 U.S. 74 (2004).

17. *Vonn*, 535 U.S. at 80 (Stevens, dissenting); *id.* at 72 (Souter, J., for majority).

18. Olmstead v. United States, 277 U.S. 438, 484–85 (1928) (Brandeis, J., dissenting). *See* Scott E. Sundby & Lucy B. Ricca, *The Majestic and the Mundane: The Two Creation Stories of the Exclusionary Rule*, 43 Tex. Tech L. Rev. 391 (2010) (interest balancing in criminal procedure exclusionary rules).

19. The data about the Supreme Court's use of the word "incentive" come from three searches in the Westlaw's Supreme Court database conducted May 20, 2014. Each search was limited to one of three time periods: 1915–1947, 1948–1980, and 1981–2013. Search terms were: "incentive /s (defendant prosecutor prosecution)."

20. Griffith v. Kentucky, 479 U.S. 314 (1986).

21. Toby Heytens, *Managing Transitional Moments in Criminal Cases*, 115 Yale L.J. 922 (2006).

22. *Griffith*, 479 U.S. at 323.

23. In Heytens's characterization, the forfeiture rule leads to "a significant amount of nonretroactivity in fact." Heytens, *supra* note 21, at 979.

24. *See* Va. S. Ct. Rules 1-1, 3A:15 (2014).

25. Fed. R. Crim. Pro. 33. For comparison, see Ariz. R. Crim. Pro. 24.2(a) (sixty-day limit); Minn. Rule Crim. Pro. 26.04(3) (fifteen-day limit). Under all variants of this rule, claims are limited to newly discovered evidence that was *not available to the parties* during the time period before the judgment. That limit implicitly speaks to party diligence; it's an example of the reliance on the parties for achieving accuracy rather than the state taking independent responsibility for ensuring it regardless of party negligence.

26. *See* Carpitcher v. Commonwealth, 641 S.E.2d 486, 492 (Va. 2007) ("recantation evidence is generally questionable in character and is widely viewed by courts with suspicion because of the obvious opportunities and temptations for fraud"); *see also* United States v. Baker, 479 P.3d 574, 578 (8th Cir. 2007); United States v. Santiago, 837 F.2d 1545, 1550 (11th Cir. 1988); United States v. Bynum, 3 F.3d 769, 773 (4th Cir. 1993).

27. *See e.g.*, the 2012 exoneration of Brian Banks, described in Mike Tierney, *At 28, Rookie Refuses to Focus on Time Lost*, N.Y. Times, Aug. 5, 2013, and at http://californiainnocenceproject.org; *see generally* National Registry of Wrongful Convictions (Univ. Mich. Law School).

28. VA. CODE §§ 19.2-327.1, -327.2 (writs of actual innocence for biological evidence, and motions for biological testing); *id.* § 19.2-327.10 (writs of actual innocence for nonbiological evidence); Va. S. Ct. Rules 5:7B & 5A:5 (petitions for writ of actual innocence); VA. CODE § 18.2-9 (specifying six classes of felonies and four of misdemeanors). *See also* District Attorney's Office for Third Judicial Dist. v. Osborne, 557 U.S. 52 (2009) (no constitutional right to test DNA evidence at defendant's own expense).
29. 443 U.S. 307 (1979).
30. Peter D. Marshall, *A Comparative Analysis of the Right to Appeal*, 22 DUKE J. COMP. & INT'L L. 1 (2011).
31. For an example of how this can matter, consider a prosecution that rests heavily on expert testimony of a prosecution witness who in fact gives unreliable or incorrect testimony. *Jackson* dictates that appellate courts credit the expert's testimony after conviction, even if error or unreliability in the testimony was not revealed because a party failed to find or produce available evidence of unreliability. (Note the prosecution might fail in this respect as well; its more thorough investigation might have revealed evidential unreliability and led prosecutors to decline to offer the evidence.)

    In addition to *Jackson*, the beyond-a-reasonable-doubt standard of proof protects defendants against inadequate evidence production by prosecutors by requiring acquittal for insufficient proof. *See In re* Winship, 397 U.S. 358 (1970) (holding the standard is required for juvenile adjudications by constitutional due process); Sullivan v. Louisiana, 508 U.S. 275 (1993) (standard required by due process in adult criminal prosecutions). Evidence rules, if parties invoke them, similarly keep certain unreliable evidence from misleading the fact-finder.
32. New York v. Hill, 528 U.S. 110, 114–15 (2000) (summarizing decisions that give attorneys professional discretion unconstrained by criminal defendant-clients for most litigation decisions except "certain fundamental rights" such as whether to plead guilty); *see also* United States v. Olano, 507 U.S. 725, 733 (1993) (client control varies with the importance of the decision or interest at issue); Brookhart v. Janis, 384 U.S. 1, 7–8 (1966) (defendant/client controls decision whether to plead not guilty); Johnson v. Zerbst, 304 U.S. 458, 464–65 (1938) (client controls right to counsel); Taylor v. Illinois, 484 U.S. 400 (1988) (lawyer has "full authority to manage the conduct of the trial"); Jones v. Barnes, 463 U.S. 745, 751 (1983) (attorney decides what legal arguments to pursue); Henry v. Mississippi, 379 U.S. 443, 451 (1965) (attorney controls evidentiary objections); United States v. McGill, 11 F.3d 223, 226–27 (C.A.1 1993) (attorney controls agreements regarding admission of evidence).
33. On constitutionality of agency costs for criminal defendants, see Maples v. Thomas, 132 S. Ct. 912, 922 (2012) ("[T]he attorney is the prisoner's agent, and under 'well-settled principles of agency law,' the principal bears the risk of negligent conduct on the part of his agent."); Coleman v. Thompson, 501 U.S. 722, 753–54 (1991); Irwin v. Department of Veterans Affairs, 498 U. S. 89, 92 (1990) ("Under our system of representative litigation, 'each party is deemed bound by the acts of his lawyer-agent.'"); Taylor v. Illinois, 484 U.S. 400 (1988) (It is not unfair to hold petitioner responsible for his lawyer's misconduct. The lawyer necessarily has full authority to manage the conduct of the trial, and the client must accept the consequences of the lawyer's trial decisions.).
34. For a sample of innumerable sources describing deficient indigent defense systems, see AMERICAN BAR ASS'N, *GIDEON'S* BROKEN PROMISE: AMERICA'S CONTINUING QUEST FOR EQUAL JUSTICE (2004) ("indigent defense in the United States remains in a state of crisis"). For examples of challenges to local indigent defense systems that describe severe deficiencies in resources, see Hurrell-Harring v. State, 930 N.E.2d 217 (N.Y. 2010) (various New York localities); State v. Peart, 621 So. 2d 780 (La. 1993) (New Orleans).
35. Vermont v. Brillon, 556 U.S. 81, 90–91 (2009).
36. *Brillon*, 556 U.S. at 91, *quoting* Polk County v. Dodson, 454 U. S. 312, 318 (1981) (citation and internal quotation marks omitted) (emphasis added).

37. Coleman v. Thompson, 501 U.S. 722, 753 (1991), subsequently cited in *Brillon*, 556 U.S. at 91.

38. Link v. Wabash R. Co., 370 U.S. 626, 633–34 (1962), *cited in* Coleman v. Thompson, 501 U.S. at 753.

39. *Brillon*, 556 U.S. at 94 (citation and internal quotation marks omitted).

40. Polk County v. Dodson, 454 U.S. 312 (1981).

41. Abraham Goldstein, *Reflections on Two Models: Inquisitorial Themes in American Criminal Procedure*, 26 STAN. L. REV. 1009 (1974) (implications of criminal litigation between two public attorneys).

42. For a critical account of U.S. prosecutors' discovery practices and motivations, see DANIEL S. MEDWED, PROSECUTION COMPLEX: AMERICA'S RACE TO CONVICT, AND ITS IMPACT ON THE INNOCENT 35–50 (2012).

43. For a study finding that indigent defendants fared worse with appointed lawyers than with full-time public defenders, see James M. Anderson & Paul Heaton, *How Much Difference Does the Lawyer Make? The Effect of Defense Counsel on Murder Case Outcomes*, 122 YALE L.J. 154 (2012) (empirical study of Philadelphia courts finding that defendants with appointed private counsel have worse sentencing outcomes than those represented by public defenders, and arguing that judges' control of attorneys' incentives is a partial cause).

44. *See, e.g.*, ARIZ. REV. STAT. § 11-582 (2014) ("The public defender shall receive that salary . . . shall be not less than seventy per cent of that paid to the county attorney."); TENN. CODE ANN. § 16-2-518 (2014) ("Any increase in local funding for positions or office expense for the district attorney general shall be accompanied by an increase in funding of seventy-five percent of the increase in funding to the office of the public defender").

45. R. v. Stinchcombe, [1991] 3 SCR 326.

46. *See* Stephen B. Bright & Sia M. Sanneh, *Fifty Years of Defiance and Resistance after Gideon* v. Wainwright, 122 YALE L.J. 2150, 2169–72 (2013); Stephen B. Bright, *Counsel for the Poor: The Death Sentence Not for the Worst Crime but for the Worst Lawyer*, 103 YALE L.J. 1835 (1994).

47. Sears v. Upton, 561 U.S. 945 (2010); Porter v. McCollum, 558 U.S. 30 (2009); Rompilla v. Beard, 545 U.S. 374 (2005); Wiggins v. Smith, 539 U.S. 510 (2003). Each of these decisions was a capital case in which lower appellate courts had found the defense attorney's failure to find and present favorable evidence for his client to be reasonable professional performance under *Strickland*.

48. *See, e.g.*, Hurrell-Harring v. State, 930 N.E.2d 217 (N.Y. 2010); State v. Peart, 621 So. 2d 780 (La. 1993).

49. Scott Sundby, *Fallen Superheroes and Constitutional Mirages: The Tale of* Brady v. Maryland, 33 McGEORGE L. REV. 643 (2002).

50. District Attorney's Office for Third Judicial Dist. v. Osborne, 557 U.S. 52 (2009) (holding state's due process disclosure duty does not apply postconviction).

51. Brady v. Maryland, 373 U.S. 83 (1963); Giglio v. United States, 405 U.S. 150 (1972); United States v. Bagley, 473 U.S. 667 (1985); Kyles v. Whitley, 514 U.S. 419 (1995); United States v. Ruiz, 536 U.S. 622 (2002).

52. Máximo Langer & Kent Roach, *Rights in the Criminal Process: A Case Study of Convergence and Disclosure Rights, in* ROUTLEDGE HANDBOOK OF CONSTITUTIONAL LAW 273 (Mark Tushnet, Thomas Fleiner, & Cheryl Saunders eds., 2013).

53. *Bagley*, 473 U.S. at 678. Arguably, materiality is a de facto rather than formal limit. The Supreme Court sometimes suggests that prosecutors must disclose *all* exculpatory evidence. But a right is usually only as meaningful as its remedy, and a remedy is provided only in when a failure to disclose involved *material* evidence.

54. *Ruiz*, 536 U.S. at 631–32 (some internal quotation marks omitted).

55. R. v. Stinchcombe, [1991] 3 SCR 326.

56. Canadian Charter of Rights and Freedoms § 7.

57. *Stinchcombe* [1991] 3 SCR 326 at ¶ 28; *see also id.* at ¶ 17 (*quoting* Marshall Commission Report recommending the same).

58. *Stinchcombe* [1991] 3 SCR 326 at ¶ 28.

59. *Id.* at ¶ 20.

60. *Id.* at ¶ 12 (emphasis added).

61. *Brady*, 383 U.S. at 87 ("Society wins not only when the guilty are convicted but when criminal trials are fair"). No reference to the prosecutor's ministerial role in *Brady*, 373 U.S. 83, Giglio v. United States, 405 U.S. 150 (1972), United States v. Agurs, 427 U.S. 97 (1976), *Bagley*, 473 U.S. 667; *Kyles*, 514 U.S. 419, or Banks v. Dretke, 540 U.S. 668 (2004).

62. *See* Weigend, *supra* note 13, at 185–87.

63. *In re* Davis, 557 U.S. 952, 955 (2009) (Scalia, J., dissenting); *see also* Kansas v. Marsh, 548 U.S. 163 (2006) (Scalia, J., concurring).

64. For examples and perspectives of more active roles judges can play, see Judith Resnik, *Managerial Judges*, 96 Harv. L. Rev. 374 (1982); Neal Devins & Saikrishna B. Prakash, *Reverse Advisory Opinions*, 80 U. Chi. L. Rev. 859 (2013) (describing—and criticizing—federal judges' orders that executive officials answer judicially posed questions). Comparable developments in English judicial practice apparently followed the Criminal Procedure and Investigations Act 1996. *See* John D. Jackson & Sean Doran, *The Case for Jury Waiver*, 1997 Crim. L.R. 155, 171 (noting judges "have been drawn into a more directorial role in pretrial proceedings" and rule revisions "enable judges to ensure" trial issues are clarified and trial preparation efforts are not wasteful).

Chapter 6

* *Epigraph*: Myers v. United States, 272 U.S. 52, 292–93 (1926) (Brandeis, J., dissenting).

1. Tony Judt, *What Is Living and What Is Dead in Social Democracy?*, N.Y. Rev. of Books, Dec. 17, 2009.

2. Myers v. United States, 272 U.S. 52, 84–85 (1926) (Brandeis, J., dissenting).

3. *Symposium: The Vanishing Trial*, 1 J. Emp. Legal Studies 459–984 (No. 3) (2004). Owen Fiss, *Against Settlement*, 93 Yale L.J. 1073 (1984).

4. *See Pareto Efficiency*, *in* A Dictionary of Economics (John Black et al. eds., 4th ed. 2012) ("Pareto efficiency [is a] form of efficiency for an economic allocation. An allocation is Pareto efficient if there is no feasible reallocation that can raise the welfare of one economic agent without lowering the welfare of any other economic agent.").

5. *Efficiency*, *in* A Dictionary of Economics, *id.*

6. *Efficiency*, *in* A Dictionary of Economics, *id.* (offering "efficiency" definitions for other contexts, including "efficiency in consumption means allocating goods between consumers so that it would not be possible by any reallocation to make some people better off without making anybody else worse off").

7. This follows the assumption of the standard demand function, according to which demand is determined by price and increases as the price of a good or service decreases, holding aside nonprice determinants of demand. *See generally* Paul Krugman & Robin Wells, Microeconomics 62–77, 147–52 (2d ed. 2009) (offering an overview of demand and supply curves and price elasticity of demand); *Law of Demand*, *in* 5 The New Palgrave Dictionary of Economics (Steven N. Durlauf & Lawrence E. Blume eds., 2d ed. 2008).

8. *See generally* Krugman & Wells, *supra* note 7, at 62–71 (describing factors affecting demand, including nonprice factors).

9. With respect to energy usage, the consensus seems to be that rebound effects are real but in most settings do not fully offset reductions from increased efficiency. For debates about rebound effects in energy contexts, see Lee Schipper & Michael Grubb, *On the Rebound? Feedback Between Energy Intensities and Energy Uses in IEA Countries*, 28 Energy Pol'y 367 (2000) (special issue on rebound effects); *see also* John M. Polimeni

& Raluca Iorgulescu Polimeni, *Jevons' Paradox and the Myth of Technological Liberation*, 3 ECOLOGICAL COMPLEXITY 344 (2006); James Barrett, *Rebounds Gone Wild*, NAT'L GEOGRAPHIC, Dec. 20, 2010, http://www.greaterenergychallengeblog.com/2010/12/rebounds-gone-wild/.

10. On Jevons or rebound effects, see Blake Alcott, *Jevons' Paradox*, 54 ECOLOGICAL ECON. 9 (2005); Kenneth A. Small & Kurt Van Dender, *Fuel Efficiency and Motor Vehicle Travel: The Declining Rebound Effect*, 28 ENERGY J. 25 (2007); LEE SCHIPPER ED., ENERGY EFFICIENCY (2000). The original argument for rebound effects (since rejected in the specific context) is found in W. STANLEY JEVONS, THE COAL QUESTION; AN INQUIRY CONCERNING THE PROGRESS OF THE NATION, AND THE PROBABLE EXHAUSTION OF OUR COAL-MINES 122–37 (2d ed. 1866).

11. On caseloads and plea bargaining, see GEORGE FISHER, PLEA BARGAINING'S TRIUMPH: A HISTORY OF PLEA BARGAINING IN AMERICA (2003) (concluding that rising civil and criminal caseloads in the nineteenth century played a big part in shaping prosecutors and judges' joint professional interests in adopting plea bargaining); LAWRENCE M. FRIEDMAN & ROBERT V. PERCIVAL, THE ROOTS OF JUSTICE: CRIME AND PUNISHMENT IN ALAMEDA COUNTY, CALIFORNIA 1870–1910, at 192–95 (1981) (attributing bargaining to shifting focus from the crime to the criminal, and to the increased involvement of police and prosecutors in adjudication).

12. *See* the discussion of this point in chapter 4.

13. *See* discussion in chapter 4, which cited, *inter alia*, MALCOLM M. FEELEY, THE PROCESS IS THE PUNISHMENT: HANDLING CASES IN A LOWER CRIMINAL COURT 244–77 (1992) (arguing against caseload pressure as explanation for bargaining); MILTON HEUMANN, PLEA BARGAINING: THE EXPERIENCES OF PROSECUTORS, JUDGES, AND DEFENSE ATTORNEYS 156–57 (1978); Milton Heumann, *A Note on Plea Bargaining and Case Pressure*, 9 LAW & SOC'Y REV. 515 (1975) (surveying caseload-pressure arguments/studies); MIKE MCCONVILLE & CHESTER L. MIRSKY, JURY TRIALS AND PLEA BARGAINING: A TRUE HISTORY (2005) (in a study of nineteenth-century New York City courts, attributing bargaining to changes in local political and social structures, macro-political economy, and emerging state interest in social control); MARY E. VOGEL, COERCION TO COMPROMISE: PLEA BARGAINING, THE COURTS, AND THE MAKING OF POLITICAL AUTHORITY 8–15 (2007); Mary E. Vogel, *The Social Origins of Plea Bargaining: Conflict and the Law in the Process of State Formation, 1830–1860*, 33 LAW & SOC'Y REV. 161 (1999).

14. MCCONVILLE & MIRSKY, *supra* note 13 (summarizing accounts of professionalization of criminal courts and noting quick trials in nineteenth-century New York, including juries that would decide multiple cases per day without deliberating before verdicts); Richard A. Posner, *The Cost of Rights: Implications for Central and Eastern Europe—and for the United States*, 32 TULSA L.J. 1, 7 (1996) ("The creation of these countervailing rights made the criminal justice system cumbersome, expensive—and quite possibly less effective in deterring crime."); William J. Stuntz, *The Political Constitution of Criminal Justice*, 119 HARV. L. REV. 780, 782 (2006) (hereafter *Political Constitution*) (describing constitutional criminal procedure as "political taxes" making process more costly); William J. Stuntz, *The Uneasy Relationship Between Criminal Procedure and Criminal Justice*, 107 YALE L.J. 1, 27–31 (1997) (discussing why it is cheaper to prosecute lower-income individuals); Ronald F. Wright, *How the Supreme Court Delivers Fire and Ice to State Criminal Justice*, 59 WASH. & LEE L. REV. 1429, 1432 (2002) (describing how Warren Court criminal justice rulings made process more expensive); *see also* JOHN H. LANGBEIN, TORTURE AND THE LAW OF PROOF: EUROPE AND ENGLAND IN THE ANCIEN RÉGIME (2006).

15. For suggestions about trial reforms, see John Rappaport, *Unbundling Criminal Trial Rights*, 82 U. CHI. L. REV. 181 (2015); Gregory M. Gilchrist, *Trial Bargaining*, 101 IOWA L. REV. (forthcoming 2015); Gregory M. Gilchrist, *Counsel's Role in Bargaining for Trials*, 99 IOWA L. REV. 1979 (2014); Stephen J. Schulhofer, *Is Plea Bargaining*

Inevitable?, 97 Harv. L. Rev. 1037 (1984). Historical research suggests that typical trials in late-eighteenth-century England may have averaged twenty minutes. *See* John Langbein, The Origins of the Adversary Criminal Trial at 16–18 (2003); J. M. Beattie, Policing and Punishment in London, 1660–1750, at 259–60 (2001); J. M. Beattie, Crime and the Courts in England, 1660–1800, at 378 (1986).

16. *See* Stephanos Bibas, The Machinery of Criminal Justice 59–127 (2012) (describing and criticizing costs to defendants, victims, and public interests in prevailing plea-based adjudication). For arguments in favor on juries, see Laura I. Appleman, Defending the Jury: Crime, Community, and the Constitution (2015); Jeffrey Abramson, *Four Models of Jury Democracy*, 90 Chi.-Kent L. Rev. 825 (2015), available on http://ssrn.com; Jenny E. Carroll, *Nullification as Law*, 102 Geo. L.J. 579 (2014); Jenny E. Carroll, *The Jury's Second Coming*, 100 Geo. L.J. 657 (2012).

17. *See, e.g.*, Santobello v. New York, 404 U.S. 257, 260 (1971) ("[Plea bargaining] is an essential component of the administration of justice. . . . If every criminal charge were subjected to a full-scale trial, the States and the Federal Government would need to multiply by many times the number of judges and court facilities."); *Ruiz*, 536 U.S. 622, 629–32 (2002). More specifically, in its *decisions related to plea bargaining* the Court speaks of the avoidance of jury trials in positive terms. Elsewhere, such as in the context of sentencing or witness confrontation rights, it puts greater emphasis on the positive contributions of jury decision making. *See, e.g.*, Apprendi v. New Jersey, 530 U.S. 466 (2000) (certain sentencing factors must be found by juries, not judges); Crawford v. Washington, 541 U.S. 36 (2004) (constitutional right to confront witnesses).

18. *See* Stephen Schulhofer, *Is Plea Bargaining Inevitable?*, 97 Harv. L. Rev. 1037 (1984).

19. *See, e.g.*, Lafler v. Cooper, 132 S. Ct. 1376, 1397 (2012) (Scalia, J., dissenting) (describing plea bargaining as a "necessary evil"); Blackledge v. Allison, 431 U.S. 63, 71 (1977) ("[T]he fact is that the guilty plea and the . . . plea bargain are important components of this country's criminal justice system. . . . Judges and prosecutors conserve vital and scarce resources."); Santobello v. New York, 404 U.S. 257, 260 (1971) (describing plea bargaining as "an essential component of the administration of justice" that prevents the "need to multiply by many times the number of judges and court facilities"); Ronald Wright & Marc Miller, *The Screening/Bargaining Tradeoff*, 55 Stan. L. Rev. 29, 40 (2002) (describing caseload pressures as the "primary engine behind the shift from trials to plea bargaining").

20. *See* Feeley, *supra* note 13; Friedman & Percival, *supra* note 11; Heumann, Plea Bargaining, *supra* note 13.

21. *See* Randolph Roth, American Homicide (2012).

22. Professor Steinberg describes increasing public violence and social disorder in mid-nineteenth-century Philadelphia, leading to more prosecutions. Allen Steinberg, The Transformation of Criminal Justice: Philadelphia, 1800–1880, at 177–87 (1989). Professor George Fisher describes rising numbers of alcohol violations, among other offenses, driving up caseloads in nineteenth-century Middlesex County. *See* Fisher, *supra* note 11, at 40–61.

23. *See generally* Douglas Husak, Overcriminalization: The Limits of the Criminal Law (2009).

24. For change in rates of crime over the last half century, see 5 Historical Statistics of the United States: Earliest Times to the Present, 5-224 tbl. Ec11-20 (2006) (estimated rates per 100,000 population of crime known to police, 1960–1997, showing an increase in all categories of crime until the 1990s, when rates start to decline); *see also* U.S. Dep't of Just., Bureau of Justice Statistics, *Sourcebook of Criminal Justice Statistics—1998*, at 260 tbl.3.114 (Kathleen Maguire & Ann L. Pastore eds., 1999).

25. Richard S. Frase, *The Decision to File Federal Criminal Charges: A Quantitative Study of Prosecutorial Discretion*, 47 U. Chi. L. Rev. 246, 247 (1980); Marc L. Miller & Ronald F. Wright, *The Black Box*, 94 Iowa L. Rev. 125, 132 (2008); Michael Edmund

O'Neill, *Understanding Federal Prosecutorial Declinations: An Empirical Analysis of Predictive Factors*, 41 AM. CRIM. L. REV. 1439, 1442 (2004); U.S. Dep't of Just., *U.S. Attorneys' Written Guidelines for the Declination of Alleged Violations of Federal Criminal Laws: A Report to the U.S. Congress* (Nov. 1979).

26. *See* James M. Cole, Deputy Attorney Gen., *Memorandum for all United States Attorneys: Guidance Regarding Marijuana Enforcement* (Aug. 29, 2013), *available at* http://www.justice.gov; James M. Cole, Deputy Attorney Gen., *Memorandum for United States Attorneys: Guidance Regarding the Ogden Memo in Jurisdictions Seeking to Authorize Marijuana for Medical Use* (June 29, 2011), *available at* http://www.justice.gov.

27. On Seattle's policy, see Mayor's Blog, *An FAQ on Marijuana Enforcement in Seattle* (Sept. 1, 2010, 12:56 P.M.), http://mayormcginn.seattle.gov/an-faq-on-marijuana-enforcement-in-seattle ("Enforcement of 'personal use' possession is the lowest priority for both the Seattle City Attorney's Office and the Seattle Police Department."). On New York's stop-and-frisk policy, see Joseph Goldstein, *Police Stop-and-Frisk Program in Bronx Is Ruled Unconstitutional*, N.Y. TIMES, Jan. 9, 2013, at A17; Harry G. Levine & Deborah Peterson Small, *N.Y. Civil Liberties Union, Marijuana Arrest Crusade: Racial Bias and Police Policy in New York City 1997–2007*, at 4 (2008), http://www.nyclu.org/files/MARIJUANA-ARREST-CRUSADE_Final.pdf; *Stop and Frisk in NYC: A Decade of Rising Numbers*, ASSOCIATED PRESS, Oct. 16, 2012, http://www.bigstory.ap.org/article/stop-and-frisk-nyc-decade-rising-numbers (noting number of pedestrian stops by New York City police officers rose from 97,296 in year in 2002 to 685,724 in 2011).

28. Andrew V. Papachristos et al., *Desistance and Legitimacy: The Impact of Offender Notification Meetings on Recidivism Among High Risk Offenders* (Mar. 27, 2013) (Offender Notification Forums is associated with a significant lengthening of the time that offenders remain on the street and out of prison), Columbia Public Law Research Paper No. 13-343, *available at* http://ssrn.com/abstract=2240232; Natalie Kroovand Hipple et al., *The High Point Drug Market Initiative: A Process and Impact Assessment* i (2010), http://www.drug-marketinitiative.msu.edu/HighPointMSUEvaluationPSN12.pdf (describing "problem solving intervention" in local drug markets that emphasized social supports and informal controls over arrest and prosecution); Andrew V. Papachristos, Tracey Meares, & Jeffrey Fagan, *Attention Felons: Evaluating Project Safe Neighborhoods in Chicago*, 4 J. EMPIRICAL LEGAL STUDIES 223 (2007). For a description of a "problem-oriented" gun-control project in Boston, see Harvard Kennedy Sch., *Operation Ceasefire: Boston Gun Project*, http://www.hks.harvard.edu/programs/criminaljustice/research-publications/gangs,-guns,-urban-violence/operation-ceasefire-boston-gun-project. For a description of another problem-oriented approach to crime reduction, see Anthony A. Braga et al., *The Strategic Prevention of Gun Violence Among Gang-Involved Offenders*, 25 JUSTICE Q. 132 (2008). Allegra M. McLeod, *Decarceration Courts: Possibilities and Perils of a Shifting Criminal Law*, 100 GEO. L.J. 1587–674 (2012); Hipple et al., *supra*, at i (finding that crime declines in the wake of "problem solving intervention" in local drug markets that emphasized social supports and informal controls over arrest and prosecution). On drug courts' alternatives to traditional punishments for drug crimes, see C. West Huddleston III et al., *Painting the Current Picture: A National Report Card on Drug Courts and Other Problem-Solving Court Programs in the United States* (U.S. Bureau of Justice Assistance, May 2008). On federal firearms enforcement policy, see Daniel C. Richman, *"Project Exile" and the Allocation of Federal Law Enforcement Authority*, 43 ARIZ. L. REV. 369 (2001).

29. *See* Memorandum from Janet Napolitano, Sec'y of Homeland Sec., to David V. Aguilar, Acting Comm'r, U.S. Customs & Border Protection et al. (June 15, 2012) (specifying, as an "exercise of our prosecutorial discretion," a policy of not enforcing immigration laws against children who entered the United States illegally), *available at* http://graphics8.nytimes.com/packages/pdf/politics/s1-exercising-prosecutorial-discretion-individuals-who-came-to-us-as-children.pdf?ref=us.

30. Richman, *supra* note 28, at 369.

31. *See* Steven M. Graves & Christopher L. Peterson, *Usury Law and the Christian Right: Faith-Based Political Power and the Geography of American Payday Loan Regulation*, 57 CATH. U. L. REV. 637, 667–68 (2008).

32. Lucia Zedner, *Pre-Crime and Post-Criminology?*, 11 THEORETICAL CRIMINOLOGY 261 (2007); Lucia Zedner, *Securing Liberty in the Face of Terror: Reflections from Criminal Justice*, 32 J.L. & SOC'Y 507 (2005); Jacqueline Hodgson & Victor Tadros, *How to Make a Terrorist Out of Nothing*, 72 MOD. L. REV. 984 (2009).

33. Gilles Duranton & Matthew A. Turner, *The Fundamental Law of Road Congestion: Evidence from US Cities*, 101 AM. ECON. REV. 2616 (2011); Anthony Downs, *The Law of Peakhour Expressway Congestion*, 16 TRAFFIC Q. 393 (1962).

34. *See, e.g.*, Blackledge v. Allison, 431 U.S. 63, 71 (1977) ("[T]he . . . plea bargain [is an] important component[] of this country's criminal justice system. . . . Judges and prosecutors conserve vital and scarce resources."); Santobello v. New York, 404 U.S. 257, 260–61 (1971) (plea bargaining is "essential" and prevents the "need to multiply by many times the number of judges and court facilities"); Wright & Miller, *supra* note 19, at 40 (caseload pressures are the "primary engine behind the shift from trials to plea bargaining").

35. As Fisher recounts, that fact convinced Massachusetts legislators who first objected to the new practice to accept it as better than the alternatives. FISHER, *supra* note 11.

36. WILLIAM J. NOVAK, THE PEOPLE'S WELFARE: LAW AND REGULATION IN NINETEENTH-CENTURY AMERICA 155–56 (1996).

37. FISHER, *supra* note 11, at 8 (noting that in the Prohibition era, "the nation's courts sank beneath the sheer weight of liquor cases"); *id.* at 4–8, 21–27 (discussing alcohol prosecutions in other eras); DANIEL OKRENT, LAST CALL: THE RISE AND FALL OF PROHIBITION 112, 264 (2010) (describing caseload strains on courts and guilty plea increases during Prohibition).

38. The same story applies to use of criminal law for other social regulation efforts, from prosecutions for public drunkenness, vagrancy, unemployment, and prostitution, to fire- and building-safety codes, operation of dance halls, and environmental regulations. For discussions and examples of such regulatory statutes in the nineteenth and twentieth centuries, see Booth v. Illinois, 184 U.S. 425 (1902) (affirming conviction under a state law criminalizing options contracts on commodities); Davis v. Beason, 133 U.S. 333, 341 (1890) ("Bigamy and polygamy are crimes by the laws of all civilized and Christian countries. . . . They tend to destroy the purity of the marriage relation, to disturb the peace of families, to degrade woman and to debase man. Few crimes are more pernicious to the best interests of society and receive . . . more deserved punishment."); Donna I. Dennis, *Obscenity Law and Its Consequences in Mid-Nineteenth-Century America*, 16 COLUM. J. GENDER & L. 43 (2007); Louis Henkin, *Morals and the Constitution: The Sin of Obscenity*, 63 COLUM. L. REV. 391 (1963); NOVAK, *supra* note 36. *See generally* Markus Dirk Dubber, *Policing Possession: The War on Crime and the End of Criminal Law*, 91 J. CRIM. L. & CRIMINOLOGY 829 (2001) (analyzing the success of the war on crime and arguing that arrests for possession have replaced vagrancy laws as law enforcement's main tool for social control).

39. U.S. Dep't of Justice, Bureau of Justice Statistics, *Sourcebook of Criminal Justice Statistics—2010* tbl. 5.22, *available at* http://www.albany.edu/sourcebook/pdf/t5222010.pdf

40. *Sourcebook of Criminal Justice Statistics—2010, id.*, at tbl. 5.8.

41. U.S. Dept. of Justice, Exec. Office for U.S. Attorneys, *United States Attorneys' Annual Statistical Report 2000*, at 14 & chart 8; *United States Attorneys' Annual Statistical Report 2010*, at 10.

42. *See* Mark Motivans, Bureau of Justice Statistics, Federal Justice Statistics 2009— Statistical Tables 18 tbl.4.2 (Dec. 2011), http://bjs.ojp.usdoj.gov/content/pub/pdf/fjs09st.pdf (96.7 percent of convictions resulted from guilty pleas in 2009); Ronald

F. Wright, Federal Criminal Workload, Guilty Pleas, and Acquittals: Statistical Background app. 1 (2005), http://papers.ssrn.com/sol3/papers.cfm?abstract_id=809124 (85.57 percent guilty plea rate in 1970, based on data from the Administrative Office of the U.S. Courts). On "fast-track" plea bargaining policy, see PROTECT Act, Pub. L. No. 108-21, § 401(m)(2)(B), 117 Stat. 650, 675 (2003) (directing U.S. Sentencing Commission to promulgate guidelines with greater discounts for fast-track bargains); U.S. Sentencing Guidelines Manual § 5K3.1 (2012); James M. Cole, Deputy Attorney Gen., *Memorandum for all United States Attorneys: Department Policy on Early Disposition or "Fast-Track" Programs* (Jan. 31, 2012) (describing Department of Justice fast-track policies and authority for them), *available at* http://www.justice.gov/dag/fast-track-program.pdf.

43. U.S. Sent. Comm'n, 2010 Annual Report, at 44 tbl.11 (2011). Fast-track plea policies for immigration charges also dropped the median number of days between charging and disposition well below the average for federal crimes—to thirty-seven days in 2004, compared to three hundred days for narcotics offenses. *See* Transactional Records Access Clearinghouse (TRAC), Prosecution Time by Department of Justice Program Category, http://www.trac.syr.edu/tracins/highlights/v04/protimeprogcat.html (last visited Dec. 31, 2013), *cited in* Mary Fan, *The Law of Immigration and Crime, in* The Oxford Handbook on Ethnicity, Crime, and Immigration 628, 638 (Sandra Bucerius & Michael Tonry eds., 2013).

44. *See* James C. Duff, *Judicial Business of the United States Courts: 2010 Annual Report of the Director* 22 & 222 tbl.D-2 (2011).

45. On the decline in unauthorized migration up to 2010, see Jeffrey S. Passel & D'Vera Cohn, *U.S. Unauthorized Immigration Flows Are Down Sharply Since Mid-Decade* i (2010). For an excellent overview discussing these developments, see Fan, *supra* note 43.

46. *See* Brandon Garrett, Too Big to Jail (2014).

47. For the most recent federal policy intended to reduce use of Section 851 enhancements, see U.S. Attorney General Eric Holder, *Memorandum: Department Policy on Charging Mandatory Minimum Sentences and Recidivist Enhancements in Certain Drug Cases, Aug. 12, 2013* (advising that enhanced sentences should be limited to "high-level or violent traffickers").

48. *See* William J. Stuntz, The Collapse of American Criminal Justice 299, 390 n.42 (2011) (providing these figures and sources for them, primarily data from the U.S. Bureau of Justice Statistics and from the National Center for State Courts). The U.S. incarceration rate rose from 104 to 492 per 100,000 between 1974 and 2005. *See* Margaret Werner Cahalan, *Historical Corrections Statistics in the United States 1850–1984*, at 35 tbl.3–7 (1986) (reporting incarceration rates for 1925–1982); E. Ann Carson & William J. Sabol, *Bureau of Justice Statistics, Prisoners in 2011*, at 6 tbl.6 (2012) (reporting incarceration rates for 2000–2011).

49. For data on rising crime rates until the early 1990s and declining rates thereafter, see Steven D. Levitt, *Understanding Why Crime Fell in the 1990s: Four Factors that Explain the Decline and Six that Do Not*, 18 J. Econ. Persp. 163, 165 fig.1 & 166 tbl.2 (Winter 2004); U.S. Dep't of Just., Crime in the United States 2005: Table 1 (2006), *available at* http://www2.fbi.gov/ucr/05cius/data/table_01.html. Population figures from U.S. Census data: 295,753, 151 in 2005; 213,853,928 in 1974.

50. *See* John F. Pfaff, *The Micro and Macro Causes of Prison Growth*, 28 Ga. St. U. L. Rev. 1239 (2012); John F. Pfaff, *The Myths and Realities of Correctional Severity: Evidence from the National Corrections Reporting Program on Sentencing Practices*, 13 Am. L. & Econ. Rev. 491 (2011) (arguing that admission practices rather than longer sentences are driving prison growth); John F. Pfaff, *The Causes of Growth in Prison Admissions and Populations* (Jan. 2012) (unpublished manuscript), *available at* http://papers.ssrn.com/sol3/papers.cfm?abstract_id=1990508.

51. Lynn Bauer & Steven D. Owens, *Justice Expenditure and Employment in the United States, 2001*, at 2 (U.S. Bureau of Justice Statistics, May 2004).

52. *See* Goldstein, *Police Stop-and-Frisk Program*, N.Y. Times, Jan. 9, 2013 (noting number of pedestrian stops by New York City police officers rose from 97,296 in 2002 to 685,724 in 2011).

53. *See* Tracey L. Meares, Place *and Crime*, 73 Chi.-Kent L. Rev. 669 (1998) (analyzing police enforcement practices across various settings and describing how sting operations against drug sellers are cheaper than those against buyers); William J. Stuntz, *Privacy's Problem and the Law of Criminal Procedure*, 93 Mich. L. Rev. 1016 (1995) (describing consequences of protecting privacy in law of investigation); Williams J. Stuntz, *Race, Class, and Drugs*, 98 Colum. L. Rev. 1795 (1998) (describing how legally protected privacy correlates with class and race, with consequences for enforcement policies).

54. For arguments about the adverse effects of excessive criminal law enforcement, see Michelle Alexander, The New Jim Crow (2010); Douglas N. Husak, Overcriminalization: The Limits of Criminal Law (2008); Douglas N. Husak, The Legalization of Drugs (2005); Michael H. Tonry, Punishing Race: A Continuing American Dilemma (2011); Michael H. Tonry, Sentencing Matters (1996); Michael H. Tonry, Malign Neglect: Race, Crime, and Punishment in America (1995); Eva Bertram et al., Drug War Politics: The Price of Denial 32–54 (1996); Jeffrey A. Miron, Drug War Crimes: The Consequences of Prohibition (2004); Jeffrey Fagan & Tracey L. Meares, *Punishment, Deterrence and Social Control: The Paradox of Punishment in Minority Communities*, 6 Ohio St. J. Crim. L. 173, 183–85 (2008); Jeffrey Fagan et al., *Reciprocal Effects of Crime and Incarceration in New York City Neighborhoods*, 30 Fordham Urb. L.J. 1551, 1552–53 (2003) (hereafter *Reciprocal Effects*). For discussion of when regulatory and prevention policies without criminal sanctions can be more effective than criminal prosecutions, see John Braithwaite, Restorative Justice and Responsive Regulation 124–25, 230–31, 248 (2002); Ian Ayres & John Braithwaite, Responsive Regulation: Transcending the Deregulation Debate 36–40 (1992); John Braithwaite, To Punish or Persuade: Enforcement of Coal Mine Safety (1985).

55. On congressional regulation of federal prosecutors through budgets and monitoring via oversight hearings, see Daniel C. Richman, *Federal Criminal Law, Congressional Delegation, and Enforcement Discretion*, 46 UCLA L. Rev. 757, 791–93 (1999), Daniel Richman, *Political Control of Federal Prosecutions: Looking Back and Looking Forward*, 58 Duke L.J. 2087, 2093 (2009). Regarding legal limits on enforcement of federal firearms regulations, see Erica Goode & Sheryl Gay Stolberg, *Legal Curbs Said to Hamper A.T.F. in Gun Inquiries*, N.Y. Times, Dec. 26, 2012, at A1. Regarding enforcement by the Internal Revenue Service, see Editorial, *A Weakened I.R.S.*, N.Y. Times, Apr. 16, 2000, at WK14 (similar account of congressional restraint of IRS enforcement through budget). On tax enforcement, see David Kocieniewski, *Budget Cuts Hamper the I.R.S. in Efforts to Collect Billions in Taxes, Report Says*, N.Y. Times, Jan. 12, 2012, at B2 (describing congressional restriction of IRS tax law enforcement by cuts to IRS budget). On securities laws enforcement, see James B. Stewart, *As a Watchdog Starves, Wall St. Is Tossed a Bone*, N.Y. Times, July 16, 2011, at A1 (describing cuts to Securities and Exchange Commission budget intended to restrain its enforcement capacity). Not all enforcement budget cuts, to be sure, are driven by the desire for reduced enforcement. For examples of cuts to police enforcement that were clearly driven by a budget crisis, see Joseph Goldstein, *After Deep Police Layoffs, Camden Feels Vulnerable*, N.Y. Times, Mar. 7, 2011, at A14; Erica Goode, *Crime Increases in Sacramento After Deep Cuts to Police Force*, N.Y. Times, Nov. 4, 2012, at N26, *available at* http://www.nytimes.com/2012/11/04/us/after-deep-police-cuts-sacramento-sees-rise-in-crime.html.

56. Alex Altman, *Congress Hands a Mixed Bag to Marijuana Movement*, Time.com, Dec. 11, 2014; David Downs, *Victory: Congress Ends War on Medical Marijuana*, SFGate.com, Dec. 12, 2014; *Congress's Double-Edged Marijuana Stance*, N.Y. Times, Dec. 10, 2014.

57. For a vivid account of enforcement practices in New York, see Matthew C. Taibbi, The Divide: American Injustice in the Age of the Wealth Gap (2014); Tracey L. Meares, *The Law and Social Science of Stop and Frisk*, 10 Ann. Rev. L. and Social Sci. 335 (2014); Jeffrey Bellin, *The Inverse Relationship between the Constitutionality and Effectiveness of New York City "Stop and Frisk,"* 94 Boston Univ. L. Rev. 1495 (2014); Bernard Harcourt, *Punitive Preventive Justice: A Critique, in* Preventive Justice (Andrew Ashworth & Lucia Zedner eds., 2014); Amanda Geller & Jeffrey Fagan, *Pot as Pretext: Marijuana, Race, and the New Disorder in New York City Street Policing*, 7 J. Emp. Legal Studies 591 (2010); Andrew Gelman, Jeffrey Fagan, & Alex Kiss, *An Analysis of the NYPD's Stop-and-Frisk Policy in the Context of Claims of Racial Bias*, 102 J. Am'n Statistical Ass'n 813 (2007).

58. *See generally* Jonathan Simon, Governing Through Crime (2009). On criminogenic effects, see, e.g., Lynne M. Vieraitis et al., *The Criminogenic Effects of Imprisonment: Evidence from State Panel Data, 1974–2002*, 6 Criminology & Pub. Pol'y 589, 590 (2007); Jeffrey Fagan et al., *Reciprocal Effects, supra* note 54. On harms to third parties, see Dan Markel, Jennifer M. Collins, & Ethan J. Leib, Privilege or Punish: Criminal Justice and the Challenge of Family Ties (2009) (recognizing punishment's value as an affirmative good but expressing a willingness to tailor its contours in special circumstances to mitigate unnecessary third-party harms); Darryl K. Brown, *Third-Party Interests in Criminal Law*, 80 Tex. L. Rev. 1383, 1386–96 (2002) (describing harms to others from punishment and legal recognition of those interests).

59. Pew Center on the States, *One in 31: The Long Reach of American Corrections* 1 (2009), http://www.pewstates.org/uploadedFiles/PCS_Assets/2009/PSPP_1in31_report_FINAL_WEB_3-26-09.pdf (noting that in recent years corrections spending "was the fastest expanding major segment of state budgets, and over the past two decades, its growth as a share of state expenditures has been second only to Medicaid").

60. Bauer & Owens, *supra* note 51, at 2 (U.S. Bureau of Justice Statistics, May 2004). For more recent data, see Pew Center on the States, *Prison Count 2010: State Population Declines for the First Time in 38 Years* 1 (Apr. 2010); Ram Subramanian & Rebecca Tublitz, *Realigning Justice Resources: A Review of Population and Spending Shifts in Prison and Community Corrections* 7 (Sept. 2012) (reporting that for 2009–2010, nearly two-thirds of states responding to a survey reported declines in prison expenditures and nearly half reported decreases in prison populations, whereas 83 percent reported prison spending increases for years 2006–2010). For an analysis suggesting that increased state prison spending comes at the cost of other priorities funded by state general funds, see Prerna Anand, *Winners and Losers: Corrections and Higher Education in California* (Sept. 5, 2012), http://www.cacs.org/ca/article/44 (reporting that, following the 2007 recession, California state spending on prisons exceeded spending on higher education for the first time); NAACP, *Misplaced Priorities: Over Incarcerate, Under Educate* 1 (2d ed. May 2011) (reporting that "[o]ver the last two decades, . . . state spending on prisons grew at six times the rate of state spending on higher education").

61. Cahalan, *supra* note 48, at 35 tbl.3–7 (reporting incarceration rates for 1925–1982); Carson & Sabol, *supra* note 48, at 6 tbl.6 (reporting data and rates for 2000–2011). For timeline charts based on BJS data, see *The Sentencing Project, Incarceration*, http://www.sentencingproject.org/template/page.cfm?id=107 (last visited Jan. 3, 2014). These incarceration figures include only those sentenced to prison and exclude jail detainees. Adding the latter group, the U.S. incarceration rate for 2008 rises to 756 per 100,000. *See* Roy Walmsley, World Prison Population List 3 tbl.2 (8th ed. 2008), http://www.prisonstudies.org/sites/prisonstudies.org/files/resources/downloads/wppl-8th_41.pdf.

62. Bauer & Owens, *supra* note 51, at 2. Spending on police increased at the slowest rate, by 202 percent for 1982–2001, but started from a much higher per capita funding level, more than double the level of spending on either corrections or courts and prosecutors. *Id.* Regarding federal spending alone in this period, justice personnel spending went up

636 percent, while corrections spending went up 861 percent. *Id.* at 3. Personnel and institutions in each category are defined on pages 8–9. For raw data on the same budget trends for these three categories extended through 2007, see Tracey Kyckelhahn, *Justice Expenditures and Employment, FY 1982–2007—Statistical Tables* (Dec. 2011), http://www.bjs.gov/content/pub/pdf/jee8207st.pdf.

63. Professor Bill Stuntz did the most to develop this insight, and the recognition that adding certain kinds of new offenses can also sometimes lower enforcement costs. *See* Stuntz, *Political Constitution, supra* note 14, at 782, 810; William J. Stuntz, *The Pathological Politics of Criminal Law*, 100 MICH. L. REV. 505, 529–40 (2001).

64. *See* Nat'l Ass'n of State Budget Officers, *State Expenditure Report: Examining Fiscal 2010–2012 State Spending* 51–52 (2012) (documenting that corrections budgets are funded overwhelmingly from state general funds; also reporting that total state spending on corrections grew in FYs 2011 and 2012 but at much lower rates than in previous years).

65. For a sample of Supreme Court statements on the virtues of jury judgments and the value of moral—as distinct from legal—verdicts in criminal cases, see, e.g., Old Chief v. United States, 519 U.S. 172, 187–88 (1997) (endorsing jurors' need for sufficient evidence to "to implicate the law's moral underpinnings" so that its "guilty verdict would be morally reasonable" rather than a rational proof of "the discrete elements of a defendant's legal fault"). Saffle v. Parks, 494 U.S. 484, 499 n.3 (1990) (Brennan, J., dissenting) (lauding "the jury's moral judgment about the defendant's actions"). Penry v. Lynaugh, 492 U.S. 302, 319, 328 (1989) (holding habeas petitioner could present claim that a death penalty statute deprived him of an individualized sentencing determination by limiting the effect the jury could give to relevant mitigating evidence), abrogated on other grounds by Atkins v. Virginia, 536 U.S. 304 (2002); California v. Brown, 479 U.S. 538, 545–46 (1987) (O'Connor, J., concurring). Law regarding jury selection procedures reinforce the public value, independent of verdict accuracy, of diverse and representative jury membership. *See* Duren v. Missouri, 439 U.S. 357, 364 (1979) (specifying requirements of fair-cross-section claims); Taylor v. Louisiana, 419 U.S. 522, 530, 538 (1975) (defining constitutional fair-cross-section doctrine).

66. *See, e.g.,* Josh Bowers, *The Normative Case for Normative Grand Juries*, 47 WAKE FOREST L. REV. 319 (2012); BIBAS, *supra* note 16, at 147–64 (proposing citizen monitors of police and prosecutors).

67. Bowers, *supra* note 66 (describing speedy resolutions of misdemeanor cases that preclude evidence discovery).

68. Gerard E. Lynch, *Our Administrative System of Criminal Justice*, 66 FORDHAM L. REV. 2117 (1998); Gerard E. Lynch, *Screening versus Plea Bargaining: Exactly What Are We Trading Off?*, 55 STAN. L. REV. 1399, 1403–04 (2003).

69. For a good overview based on a systemic study of prosecutor misconduct in one state, see George Thomas et al., *Trial and Error: A Comprehensive Study of Prosecutorial Conduct in New Jersey* (2012) (ACLU report). *See also* Peter A. Joy, *The Relationship Between Prosecutorial Misconduct and Wrongful Convictions: Shaping Remedies for a Broken System*, 2006 WISC. L. REV. 399; Susan A. Bandes, *The Lone Miscreant, the Self-Training Prosecutor, and Other Fictions: A Comment on* Connick v. Thompson, 80 FORDHAM L. REV. 715 (2012).

70. Kyron Huigens, *Liberalism, Normative Expectations, and the Mechanics of Fault*, 69 MOD. L. REV. 462, 477 (2006). *See also* Kyron Huigens, *Law, Economics, and the Skeleton of Value Fallacy*, 89 CALIF. L. REV. 537, 564–65 (2001); ROBERT P. BURNS, THE DEATH OF THE AMERICAN TRIAL 30–39 (2009); Mike Redmayne, *Theorising Jury Reform, in* 2 THE TRIAL ON TRIAL: JUDGMENT AND CALLING TO ACCOUNT 99, 99–102 (Antony Duff et al. eds., 2006); BIBAS, *supra* note 16, at 69–81, 114–27 (offering arguments for the moral significance of adjudication procedures).

71. On moral as distinct legal judgments, see, e.g., *Old Chief*, 519 U.S. 172, 187–88; Saffle v. Parks, 494 U.S. 484, 499 n.3 (1990) (Brennan, J., dissenting); Penry v. Lynaugh, 492 U.S. 302, 319, 328 (1989).

72. *See* Huigens, *supra* note 70, at 546.
73. Joseph E. Stiglitz et al., *Report by the Commission on the Measurement of Economic Performance and Social Progress* 7 (2009) (Fr.), *available at* http://www.stiglitz-sen-fitoussi.fr/documents/rapport_anglais.pdf. For other prominent criticisms of GDP and arguments for alternative measures, see, e.g., Lew Daly & Stephen Posner, Demos, Beyond GDP: New Measures for a New Economy 2–3, 10 (2011); Panel to Study the Design of Nonmarket Accounts, Nat'l Res. Council, Beyond the Market: Designing Nonmarket Accounts for the United States 1–8 (Katharine G. Abraham & Christopher Mackie eds., 2005). *See also* Beyond GDP: Measuring Progress, True Wealth, and the Well-Being of Nations, Eur. Comm'n, http://www.ec.europa.eu/environment/beyond_gdp/index_en.html (last visited Jan. 3, 2014) (describing a European initiative that began in 2007); The Global Project on Measuring the Progress of Societies, Org. Econ. Co-operation & Dev., http://www.wikiprogress.org/index.php/The_Global_Project_on_Measuring_the_Progress_of_Societies (last updated July 25, 2013) (describing a project established in 2008). For the 2011 resolution of the European Parliament supporting alternative GPD measures, see Resolution on GDP and Beyond—Measuring Progress in a Changing World, Eur. Parl. Doc. P7_TA(2011)0264 (2011), *available at* http://www.europarl.europa.eu/sides/getDoc.do?type=TA&reference=P7-TA-2011-0264&language=EN.
74. United States v. Hasting, 461 U.S. 499, 527 (1983) (Brennan, J., dissenting).
75. Taylor v. United States, 493 U.S. 906 (1989) (Stevens, J., concurring in denial of certiorari) (Justice Stevens agreed that the Supreme Court should not grant certiorari to review circuit court's sentencing decision that was incorrect under the circuit's own precedent, in the absence of a conflict between circuits. Acknowledging this outcome allowed an unlawfully harsh sentence to stand, he observed: "That . . . is the kind of burden that the individual litigant must occasionally bear when efficient management is permitted to displace the careful administration of justice in each case. Perhaps it is not too late for the Court of Appeals to exercise additional care in the administration of justice in this case."). *See also* Ludwig v. Massachusetts, 427 U.S. 618, 627–28 (1976) (holding that harsher sentence for defendant who demanded a jury trial de novo after conviction at a bench trial does not unconstitutionally discourage assertion of the jury trial right, due to the interest of the state in efficient criminal procedure); *cited in* Corbitt v. New Jersey, 439 U.S. 212, 220 (1978).

Chapter 7

* *Epigraph:* United States v. Hensley, 469 U.S. 221, 229 (1985).
1. William Blackstone, Commentaries on the Law of England, vol. III at 379 & vol. IV at 350 (Thomas Green ed.; facsimile of first edition 1765–69; U. Chicago Press 1979).

    For an account of the American founders' views on the jury's importance as a governing institution, see Akhil Amar, The Constitution and Criminal Procedure: First Principles (1998). *See* Edward Glaeser & Andrei Shleifer, *Legal Origins*, 117 Q.J. Econ. 1193 (2002) (describing the rise of juries in England as a means to limit the king's influence over judges and thereby reduce bias in adjudication and advance fair and efficient dispute resolution).
2. *See generally* Jonathan Simon, Governing Through Crime (2007).
3. U.S. Const., preamble & amend. II.
4. *See generally* Lucia Zedner, Security 1–7 (2009).
5. Mattox v. United States, 156 U.S. 237 (1895).
6. *See* DeShaney v. Winnebago County, 489 U.S. 189 (1989).
7. *See* R(FB) v. DPP, 1 Cr. App. R. 38 [2009] EWHC 106 (Admin) (Toulson, L.J.); Nikolova v. Bulgaria, [2007] E.C.H.R. 1128, at [57] (ECHR Article 2 requires that national

criminal justice processes "must satisfy the requirements of the positive obligation to protect lives through the law"); MC v. Bulgaria (2005) 40 E.H.R.R. 20 (holding that Bulgaria violated Article 3 by failing to administer an effective criminal justice system to punish rape).

8. ANDREW ASHWORTH & LUCIA ZEDNER, PREVENTIVE JUSTICE 7–13 (2012) (duty of states to prevent harm).

9. Tennessee v. Garner, 471 U.S. 1, 2627 (1985) (O'Connor, J., dissenting); *see also* Texas v. Cobb, 532 U.S. 162 (2001), United States v. Ewell, 383 U.S. 116 (1966); Imbler v. Pachtman, 424 U.S. 409, 427 (1976) ("vigorous and fearless performance of the prosecutor's duty [is] essential"). Herbert Packer's classic "two models of crime control" captures the dual duties of the state as well as competing trade-offs in procedure. *Cf.* Herbert Packer, *Two Models of the Crime Process*, in THE LIMITS OF THE CRIMINAL SANCTION (1968).

10. *See* Roviaro v. United States., 353 U.S. 53, 59 (1957); *also* Branzburg v. Hayes, 408 U.S. 665 (1972); Rugendorf v. United States, 376 U.S. 528 (1964); United States v. Mendenhall, 446 U.S. 544, 565 (1980) (Powell, concurring).

11. Frank v. Mangum, 237 U.S. 309, 337 (1915).

12. Zurcher v. Stanford Daily, 436 U.S. 547, 560–61 (1978). *See also* United States v. Sells Engineering, Inc., 463 U.S. 418 (1983) (Burger, dissenting) ("investigations of criminal activity . . . play a major role in protecting the nation.").

13. BERNARD HARCOURT, THE ILLUSION OF FREE MARKETS: PUNISHMENT AND THE MYTH OF NATURAL ORDER (2011).

14. MARKUS DIRK DUBBER, THE POLICE POWER: PATRIARCHY AND THE FOUNDATIONS OF AMERICAN GOVERNMENT (2005); WILLIAM J. NOVAK, THE PEOPLE'S WELFARE: LAW AND REGULATION IN NINETEENTH-CENTURY AMERICA (1996).

15. Carol S. Steiker, *Punishment and Procedure: Punishment Theory and the Criminal-Civil Procedural Divide*, 85 GEO. L.J. 775 (1997); PETER RAMSAY, THE INSECURITY STATE: VULNERABLE AUTONOMY AND THE RIGHT TO SECURITY IN THE CRIMINAL LAW (2012); Christopher Slobogin, *A Jurisprudence of Dangerousness*, 98 Nw. U. L. REV. 1 (2003).

16. KATHERINE BECKETT, MAKING CRIME PAY: LAW AND ORDER IN CONTEMPORARY AMERICAN POLITICS (1997); Vesla Weaver & Amy Lerman, *Race and Crime in American Politics: From Law and Order to Willie Horton and Beyond*, in OXFORD HANDBOOK OF RACE, ETHNICITY, IMMIGRATION, AND CRIME (Sandra Bucerius & Michael Tonry eds., 2014); Vesla Weaver, *Frontlash: Race and the Development of Punitive Crime Policy*, 21 STUDIES IN AM. POLITICAL DEV'T 230 (2007).

NICOLA LACEY, THE PRISONERS' DILEMMA: POLITICAL ECONOMY AND PUNISHMENT IN CONTEMPORARY DEMOCRACIES (2008); Katherine Beckett & Bruce Western, *Governing Social Marginality: Welfare, Incarceration, and the Transformation of State Policy*, 3 PUNISH. & MOD. SOC'Y 43–59 (2001) (describing correlation in U.S. states between high incarceration rates and weak social welfare systems). JULIAN V. ROBERTS ET AL., PENAL POPULISM AND PUBLIC OPINION: LESSONS FROM FIVE COUNTRIES (2002).

17. DAVID GARLAND, THE CULTURE OF CONTROL: CRIME AND SOCIAL ORDER IN CONTEMPORARY SOCIETY (2001); *see also* JAMES Q. WHITMAN, HARSH JUSTICE: CRIMINAL PUNISHMENT AND THE WIDENING DIVIDE BETWEEN AMERICA AND EUROPE (2003).

18. SIMON, *supra* note 2.

19. Kansas v. Hendricks, 521 U.S. 346 (1997); RAMSAY, *supra* note 15; Slobogin, *supra* note 15.

20. BERNARD E. HARCOURT, AGAINST PREDICTION: PROFILING, POLICING, AND PUNISHING IN AN ACTUARIAL AGE (2003).

21. ASHWORTH & ZEDNER, *supra* note 8, at 7–50; G. R. SULLIVAN & IAN DENNIS EDS., SEEKING SECURITY: PRE-EMPTING THE COMMISSION OF CRIMINAL HARMS (2012);

IAN LOADER & NEIL WALKER, CIVILIZING SECURITY (2007); LUCIA ZEDNER, CRIMINAL JUSTICE 283–306 (2004); Malcom Feeley & Jonathan Simon, *Actuarial Justice: The Emerging New Criminal Law, in* THE FUTURES OF CRIMINOLOGY 173 (David Nelkin ed., 1994); CRIME, RISK AND INSECURITY (Tim Hope & Richard Sparks eds., 2000); Ian Loader, Benjamin J. Goold, & Angélica Thumala, *The Moral Economy of Security,* 18 THEORETICAL CRIMINOLOGY No. 3 (2014), *available at* http://ssrn.com/abstract=2431339; RAMSAY, *supra* note 15; Lucia Zedner, *Pre-Crime and Post-Criminology?,* 11 THEORETICAL CRIMINOLOGY 261 (2007); Lucia Zedner, *Preventive Justice or Pre-Punishment? The Case of Control Orders,* 59 CURRENT LEGAL PROBS. 174 (2007); Lucia Zedner, *Securing Liberty in the Face of Terror: Reflections from Criminal Justice,* 32 J.L. & SOC'Y 507 (2005); Jacqueline Hodgson & Victor Tadros, *How to Make a Terrorist Out of Nothing,* 72 MOD. L. REV. 984–98 (2009); Victor Tadros, *Crimes and Security,* 71 MOD. L. REV. 940 (2008).

22. BLACKSTONE, COMMENTARIES ON THE LAWS OF ENGLAND, vol. IV, *supra* note 1, at 248–53; ASHWORTH AND ZEDNER, *supra* note 8, at 27–50. *See also* Papachristou v. City of Jacksonville, 405 U.S. 156 (1972) (overturning a statute prohibiting "rogues, vagabonds . . . night walkers . . . lascivious persons," among other descriptors).

23. London's was the first modern police force, established in 1829. But organized slave patrols in southern U.S. cities preceded the London police. *See* G. EDWARD WHITE, LEGAL HISTORY: A VERY SHORT INTRODUCTION (2013) (describing early police forces in the United States, including slave patrols in southern cities in the early 1800s). On the advent of modern prisons, see DAVID J. ROTHMAN, THE DISCOVERY OF THE ASYLUM: SOCIAL ORDER AND DISORDER IN THE NEW REPUBLIC xxx–xl & 55–76 (1970; rev. 1990); HARCOURT, *supra* note 13, at 215–17; MICHEL FOUCAULT, DISCIPLINE & PUNISH: THE BIRTH OF THE PRISON (Alan Sheridan trans., 2d ed. 1995).

24. DUBBER, *supra* note 14; NOVAK, *supra* note 14.

25. *See generally* GORDON S. WOOD, EMPIRE OF LIBERTY: A HISTORY OF THE EARLY REPUBLIC, 1789–1815 (2009).

26. RANDOLPH ROTH, AMERICAN HOMICIDE 9, 22, 299 (2009).

27. *See generally* CHARLES SELLERS, THE MARKET REVOLUTION (1993); WOOD, *supra* note 25; DANIEL WALKER HOWE, WHAT HATH GOD WROUGHT: THE TRANSFORMATION OF AMERICA, 1815–1848 (2007); JOHN LAURITZ LARSON, THE MARKET REVOLUTION IN AMERICA: LIBERTY, AMBITION, AND THE ECLIPSE OF THE COMMON GOOD (2009).

28. ROTH, *supra* note 26, at 299.

29. *Id.,* at 22, 299.

30. ROTHMAN, *supra* note 23, at xxx–xl & 55–76 (quotations from page 60 and the 1990 preface at xxxiv–xl).

31. Mary E. Vogel, *The Social Origins of Plea Bargaining: Conflict and the Law in the Process of State Formation,* 33 LAW & SOC'Y REV. 161, 164, 196–204 (1999).

32. ALLEN STEINBERG, TRANSFORMATION OF CRIMINAL JUSTICE, PHILADELPHIA, 1800–1880, at 92–119 (1989).

33. MIKE MCCONVILLE & CHESTER MIRSKY, JURY TRIALS AND PLEA BARGAINING: A TRUE HISTORY 15–35, 309–25 (2005). New York's population grew six-fold in the four decades before 1845. McConville and Mirsky emphasize officials' intentions to advance their enforcement capacity and control in the context of these developments, while Rothman and Steinberg put more emphasis on social disorder to which criminal law was an obvious and perhaps inevitable response. For another account of the expansion of criminal law and punishment as a response to concern about social order, see MARK E. KANN, PUNISHMENT, PRISONS, AND PATRIARCHY: LIBERTY AND POWER IN THE EARLY AMERICAN REPUBLIC (2005).

34. MICHAEL H. TONRY, PUNISHING RACE: A CONTINUING AMERICAN DILEMMA (2011); MICHELLE ALEXANDER, THE NEW JIM CROW (2012); Amanda Geller & Jeffrey Fagan, *Pot as Pretext: Marijuana, Race, and the New Disorder in New York City Street Policing,*

7 J. Emp. Legal Studies 591 (2010); Jeffrey Fagan & Tracey L. Meares, *Punishment, Deterrence and Social Control: The Paradox of Punishment in Minority Communities*, 6 Ohio St. J. Crim. L. 173, 183–85 (2008); Jeffrey Fagan et al., *Reciprocal Effects of Crime and Incarceration in New York City Neighborhoods*, 30 Fordham Urb. L.J. 1551, 1552–53 (2003).

35. Roth, *supra* note 26, at 17–26, 297–300; *see generally* Brian Balogh, A Government Out of Sight: The Mystery of National Authority in Nineteenth Century America 11, 42 (2009). On Reconstruction, *see* Eric Foner, A Short History of Reconstruction (1990).

36. Roth, *supra* note 26, at 17–26.

37. Perhaps the strongest statement by the U.S. Supreme Court of the jury as a check on distrusted government officials is in *Duncan v. Louisiana*, 391 U.S. 145, 155–66 (1968). The jury trial right, the Court says, guards against "oppression by the government," "unchecked power," and "arbitrary law enforcement," and was viewed by the Constitution's drafters as "necessary to protect against unfounded criminal charges brought to eliminate enemies" by "the corrupt or overzealous prosecutor" or "the compliant, biased or eccentric judge."

38. *See, e.g.,* Daniel J. Solove, Nothing to Hide: The False Tradeoff between Privacy and Security (2013); Christopher Slobogin, Privacy at Risk: The New Government Surveillance and the Fourth Amendment (2007).

39. *See generally* Alexander, *supra* note 34; Desmond S. King & Rogers M. Smith, Still a House Divided: Race and Politics in Obama's America 215–49 (2011); Tonry, *supra* note 34.

40. John Langbein, The Origins of the Adversary Criminal Trial (2002).

41. *See generally* Roberts et al., *supra* note 16; Richard S. Frase, *Comparative Perspectives on Sentencing Policy and Research*, *in* Sentencing and Sanctions 259, 276–77 (Michael Tonry & Richard S. Frase eds., 2001); Julian V. Roberts & Jane B. Sprott, *Exploring the Differences Between Punitive and Moderate Penal Policies in the United States and Canada*, *in* 4 Crime and Crime Policy: International Perspectives on Punitivity 55, 71–72 (Helmut Kury & Theodore N. Ferdinand eds., 2008).

42. *See* David Garland, Peculiar Institution: America's Death Penalty in an Age of Abolition (2010) (identifying local, democratic governance as a key explanation for persistence of the death penalty in the United States); Simon, *supra* note 2; Bernard E. Harcourt, *Neoliberal Penality: A Brief Genealogy*, 14 Theoretical Criminology 74 (2010).

43. Roberts et al., *supra* note 16; Franklin E. Zimring and Gordon Hawkins, Punishment and Democracy: Three Strikes and You're Out in California (2003); Marie Gottschalk, Caught: The Prison State and the Lockdown of American Politics (2014).

44. *See* Jed Rubenfeld, *The Two World Orders*, 27 Wilson Q. 22 (Fall 2003); *see also* Edward J. Eberle, *The German Idea of Freedom*, 10 Ore. Rev. Int'l L. 1 (2008).

45. Vanessa Barker, The Politics of Imprisonment How the Democratic Process Shapes the Way America Punishes Offenders (2009); John L. Campbell & Ove K. Pedersen, *Knowledge Regimes and Comparative Political Economy*, *in* Ideas and Politics in Social Science Research 167–90 (Daniel Béland & Robert Cox eds., 2011) (describing how expertise and information sources for U.S. public policymaking is often comes from more partisan political sources than in the United Kingdom or European nations); John L. Campbell & Ove K. Pedersen, The National Origins of Policy Ideas: Knowledge Regimes in the United States, France, Germany and Denmark (2014) (same, with different national comparisons and greater detail).

46. *See* Robert P. Burns, The Death of the American Trial (2009) (describing the full development of factual records and their close consideration in trial compared to weaker evidentiary accounts upon which lawyers commonly rely to negotiate settlements).

47. Paul Robinson & John M. Darley, Justice, Liability and Blame: Community Views and the Criminal Law (1996); Paul Robinson & Michael T. Cahill, Law without Justice: Why Criminal Law Doesn't Give People What They Deserve (2005).

48. Scott Ashworth, *Electoral Accountability: Recent Theoretical and Empirical Work*, 15 Ann. Rev. Pol. Sci. 183 (2012).

49. Voters do—rarely—punish prosecutors for contributing to wrongful convictions, but only in rare settings where such an event becomes highly visible. For an example, see Pamela Colloff, *Why John Bradley Lost*, Tex. Monthly, Daily Post blog, May 30, 2012 (Williamson County, Texas, prosecutor lost re-election after fighting against efforts to overturn a conviction proven by DNA evidence to be erroneous), at http://www.tmdailypost.com/article/criminal-justice/why-john-bradley-lost.

50. Abby L. Dennis, *Reining in the Minister of Justice: Prosecutorial Oversight and the Superseder Power*, 57 Duke L.J. 131, 157–58 (2007) (describing N.Y. Governor George Pataki's removal of Bronx County District Attorney Robert Johnson from a potential death penalty case involving a slain police officer after Johnson declined to seek the death penalty against the accused); Terence Hallinan, a former criminal defense lawyer, was twice elected as the district attorney of San Francisco on an openly liberal platform. *See, e.g.*, Ilene Lelchuk, *D.A. Race Could Hinge on Police Indictments*, S.F. Chron., Mar. 10, 2003, at A1 (stating that Hallinan has been referred to as the country's most progressive district attorney and that he overcame reports during his 1999 election that "his office had won convictions in only 35.5 percent of the homicide, rape, robbery and assault cases police brought to his office"); Maura Dolan, *In Land of Liberals, D.A. Race Takes Twist*, L.A. Times, Dec. 13, 1999, at A3 (describing the San Francisco district attorney's race in 1999); William Yardley, *Some Find Hope for Shift in Drug Policy*, N.Y. Times, Feb. 15, 2009, at A13 (describing Seattle police chief Gil Kerlikowske's policy that made marijuana a low enforcement priority). Lisa N. Sacco & Kristin Finklea, *State Marijuana Legalization Initiatives: Implications for Federal Law Enforcement* 5–6 (Cong'l Res. Serv., Dec. 2014) (reporting that, since a California voter initiative started the trend in 1996, more than half of U.S. states have decriminalized medical marijuana use in some form as of November 2014). For a good general discussion of prosecutors and local politics, see Daniel S. Medwed, *The Zeal Deal: Prosecutorial Resistance to Post-Conviction Claims of Innocence*, 84 B.U. L. Rev. 125, 150 (2004) ("the institutional culture of prosecutorial agencies is determined, to some extent, by the political landscape of the particular community").

51. *See* McConville & Mirsky, *supra* note 33, at 38 (listing prominent political figures including Alexander Hamilton, Aaron Burr, and Edward Livingston as criminal defense attorneys). Future President John Adams served as defense counsel to British soldiers charged in the wake of the 1770 "Boston massacre," and former President John Quincy Adams served as counsel for the black defendants seized in the 1841 *Amistad* case. For an account of the latter Adams's role in that case, see Marcus Rediker, The Amistad Rebellion: An Atlantic Odyssey of Slavery and Freedom 180–92 (2013).

52. *See* McConville & Mirsky, *supra* note 33, at 287–314.

53. *See, e.g.*, Beckett, *supra* note 16, at 51 (describing how politicians' initiatives drive public opinion on crime, and conversely how politicians to compete to appear "tougher" on crime); Desmond King, *Ironies of State Building: A Comparative Perspective on the American State*, 61 World Politics 547 (July 2009) ("Over the course of American history, race has both inhibited national state growth through federalism and enhanced state building, through the development of repressive capacity and the more positive deployment of force to protect rights and promote democratization."); Desmond King & Rogers Smith, *Strange Bedfellows? Polarized Politics? The Quest for Racial Equity in Contemporary America*, 61 Political Res. Q. 686 (2008) ("A racial orders analysis shows that the policy conflicts, the contesting coalitions, and the broader ideologies of

America's racial alliances have altered over time, in ways that have taken some types of racial inequality off the agenda. The ones that persist, including welfare, educational, and criminal justice policies with grossly disparate racial impacts, are very serious, but not tantamount to slavery or de jure segregation."); Weaver & Lerman, *Race and Crime, supra* note 16; Weaver, *Frontlash, supra* note 16.

54. *See, e.g.,* Papachristou v. City of Jacksonville, 405 U.S. 156 (2972).

55. William J. Stuntz, *Substance, Process, and the Civil-Criminal Line,* 7 J. CONTEMP. LEGAL ISSUES 1, 17–18, 21 (1996); *see also* William J. Stuntz, *The Pathological Politics of Criminal Law,* 100 MICH. L. REV. 505, 559–60 (2001).

56. Markus D. Dubber, *Policing Possession: The War on Crime and the End of Criminal Law,* 91 J. CRIM. L. & CRIMINOLOGY 829 (2002).

57. 18 U.S.C. § 371 (2014) (conspiracy); 18 U.S.C. §§ 2339A, 2339B (2014) (material support for terrorism); 31 U.S.C. § 3524; 26 U.S.C. § 6050I; 18 U.S.C. §§1956-1957 (2014) (money laundering and related reporting offenses).

58. *See* BRANDON GARRETT, TOO BIG TO JAIL (2014).

59. On the trial's virtues for fact development compared to lawyer-controlled discovery and settlement, see BURNS, *supra* note 46. For an account of how trial juries may have fuller factual accounts than prosecutors because the latter have limited access to defendants and defense witnesses, see DAN GIVELBER & AMY FARRELL, NOT GUILTY: ARE THE ACQUITTED INNOCENT? 54–55 (2012). For a history of different procedures when the crime is *flagrante* (the defendant caught in the act), see STEPHEN C. THAMAN, COMPARATIVE CRIMINAL PROCEDURE 4–7 (2d ed. 2008).

60. The vagrancy offense language is from city ordinance invalidated in Papachristou v. City of Jacksonville, 405 U.S. 156 (1972). On "scheme to defraud," see 18 U.S.C. § 1341.

61. *See generally* National Research Council, *Strengthening Forensic Science in the United States: A Path Forward* (2009); SIMON A. COLE, SUSPECT IDENTITIES: A HISTORY OF FINGERPRINTING AND SUSPECT IDENTIFICATION (2002); Jennifer Mnookin, *Scripting Expertise: The History of Handwriting Identification Evidence and the Judicial Construction of Expertise,* 87 VA. L. REV. 1723–845 (2001).

62. BURNS, *supra* note 46 (describing advantages of trials for fact development).

63. John Langbein, *The Disappearance of Civil Trial in the United States,* 122 YALE L.J. 522 (2012).

64. For rich accounts of the jury trial's purposes and virtues, see BURNS, *supra* note 46; Stephan Landsman, *So What? Possible Implications of the Vanishing Trial Phenomenon,* 1 J. EMPIRICAL LEGAL STUD. 980 (2004). Burns also provides a compelling argument for the trial's greater fact-development capacity. On that topic, see also Marc Galanter, *A World Without Trials?,* 2006 J. DISP. RESOL. 7, 26; Stephen B. Burbank, *Vanishing Trials and Summary Judgment in Federal Civil Cases: Drifting Toward Bethlehem or Gommorah?,* 1 J. EMPIRICAL LEGAL STUD. 597, 626 (2004) (arguing, in the context of civil litigation, that "the law development through summary judgment will be arid, divorced from the full factual context that has in the past given our law life and the capacity to grow").

65. For accounts of how adjudication is constitutive of legal judgments and substantive justice specifically in criminal law, see Kyron Huigens, *Law, Economics, and the Skeleton of Value Fallacy,* 89 CAL. L. REV. 537 (2001). For somewhat broader accounts with different emphases, see Richard H. Fallon Jr., *Constitutional Precedent Viewed Through the Lens of Hartian Positivist Jurisprudence,* 86 N.C. L. REV. 1107, 1119–37 (2008); Patrick Higginbotham, *So Why Do We Call Them Trial Courts?,* 55 SMU L. REV. 1405, 1419 (2002) (discussing role of juries when legal standards are indeterminate); David Luban, *Settlement and the Erosion of the Public Realm,* 83 GEO. L.J. 2619, 2628–35 (1995). The U.S. Supreme Court has implied its recognition that adjudication process, and the choice of adjudicators, affects substantive outcomes as well, especially with reference to juries. *See, e.g.,* McClesky v. Kemp, 481 U.S. 279, 311 (1987) ("it is the jury's function to make the difficult and uniquely human judgments that defy codification"); Duncan

v. Louisiana, 391 U.S. 145, 156 (1968) (describing the legitimacy of the jury's "common sense judgment" compared to judges' "perhaps less sympathetic reaction of the single judge" to defendants); Saffle v. Parks, 494 U.S. 484. 499–503 (1990) (Brennan, J., dissenting) (describing jury's "reasoned moral judgment" as critical to judgments of culpability in capital cases).

66. *See generally* Peter W. Singer, Corporate Warriors: The Rise of the Privatized Military Industry (2007); Peter W. Singer, *Can't Win With 'Em, Can't Go To War Without 'Em: Private Military Contractors and Counterinsurgency* (Brookings Inst'n Policy Paper Sept. 2007).

67. One traffic-camera firm is RedFlex Traffic Systems, which claimed to operate in 220 U.S. and Canadian localities in 2014 and offers "turnkey safety programs [that] typically include all hardware, installation, maintenance, software, citation processing, mailing, adjudication services, payment possessing, collections, process serving, public outreach and training." *See* http://www.Redflex.com. David McNair, *County's Red Light Camera System Goes Live*, The Hook, Nov 12, 2010 (describing traffic camera in Virginia operated by RedFlex).

68. New Zealand's Crown Solicitors Network has sixteen Crown Solicitors who are partners in private firms, appointed for prosecution duties in regional districts. *See* website of New Zealand Crown Law Office, http://www.crownlaw.govt.nz/ (visited May 29, 2015); New Zealand Law Commission, *Report 66: Criminal Prosecution* (Oct. 2000). American police and prosecutors, it bears noting, have largely avoided U.S. policy efforts directed at other public employees, notably teachers, to tie job review, pay, and employment security more closely to measurable proxies for productivity. Ideas along these lines exist in scholarly literature but have gained little traction. *See, e.g.,* Gary Becker & George J. Stigler, *Law Enforcement, Malfeasance and Compensation of Enforcers*, 3 J. Legal Stud. 3 1–18 (1974). One example of incentives for private actors to support law enforcement and court interests are private bounty hunters acting on behalf of sureties for suspects granted pretrial release on bail. *See* J. A. Chamberlin, *Bounty Hunters: Can the Criminal Justice System Do Without Them?*, Univ. Ill. L. Rev. 1175 (1998). Another example, applied directly to police, are the widespread and controversial policies that direct criminal forfeiture proceeds to law enforcement budgets. Those policies incentivize police departments and prosecutors to pursue cases in which forfeiture proceeds are likely to be large, with little incentive to forgo proceeds as a matter of discretion despite their expansive statutory definitions. Eric Blumenson & Eva Nilsen, *Policing for Profit: The Drug War's Hidden Economic Agenda*, 65 U. Chi. L. Rev. 35 (1998). Magnuson-Stevens Fishery Conservation and Management Act, P.L. 94-265, 16 U.S.C. §§ 1801–1884 (2012) (allows federal to retain fines recovered from enforcing certain marine resources statutes).

69. A significant concern about private actors' power to prosecute stems from uncertainty about their interests and motives. Risks of abuse of private prosecution authority are addressed in code provisions that authorize it, although with the effect of greatly discouraging private charging. In Germany, rules require private prosecutors to attempt mediation before trial, to post a bond upon filing charges, and to face a "loser pays" rule for attorneys' litigation costs. *See* StPO §§ 374-394 (German Criminal Procedure Code).

70. Sarah Stillman, *Get Out of Jail, Inc.*, New Yorker, June 23, 2014, at 49 (private probation contractors); Sharon Dolovich, *How Privatization Thinks: The Case of Prisons*, in Government by Contract: Outsourcing and American Democracy 128 (Jody Freeman & Martha Minow eds., 2009). Earlier versions of the idea can be found in the history of convict leasing systems; private employers paid states, and took custody of inmates, to gain prisoners' labor. David M. Oshinsky, Worse than Slavery: Parchman Farm and the Ordeal of Jim Crow Justice (1997).

71. On private security contractors for federal agencies during the Iraq War, see Special Inspector General for Iraq Reconstruction, Letter for Secretary of State et al., *Monitoring Responsibilities for Serious Incidents Involving Private Security Contractors Once U.S.*

Military Forces Leave Iraq Have Not Been Determined, July 29, 2011 (SIGIR 11-019) (describing use of private security contractors including Blackwater, Inc. and Aegis Defense Services, Ltd. by State Department and other federal agencies in Iraq); JEREMY SCAHILL, BLACKWATER: THE RISE OF THE WORLD'S MOST POWERFUL MERCENARY ARMY (rev. ed. 2008).

72. *See generally* DAVID A. SKLANSKY, DEMOCRACY AND THE POLICE (2007).

73. On private security and policing, see David A. Sklansky, *The Private Police*, 46 UCLA L. REV. 1165 (1999).

   Additional examples of private action in policing might include law enforcement use of private informers. For a critical overview, see ALEXANDRA NATAPOFF, SNITCHING: CRIMINAL INFORMANTS AND THE EROSION OF AMERICAN JUSTICE (2009). Reliance on the private bail bond system to supervise defendants pending trial is another example. Timothy R. Schnacke, *Fundamentals of Bail: A Resource Guide for Pretrial Practitioners and a Framework for American Pretrial Reform* (U.S. Dep't of Justice, Nat'l Inst. of Corrections 2014).

74. *See generally* Sandra Guerra Thompson, *The White-Collar Police Force: "Duty to Report" Statutes in Criminal Law Theory*, 11 WM. & MARY BILL RTS. J. 3 (2002). On the common law offense "misprision of felony" failing to report, see P. R. Glazebrook, *Misprision of Felony—Shadow or Phantom*, 8 AM. J. LEGAL HIST. 189 (1964); *cf.* McCONVILLE & MIRSKY, *supra* note 33, at 31 (duty to serve as night watchman); *id.* at 171 (duty to prosecute).

75. Private prison contractors' self-interested goals of maximizing profits can be poorly aligned with state interests in humane treatment (to which the state may lack full commitment as well, for familiar political reasons). The route to increasing returns may include understaffing, inadequate staff training, minimal spending on food or health care, or methods of housing and discipline, any of which may result in unduly harsh treatment. *See* ACLU Report, *Warehoused and Forgotten: Immigrants Trapped in Our Shadow Private Prison System* (June 2014) (describing "shocking abuse and mistreatment . . . and the excessive use of solitary confinement" in privately run federal detention facilities).

76. ROBERT ELLICKSON, ORDER WITHOUT LAW: HOW NEIGHBORS SETTLE DISPUTES (1994).

77. HARCOURT, *supra* note 13, at 146 *passim*.

78. All nations punish less than the United States, and many rely on criminal law less because they rely on other policy options—especially social welfare and public health systems—more. LACEY, *supra* note 16; Beckett & Western, *supra* note 16.

Chapter 8

1. The U.S. Justice Department—not created until after the Civil War—began to shift to a civil service system for staff prosecutors only in the late nineteenth century, and chief prosecutors in each federal district remain political appointees. Jed Handelsman Shugerman, *The Creation of the Department of Justice: Professionalization Without Civil Rights or Civil Service*, 66 STAN. L. REV. 121 (2014). Prosecution agencies in many state justice systems never professionalized to the same degree as their federal counterparts. Staff prosecutors often continue to serve at the pleasure of an elected local prosecutor, who is usually autonomous from the state attorney general.

2. Jed Handelsman Shugerman, *The Dependent Origins of Independent Agencies: The Interstate Commerce Commission and the Rise of Modern Campaign Finance and Capture* (working paper Mar. 2015, available on http://ssrn.com); FRANCIS FUKUYAMA, POLITICAL ORDER AND POLITICAL DECAY 174–90, 509–12 (2014); STEPHEN SKOWRONEK, BUILDING A NEW AMERICAN STATE: THE EXPANSION OF NATIONAL ADMINISTRATIVE CAPACITIES, 1877–1920, at 151 (1982).

3. Regulatory effectiveness and professional competence vary across agencies. Some have well-qualified staffs and are mostly free of political influence; others less so. NASA, the Centers for Disease Control, and the Defense Department are often cited examples of the first type; the Forest Service and Federal Emergency Management Agency have been, at times, examples of the latter. FUKUYAMA, *supra* note 2, at 464–80 & 508.

4. *See, e.g.*, FUKUYAMA, *supra* note 2, at 464–544; PAUL LIGHT, A GOVERNMENT ILL EXECUTED: THE DECLINE OF THE FEDERAL SERVICE AND HOW TO REVERSE IT (2009).

5. FUKUYAMA, *supra* note 2, at 478–79.

6. FUKUYAMA, *supra* note 2, at 480.

7. For a compelling account of an urban area plagued by gang violence in which police could not maintain order or make arrests in most homicide cases, see JILL LEOVY, GHETTOSIDE: A TRUE STORY OF MURDER IN AMERICA (2015). An earlier, equally compelling account in the same genre is DAVID SIMON, HOMICIDE: A YEAR ON THE KILLING STREETS (2006); *see also* SUDHIR VENKATESH, GANG LEADER FOR A DAY (2008) (study of Chicago drug gangs).

8. *See* Owen Bowcott, *Campaigners Win Right to Challenge Assisted Dying Prosecution Policy*, THE GUARDIAN, Apr. 28, 2015 (describing *Kenward v. Director of Public Prosecutions*, CO/199/2015), *available at* http://www.theguardian.com. Although no equivalent process exists for U.S. prosecution policies, well-organized private interest groups can sometimes exert informal influence. The clearest example of corporate interest groups successfully pushing back against Justice Department policies is probably the debate about guidelines (in the 2003 "Thompson Memo") regarding waiver of attorney-client privilege or corporate nonreimbursement of defense fees as a condition for leniency. *See* Julie Rose O'Sullivan, *The Last Straw: The Department of Justice's Privilege Waiver Policy and the Death of Adversarial Justice in Criminal Investigations of Corporations*, 57 DEPAUL L. REV. 329 (2008); Darryl K. Brown, *Executive Branch Regulation of Criminal Defense Counsel and the Private Contract Limit on Prosecutor Bargaining*, 57 DEPAUL L. REV. 365 (2008).

9. Perhaps coincidentally, the Supreme Court began defining the law of guilty pleas and plea bargaining almost immediately upon the 1969 retirement of Chief Justice Earl Warren. That body of law commences with Boykin v. Alabama, 395 U.S. 238 (1969); Brady v. United States, 397 U.S. 742 (1970); and Santobello v. New York, 404 U.S. 257 (1971).

10. Constitutional limits on state judicial offices are minimal; judges cannot, for example, have a financial interest in a prosecution over which they preside. Tumey v. Ohio, 273 U.S. 510 (1927).

11. H. L. A. HART, THE CONCEPT OF LAW (1961); Brian Leiter, *The Radicalism of Legal Positivism*, 66 NAT. L. GUILD REV. 165 (2009); Scott Shapiro, *What Is the Rule of Recognition (and Does It Exist)?*, *in* THE RULE OF RECOGNITION AND THE U.S. CONSTITUTION 235 (Matthew D. Adler & Kenneth E. Himma eds., 2009); Robert S. Summers, *H.L.A. Hart's Concept of Law*, 1963 DUKE L.J. 929.

12. Mooney v. Holohan, 294 U.S. 103, 112 (1935); Rochin v. California, 342 U.S. 165, 173 (1952); Trop v. Dulles, 356 U.S. 86, 101 (1958).

13. *See generally* JACK M. BALKIN, LIVING ORIGINALISM (2014); JACK M. BALKIN, CONSTITUTIONAL REDEMPTION: POLITICAL FAITH IN AN UNJUST WORLD (2011); LARRY D. KRAMER, THE PEOPLE THEMSELVES: POPULAR CONSTITUTIONALISM AND JUDICIAL REVIEW (2004).

14. *See* United States v. Ruiz, 536 U.S. 622, 631 (2002) (*citing* Ake v. Oklahoma, 470 U.S. 68, 77 (1985)).

15. *See Ruiz*, 536 U.S. 622.

16. New State Ice Co. v. Liebmann, 285 U.S. 262, 311 (1932) (Brandeis, J., dissenting).

17. *See, e.g.*, Lord Justice Gross, *Review of Disclosure in Criminal Proceedings* (Sept. 2011) (report for Judiciary of England and Wales that extensively investigates U.S. federal court

disclosure practices); Jessica de Grazia, *Review of the Serious Fraud Office, Final Report* (June 2008) (U.S. federal prosecutor retained to review U.K. Serious Fraud Office).

18. *See generally* THOMAS PIKETTY, CAPITAL IN THE TWENTY-FIRST CENTURY (2014); DANIEL T. RODGERS, AGE OF FRACTURE (2011).

19. *See* Adam Bonica, Nolan McCarty, Keith T. Poole, & Howard Rosenthal, *Why Hasn't Democracy Slowed Rising Inequality?*, 27 J. ECON. PERSPECTIVES 103 (Summer 2013) (analysis concluding that political parties in the U.S. Congress are more polarized than any time since the decade after 1865). Further data at http://Voteview.com.

20. NICOLA LACEY, THE PRISONERS' DILEMMA: POLITICAL ECONOMY AND PUNISHMENT IN CONTEMPORARY DEMOCRACIES (2008).

21. BERNARD HARCOURT, THE ILLUSION OF FREE MARKETS: PUNISHMENT AND THE MYTH OF NATURAL ORDER (2011).

22. TIMOTHY NOAH, THE GREAT DIVERGENCE: AMERICA'S GROWING INEQUALITY CRISIS AND WHAT WE CAN DO ABOUT IT (2012).

23. United States v. Gonzalez-Lopez, 548 U.S. 140, 146 (2006) (right "to have the Assistance of Counsel" requires that "the accused be defended by the counsel he believes to be best" and "can afford to hire"); *see also* Caplin & Drysdale v. United States, 491 U.S. 617, 624–25 (1989).

24. *Federalist No. 10* (Madison), *in* THE FEDERALIST PAPERS 77 (Clinton Rossiter ed., 1961).

25. *In re* Davis, 557 U.S. 952, 955 (2009) (Scalia, J., dissenting); *see also* Kansas v. Marsh, 548 U.S. 163 (2006) (Scalia, J., concurring).

26. U.S. CONST., amend. V ("No person ... shall be ... deprived of life, liberty, or property, without due process of law"); amend. XIV ("[N]or shall any state deprive any person of life, liberty, or property, without due process of law."). Some justices disapprove of substantive due process doctrine. McDonald v. City of Chicago, Ill., 561 U.S. 742, 811 (2010) (Scalia, J., concurring) ("The one theme that links the Court's substantive due process precedents together is their lack of a guiding principle to distinguish 'fundamental' rights that warrant protection. ..."); Albright v. Oliver, 510 U.S. 266, 275 (1994) (Scalia, J., concurring) ("Except insofar as our decisions have included within the Fourteenth Amendment certain explicit substantive protections of the Bill of Rights ... I reject the proposition that the Due Process Clause guarantees certain (unspecified) liberties, rather than merely guarantees certain procedures."). And the Court's notorious *Lochner*-era decisions were once within the doctrine. Lochner v. New York, 198 U.S. 45 (1905) (state labor law limiting bakery employees to sixty-hour work weeks unconstitutional). But the doctrine remains a basis for significant substantive rights. *See, e.g.*, BMW of North America, Inc. v. Gore, 517 U.S. 559 (1996) (substantive due process prohibits "grossly excessive" civil damages judgments such as $2 million punitive damages award for failure to disclose repainting of automobile); Roe v. Wade, 410 U.S. 113 (1973) (holding state prohibition on abortions at any stage of pregnancy except to save the life of the mother is unconstitutional), holding modified by Planned Parenthood of Se. Pennsylvania v. Casey, 505 U.S. 833 (1992).

27. U.S. CONST., art. III, § 2 (emphasis added); *see* AKHIL REED AMAR, AMERICA'S CONSTITUTION: A BIOGRAPHY 240–42 (2005).

28. In Emma Rothschild's words, this is an uncontested "society of universal commerce." EMMA ROTHSCHILD, ECONOMIC SENTIMENTS: ADAM SMITH, CONDORCET, AND THE ENLIGHTENMENT 2, 251 (2001).

29. T. H. Marshall, *Value Problems of Welfare Capitalism*, 1 J. SOC. POL'Y 19, 20 (1972), *quoted in* NEIL GILBERT, TRANSFORMATION OF THE WELFARE STATE: THE SILENT SURRENDER OF PUBLIC RESPONSIBILITY 135 (2002).

30. KENNETH CULP DAVIS, DISCRETIONARY JUSTICE: A PRELIMINARY INQUIRY 224–25 (1969).

31. *See, e.g.*, 21 U.S.C. § 851 (federal prosecutor power to trigger recidivist sentencing enhancement); N.J. REV. STAT. § 2C:35-12 (2013) (state judge must impose mandatory

sentences unless prosecutor authorizes an exception); Mont. Code § 46-16-130 (state prosecutor controls access to diversion program focused on rehabilitation and treatment); Howard N. Snyder et al., Juvenile Transfers to Criminal Courts in the 1990s (Nat'l Cen. for Juv. Justice, Aug. 2000) (summarizing studies of state systems and describing state statutes that give prosecutors the power, without judicial review, to file juvenile cases in juvenile or adult criminal courts).

32. John C. Jeffries Jr., *The Liability Rule for Constitutional Torts*, 99 Va. L. Rev. 207, 220–32 (2013); Connick v. Thompson, 563 U.S. 51, 131 S. Ct. 1350 (2011).

33. Herbert L. Packer, The Limits of Criminal Sanction 149–246 (1968). An earlier version is Herbert L. Packer, *Two Models of Criminal Process*, 113 U. Pa. L. Rev. 1 (1964). For an insightful reconsideration of Packer's framework, see Erik Luna, *The Models of Criminal Procedure*, 2 Buffalo Crim. L. Rev. 389 (1999).

34. Packer, Limits of Criminal Sanction, *supra* note 33 at 159–62 & 209.

35. United States v. Mezzanatto, 513 U.S. 196, 208 (1995).

36. On the Crown Prosecution Service and English procedural rules including plea bargain discounts, see chapter 2. For a general overview that includes sentencing trends, see *Falling Crime: Where have All the Burglars Gone?*, The Economist, July 20, 2013, *available at* http://www.economist.com/news/briefing/21582041-rich-world-seeing-less-and-less-crime-even-face-high-unemployment-and-economic; Ministry of Justice, *Story of the Prison Population: 1993–2012 England and Wales* 1 (Jan. 2013) ("Between June 1993 and June 2012 the prison population in England and Wales increased by 41,800 prisoners to over 86,000.").

37. Carol S. Steiker, *Why We're So Tough on Crime*, Boston Rev. (Oct./Nov. 2003) (reviewing James Q. Whitman, Harsh Justice).

38. For surveys of executive clemency practices in the twentieth century, including its declining use since the 1970s, see Elizabeth Rapaport, *Retribution and Redemption in the Operation of Executive Clemency*, 74 Chi.-Kent L. Rev. 1501, 1508–09 (2000); Michael L. Radelet & Barbara A. Zsembik, *Executive Clemency in Post-Furman Capital Cases*, 27 U. Rich. L. Rev. 289, 290 (1993). As of this writing, in May 2015, the Nebraska legislature voted by a two-thirds majority to abolish the state's death penalty, becoming the seventh state in eight years to eliminate capital punishment.

39. *See* James M. Cole, Deputy Attorney Gen., *Memorandum for all United States Attorneys: Guidance Regarding Marijuana Enforcement* (Aug. 29, 2013); U.S. Attorney General Eric Holder, *Memorandum: Department Policy on Charging Mandatory Minimum Sentences and Recidivist Enhancements in Certain Drug Cases, Aug. 12, 2013* (advising that enhanced sentences should be limited to "high-level or violent traffickers").

40. Miller v. Alabama, 132 S. Ct. 2455 (2012) (barring life-without-parole sentences for all juvenile offenders); Graham v. Florida, 560 U.S. 48, 130 S. Ct. 2011 (2010) (barring life-without-parole sentences for juveniles convicted of crimes excluding murder).

INDEX